ALL ROCKED OUT

**500 Deceased Stars of Rock & Pop
Remembered**

John Sydenham

Forever In Print Ltd
London

Forever In Print
King Street, London W6

First published in Great Britain 2023

This Edition published 2023

Copyright © John Sydenham 2023

Printed and bound by CPI Group (UK) Ltd, Croydon, CR0 4YY

INTRODUCTION

Welcome to ALL ROCKED OUT, an extensive collection of obituaries of the deceased stars of pop & rock music.

We are defining a "Pop Star" here as someone who has achieved significant success on the Pop singles charts in the U.K. or U.S.A; these charts first appearing in the nineteen fifties. Rock Stars are those who have predominantly enjoyed high sales of albums and/or sold-out concert tours at various times since the late Nineteen Sixties.

Strikingly, the average age at death of the stars in this collection is around only fifty-nine years of age. Compared with life expectancy of the general population (U.K. 81 years, U.S.A. 79 years) our stars are dying twenty years younger than the average deceased person. You will find the deceased stars in this book in alphabetical order of their surnames.

CONTENTS

DEAD STARS A - E

Michael Lee Aday   Meat Loaf

Michael Lee Aday, Meat Loaf, died aged seventy-four in Nashville, Tennessee, USA on the twentieth of January, 2022 . He was survived by his wife, Leslie and daughters, Amanda and Pearl. He was reportedly ill with COVID-19 earlier in the month and is thought to have died from COVID-19 complications.

Michael was born in Dallas, Texas, on twenty-seventh of September 1947. He stated in an interview that when he was born, he was "bright red and stayed that way for days" and that his father said he looked like "nine pounds of ground chuck", and convinced hospital staff to put the name "Meat" on his crib. He was later called "M.L." in reference to his initials, but when his weight increased, his seventh-grade classmates referred to him as "Meatloaf", referring to his short and heavy stature.

In 1965, Michael graduated from High School, after having appeared in school stage productions including Where's Charley? and The Music Man. In Los Angeles, Michael formed his first band, Meat Loaf Soul. In 1968, he joined the cast of the musical, Hair, in various replacement parts.   .

In the 1970s, with the publicity generated from Hair, Meat Loaf accepted an invitation by Motown, in Detroit, to record only the vocals with fellow Hair performer Shaun "Stoney" Murphy on an album of songs written and selected by the Motown production team.

In December 1972, Michael was in the original off-Broadway production of Rainbow at the Orpheum Theatre in New York. After the tour, He rejoined the cast of Hair. In late 1973, He was cast in the original L.A. Roxy cast of The Rocky Horror Show, playing the parts of Eddie and Dr. Everett Scott.

Jim Steinman and Michael began working on Bat Out of

Hell in 1972, but did not get serious about it until the end of 1974. Michael and Jim Steinman formed the band Neverland Express to tour in support of Bat Out of Hell. Their first gig was opening for Cheap Trick in Chicago. Michael gained national exposure as the musical guest on Saturday Night Live on the 25th of March, 1978. Also in 1978, he jumped off a stage in Ottawa, Ontario, breaking his leg and finished his tour performing in a wheelchair. The album, Bat Out of Hell, has sold an estimated forty-three million copies globally, including fifteen million in the United States, making it one of the best-selling albums of all time.

Bad money management as well as forty-five lawsuits totalling eighty million dollars, including ones from Steinman, resulted in Michael filing for personal bankruptcy in 1983. The bankruptcy resulted in Meat Loaf losing the rights to his songs, although he received royalties for Bat Out of Hell in 1997.

In 1984, Michael went to England, where he felt increasingly at home, to record the album Bad Attitude where it was released that year. In 1995, Meat Loaf released his seventh studio album, Welcome to the Neighbourhood. The album went platinum in the United States and the United Kingdom. In 1998, Michael released an album called The Very Best of Meat Loaf. In 2003, Meat Loaf released his album Couldn't Have Said It Better.

On the 17th of November, 2003, during a performance at London's Wembley Arena, on his Couldn't Have Said It Better tour, Michael collapsed of what was later diagnosed as Wolff–Parkinson–White syndrome.

Martin Allcock   Fairport Convention

Martin Allcock died of body malfunction aged sixty-one on the 16th of September 2018. He was a musician, multi-instrumentalist and record producer who played guitar, keyboards, violin, bass guitar and pipes.

Martin was born on the 5th of January 1957 in Middleton, Lancashire, United Kingdom and studied music at Huddersfield and Leeds. He began playing professionally in January 1976, playing in dance bands and folk clubs. His first tour was in 1977 with Mike Harding as one of the Brown Ale Cowboys. He went to Brittany in 1978, for a temporary stay, but ended up remaining longer than intended, and learned to cook while there. On returning to Manchester he studied to become a chef and later qualified as one and worked as a chef in the Shetland Islands in 1980.

In 1981 he joined the Bully Wee Band, a Celtic folk group, which led to an eleven-year stint as lead guitarist with British folk rock band Fairport Convention from October 1985 to December 1996, and concurrently four years as keyboardist with rock band Jethro Tull from January 1988 to December 1991. In summer 1991 he also played keyboards for The Mission. From the early 2000's he began working freelance from his home on the west coast of Snowdonia as a session man and record producer with the Welsh language Sain record label.

In 2018, it was announced that Martin had been diagnosed with liver cancer and would make his final live performance before retirement at the 2018 Cropredy Festival, an event which is held annually near Banbury, Oxfordshire, United Kingdom.

Martin Allcock's session career included more than two hundred albums, including those of Robert Plant, Beverley Craven, Judith Durham, Breton guitarist Dan Ar Braz, Ralph McTell and Cat Stevens.

Gregg Allman   The Allman Brothers

Gregg Allman died aged sixty-nine at his home in Savannah, Georgia, U.S.A. on 27th May 2017, due to complications from liver cancer. He was survived by sons Elijah, Devon and Michael and daughters Layla and Delila His funeral took place at Snow's Memorial Chapel in Macon,

Georgia on 3rd June that year and was attended by once-estranged bandmate Dickey Betts, his ex-wife Cher, and former American President, Jimmy Carter, amongst others. He was buried at Rose Hill Cemetery in Macon, beside his brother Duane, and fellow band member Berry Oakley.

Gregg was born Gregory LeNoir Allman on the eighth of December 1947 in Nashville, Tennessee. Later on Gregg and his brother Duanne began meeting various musicians in the Daytona Beach area of Florida. They later formed their first band which performed a mix of top forty and rhythm and blues music at clubs around the town. Duane, who took the lead vocal role on early demos, encouraged his younger brother to sing instead.

After Duane's death in 1971, the band held a meeting to discuss their future. It was clear all wanted to continue and after a short period, they returned to touring and completed their third studio album, Eat a Peach, that winter.

The Allman Brothers band played mostly in arenas and stadiums and in 1974, the band was regularly taking in one hundred thousand dollars per show. In January 1975, Gregg began a relationship with pop star Cher. The sessions that produced 1975's Win, Lose or Draw, the last album by the original Allman Brothers Band, were disjointed and inconsistent, partly because Gregg was spending more time in Los Angeles with Cher.

Gregg married Cher in June 1975, and the two lived in Hollywood during their years together as tabloid favourites. Their marriage produced one son, Elijah Blue Allman, who was born in July 1976. Gregg recorded his second solo album, Playin' Up a Storm, with the Gregg Allman Band, and it was released in May 1977.

Gregg spent much of the 1980s adrift and living in Sarasota, Florida with friends Marcia and Chuck Boyd. His alcohol abuse was at one of its worst points, with Gregg consuming "a minimum of a fifth of vodka a day." He felt the local police pursued him heavily, due to his tendency to get inebriated and "go jam anywhere". He was arrested and charged with driving while intoxicated and, as a result, he spent five days in jail and was fined one thousand dollars. The Allman Brothers Band celebrated its twentieth anniversary in 1989, and the band reunited for a summer tour.

For much of the nineteen-nineties , Gregg lived in Marin County, California, spending his free time with close friends and riding his motorcycle. The band was inducted into the Rock and Roll Hall of Fame in January 1995. Gregg however, was so severely inebriated that he could not make it through his acceptance speech. Seeing the ceremony broadcast on television later, Gregg was mortified, providing a catalyst for his final, successful attempt to quit alcohol and substance abuse. He hired two in-home nurses that switched twelve-hour shifts to help him through the process. He was immensely happy to finally quit alcohol.

Gregg recorded a fifth solo album, Searching for Simplicity, which was quietly released on 550 Music. Gov't Mule, feeling as though a break was imminent with the Allman Brothers Band.

Gregg moved to Richmond Hill, Georgia, in the year 2000, purchasing five acres on the Belfast River. The last incarnation of the Allman Brothers Band was well-regarded among fans and the general public, and remained stable and productive. The band released their final studio recording, Hittin' the Note, in 2003 to critical acclaim.

Gregg was diagnosed with hepatitis C in 2007 which he blamed on a dirty tattoo needle. By the next year, three tumors were found in his liver, and he was recommended to the Mayo Clinic in Jacksonville by a Savannah doctor for a liver transplant. He went on a waiting list and after five months, he underwent a successful liver transplant in 2010. Gregg went to rehab in 2012 for addiction following his medical treatments. Later that year, he released his memoir.

After the dissolution of the Allman Brothers, Gregg kept busy performing music, releasing the live album Gregg Allman Live. Gregg also attempted to grow healthier, switching to a gluten-free vegan diet. He also tried to keep a light schedule at the advice of doctors, who warned that too many performances might intensify his conditions.

Barbara Alston   The Crystals

Barbara Alston died aged seventy-four on 16th February 2018 from influenza in North Carolina, U.S.A. She was survived by her sons, Tony and Kenneth and her daughters, Donielle and Kemberley.

Barbara was born Barbara Ann Alston in Baltimore, U.S.A. in 1943 and moved as a child with her mother to New York. After entering talent shows at school, her uncle Benny Wells, a former big-band musician, offered to help her to form a group. With her friends Mary and Myrna on board, the uncle recruited Dee Dee Kenniebrew, aged fifteen, and Patsy Wright, seventeen, whose baby niece Crystal provided the group with its name, "The Crystals".

With some reluctance Barbara agreed to be the lead singer. She stated that her uncle said he needed background singers and that was why she agreed. She said that she could do harmony by ear and loved making up dance routines and that was her forte and that everyone else at the time was too shy to give the lead a shot.

They were rehearsing in the Brill Building in New York when producer Phil Spector put his head round the door and offered to produce them. Within months the Crystals were in the Top 20 pop charts and appearing on-stage at the Apollo Theatre in Harlem.

Despite a string of hit records over the next three years, tensions mounted between the group and Phil Spector, who was spending increasing amounts of his time with their rivals, Ronettes. Following a tour of Britain in 1964, where the song "Then He Kissed Me" reached number two in the pop charts, the Crystals broke with Phil Spector and before the end of that year, Barbara Alston had left the group. She moved to Charlotte, North Carolina, where she raised her four children and worked for an insurance company. According to her daughter Donielle, Barbara spent her later years contentedly singing her hits while doing chores.

Eddie Amoo   The Real Thing

Eddie Amoo died of natural causes on the 23rd of February 2018 while visiting family in Australia. Eddie was survived by his wife Sylvia and their four daughters; Dionne, Sara, Michaela and Marlene.

Eddie was born Edward Robert Amoo, in Toxteth, Liverpool, U.K. on the 4th of May 1944. In 1976, the Real Thing topped the UK charts with You to Me Are Everything, a song that became a disco classic.

In the early 1960s, Eddie had befriended Joey and Edmund Ankrah, the sons of a minister, and together with Alan Harding and Nat Smeeda they formed a doo-wop group called the Chants. During 1975 Chris Amoo formed his own band, the Real Thing, which won ITV television's Opportunity Knocks competition and he suggested that Eddie, now playing guitar and keyboards, should join them. Eddie coached the band, which included Dave Smith and Ray Lake, and they toured with David Essex, who used them on the hit album, All the Fun of the Fair, in 1975. The Real Thing's first hits, You to Me Are Everything and Can't Get By Without You, the latter of which reached Number 2, were written and produced by Ken Gold, but their subsequent successes, You'll Never Know What You're Missing, Love's Such a Wonderful Thing and Can You Feel the Force?, were written by the Amoo brothers.

Andy Anderson   The Cure

Andy Anderson died aged sixty-eight on twenty-sixth of

February 2019, after he had been diagnosed with terminal cancer earlier in the month.

Andy was born, Clifford Leon Anderson on the thirtieth of January 1951 in West Ham, East London, U.K. Andy joined Steve Hillage's band and appeared on the two 1979 Hillage albums, Live Herald and Open. Then, after a few years as a session musician, Andy had a brief period in Hawkwind in 1983, but did not record with them.

Andy then played with the Glove on their only album 'Blue Sunshine'. This led to him joining the Cure later that year, when their original drummer Lol Tolhurst moved to keyboards. Andy Anderson recorded on the Cure albums 'Japanese Whispers', 'The Top', and 'Concer' in addition to the singles "Love Cats" and "The Caterpillar".

Louis Armstrong   The Allstars

Louis Armstrong died of a heart attack in his sleep on the 6th of July 1971, a month before his seventieth birthday. He had been in his home in Corona, Queens, New York City, U.S.A. and was interred in Flushing Cemetery, Flushing, in Queens, New York City. His honorary pallbearers included Bing Crosby, Ella Fitzgerald, Dizzy Gillespie, Pearl Bailey, Count Basie, Harry James, Frank Sinatra, Ed Sullivan, Earl Wilson, Alan King, Johnny Carson and David Frost. Peggy Lee sang The Lord's Prayer at the services while Al Hibbler sang "Nobody Knows the Trouble I've Seen" and Fred Robbins, a long-time friend, gave the eulogy.

Against his doctor's advice, Louis had played a two-week engagement during March nineteen seventy-one at the Waldorf-Astoria's Empire Room in New York. At the end of it he was hospitalized for a heart attack but was released from the hospital the following May, and soon resumed practicing his trumpet playing, whilst hoping to get back on the road.

Louis Armstrong was born in New Orleans on the 4th of

August 1901. His father, William Armstrong, abandoned the family shortly after Louis was born. Louis' maternal grandmother, Josephine, however, raised him until he was about five. At the age of six he began attending the Fisk School for Boys, where he acquired literacy and gained early exposure to music. Most schools were racially segregated in New Orleans but, Fisk, however. was located in his neighbourhood and enrolled African-American children. During his school years, Louis continued to bring in money delivering coal and other odd jobs working for the Karnoffskys, a family of Lithuanian Jews. He sold coal for a nickel per bucket, in many cases, to the brothels in Storyville. Making the rounds with the Karnoffsky family while delivering coal exposed Louis to music by spasm bands, and the house musicians playing at brothels and dance halls.

The Karnoffskys took Louis in and treated him like family and knowing he lived without a father, they fed and nurtured him after which Louis wore a Star of David pendant for the rest of his life. Morris Karnoffsky advanced the young Louis two dollars toward the purchase of a five dollar cornet from a pawn shop and in general, the family encouraged Louis' musical pursuits.

Louis dropped out of school at age eleven and at around the same time, Mary Albert moved to a one-room house with Louis, her daughter Lucy, and her common-law husband. Louis joined a quartet of boys who sang in the streets for money but he also began to get into trouble with the law.

Louis was arrested in December 1912 for firing a revolver into the air. He had gone to sing on the streets for money, and had taken his stepfather's handgun, without permission. The round fired was only a blank but Louis was held overnight at the New Orleans Juvenile Court. The following day, Louis was sentenced to detention at the Coloured Waif's Home. Lodgings and meals there were basic since there were no mattresses and they often ate only bread and molasses.

At the Coloured Waif's home, Louis developed his cornet playing skills by playing in the band with other residents and a professor there who provided discipline and musical training to the otherwise self-taught Louis. Eventually, Louis was made the band leader. This home band played around New Orleans and the thirteen-year-old Louis began to draw attention for his cornet playing, launching him onto a musical career.

In 1914, Louis was released into the custody of his father and his new stepmother, Gertrude. He lived in their household, with two stepbrothers, for several months. When Gertrude gave birth to a daughter, however, Louis' father no longer welcomed him, so he returned to live with his birth mother, Mary Albert. The house was so cramped that he had to sleep in the same bed with his mother and sister. His mother still lived in the same part of the rough neighborhood, which left him exposed to old temptations. But Louis continued to seek work as a musician until he found his first dance hall job at Henry Ponce's, a club whose owner had ties to organized crime. At this time, Louis met an extremely tall drummer called Black Benny, who became his protector and guide.

Louis played in brass band parades in New Orleans and he also took the opportunity to take in the music of local musicians, such as Kid Ory, and also his idol, "King" Oliver. Louis eventually received an invitation to go to New York City to play with the Fletcher Henderson Orchestra, the top African-American band of the time. Louis then switched from cornet to the trumpet to blend in better with the other musicians in his section.

Louis quickly adapted to the more tightly controlled style of the Henderson band, playing trumpet and even experimenting with the trombone. The other members quickly took up Louis's emotional, expressive pulse. Soon his act included singing and telling tales of New Orleans characters, especially preachers. The Henderson Orchestra was playing in prominent venues for white-only patrons, including the famed Roseland Ballroom, featuring the arrangements of Don Redman. Duke Ellington's orchestra would go to Roseland to catch Louis's performances and young horn men around town tried in vain to outplay him.

During this time, Louis Armstrong made many recordings on the side, arranged by an old friend from New Orleans, pianist Clarence Williams; these included small jazz band sides with the Williams Blue Five and a series of accompaniments with blues singers, including Bessie Smith, Ma Rainey, and Alberta Hunter.

Tony Ashton   Ashton, Gardner & Dyke

Tony Ashton died aged fifty-five from cancer on the 28th of May 2001 at his home in London, United Kingdom. He was survived by his wife Sandra and his step-daughter, Indira.

Tony was born in Blackburn, Lancashire,United Kingdom on the 1st of March 1946 and spent his formative years in the seaside town of Blackpool where his parents had an upright piano. As a child, his mother sent him to piano lessons and at the age of thirteen, in 1959, whilst a student in Blackpool, he joined a local group called The College Boys, playing both rhythm guitar and piano.

When Tony Ashton left school at the age of fifteen he was already an accomplished pianist and after playing with various Blackpool bands he was invited to join a Liverpool group called The Remo Four as an organist and vocalist. The group spent some time as the resident band at the Star Club in Hamburg, Germany. They followed this with a US tour accompanying the Beatles.

At the end of the 1960s, Tony Ashton formed a fresh group with Remo drummer Roy Dyke and bass player Kim Gardner and they called themselves Ashton, Gardner and Dyke. The music, however, was all composed by Tony Ashton.

Tony met Deep Purple in the early 1970s, when the last recording of Ashton, Gardner and Dyke was a collaboration with keyboardist Jon Lord on the soundtrack for a b-movie called 'The Last Rebel'. In the meantime, Tony Ashton had appeared on Jon Lord's first solo album Gemini Suite in 1971. In 1973, Tony Ashton joined the group Family for their last album and tour.

In August 1976, when Deep Purple split, Jon Lord and Ian Paice found themselves with a lot of free time on their hands and a need to steer away from the hard rock scene. The logical step to take was to call on their old friend Tony Ashton. The result was the formation of the Paice Ashton Lord band.

During the nineteen-eighties Tony Ashton co-hosted a TV show with Rick Wakeman called "GasTank" which was aired once each two weeks. Following that, Tony Ashton went through some hard times due to ill health and lack of work. Although he continued to gig occasionally, he did not release any more recordings until 1988 with a single called "Saturday Night and Sunday Morning".

In 1986 Tony married Sandra Naidoo and adopted her daughter Indira. In 1999, when Tony became seriously ill, a special benefit concert was recorded and filmed at EMI's Abbey Road Studios, featuring the many diverse talents of a number of Tony's friends and colleagues over the years, including Jon Lord, Ian Paice, Micky Moody, Bernie Marsden, Howie Casey, Chris Barber, John Entwistle, Zak Starkey, Pete York, Zoot Money, Joe Brown, Geoff Emerick, Mike Figgis and Ewan McGregor.

Kevin Ayres   **The Soft Machine**

Kevin Ayres died aged sixty-eight in his sleep on the 18th of February 2013 in Montolieu, France. Kevin was born on the 16th of August 1944 in Herne Bay, Kent, United Kingdom. He was the son of a BBC producer named Rowan Ayers. Following his parents' divorce and his mother's subsequent marriage to a British civil servant, Kevin spent most of his childhood in Malaya.

Kevin returned to England at the age of twelve. In his early college years he took up with the burgeoning musicians' scene in the Canterbury area and he was quickly drafted into the Wilde Flowers, a band that featured Robert Wyatt and Hugh Hopper.

The Wilde Flowers evolved into two bands, these being Caravan and Soft Machine. Kevin played bass and guitar and shared vocals with the drummer Robert Wyatt. They released their debut single in February 1967. Their debut album, The Soft Machine, was recorded in the USA for ABC/Probe and released in 1968. It is considered a classic of its genre.

After an extensive tour of the United States opening for Jimi Hendrix, a weary Kevin sold his white Fender Jazz Bass and retreated to the beaches of Ibiza in Spain. However, a second album, Shooting at the Moon, quickly followed. For this record Kevin assembled a band that he called The Whole World, including a young Mike Oldfield on bass and occasionally lead guitar, avant-garde composer David Bedford on keyboards and improvising saxophonist, Lol Coxhill. Once again Kevin came up with a batch of engaging songs interspersed with avant-garde instrumentals and a heavy dose of quirkiness.

The Whole World was reportedly an erratic band live, and Kevin was not suited for life on the road touring. The band broke up after a short tour, with no hard feelings, as most of the musicians guested on Kevin's next album, Whatevershebringswesing, which is regarded as one of his best, featuring the mellifluous eight-minute title track that would become Kevin's signature sound for the nineteen-seventies. Bananamour was the fourth studio album by Kevin Ayers and it featured some of his most accessible recordings, including "Shouting in a Bucket Blues" and his whimsical tribute to Syd Barrett, "Oh! Wot A Dream".

On the 1st of June 1974, Kevin headlined a heavily publicised concert at the Rainbow Theatre, London, accompanied by John Cale, Nico, Brian Eno and Mike Oldfield. The late 1970s and 1980s saw Kevin Ayers as a self-imposed exile in warmer climes.

In 1993 Kevin toured America twice, most often performing solo with occasional guests, including Daevid Allen, who was also touring America at the same time. Aside from a few New York shows in 1980 with Ollie Halsall, these tours were Kevin Ayers' first live performances in America since 1968.

In the late 1990s, Kevin Ayers was living the life of a recluse in the South of France. At the Sculpture Centre he met American artist Timothy Shepard, who had been invited to use studio space there, and the two became friends. Kevin began to show up at Shepard's house with a guitar, and by 2005 passed some new recordings on to Shepard, most of them taped on a cassette recorder at his kitchen table.

Charles Aznavour   Solo Artiste

Charles Aznavour died aged ninety-four on the first of October 2018 in his bathtub at home at Mouries in France. He was survived by his wife, Ulla and by his sons, Patrick, Mischa and Nicolas and his daughters, Katia and Seda.

An autopsy report concluded that he died of cardiorespiratory arrest complicated by an acute pulmonary edema. On the fifth of October 2018, Charles Aznavour was honoured with a state funeral at Les Invalides military complex in Paris, with president Emmanuel Macron lauding him as one of the most important "faces of France". His coffin was lifted away at the end to the sound of his recording "Emmenez-Moi".

In April 2018, shortly before his ninety-fourth birthday, Charles was taken to hospital in Saint Petersburg after straining his back during a rehearsal prior to a concert in the city. The concert was postponed until the following season, but eventually cancelled since he died.

Charles was already familiar with performing on stage

by the time he began his career as a musician. At the age of nine, he had roles in a play called Un Petit Diable à Paris and a film entitled La Guerre des Gosses. He then turned to professional dancing and performed in several nightclubs. In 1944, he and actor Pierre Roche began a partnership and in collaborative efforts performed in numerous nightclubs. It was through this partnership that Charles began to write songs and sing. The partnership's first successes were in Canada in 1948-1950. Meanwhile, Charles wrote his first song entitled J'ai Bu in 1950.

In 1974 Charles became a major success in the United Kingdom when his song "She" was number one on the UK Singles Chart for four weeks during a fourteen week run. His other well-known song in the UK was the 1973 "The Old Fashioned Way" which was on UK charts for 15 weeks. Artists who have recorded his songs and collaborated with Charles Aznavour include Édith Piaf, Fred Astaire, Frank Sinatra, Andrea Bocelli, Bing Crosby, Ray Charles, Bob Dylan, Dusty Springfield, Liza Minnelli, Mia Martini, Elton John, Dalida, Serge Gainsbourg, Josh Groban, Petula Clark, Tom Jones, Shirley Bassey, José Carreras, Laura Pausini, Nana Mouskouri and Julio Iglesias.

On 25th October 2013 Charles performed in London for the first time in 25 years at the Royal Albert Hall. Demand was so high that a second concert at the Royal Albert Hall was scheduled for June 2014. In November 2013, He appeared with Achinoam Nini in a concert, dedicated to peace, at the Nokia Arena in Tel Aviv to which the audience, including Israeli president Shimon Peres, sang along. In December 2013 Charles gave two concerts in the Netherlands at the Heineken Music Hall in Amsterdam, and again in January 2016.

Robbie Bachman   Bachman Turner Overdrive

Robbie Bachman died aged sixty-nine on the twelfth of January 2023. He was survived by his wife Chrissy.

While growing up, Robbie practised the drums at home, often playing along with his older brother Randy. In 1971, Randy offered the Brave Belt drumming job to his then eighteen year old brother, and Robbie accepted. Other members of Brave Belt were Chad Allan and Fred Turner. In 1972, another Bachman brother, Tim, joined Brave Belt after the departure of Allan.

When Brave Belt changed their name to Bachman–Turner Overdrive (BTO) in 1973, Robbie was credited with designing the BTO 'gear' logo. BTO enjoyed a period of peak popularity between 1973 and 1976, releasing five Top 40 albums, six U.S. Top 40 singles, and eleven Top 40 singles in Canada. Robbie co-wrote one of Bachman–Turner Overdrive's biggest hits, "Roll On down the Highway".

Tim Bachman   **Bachman Turner Overdrive**

Tim Bachman died of cancer, aged seventy-one, on the 28th of April , 2023. He was survived by his wife, Laurie and his son, Paxton and daughter, Madison.

Tim originally played guitar in a few Winnipeg-area bands, some with his younger brother Robbie on drums. He later briefly quit music, feeling that the Winnipeg scene had become stagnant and he obtained a job and began attending college. Tim returned to music in 1972, when his older brother Randy was looking to add a second guitar to his band, Brave Belt.

Tim wrote or co-wrote several songs during his tenure with Brave Belt and Bachman Turner Overdrive, including "Put It in a Song" for the Brave Belt II album, "Down and Out Man" for the first BTO album, and "Blown" and "I Don't Have To Hide" for Bachman–Turner Overdrive II.

Tim Bachman left Bachman Turner Overdrive in 1974, shortly after the release of their Bachman–Turner Overdrive II album and he was replaced by Blair Thornton but rejoined them, along with Randy Bachman, Fred Turner, and Garry Peterson, for a 1984 reunion album and supporting tours. These included a high-profile world tour opening for Van Halen.

Ginger Baker   Cream, & Blind Faith

Ginger Baker died from chronic obstructive pulmonary disease aged eighty years on the 6th of October 2019, at the Kent & Canterbury hospital in Canterbury, Kent, England. Ginger was survived by his first wife, Liz, his son, Kofi and his daughters, Ginette, Nettie and Leda.

Ginger was born Peter Edward Baker in Lewisham, South London, United Kingdom in 1939 and was nicknamed "Ginger" for his shock of flaming red hair. He began playing drums at about fifteen years old and in the early 1960's, he took lessons from a leading British jazz drummer of the post-war era. Ginger gained early fame as a member of the Graham Bond Organisation with future Cream bandmate Jack Bruce, an r&b group with strong jazz leanings.

Ginger co-founded the rock band Cream in 1966 with bassist Jack Bruce and guitarist Eric Clapton. Playing a fusion of blues, psychedelic rock and hard rock, the band released four albums in slightly over two years before disbanding in 1968. Ginger then joined the short-lived "supergroup" Blind Faith, composed of Eric Clapton, bassist Ric Grech from Family, and Steve Winwood from Traffic on keyboards and vocals. They released only one album, the eponymous 'Blind Faith, before disbanding.

In 1980, Ginger joined Hawkwind after initially playing as a session musician on the album Levitation. He left in 1981, after a tour. Ginger moved to Los Angeles in the late 1980s intending to become an actor and appeared in the 1990 TV series Nasty Boys.

Ginger lived in Parker, Colorado, USA between 1993 and 1999, partly due to his passion for polo where he participated in polo events at the Salisbury Equestrian Park there.

Long John Baldry died aged sixty-five of a severe chest infection in Vancouver General Hospital, Vancouver, British Columbia, Canada. He was survived by his partner, Felix "Oz" Rexach, a brother, Roger, and a sister, Margaret.

John was born in January 1941 and his early life was spent in Edgware, Middlesex, UK. He grew to six feet & seven inches, resulting in the nickname "Long John" and he was one of the first British vocalists to sing blues in clubs. He appeared quite regularly in the early 1960s in the Gyre & Gimble coffee lounge, around the corner from Charing Cross railway station in London and at the Brownsville R & B. Club, Manor House, London.

In the early 1960's, John sang with Alexis Korner's Blues Incorporated, with whom he recorded the first British blues album in 1962, called R&B from the Marquee. When The Rolling Stones made their debut at the Marquee Club in July 1962, John put together a group to support them. Later, he was the announcer introducing the Stones on their US-only live album, Got Live If You Want It!, in 1966.

John became friendly with Paul McCartney after a show at the Cavern Club in Liverpool in the early 1960s, leading to an invitation to sing on one of The Beatles 1964 TV specials, Around The Beatles. In the special, he performs "Got My Mojo Workin'.

In 1963, Long John joined the Cyril Davies R&B All Stars with
Nicky Hopkins playing piano. He took over in 1964 after the death of Cyril Davies, and the group became Long John Baldry and his Hoochie Coochie Men.

In 1965, the Hoochie Coochie Men became Steampacket but after that group broke up in 1966, John formed Bluesology featuring Reg Dwight on keyboards and Elton Dean, later of Soft Machine. When Elton John and Bluesology left John without a backing group he was in the Mecca at Shaftesbury Avenue where he was watching a five piece harmony group from Plymouth, Devon called "Chimera" who had then recently turned professional. John approached them after their set and said how impressed he was by the vocal harmonies and that they would be ideal to back him on the cabaret circuit he was currently embarked on, which they did.

John was openly gay during the early 1960s, at least amongst his friends and industry peers. However, he did not make a formal public acknowledgement of this until the 1970s. John had a brief relationship with lead-guitarist of The Kinks, Dave Davies, and supported Elton John in coming to terms with his own sexuality. In 1978 his then-upcoming album Baldry's Out announced his formal coming out, and he addressed sexuality problems with a cover of Canadian songwriter Bill Amesbury's "A Thrill's a Thrill".

In 1967, he recorded a pop song "Let the Heartaches Begin" that went to number one in the British charts, followed by a 1968 top 20 hit titled "Mexico", which was the theme of the UK Olympic team that year. "Let the Heartaches Begin" made the lower reaches of the Billboard Hot 100 in the USA.

Bluesology broke up in 1968, with John continuing his solo career. Following the departure of Elton John and Bluesology, John was left without a backup band. Attending a show in the Mecca at Shaftesbury Avenue, he saw a five piece harmony group called Chimera from Plymouth, Devon, who had recently turned professional. He approached them after their set and said how impressed he was by their vocal harmonies and that they would be ideal to back him on the cabaret circuit he was currently embarked on. This they did. John, however, had mental health problems and was institutionalised for a brief time in 1975. The 1979 album Baldry's Out was recorded after his release.

After time in New York City and Los Angeles in 1978, Long John settled in Vancouver, British Columbia, where he became a Canadian citizen. He toured the west coast, as well as the US Northwest.

Long John played his last live show in Columbus, Ohio, on the 19th of July 2004, at Barristers Hall with guitarist Bobby Cameron. In 2003 John headlined the British Legends of Rhythm and Blues UK tour, alongside Zoot Money, Ray Dorset and Paul Williams.

Long John Baldry's final UK Tour as 'The Long John Baldry Trio' concluded with a performance on Saturday the thirteenth of November 2004 at The King's Lynn Arts Centre, King's Lynn, Norfolk, UK.

Marty Balin   Jefferson Airplane

Marty Balin died aged seventy-six on the twenty-seventh of September 2018 while being taken to hospital in Tampa, Florida, U.S.A. from actual causes which remain a mystery. He was survived by his wife, Susan and daughters, Delaney and Jennifer.

In 1962, then named Martyn Jerel Buchwald, He changed his name to Marty Balin and began recording, releasing singles called "Nobody But You" and "I Specialize in Love" and by 1964, he was leading a folk music quartet called The Town Criers.

Marty was the primary founding member of Jefferson Airplane and was also one of its lead vocalists and songwriters from 1965 to 1971. In the group's 1966–1971 lineup, Marty served as co-lead vocalist alongside Grace Slick and rhythm guitarist Paul Kantner. He played with Jefferson Airplane at the Monterey Pop Festival in 1967 and at the Woodstock Festival in 1969.

In April 1971, Marty formally departed Jefferson Airplane. However, he remained active in the San Francisco Bay Area rock scene, managing and producing an album for the Berkeley-based sextet Grootna before briefly joining funk-inflected hard rock ensemble Bodacious DF as lead vocalist on their eponymous 1973 debut album.

The following year, Paul Kantner asked Marty Balin to write a song for his new Airplane off-shoot group, Jefferson Starship. Together, they wrote the early power ballad "Caroline", which appeared on the album Dragon Fly with Marty Balin as guest lead vocalist.

Rejoining the team he had helped to establish, Marty became a permanent member of Jefferson Starship in 1975. over the next three years. Ultimately, Marty Balin's relationship with Jefferson Starship was beleaguered by interpersonal problems and he abruptly left them in October 1978 shortly after Grace Slick's departure from the band.

Marty continued with EMI as a solo artist and in 1981 he released his first solo album, ,Marty Balin. There was in 1983 a second solo album, 'Lucky', but his contract with EMI ended shortly thereafter.

In 1985, Marty teamed with Paul Kantner and Jack Casady to form the KBC Band.Marty continued recording solo albums in the years following the reunion, and reunited with Paul Kantner in the most recent incarnation of Jefferson Starship.

Dave Ball   Procol Harum

Dave Ball died of bowel cancer, aged sixty-five, on first of April 2015. He was survived by two sons and a daughter.

Dave was born in 1950 in Handsworth, Birmingham, U.K. In April 1971, he joined Procol Harum on guitar after he saw an advertisement in the Melody Maker music paper. At this point he replaced Robin Trower, and can be heard on Procol Harum's live album, 'Procol Harum Live' with the Edmonton Symphony Orchestra. Dave left the group in September 1972 during the recording sessions for their album Grand Hotel and then formed the group Bedlam with his brother Dennis and drummer Cozy Powell. They released an album on Chrysalis Records, but disbanded soon after. Dave also recorded on Long John

Baldry's 1973 album 'Good to Be Alive' and also played in the Nickey Barclay Band in London in the 1980s.

Dave last played with Gary Brooker of Procol Harum in London, in July 2007 and he also occasionally played with The Palers, a Procol Harum tribute band. In 2012 he released a solo album entitled 'Don't Forget Your Alligator'.

Kenny Ball   Jazzmen

Kenny Ball died of pneumonia, aged eighty-three, on the seventh of March 2013 in an Essex hospital in hte United Kingdom. He was survived by his second wife, Michelle; his stepdaughters Nicole and Sophie; and his children from his first marriage; daughters Gillian and Jane and son Keith.

Kenny was born in Ilford, Essex, U.K. in 1930. At the age of fourteen he left school to work as a clerk in an advertising agency, but also started taking trumpet lessons. He began his career as a semi-professional sideman in bands, whilst also working as a salesman and for the advertising agency. He turned professional in 1953 and played the trumpet in bands led by Sid Phillips, Charlie Galbraith, Eric Delaney and Terry Lightfoot before forming his own trad jazz band, Kenny Ball and his Jazzmen. In 1958. Kenny's Dixieland band was at the forefront of the 1960's United Kingdom jazz revival.

During 1963 Kenny became the first British jazzman to become an honorary citizen of New Orleans, USA. Kenny and his band enjoyed one of the longest unbroken spells of success for trad jazz bands and he had numerous Top 50 hit singles in the UK alone.

Florence Ballard   The Supremes

Florence Ballard died of coronary thrombosis, aged thirty-two, on the22nd of February 1976 at the Mt. Carmel Mercy Hospital in Detroit, Michigan, U.S.A.

Florence married in Hawaii in 1968 and had three daughters: Michelle Denise and Nichole Rene[and Lisa Sabrina. She was born in Detroit, Michigan in 1943 and had 12 siblings; Bertie, Cornell, Jesse, Jr., Gilbert, Geraldine, Barbara, Maxine, Billy, Calvin, Pat, Linda and Roy. Florence was coached vocally by a voice teacher and met future singing partner Mary Wilson during a middle-school talent show and became friends while attending High School.

From an early age, Florence aspired to be a singer and agreed to audition for a spot on a sister group of the local Detroit attraction, the Primes, who were managed by Milton Jenkins. After she was accepted, Florence recruited Mary Wilson to join Jenkins' group. Mary then enlisted another neighbour, Diana Ross. Betty McGlown completed the original lineup then named "The Primettes". The group performed at talent showcases and at school parties before auditioning for Motown Records in 1960. Berry Gordy, head of Motown, advised the group to graduate from high school before auditioning again.

Chris Barber   Jazzband

Chris Barber died aged ninety on 2nd March 2021 after suffering dementia in the period before his death. He was survived by his fourth wife, Kate, his son, Christopher Jnr and his daughter, Caroline.

Chris was born in Welwyn Garden City, Hertfordshire, United Kingdom and began learning to play the violin when he was seven years old. After the end of the Second World War, he attended a school in London, and began visiting clubs to hear jazz groups. He then spent three years at the Guildhall School of Music, and started playing music with friends he met there, including Alexis Korner.

In 1950 Chris Barber formed the New Orleans Jazz Band, a non-professional group of up to eight musicians, including Alexis Korner on guitar and himself on double bass and trombone, to play both trad jazz and blues tunes. He decided then to leave his job in an insurance office in 1951 and the following year he became a professional musician.

In 1959, the band's October 1956 recording of Sidney Bechet's "Petite Fleur", a clarinet solo by Monty Sunshine with Dick Smith on bass, Ron Bowden on drums and Dick Bishop on guitar, spent twenty-four weeks in the UK Singles Charts, making it to number 3 and selling over one million copies. It was awarded a gold disc. After 1959, Chris toured the United States several times where "Petite Fleur" charted at number five.

Peter Bardens   Camel

Peter Bardens died aged fifty seven on 22nd January 2002 from lung cancer in Malibu, California, U.S.A. He was survived by his ex-wife, Julia, his son, Sam and his daughter, Tullulah.

Peter Bardens was born in Westminster, London, U.K. and grew up in London's Notting Hill. He studied fine art at Byam Shaw School of Art, and learned the piano, before switching to the Hammond organ after listening to organist Jimmy Smith. In 1965, he joined the rock/pop band 'Them'.

Peter formed Camel in 1972 but left Camel in 1978 to join Van Morrison's band. By the end of the 1970s, he began exploring electronica and released the album Heart to Heart in 1979.

In 1984, Peter became a member of Keats, an Alan Parsons Project offshoot, and released an album with them. He continued to release a number of solo electronic albums including 'Seen One Earth' in 1987, which found chart success in the United States. The first single from the album, "In Dreams", was met with commercial success as well. The song enjoyed heavy airplay on rock stations in the U.S.A. and Australia.

Peter released Water Colours in 1991, an album that featured his former Camel bandmate Andy Ward and Caravan's Dave Sinclair. Peter formed the band Mirage and released a new album, Big Sky in 1994. His last concert, prior to being diagnosed with a brain tumour, was in Los Angeles in the summer of 2001.

Paul Barrere   Little Feet

Paul Barrere died aged seventy-one on the 26th of October, 2019 in Los Angeles, California, U.S.A. after, in 2015, having been diagnosed with liver cancer. He was survived by his wife, Pam and his son, Gabriel and his daughters, Genevieve and Gillian.

Paul's best known contributions to Little Feat as a songwriter include "Skin It Back", and "Feats Don't Fail Me Now" from the album Feats Don't Fail Me Now. Paul was a guitarist who played a wide variety of styles of music including blues, rock, jazz, and cajun music and was also proficient as a slide guitarist. He also recorded and toured as an acoustic duo with fellow Little Feat member Fred Tackett.

Syd Barrett   Pink Floyd

Syd Barrett died from pancreatic cancer, aged 60, on the 7th of July, 2006 at his home in Cambridge, UK. He was survived by his his sister, Rosemary.

Syd was born Roger Keith Barrett in Cambridge UK in 1946. As a child, he played piano occasionally, but usually preferred writing and drawing. However, Syd got a ukulele at ten, a banjo at eleven and a Hofner acoustic guitar at age fourteen. Just on year after he got his first acoustic guitar, he bought his first electric guitar and built his own amplifier.

In September 1962, Syd took a place at the Cambridge Technical College art department, where he met future collaborator, Dave Gilmour. Syd then decided to apply for Camberwell College of Arts in London and enrolled there in the summer of 1964 to study painting.

In 1966, a new rock concert venue, the UFO, opened in London and quickly became a haven for British psychedelic music lovers. Pink Floyd, the house band, was its most popular attraction and after making appearances at the rival Roundhouse, became the most popular musical group of the London psychedelic music scene.

At the beginning of 1967, Syd Barrett was dating a girl named Jenny, however, through late 1967 and early 1968, his behaviour became increasingly erratic and unpredictable, partly as a consequence of his reported heavy use of psychedelic drugs, most prominently LSD. He is said to have become unable to recognize old friends that he had known for years.

After leaving Pink Floyd, Syd Barrett was out of the public eye for a year, then, in 1969, at the behest of his record company, he embarked on a brief solo career and released two solo albums.

In 1978, when Syd's money ran short, he moved back to Cambridge to live with his mother, returning to live in London again in 1982 for a few weeks, then soon returned to Cambridge for good.

Syd made a final public acknowledgement of his musical past in 2002 when he autographed 320 copies of photographer Mick Rock's book Psychedelic Renegades, which contained a number of photos of Syd. Having reverted to his birth name of Roger, he signed simply, Barrett.

Fontella Bass   Solo Artiste

Fontella Bass died aged seventy-two on the 26th December 2012 at a hospital in St. Louis, Missouri, U.S.A. from complications of a heart attack suffered earlier in the month.

Fontella was born in St. Louis, Missouri, U.S.A. the

daughter of gospel singer Martha Bass and, at an early age, Fontella showed great musical talent. At the age of five, she provided the piano accompaniment for her grandmother's singing at funeral services, she sang in her church's choir at six, and by the time she was nine, she had accompanied her mother on tours throughout the South and south-west USA.

Fontella continued touring with her mother until the age of sixteen. As a teenager, Fontella was attracted by more secular music and she began singing Rythm & Blues songs at local contests and fairs while attending high school from which she graduated in 1958. At seventeen, she started her professional career working at the Showboat Club near Chain of Rocks, Missouri.

With the support of the manager of St. Louis radio station KATZ, Fontella recorded several songs released through Bobbin Records She was produced by Ike Turner when she recorded on his labels Prann and Sonja. Her single "Poor Little Fool" released from Sonja in 1964 features Tina Turner. It was also during this period she met and subsequently married the jazz trumpeter Lester Bowie.

Two years later, she quit the Milton band and moved to Chicago after a dispute with Oliver Sain. She auditioned for Chess Records, who immediately signed her as a recording artist to the subsidiary label Checker Records. Her first works with the label were several duets with Bobby McClure, who had also been signed to the label. Released early in 1965, their recording "Don't Mess Up a Good Thing" found immediate success.

Fontella and McClure followed their early success with "You're Gonna Miss Me", that summer, a song that had mild success, reaching the Top 30 on the R&B chart, although it made no significant impression on the pop chart. After a brief tour, Fontella returned to the studio. The culmination of one particular session was an original composition with an aggressive rhythm section. The resulting song, "Rescue Me" shot up the charts in the fall and winter of 1965. After a month-long run at the top of the R&B charts, the song reached number 4 on the US pop charts and number 11 in the UK, and gave Chess its first million-selling single for a decade .

Skip Battin   The Byrds

Skip Battin died aged sixty-nine from the complications of Alzheimer's disease on the 6th of July, 2003. He was survived by his wife Patricia and his sons Brent and John-Clyde and his daughter, Susanna.

Skip discovered the electric bass when he was seventeen years old and he was a member of the Byrds from 1970 to 1973. After the breakup of the Byrds, Skip recorded a solo album called 'Skip'. In February 1973, Skip was invited to join the country-rock group New Riders of the Purple Sage, with whom he recorded three albums between 1974 and 1976.

Jeff Beck   The Yardbirds

Jeff Beck died aged seventy-eight on the 10th of January 2023 while in hospital with a bacterial meningitis infection. He was survived by his wife, Sandra.

As a teenager Jeff learned to play on a borrowed guitar and made several attempts to build his own instrument. After leaving school, he attended art college then was briefly employed as a painter and decorator, a groundsman on a golf course, and a car paint sprayer. While attending Wimbledon College of Art, Jeff played in a succession of groups, including Screaming Lord Sutch and the Savages during 1962. Later in 1963, he joined the Tridents, a band from the Chiswick area of London.

In March 1965, he was recruited by the Yardbirds who recorded most of their Top 40 hit songs during Jeff's short but significant twenty months with the band. In May 1966, he recorded a solo instrumental entitled "Beck's Bolero".

Jeff's solo album, Blow by Blow, in March 1975, show-cased his technical prowess in jazz-rock. The album reached number four in the charts and is his most commercially successful release. Jeff returned to the studio and recorded Wired in 1976 which used a jazz-rock fusion style.

Walter Becker   Steely Dan

Walter Becker died aged sixty-seven of esophageal cancer at his home in Manhattan, New York, U.S.A. on the third of September 2017. He was survived by his wife, Elinor, his adopted daughter, Sayan and son, Kawai. Musicians including Julian Lennon, Steve Lukather, and John Darnielle of the Mountain Goats made public statements mourning Walter's death.

Walter was raised in Queens, NewYork. U.S.A. by his father and grandmother and graduated from high school in 1967. After starting out on saxophone, he switched to guitar and received instruction in blues technique from a neighbour.

Walter left school in 1969 before completing his degree and moved with Donald Fagen to Brooklyn, where the two began to build a career as a songwriting duo. In 1971, they moved to Los Angeles and formed Steely Dan with guitarists Denny Dias and Jeff "Skunk" Baxter, drummer Jim Hodder, and vocalist David Palmer.

Donald Fagen played keyboards and sang, while Walter Becker played bass guitar. Steely Dan spent the next three years touring and recording before quitting touring in 1974, confining themselves to the studio with personnel that changed for every album. In addition to co-writing all of the band's material, Walter played guitar and bass guitar and sang background vocals.

Despite the success of the album "Aja" in 1977, Walter endured some setbacks during this period, including an addiction to narcotics. After the duo returned to New York in 1978, Walter's girlfriend, Karen, died of a drug overdose in his apartment, resulting in a wrongful death lawsuit against him. Soon after, Walter was hit by a cab in Manhattan while crossing the street and was forced to walk with crutches while recovering. His exhaustion was made worse by commercial pressure and the complicated recording of the album Gaucho. Walter Becker and Fagen suspended their partnership in June 1981.

Following Steely Dan's breakup, Walter Becker and his family moved to Maui in Hawaii where Walter ceased using drugs, stopped smoking and drinking, and became a self-styled critic of the contemporary scene.

Harry Belefonte   Solo Artiste

Harry Belafonte died aged ninety-six from congestive heart failure on the 25th of April, 2023 at his home on the Upper West Side of Manhattan, New York City. He was survived by his second wife, Julie, his son, David, his daughters, Adrienne, Shari and Gina and five grand-children. His interment was at Ferncliff Cemetery and Mausoleum in Hartsdale, New York, USA. Harry had suffered a stroke in 2004, which diminished his inner-ear balance and from 2019, his health had been in decline.

Harry began his career in music as a club singer in New York to pay for acting classes and the first time he appeared in front of an audience, he was backed by the Charlie Parker band. With guitarist and friend Millard Thomas, Harry soon made his debut at the legendary jazz club The Village Vanguard. He signed a contract with RCA Victor in 1953, recording regularly for them until 1974. Harry's first widely released single, which went on to become his "signature" song in most of his live performances, was "Matilda", recorded during April, 1953.

Harry Belafonte's breakthrough album, Calypso in 1956, became the first long playing album in the world to sell over one million copies in a year and was the first million-selling album ever in the UK. Calypso introduced American audiences to calypso music, which originated from Trinidad and Tobago in the early nineteenth century. Harry was then dubbed the "King of Calypso", a title he wore with some reservations. One of the songs included in the album is the well known "Banana Boat Song", which reached number five on the pop chart, and featured its signature lyric "Day-O".

In 1961, Harry was one of many entertainers recruited by Frank Sinatra to perform at the inaugural gala of President John F. Kennedy. Later that year, RCA Victor released another calypso album, Jump Up Calypso, which went on to become another million seller.

Harry's fifth and final calypso album, Calypso Carnival, was issued by RCA in 1971, however, his recording activity slowed considerably after releasing his final album for RCA in 1974. From the mid-1970s to early 1980s, Harry spent the greater part of his time on tour, which included concerts in Japan, Europe, and Cuba.

In 1988, Harry released his first album of original material in over a decade called Paradise in Gazankulu, which contained ten protest songs against the South African former Apartheid policy, and was his last studio album.

Ronald Bell   Kool & the Gang

Ronald Bell died aged sixty-eight on the ninth of September 2020 at his home in the Virgin Islands with no cause of death being given. He was survived by his third wife, Tia, and ten children.

Kool & the Gang, a band Ronald formed with his brother, Robert, were one of the first fully fledged funk ensembles, their distinctive sound emphasised by bright horns, percussive congas and cowbells.

Ronald was born in Youngstown, Ohio, United States of America but when Ronald was still a boy the family moved to Jersey City, New Jersey, in 1961. Whilst attending Lincoln school, Ronald and Robert formed their first band, the Jazziacs, with fellow pupils, and played in jazz clubs and bars. Their sound began to change when, in 1968, they became part of the Soul Town Band, learning recent soul hits to accompany singers. Then, deciding to perform under Robert's nickname, they finally settled on Kool & the Gang as their name.

Chester Bennington   Linkin Park

Chester Bennington died from suicide at age forty-one on the 20th of July 2017 by hanging himself at his home in Palos Verdes Estates, California. Chester's death occurred on what would have been Chris Cornell's 53rd birthday. Cornell, a close friend of Chester's, had also died by suicide when hanging himself two months earlier. Chester was survived by his wife, Talinda and his sons, Tyler Lee, Jaime, Draven and Isaiah and his daughters, Lily and Lila.

Chester was plagued with poor health during the making of the album Meteora, and struggled to attend some of the recording sessions. In the summer of 2003, he began to suffer from extreme abdominal pain and gastrointestinal issues while filming the music video for "Numb" in Prague. He was forced to return to the United States for surgery, and filmed the remainder of the music video in Los Angeles.

Chester was born Charles Bennington in 1976 in Phoenix, Arizona, U.S.A. He worked at a Burger King before starting his career as a professional musician. Chester first began singing with a band with Sean Dowdell and they released a three-track cassette in 1993. Later, Sean Dowdell and Chester moved on to form a new band, Grey Daze, a post-grunge band based in Phoenix, Arizona and they recorded three albums; 'Demo' in 1993, 'Wake/ Me' in 1994, and 'No Sun Today' in 1997 before Chester left Grey Daze in 1998.

On October 24th 2000, Linkin Park released their debut album, Hybrid Theory, through Warner Bros. Records. Chester primarily served as Linkin Park's lead vocalist.

Renaldo Obie Benson   The Four Tops

Renaldo "Obie" Benson died aged sixty-nine of lung cancer and other illnesses on the 1st of July 2005. His leg had been amputated earlier in 2005 due to circulation problems. He was survived by two daughters. His last performance as a Four Top was on the 8th of April 2005. He was interred at Woodlawn Cemetery, Detroit, Michigan, U.S.A.

Renaldo attended High School in Detroit, Michigan, U.S.A. with Lawrence Payton. The pair met Levi Stubbs and Abdul "Duke" Fakir while singing at a friend's birthday party in 1954 and decided to form a group called the Four Aims. The group changed their name to the Four Tops to avoid confusion with the Ames Brothers and had one single called "Kiss Me Baby" released through Chess Records which failed to chart.

In 1963 the Four Tops signed with Tamla Motown and worked with Holland-Dozier-Holland who wrote and produced a number of soul music hits for them over the next few years, including "I Can't Help Myself" and "Reach Out I'll Be There" which both topped the US and UK pop charts.

Chuck Berry   Solo Artiste

Chuck Berry died of a cardiac arrest aged ninety on the 18th of March 2017 at his home in Missouri, U.S.A. He was survived by his wife, Themetta and his son, Charles and his daughter, Ingrid.

Chuck Berry's funeral was held on 9th April 2017, at The Pageant, in his hometown of St. Louis, Missouri, U.S.A. He was remembered in rock 'n' roll style with a public viewing by family, friends, and fans in The Pageant, a music club where he often performed, with his beloved cherry-red guitar bolted to the inside lid of the coffin and with flower arrangements that included one sent by English R&B band the Rolling Stones in the shape of a guitar. Afterwards a private service was held in the club celebrating Chuck

Berry's life and musical career, with the Berry family inviting 300 members of the public into the service. The night before, many St. Louis area bars held a mass toast at 10 pm in Chuck Berry's honour.

Chuck Berry was born Charles Edward Anderson Berry in 1926 in St. Louis, Missourii, U.S.A. where he was the fourth child in a family of six.

Chuck initially supported his family by taking various jobs in St. Louis, working briefly as a factory worker at two automobile assembly plants and as a janitor in the apartment building where he and his wife lived.

By the end of the 1950s, Chuck Berry was a high-profile established star with several hit records and film appearances and a lucrative touring career. In May 1964, he made a successful tour of the UK.

Chuck announced on his 90th birthday that his first new studio album since Rock It in 1979, entitled 'Chuck', would be released in 2017. His first new record in 38 years, it includes his children, Charles and Ingrid, on guitar and harmonica, with songs "covering the spectrum from hard-driving rockers to soulful thought-provoking time capsules of a life's work".

Acker Bilk   Paramount Jazz Band

Acker Bilk died aged eighty-five in Bath, Somerset, UK on the 2nd of November 2014. He was survived by his wife, Jean and his son, Peter and his daughter, Jenny. His last recorded interview was for a Cornish community radio station.

Acker Bilk was born Bernard Stanley Bilk in 1929 in Somerset, UK. and he earned the nickname "Acker" from the Somerset slang for "friend" or "mate". He lost two front teeth in a school fight and half a finger in a sledging accident, both of which he claimed affected his eventual clarinet style.

Acker played with friends on the Bristol jazz circuit and

in 1951 moved to London to play with Ken Colyer's band. Acker disliked London, so returned west and formed his own band in Pensford called the Chew Valley Jazzmen.

Acker Bilk was not an internationally known musician until 1962, when the experimental use of a string ensemble on one of his albums and the inclusion of a composition of his own as its keynote piece won him an audience outside the UK. He had composed a melody, entitled "Jenny" after his daughter, but was asked to change the title to "Stranger on the Shore" for use in a British television series. He went on to record it as the title track of an album.

Acker continued to tour with his Paramount Jazz Band, as well as performing concerts with his two contemporaries, Chris Barber and Kenny Ball. In 2005 Acker was awarded the BBC Jazz Awards' "Gold Award". In 2012 Acker is known to have said that, after fifty years, he was "fed up" with playing "Stranger on the Shore", his most famous tune.

Cilla Black   Solo Artiste

Cilla Black died of a stroke, aged seventy-two on the 1st of August 2015 at her holiday home near Estepona in Spain. She was survived by her sons, Robert, Ben and Jack. In the days following her death, a book of condolence was opened at the Liverpool Town Hall.

Cilla was born Priscilla Maria Veronica White in 1943 in Liverpool, UK. She was raised in a Roman Catholic household, and attended a school where she learned office skills. Determined to become an entertainer, Cilla gained a part-time job as a cloakroom attendant at Liverpool's Cavern Club, best known for its connection with the Beatles. Her impromptu performances there impressed the Beatles and others and she was encouraged to begin singing by a Liverpool promoter, Sam Leach, who booked her first gig at the Casanova Club, on London Road, where she appeared as "Swinging Cilla". She also became a guest singer with local

Merseybeat bands. Meanwhile, she worked as a waitress at the Zodiac coffee lounge, where she later met her future husband Bobby Willis.

Cilla had signed her first contract with long-time friend and neighbour, Terry McCann, but this contract was never honoured as it was made when she was under age and her father subsequently signed her with Brian Epstein. Brian Epstein's attempts to make Cilla Black a film actress were less successful. A brief appearance in the film Ferry 'Cross the Mersey in 1965 and a leading role alongside David Warner in the psychedelic comedy Work Is a Four-Letter Word in 1968 were largely ignored by film critics.

Cilla's Black's boyfriend and songwriter Bobby Willis assumed management responsibilities after Brian Epstein died and in 1993 Cilla released Through the Years, an album of new material featuring duets with Dusty Springfield, Cliff Richard and Barry Manilow. Ten years later, in 2003, she released the album Beginnings. Greatest Hits and New Songs.

Cilla Black was one of the best-selling British female recording artist in the UK during the 1960s, releasing a total of 15 studio albums and 37 singles.

Jet Black   The Stranglers

Jet Black died aged eighty-four from respiratory problems on the sixth of December 2022 at his home in Wales, United Kingdom. He was survived by his second wife Helena, from whom he was separated.

Jet was born as Brian John Duffy in Ilford, Essex, UK. and became a full-time professional musician in the mid nineteen seventies and joined Hugh Cornwell in the Stranglers in 1974.

During his extensive career as a drummer, Jet became aware of certain practical limitations inherent in the basic kit design and set about addressing the issue in the form of the now patented 'Jet Black Power Bass Drum Pedal'.

which enables the bass drum to be placed anywhere and yet remain playable.

In March 2007, Jet suffered from atrial fibrillation and stopped playing with the Stranglers until he had recovered. He returned to playing with the band in June, but it was at this time that he retired from performing outside of the United Kingdom due to health issues exacerbated by lengthy travel. However, he returned to full rehearsals and began touring with the band again that October but in March 2012, he was taken to hospital shortly before a Stranglers concert at the O2 Academy Oxford.

Marc Bolan   T Rex

Marc Bolan died in a motor accident, aged twenty-nine, on the 16th of September 1977. He had been a passenger in a car driven by his girlfriend, Gloria, as they drove home from a restaurant in Berkeley Square, London. Gloria lost control of the car and it hit a steel reinforced fence post before coming to rest against a tree near Barnes in southwest London. Neither occupant was wearing a seat belt and Marc was killed instantly. Gloria Jones suffered a broken arm and broken jaw and spent time in hospital.

Marc was survived by his wife, June, who died in 1994, and his son, Rolan.

At Marc's funeral, attended by David Bowie, Rod Stewart, Tony Visconti, and Steve Harley, a swan-shaped floral tribute was displayed outside the service in recognition of his breakthrough hit single "Ride a White Swan". His funeral service was at the Golders Green Crematorium, in north London, where his ashes were buried. The car crash site has subsequently become a shrine to his memory, where fans leave tributes beside the tree.

Marc Bolan was born Mark Feld on the 30th of September 1947 and grew up in East London, UK. At the age of nine, Marc was given his first guitar and began a skiffle band. Marc briefly joined a modelling agency and appeared in a clothing catalogue for a menswear store.

After changing his name to Marc Bolan, he signed to Decca Records in August 1965 and recorded his debut single "The Wizard." In 1966, Marc turned up at Simon Napier-Bell's front door with his guitar and proclaimed that he was going to be a big star and he needed someone to make all of the arrangements. Simon invited Marc in and listened to his songs. A recording session was immediately booked and the songs were very simply recorded and most of them not actually released until 1974.

In 1969, Marc published his first and only book of poetry entitled The Warlock of Love. In keeping with his early rock&roll interests, Marc began bringing amplified guitar lines into his music, buying a white Fender Stratocaster decorated with a paisley teardrop motif.

In 1972, Marc achieved two British number ones with "Telegram Sam" and "Metal Guru" and two more number twos in "Children of the Revolution" and "Solid Gold Easy Action". In that same year he appeared in Ringo Starr's film Born to Boogie. At this time T. Rex record sales accounted for about six percent of total British domestic record sales.

Eventually, the original T. Rex line-up disbanded and Marc's marriage to June came to an end because of his affair with backing singer Gloria who gave birth to his son Rolan in 1975. He also had spent a lot of his time in the USA

Trevor Bolder   **Uriah Heep**

Trevor Bolder died aged sixty-two from cancer on twenty-first of May 2013 in hospital at Cottingham, Yorkshire, after having undergone surgery for pancreatic cancer earlier in the year. He was survived by his wife Shelly, his sons James and Ashley and his daughter Sarah.

Trevor was born in Kingston upon Hull, East Riding,

Yorkshire, U.K. His father was a trumpet player and other members of his family were also musicians. He played cornet in the school band and was active in his local R&B scene in the mid 1960's. Then inspired by The Beatles, in 1964 he formed his first band with his brother and took up the bass guitar.

Trevor first came to prominence in a band which also featured guitarist Mick Ronson. In 1971 he was asked to replace the guitarist in David Bowie's backing band, which was soon be known as 'The Spiders from Mars'.

Trevor Bolder's bass playing and occasional trumpet work appeared on the studio albums Hunky Dory from 1971, The Rise and Fall of Ziggy Stardust and the Spiders from Mars, from 1972, Aladdin Sane and Pin Ups from 1973. He went on to play on Mick Ronson's 1974 album Slaughter on 10th Avenue which made the British Top Ten.

In 1976 Trevor Bolder joined Uriah Heep, replacing John Wetton. He worked on the albums 'Firefly', 'Innocent Victim', 'Fallen Angel' and 'Conquest'. When the line-up that had recorded the latter disbanded, Trevor alone was left with Mick Box, guitarist, founder-member and legal owner of the band's name. The attempt to put a new line-up together temporarily stalled and Trevor Bolder, needing to earn a living, accepted an offer in 1981 to join Wishbone Ash but by 1983 he had returned to play with Uriah Heep.

John Bonham   Led Zeppelin

John Bonham choked to death aged thirty-two on the twenty-fifth of September 1980 in Winsor, UK. He was survived by his wife, Pat, by his son, Jason and daughter, Zoe.

John had been picked up the day before by a Led Zeppelin assistant to attend rehearsals prior to a tour of North America. During the journey, John asked to stop for breakfast, where he drank four quadruple vodka Screwdrivers and then continued to drink heavily after arriving at rehearsals. The band stopped rehearsing late in the evening and then went to Jimmy Page's house, the Old Mill House in Clewer, Windsor. After midnight John fell asleep; someone took him to bed and placed him on his side. Led Zeppelin's tour manager found him unresponsive the next afternoon and he was later pronounced dead.

The inquest on the twenty-seventh of October 1980 showed that in four hours, John had consumed around forty shots of 40 percent ABV vodka, after which he vomited and choked. The finding was accidental death and an autopsy found no other drugs in his corpse.

John was born John Henry Bonham on the thirty-first of May 1948 in Redditch, Worcestershire, United Kingdom. He began learning to play drums at five years old, making a kit of containers and coffee tins and imitating his idols Max Roach, Gene Krupa and Buddy Rich. John's mother gave him a snare drum when he was ten and he received his first drum kit from his father at age fifteen, a Premier set. John never took formal drum lessons, though as a teenager he listened to advice from other Redditch drummers.

John attended a Secondary Modern School, where his headmaster reported that he would either end up a dustman or a millionaire. After leaving school in 1964, John worked for his father as an apprentice carpenter in-between drumming for local bands. In 1964, he joined his first semi-professional band, Terry Webb and the Spiders, and met his future wife Pat around the same time. He also played in other Birmingham bands and in 1964 he took up drumming full-time. Two years later, he joined a band which soon broke-up and needing a regular income he joined a blues group called Crawling King Snakes whose lead singer was Robert Plant.

In 1967 Robert Plant formed Band of Joy and chose John as the drummer. In 1968, American singer Tim Rose toured Britain and asked Band of Joy to open his concerts. When Tim Rose returned months later, John was invited by the singer to drum for his band, which provided a regular income.

After leaving The Yardbirds, guitarist Jimmy Page formed another band and recruited Robert Plant, who then recommended John as drummer. On hearing John he was convinced he was perfect for the project, first known as the New Yardbirds and later as Led Zeppelin.

During Led Zeppelin's first tour of the United States in December 1968, John became friends with Vanilla Fudge's drummer, Carmine Appice. Appice introduced him to Ludwig drums, which he then used for the rest of his career. John used the longest and heaviest sticks which he called his trees.

Sonny Bono   Sonny & Cher

Sonny Bono died aged sixty-two on the fifth of January 1998 of injuries he sustained by striking a tree while skiing in California, U.S.A. He was survived by his wife, Mary and his sons, Chaz, Chesare and Sean and his daughters, Christy and Chianna. Cher gave an eulogy at Sonny's funeral and his remains were buried at Desert Memorial Park in Cathedral City, California. The epitaph on Sonny Bono's headstone reads: "AND THE BEAT GOES ON".

Sonny was born Salvatore Phillip Bono on the 16th of February, 1935 in Detroit, Michigan, U.S.A. He began his music career as a songwriter at Specialty Records, where his song "Things You Do to Me" was recorded by Sam Cooke, and went on to work for record producer Phil Spector in the early 1960s as a promotion man, percussionist and "gofer". One of his earliest songwriting efforts, "Needles and Pins" was co-written with Jack Nitzsche, another member of Spector's production team. Later in the same decade, Sonny achieved commercial success with his then-wife Cher in the singing duo Sonny and Cher. Sonny wrote, arranged, and produced a number of hit records including the singles "I Got You Babe" and "The Beat Goes On".

Sonny continued to work with Cher through the early and mid-1970s, starring in a popular television variety show, The Sonny and Cher Comedy Hour, which ran on America's CBS from 1971 to 1974, then, from 1976 to 1977, the duo, then divorced, returned to perform together on The Sonny and Cher Show. Their last appearance together was on television in 1987 on which they sang "I Got You Babe".

David Bowie   Spiders From Mars

David Bowie died aged sixty-nine from liver cancer on the tenth of January 2016 in his city apartment in New York, U.S.A., just two days after the release of his final album, 'Blackstar'. He was survived by his wife, Inman and his son, Duncan and his daughter, Alexandria.

David Bowie was born David Robert Jones in 1947, in Brixton, South East London, UK. In 1953, David moved with his family to the suburb of Bromley, where, two years later, he started attending a junior school where his voice was considered "adequate" by the school choir and he demonstrated above-average abilities in playing the recorder. At the age of nine, his dancing during the newly introduced music and movement classes was strikingly imaginative: teachers called his interpretations "vividly artistic" and his poise "astonishing" for a child. The same year, his interest in music was further stimulated when his father brought home a collection of American vinyl records. The following year he had taken up the ukulele and tea-chest bass, begun to participate in skiffle sessions with friends, and had started to play the piano.

After his half-brother introduced David to modern jazz, his enthusiasm for players like Charles Mingus and John Coltrane led his mother to give him a Grafton saxophone in 1961 and he was soon receiving lessons from a local musician.

In 1962 David formed his first band called King Bees, at the age of fifteen, playing guitar-based rock and roll at local youth gatherings and weddings.

Dissatisfied with his stage name as Davy he renamed himself after the 19th-century American pioneer James Bowie and the knife thus popularised. His April 1967 solo single, "The Laughing Gnome", using speeded-up high-pitched vocals, failed to chart. Released six weeks later, his album debut, 'David Bowie', an amalgam of pop, psychedelia, and music hall, also failed.

David contributed backing vocals to Lou Reed's 1972 solo breakthrough Transformer, co-producing the album with Mick Ronson. His own Aladdin Sane album in 1973 topped the UK chart, David's first number-one album. After breaking up the Spiders from Mars, David attempted to move on from his Ziggy persona. David was the best-selling act of 1973 in the UK. It brought the total number of David Bowie albums concurrently on the UK chart to six.

David moved to the USA in 1974, initially staying in New York City before settling in Los Angeles. The Diamond Dogs album in 1974, went to number one in the UK, spawning the hits "Rebel Rebel" and "Diamond Dogs", and number five in the USA.

David moved to Switzerland in 1976, purchasing a chalet in the hills to the north of Lake Geneva. In the new environment, his cocaine use decreased and he found time for other pursuits outside his musical career. David's duet with Mick Jagger. "Dancing in the Street" quickly went to number one on release.

In October 1990, a decade after his divorce from Angie, David Bowie and Somali-born supermodel Iman were introduced by a mutual friend. On twentieth of April 1992, David appeared at The Freddie Mercury Tribute Concert. Four days later, David and Iman were married in Switzerland and were intending to move to Los Angeles but they they settled in New York instead.

Blackstar was released on the eighth of January 2016, David's sixty-ninth birthday, and was met with critical acclaim.

After news of his death, sales of his albums and singles soared. David had insisted that he did not want a funeral, and according to his death certificate he was cremated in New Jersey, USA on the 12th of January 2016.

Laura Branagan   Solo Artiste

Laura Branigan died aged fifty-two on twenty-sixth of August 2004 from a ventricular brain aneurysm at her lodge in East Quogue, New York, U.S.A. and her ashes were scattered over Long Island Sound, the tidal estuary running between New York's Long Island and Connecticut. She was survived by her mother Kathleen and her brothers Billy and Mark and sister Susan.

Laura Ann Branigan was born on the third of July 1952 in the village of Brewster, New York, U.S.A. She attended High School from 1966 to 1970, starring in the school musical, The Pajama Game, in her senior year. Later, she attended the American Academy of Dramatic Arts in New York City between 1970 and 1972. In 1972 she participated in forming the folk-rock band Meadow who released their debut album 'The Friend Ship' featuring the singles 'When You Were Young', and 'Cane and Able'. After a fellow member committed suicide the band broke up.

In 1979, Laura was signed to Atlantic Records and her 1981 single "Looking Out for Number One", from her unreleased album Silver Dreams, made a brief appearance on the U.S. dance chart, reaching number 60. Two other early Atlantic singles, "Tell Him" and "Fool's Affair", followed. None of these three singles were included on her first album, but all four songs were eventually released on CD over thirty years later in 2014 as bonus cuts on an American CD reissue of her first album.

Laura's nine-track debut album, 'Branigan', was

released in March 1982. The first single from the album was "All Night with Me", which reached number 69 on the Billboard charts in early 1982. The album alternated four energetic up-tempo songs with five ballads, including one of the few songs written solely by Laura, "I Wish We Could Be Alone". "Gloria", an Italian love song , was released as the album's second single.

In the spring of 1983 Laura Branigan released her second album 'Laura Branigan 2'. Laura's vocals propelled her English-language version of the French song Solitaire toward the top of the U.S. charts. In 1984 "Self Control", the title track of her third album, became her biggest hit internationally, topping the charts in over six countries, most notably West Germany, where it spent six weeks at number one.

Other pop, disco, and adult contemporary hits from Laura's Self Control album include "The Lucky One", which won her a Tokyo Music Festival prize, the continental ballad "Ti Amo" and the dance hit "Satisfaction". The album also featured a version of Carole King's "Will You Still Love Me Tomorrow"; as a counterpoint to all the dance productions, it was a bare-bones piano version. In concerts and television appearances throughout her career, Laura accompanied herself on the piano for that song.

By the time Laura's fourth album was released in 1985, "Self Control" was a worldwide success. The hits continued with "Spanish Eddie", which was her sixth U.S. Billboard top 40 pop hit in two and a half years. The subsequent single release "Hold Me" was a U.S. top-40 dance hit, and Laura's introduction of the rock ballad "I Found Someone" scored even higher on the adult contemporary chart.

Laura's fifth album Touch, released in July 1987, marked a change in her career. Under new management and using different producers, Laura took a more active role in her work and in the studio, seeing her return to dance floors with the Stock-Aitken-Waterman-produced track "Shattered Glass" written by Bob Mitchell and Steve Coe, of the band Monsoon.

Laura's sixth album brought her back to the Hi-NRG charts and gay clubs with "Moonlight On Water", and she scored a top-30 adult contemporary hit with "Never in a Million Years." Laura added production to her list of credits with her cover of Vicki Sue Robinson's disco-era "Turn the Beat Around" and the atmospheric "Let Me In," a cover of an Eddie Money song. The album also includes performed at the Warwick Musical Theatre in Rhode Island.

Lee Brilleaux   Dr. Feelgood

Lee Brilleaux died aged forty-one from lymphoma at his home in Leigh-on-Sea, Essex, UK. He was survived by his wife, Shirley and his son, Nick and his daughter, Kelly.

Lee was born Lee John Collinson in 1952 in South Africa to English parents who brought him up in London, United Kingdom. They moved to Canvey Island, Essex, when Lee was thirteen years old.

Lee co-founded Dr Feelgood with Wilko Johnson in nineteen seventy-one and was the band's lead singer, harmonica player and occasional guitarist. Lee and Wilco developed a frantic act, often charismatically dressed in dark suits and loose ties, shabby rather than smart. The rough, and almost ruthless, edge which ran through his vocal and harmonica style reflected the character and philosophy of the band.

In 1976, Lee helped found Stiff Records, one of the main vehicles of the "New Wave" music of the mid- to late-1970s. Wilco Johnson left Dr Feelgood in 1977 and Lee reformed the band with different musicians in the 80s and early 90s. By 1984 he was the only founder member remaining. In 1986, he recorded the album 'Brilleaux 86', featuring songs by Johnny Cash. His last performance was in January 1994, at the Dr Feelgood Music Bar in Canvey Island, Essex, U.K.

Gary Brooker   Procol Harum

Gary Brooker died from cancer aged seventy-six on the
nineteenth of February 2022 at his home in Surrey, United
Kingdom. He was survived by his wife, Franky.

Gary was born in East London, UK, on the twenty-ninth
of May

1945. His father was a professional musician, and as a
child Gary learned to play piano, cornet, and trombone.

When Gary left school, he went to college to study zoology and botany but dropped out to become a professional
musician.

In 1966, Gary founded Procol Harum with a friend and
he wrote their huge hit record, A Whiter shade of Pale.

In May 2012, Gary fractured his skull in a fall in his hotel
room in Cape Town on his 67th birthday during a South
African tour. However, they continued touring until 2019,
playing their final gig in Switzerland.

John Brookes   The Charlatans

Jon Brookes died aged forty-four from a brain tumour on
the 13th of August 2013 in hospital following a seizure while
on tour in America. He was survived by his wife Debbie and
his daughters, Lola Primrose, Ruby Rose and Coco Dahlia.

Jon was born in 1968 in Burntwood, Staffordshire,
United Kingdom and grew up in Wednesbury, a market
town in the Black Country. He was a founding member of
the Charlatans, who formed in 1989 in the West Midlands
of the United Kingdom.

James Brown   Solo Artiste

James Brown died aged seventy-three of Congestive Heart
Failure on the 25th of December 2006. He was survived by
his sons, Teddy, James, Daryl, Larry and Terry and by his
daughters, Yamma, Venisha, LaRhonda, Deanna and Lisa.

Two days earlier, he had been feeling quite unwell and arrived at his dentist's office in Atlanta, Georgia, U.S.A. for dental implant work. During James's visit the dentist observed that James looked weak and dazed. Instead of performing the work, the dentist advised James to see a doctor immediately about his medical condition. The next day James visited a hospital in Atlanta for medical evaluation and was admitted for observation and treatment where he remained hospitalized but his condition worsened throughout the day.

After several memorial services and an unusual delay, James Brown's body was finally laid to rest seventy-six days after his death, in a crypt at the home of daughter, Deanna, on Beech Island, South Carolina, U.S.A.

James Joseph Brown was born on May 3rd 1933 in Barnwell, South Carolina,USA . James began singing in talent shows as a young child, first appearing at Augusta's Lenox Theater in 1944, winning the show after singing a ballad "So Long". While in Augusta, He learned to play the piano, guitar, and harmonica. In his teen years, James briefly had a career as a boxer. At the age of sixteen he was convicted of robbery and sent to a juvenile detention center and upon his release, he joined a gospel group.

In October 1958, James released the ballad "Try Me", which hit number one on the American Rythm & Blues chart in the beginning of 1959, becoming the first of seventeen chart-topping Rythm & Blues hits. By 1960, James Brown began multi-tasking in the recording studio involving himself, his singing group, the Famous Flames, and his band. That year the band released the top ten Rythm & Blues hit "(Do the) Mashed Potatoes" .

In 1962, James and his band scored a hit with their cover of the instrumental "Night Train", becoming not only a top five Rythm & Blues single but also James Brown's first top 40 entry on the USA Billboard Hot 100. That same year, the ballads "Lost Someone" and "Baby You're Right", the latter a Joe Tex composition, added to his repertoire and increased his reputation with Rythm & Blues audiences.

In 1963, James scored his first top 20 pop hit with his rendition of the standard "Prisoner of Love". By 1967, James's emerging sound had begun to be defined as funk music. That year he released what some critics cited as the first true funk song, "Cold Sweat", which hit number-one on the Rythm & Blues chart.

In 1973, James Brown provided the score for the blaxploitation film Black Caesar and also recorded another soundtrack for the film, Slaughter's Big Rip-Off. Following the release of these soundtracks, James acquired a self-styled nickname, "The Godfather of Soul".

Errol Brown   Hot Chocolate

Errol Brown died aged seventy-one from liver cancer at his home in the Bahamas on the 6th of May 2015. He was survived by his wife Ginette and his two daughters, Colette and Leonie.

Errol Brown was born on 12th November 1943 in Kingston, Jamaica, but moved to the UK when he was twelve years old. His break in music came in 1969 when he recorded a version of John Lennon's "Give Peace a Chance" with his band "Hot Chocolate". Unable to change the lyrics without Lennon's permission, he sent a copy to his record label, Apple, and the song was released with Lennon's approval.

The Hot Chocolate albums were produced by Mickie Most and recorded at the Rak Records studio. Errol Brown left the group in 1985 to take a hiatus from music. However, he soon went on to have a solo career, achieving success in the clubs with the 1987 single "Body Rocking".

In 2003, Queen Elizabeth II named Errol Brown a Member of the Order of the British Empire for "services to popular music for the United Kingdom". In 2004 Errol received an Ivor Novello Award for outstanding contributions to British music.

Jack Bruce died, aged seventy-one, from liver disease on the 25th of October 2014, in Suffolk, United Kingdom. He was survived by his wife, Margrit and his sons, Jonas, Malcolm and Corin and daughters, Natasha and Kyla. His funeral was held in London and was attended by noted musicians.

Jack was born in Scotland and began playing the jazz bass in his teens and won a scholarship to study cello and musical composition at the Royal Scottish Academy of Music and Drama.

In 1962 Jack became a member of the London-based band, Blues Incorporated, led by Alexis Korner, in which he played the upright bass. In 1963 the group broke up and Jack went on to form the Graham Bond Quartet with Bond, Ginger Baker and guitarist John McLaughlin. They played an eclectic range of music genres, including bebop, blues and rhythm and blues. As a result of session work at this time, Jack switched from the upright bass to the electric bass guitar.

Later, Jack joined John Mayall's Bluesbreakers, which featured guitarist Eric Clapton. In July 1966 Jack with Eric Clapton and Ginger Baker founded the power trio Cream, which gained international recognition playing blues-rock and jazz-inflected rock music. Jack sang most of the lead vocals, with Eric backing him.

Jack Bruce's first solo release, Songs for a Tailor, was issued in September 1969 and it featured Dick Heckstall-Smith and Jon Hiseman. It was a worldwide hit, but after a brief supporting tour backed by Larry Coryell and Mitch Mitchell, Jack joined the jazz fusion group Lifetime. However, Lifetime did not receive much critical or commercial acclaim at the time, and the band broke up in 1971. Jack then recorded his third solo album 'Harmony Row', but this was not as commercially successful as 'Songs for a Tailor'.

In 1972 Jack formed a blues rock power trio, West, Bruce & Laing. Besides Jack, the group included singer/guitarist Leslie West and drummer Corky Laing, both formerly of the Cream-influenced American band Mountain. West, Bruce & Laing produced two studio albums, Why Dontcha and Whatever Turns You On, and one live album, Live 'n' Kickin'.

By 1980 Jack had another new band, Jack Bruce & Friends, consisting of drummer Billy Cobham, guitarist Clem Clempson and keyboardist/guitarist David Sancious. In 1981, Jack collaborated with guitarist Robin Trower and released two power trio albums.

In 2003 Jack was diagnosed with liver cancer and he underwent a liver transplant, which was almost fatal, as his body initially rejected the new organ.

Improved health led to Jack Bruce playing a series of live outdoor concerts across the USA starting in July 2008 as part of the Hippiefest Tour. He was supported by members of the late Who bassist John Entwistle's The John Entwistle Band, and headlined at a tribute concert to the bassist. In October 2009, Jack Bruce performed at the 50th anniversary of Ronnie Scott's Club with the Ronnie Scott's Blues Band.

Jeff Buckley   Solo Artiste

Jeff Buckley drowned to death aged thirty on the 29th of May 1997. His autopsy revealed no signs of drugs or alcohol in his body and his death was ruled an accidental drowning.

Jeff grew up singing around the house and in harmony with his mother, later noting that all his family sang. His father was the musician, Tim Buckley, who died aged twenty-eight in 1975. Jeff began playing guitar at the age of five after discovering an acoustic guitar in his grandmother's closet.

At the age of twelve, he decided to become a musician, and received his first electric guitar — a black Les Paul — at the age of thirteen. He attended a High School, and played in the school's jazz band. During this time, he developed an affinity for progressive rock bands.

After graduating from high school, he moved north to Hollywood to attend the Musicians Institute, completing the one-year course at the age of nineteen.

Jeff spent the next six years working in a hotel and playing guitar in various struggling bands playing in styles from jazz, reggae, and roots rock to heavy metal.

Jeff began performing at several clubs and cafés around Lower Manhattan, New York but Sin-é in the East Village became his main venue. He first appeared at Sin-é in April 1992, and quickly earned a regular Monday night slot there. His repertoire consisted of a diverse range of folk, rock, R&B, blues and jazz cover songs, much of it music he had newly learned.

In mid-1993, Jeff began working on his first album and assembled a band, composed of a bassist and drummer. That September, the trio headed to Bearsville Studios in Woodstock, New York to spend six weeks recording basic tracks for what would become the album, 'Grace'.

In January 1994, Jeff left to go on his first solo North American tour to support Live at Sin-é followed by a ten day European tour.

Grace was released in August 1994 and Jeff spent much of the next year and a half touring internationally to promote his album.

Boz Burrell   King Crimson & Bad Company

Boz Burrell died aged sixty of a heart attack on the twenty-first of September 2006 during rehearsals in Marbella, Spain. He was survived by his wife, Kath.

Boz was born in 1946 in Holbeach, Lincolnshire, U.K. As a teen in the 1950s, he began playing rhythm guitar for a group formed with a school friend.

In 1971 Boz joined King Crimson as their vocalist, having met Robert Fripp while both were performing with

Centipede. After a last minute let down by bassist Rick Kemp, Boz, who had only limited guitar-playing ability, became the band's bass player.

Boz became a founding member of the supergroup, Bad Company, formed in 1973 along with ex Free vocalist Paul Rodgers and drummer Simon Kirke and ex Mott the Hoople guitarist, Mick Ralphs. The band debuted with the self-titled Bad Company in 1974 which eventually went Platinum, as did the 1975 follow-up, Straight Shooter and 1976's Run With the Pack.

Max Bygraves   Solo Artiste

Max Bygraves died aged eighty-nine on 31st of August 2012 at his home on Hope Island, Queensland, Australia following a diagnosis of Alzheimer's disease.

Max was born as Walter Bygraves in nineteen twenty-two in Rotherhithe, London, U.K. and he grew up in poverty in a two-room council flat with his five siblings, his parents and a grandparent.

Brought up Catholic, Max sang with his school choir at Westminster Cathedral. He left school aged fourteen and worked at the Savoy Hotel in London as a pageboy. He then became a messenger for an advertising agency in Fleet Street, before serving as a fitter in the Royal Air Force in the Second World War and working as a carpenter. He changed his name to Max in honour of comedian Max Miller.

During the 1950s and 1960s, Max Bygraves appeared as a guest on several television variety programmes, both in the UK and United States. In December, 1959, his single, Jingle Bell Rock, got to number seven on the UK hit parade.

J J Cale   Solo Artiste

J.J. Cale died of a heart attack aged seventy-four on the 26th of July 2013 in La Jolla, California, USA. He was survived by his wife, Christine.

J.J. was born John Cale in 1938 in Oklahoma. USA. Besides learning to play the guitar he began studying the principles of sound engineering while still living with his parents in Tulsa, where he built himself a recording studio. After graduation he was drafted into military service, studying at the Air Force Air Training Command in Rantoul, Illinois.

Along with a number of other young Tulsa musicians, J.J. moved to Los Angeles in the early 1960s, where he found employment as a studio engineer. While living in Los Angeles he cut a demo single in 1966 with Liberty Records of his composition "After Midnight".

In 1970, it came to his attention that Eric Clapton had recorded a cover of "After Midnight" on his debut album in 1970. As a result of this, it was suggested to J.J. that he should take advantage of this publicity and cut a record of his own. His first album, 'Naturally', established his style. Songs written by J.J. Cale have since been covered by many other musicians.

Randy California   Spirit

Randy California died aged forty-five on the 2nd of January 1997 when he drowned in the Pacific Ocean while rescuing his twelve year-old son Quinn from a rip current in Hawaii. He managed to push Quinn, who survived, towards the shore.

Randy helped found the band Spirit and their first and eponymous album was released in January 1968, one month before Randy's 17th birthday. It contained the song "Fresh Garbage" which perhaps remains their most well-known number.

Robert Calvert   HawkWind

Robert Calvert died aged forty-three from a heart attack on the 14th of August 1988 in Ramsgate, Kent, United

Kingdom. His gravestone is engraved with the line "Love's No Time's fool", from William Shakespeare's Sonnet 116. He was survived by his second wife, Pamela and his son Nicolas.

At the end of the 1960s Robert moved to London and joined the then flourishing psychedelic subculture. He co-wrote Hawkwind's hit single "Silver Machine", which reached number three in the UK singles chart in July 1972.

Robert suffered from bipolar disorder, which often caused a fractious relationship with his fellow musicians. Despite his sometimes debilitating mental health, Robert remained a fiercely creative, driven and multi-talented artist. During periods away from Hawkwind activities, he worked on his solo career; his creative output including albums, stage plays, poetry, and a novel. Robert's first solo album, Captain Lockheed and the Starfighters, a concept album, was released in 1974.

Glen Campbell   Solo Artiste

Glen Campbell died aged eighty-one of Alzheimer's disease on the eighth of August 2017 in Nashville, Tennessee, U.S.A. He was survived by his wife, Kimberly and his sons, Dylan, Shannon, Cal, Travis and Kane and his daughters, Ashley, Debbie and Kelli.

Glen was born Glen Travis Campbell in 1936 in Arkansas, USA and started playing guitar at age four after an uncle gave him a guitar as a gift and teaching him the basics of how to play and by the time he was six he was performing on local radio stations.

In nineteen fifty four, at age seventeen, Glen moved to Albuquerque, New Mexico, to join his uncle's band, known as Dick Bills and the Sandia Mountain Boys.

Glen won four Grammy Awards for "Gentle on My Mind" and "By the Time I Get to Phoenix". In the mid-nineteen-seventies, he had more hits with "Rhinestone Cowboy", "Southern Nights", "Sunflower" and "Country Boy".

Jim Capaldi   Traffic

Jim Capaldi died aged sixty from stomach cancer on the
28th of January 2005 while in Westminster, London, UK.
He was survived by his widow Aninha and his daughters,
Tabitha and Tallulah.

Jim was born Nicolas James Capaldi in 1944 in Worcestershire, UK. As a child he studied the piano and singing
with his father, a music teacher, and by his teens he was
playing drums with his friends. At age fourteen he founded
the band The Sapphires and served as their lead vocalist.
At sixteen he took an apprenticeship at a factory in
Worcester, where he met Dave Mason. In 1963 he formed
The Hellions with Mason on guitar and Gordon Jackson
on rhythm guitar, while he himself switched to drums.

Following his death, several tributes in celebration of
Jim Capaldi's life and music came out under the name
Dear Mr Fantasy.

Karen Carpenter   The Carpenters

Karen Carpenter died of Cardiac Arrest aged thirty-two on
the 4th of February 1983 in California, U.S.A. She was survived by her husband, Tom.

Karen's funeral service took place that February at a
local Methodist Church. Dressed in a rose-colored suit,
Karen Carpenter lay in an open white casket as over a
thousand mourners passed through to say goodbye.
Karen's estranged husband Tom took off his wedding ring
and placed it inside the casket. She was entombed at the
Forest Lawn Memorial Park in Cypress, California.

Karen was born in 1955 and when she entered high
school, she joined the school band. She and her brother
made their first recordings in 1965 and 1966. From 1965 to
1968 Karen, her brother Richard, and his college friend
Wes Jacobs, a bassist and tuba player, formed The Richard
Carpenter Trio and also performed as an ensemble known

as Spectrum. Spectrum focused on a harmonious and vocal sound, and recorded many demo tapes in the garage studio of a friend.

Karen started out as both the group's drummer and lead singer, and she originally sang all her vocals from behind the drum set. Because she was just 5' 4" tall, it was difficult for people in the audience to see her behind her drum kit, so she was eventually persuaded to stand at the microphone to sing the band's hits while another musician played the drums.

In addition to being a drummer and a singer, Karen could also play the electric bass guitar.

Eric Carr   Kiss

Eric Carr died of cancer, aged forty-one on 24th of November, 1991 in New York City, United States of America.

Eric's last public appearance with Kiss was at the MTV Video Music Awards in September 1991 and not long afterwards, he suffered an aneurysm and was rushed to hospital. Several days later, he suffered a brain hemorrhage and never again regained consciousness. Eric Carr died on the same day as Freddie Mercury, the lead singer of the British rock band Queen, whose death attracted far more media attention.

In keeping with Eric's accessibility to his fans, his family decided to open his funeral service to the public while reserving the interment as a private event.

While still in high school, Eric began playing with a string of bands mostly performing covers of Top 40 songs. His first band, The Cellarmen, was formed in 1965 by him and several of his friends.

In 1970, Eric joined the band Salt & Pepper, which started as a cover band playing music from multiple genres. In December 1979, Eric successfully auditioned for a four-piece rock 'n' roll cover band called Flasher and after three weeks of rehearsals, they started playing at clubs.

Besides drumming, Eric Carr also played guitar, bass guitar and piano and sang background vocals. Occasionally he sang lead vocals, such as on "Black Diamond" and "Young and Wasted" live with Kiss.

Eric's final recording with Kiss was for the song "God Gave Rock 'N' Roll To You", which featured him on backing vocals. The last time Eric worked with Kiss was in July 1991 when Kiss filmed the video for "God Gave Rock 'N Roll to You" with him playing drums.

Johnny Cash   Solo Artiste

Johnny Cash died aged seventy-one on the 12th of September 2003 from complications of diabetes while hospitalized in Nashville,Tennessee, U.S.A. less than four months after his wife's death. He was survived by his sons, John and his daughters, Rosanne, Kathy, Cindy and Tara. He was buried next to wife, June in Hendersonville Memory Gardens near his home in Tennessee.

Johnny was born in 1932 in Kingsland, Arkansas, U.S.A. and in 1955, when signing with Sun Records, he took Johnny Cash as his stage name. Johnny had enlisted in the United States Air Force in 1950. It was there he created his first band, named "The Landsberg Barbarians". He was honorably discharged as a staff sergeant on July 3rd 1954, and returned to Texas. During his military service, he acquired a distinctive scar on the right side of his jaw as a result of surgery to remove a cyst.

As his career was taking off in the late 1950s, Johnny began drinking heavily and became addicted to amphetamines and barbiturates. Although he was in many ways spiraling out of control, Johnny's frenetic creativity was still delivering hits. His rendition of "Ring of Fire" was a crossover hit, reaching Number one on the country charts and entering the Top 20 on the pop charts.

Johnny had also been arrested on May 11th, 1965, in Starkville, Mississippi, for trespassing late at night onto private property to pick flowers. He began performing concerts at prisons starting in the late 1950s and played his first famous prison concert on January 1st 1958, at San Quentin State Prison. These performances led to two highly successful live albums, 'Johnny Cash at Folsom Prison' in 1968 and 'Johnny Cash at San Quentin in 1969'.

In 1969 Johnny became an international star when he eclipsed even the Beatles by selling six and a half million albums.

Paul Cattermole   S Club 7

Paul Cattermole died aged forty-six on the 6th of April 2023. He had been found unresponsive at his home in Dorset and cause was immediately given but police said the death was not suspicious. Paul was survived by his partner, Hannah.

Paul and future S Club 7 bandmate Hannah had met as members of the National Youth Music Theatre in 1994 when Paul was 17 years old and Hannah was 14. In May 2001, the friendship between the two developed into a romantic relationship but they kept their relationship a secret for the first six months, waiting until November 2001 to make a public announcement. Their S Club colleagues were supportive of the relationship.

Paul was born in St Albans, Hertfordshire, UK. His first big break was when he landed a part in a local performance of West Side Story. When he was 16, Paul decided to go in a different musical direction and formed a heavy metal band called Skua before he was chosen to be in S Club 7 after a series of auditions. During five years together they released four number-one singles and one number-one album. They also had a series of TV shows.

S Club 7 recorded a total of four studio albums, released eleven singles and went on to sell over fourteen million albums worldwide. Their first album, S Club, had a strong 1990s pop sound, similar to many artists of their time.

However, throughout the course of their career, their musical approach changed to a more dance and R&B sound. Their television series went on to last four series, seeing the group travel across the United States and eventually ending up in Barcelona, Spain. It became popular in 100 different countries where the show was watched by over 90 million viewers.

David Cassidy   The Partridge Family

David Cassidy died aged sixty-seven of liver failure on the 21st of November 2017 in Fort Lauderdale, Florida, U.S.A. He was survived by his first, second and third ex-wives: Kay, Meryl and Sue and also by his son, Beau and daughter, Katie.

David was born in New York City, USA. In 1968, after completing one final session of summer school to obtain credits necessary to get a high school diploma, David sought fame as an actor or musician, while simultaneously working half-days in the mailroom of a textile firm.

After David signed with Universal Studios in 1969, he was introduced to Ruth Aarons, who later found her niche as a talent manager, having a theatre background. Ruth became an authority figure and close friend to David and was the driving force behind his on-screen success. After David made small wages from Screen Gems for his work on The Partridge Family during season one, Ruth discovered that he had been underage when he signed his contract. She then renegotiated the contract with far superior provisions and a rare four-year term.

In January, 1969, David made his professional debut in the Broadway musical The Fig Leaves Are Falling. It closed after four performances, but a casting director saw the show and asked David to make a screen test. In 1969, he moved to Los Angeles. After signing with Universal Studios in 1969, David was featured in episodes of the television series Ironside, Marcus Welby, M.D., Adam-12, Medical Center, and Bonanza.

In 1970, David took the role of Keith Partridge on the musical television show The Partridge Family. After demonstrating his singing talent, David was allowed to join the studio ensemble as the lead singer. The show proved popular, but the fame took its toll on David. In the midst of his rise to fame, David felt stifled by the show and trapped by the mass hysteria surrounding his every move. In May 1972, to alter his public image, he appeared nude on the cover of Rolling Stone magazine.

After "I Think I Love You", the first single released by The Partridge Family pop group, became a hit, David began work on solo albums, including 'Cherish' and 'Rock Me Baby', both released in 1972. Within the first year, he had produced his own single, "Cherish" which reached number nine in the United States, number two in the United Kingdom and number one in Australia and New Zealand. He then began tours that featured Partridge Family tunes as well as his own hits.

David achieved far greater solo chart success in the UK than in his native America, including a cover of The Young Rascals' "How Can I Be Sure" and the double A-side single "Daydreamer" coupled with "The Puppy Song" – a UK number one which failed to chart in the States.

After launching his solo musical career, David was for a short time the highest paid entertainer in the world. At the peak of his career, David's fan club was larger than that of any other pop star, including The Beatles or Elvis Presley.

Danny Cedrrone   The Comets

Danny Cedrone died aged thirty-three from a broken neck on the 17th of June, 1954 in Philadelphia, Pennsylvania, United States of America. He was survived by his wife, Millie and their four daughters.

Danny Cedrone was born with the birth-name Donato Joseph Cedrone in Jamesville, New York, United States of America. Danny's musical career began in the 1940's, but he came into his own in the early 1950s, first as a session guitarist hired by what was then a country and western musical group based out of Chester, Pennsylvania called Bill Haley and His Saddlemen. In 1951, Danny played lead on their recording of "Rocket 88" which is considered one of the first acknowledged rock and roll recordings. At around this time, Danny formed his own group, The Esquire Boys, and this is believed to be one of the reasons why he did not join Bill Haley's group as a full-time member. In 1952, Danny played lead guitar on Bill Haley's version of "Rock the Joint", and his swift guitar solo, which combined a jazz-influenced first half followed by a lightning-fast down-scale run, was a highlight of the recording.

Danny's involvement with the Esquire Boys kept him off of Bill Haley's recording schedule for most of 1952 and 1953. During this time, Danny made a number of recordings with the Esquires, most notably two versions of the Bill Haley composition, "Rock-A-Beatin' Boogie", several years before Bill Haley recorded it himself. The Esquire Boys recorded a second version of "Rock-A-Beatin' Boogie" in 1954 which reached number 42 on the Cashbox pop singles chart. "Rock-A-Beatin' Boogie" was recorded by Bill Haley and his Comets in 1955 on Decca.

Danny returned to work with Bill Haley's group in 1954, by which time it had been renamed The Comets. He played a key role in the band's first recording session for Decca Records in April, 1954 when they recorded "Rock Around the Clock" in New York City. Ten days after this session, Danny died after falling down a staircase.

Eight months after Danny Cedrone's death, "Rock Around the Clock" was included on the opening credits of the film 'Blackboard Jungle' and became the first rock and roll recording to hit the top of the American charts.

Chas Chandler   The Animals

Chas Chandler died aged fifty-eight of an aortic aneurysm

on the 17th of July, 1996 in hospital in Newcastle, U.K. He was survived by his wife, Madeleine and his sons Steffan and Alex and his daughters, Elizabeth and Katherine.

Chas was born Bryan James Chandler in Newcastle upon Tyne, UK. in 1938. After leaving school, he worked as a turner in the Tyneside shipyards. Having originally learned to play the guitar, he became the bass player with The Alan Price Trio in 1962. After Eric Burdon joined the band, the Alan Price Trio was renamed The Animals.

After The Animals underwent personnel changes in 1966, Chas Chandler turned to becoming a talent scout, artist manager, and record producer. During his final tour with The Animals, Chas Chandler saw a then-unknown Jimi Hendrix play in a New York City nightclub and brought him to England and international fame.

The Animal's UK chart hits included: "The House of the Rising Sun" in 1964, "Don't Let Me Be Misunderstood" in 1965, "It's My Life" in 1965, "Inside Looking Out" in 1966 and "Don't Bring Me Down" in 1966.

Ray Charles   **Solo Artiste**

Ray Charles died of liver disease aged seventy-three on the 10th of June, 2004 in California, U.S.A. He was survived by his second wife, Della and his sons, Ray, Wayne, Ryan, Vincent, Robert and David and his daughters, Sheila, Robyn, Raenee, Evelyn, Alexandra and Reatha.

Ray had been born Raymond Charles Robinson in Georgia, U.S.A. He began losing his sight at the age of four or five, and was blind by the age of seven, likely as a result of glaucoma.

After leaving school, Ray moved to Jacksonville and began to build a reputation as a musician there.

In 1953, "Mess Around" became Ray's first hit for Atlantic; during the next year, he had hits with "It Should've Been Me" and "Don't You Know". He also recorded the songs "Midnight Hour" and "Sinner's Prayer" around this time.

Late in 1954, Charles recorded "I've Got a Woman". With "Georgia on My Mind", his first hit single for ABC-Paramount in 1960, Ray received national acclaim and four Grammy Awards. Ray earned another Grammy for the follow-up track "Hit the Road Jack".

By late 1961, Ray had expanded his small road ensemble to a big band, partly as a response to increasing royalties and touring fees, becoming one of the few black artists to cross over into mainstream pop with such a level of creative control.

Mannie Charlton   Nazareth

Manni Charlton died aged eighty from a head trauma on the 5th of July 2022 whilst in Texas, USA. He was survived by his second wife, Julie.

Manni was born in Andalusia, Spain. Prior to joining Nazareth, he had played in a few bands until joining the local semi-pro Dunfermline band The Shadettes who, in 1968, changed their name to Nazareth.

Manni played a big part in Nazareth's worldwide success. After leaving Nazareth in 1990, Manni played some solo shows on the Scottish club circuit, and released his first solo album Drool in 1997, on the Red Steel record label with Neil Miller on vocals. The following year, he relocated to Texas, where he formed the Manny Charlton Band (MCB).

Alex Chilton   The Box Tops & Big Star

Alex Chilton died aged fifty-nine of a heart attack on the 17th of March 2010 whilst in hospital in New Orleans, U.S.A. He was survived by his wife, Laura, a son, Timothee, and a sister, Cecilia.

Alex had been scheduled to play a concert with Big Star at the South by Southwest music festival in Austin, Texas, that March but the show instead took place as a tribute to him.

Alex was born William Alexander Chilton in 1950. He was an American singer-songwriter, guitarist, and record producer, best known as the lead singer of the Box Tops and Big Star.

Don Ciccone   The Four Seasons

Don Ciccone died aged seventy on the 8th of October, 2016 of a heart attack in Idaho, United States of America. He was survived by his wife, Stephanie and his son, D'Arcey.

Don was born, Donald Joseph Ciccone, in Jersey City, New Jersey in 1946. In the 1970s, Don joined the Four Seasons, where he played guitar and bass and also contributed lead vocals to songs including "December, 1963 (Oh, What a Night)" and "Rhapsody." After he left the Four Seasons, he joined Tommy James and the Shondells as their bassist.

Gene Clark   The Byrds

Gene Clark died aged forty-six on the 24th of May 1991 of causes brought on by a bleeding ulcer. He was survived by his wife, Carlie and his sons, Kelly and Kai.

Gene wrote or co-wrote many of the Byrds' best-known original songs from their first three albums, including "I'll Feel a Whole Lot Better".

The Byrd's UK chart hits include: "Mr Tambourine Man" in 1965, "All I Really Want to Do" in 1965, "Turn, Turn, Turn" in 1965, "Eight Miles High" in 1966 and "Chestnut Mare" in 1971.

Steve Clark   Def Leppard

Steve Clark died on the 8th of January 1991 from blood poisoning by alcohol and a mix of prescription drugs in his London home.

Steve joined Def Leppard more than two decades after they were formed. He became their lead guitarist following a successful audition and wrote or co-wrote more than 90% of the band's songs throughout his career with them. At times, Steve struggled with alcoholism and drug addiction.

Just days before his passing, Steve appeared in the recording sessions of 'When Love & Hate Collide.'

Eddie Clarke   Motorhead

Eddie Clarke died of pneumonia aged sixty-seven on the 10th of January 2018 in a hospital where he was being treated. He was survived by his wife, Mariko.

Eddie played guitar as a youth and by the time he was fifteen years old, he had played in a number of local bands including 'The Bitter End'. Eddie continued playing local gigs until 1973, when he turned professional by joining Curtis Knight's blues prog rock band, Zeus.

Eddie was working on re-fitting a houseboat, when he met drummer Phil Taylor, who had recently joined Motörhead. In the early days Eddie rehearsed with Motörhead, before going on the road, at Snobs Rehearsal Studios, part of a converted brewery on the corner of Kings Road and Lots Road, Chelsea, known as the "Furniture Cave". Motörhead's popularity increased along with their UK chart successes. The threesome (Lemmy, Clarke, Taylor) are considered the classic Motörhead line-up and have the Motörhead, Overkill, Ace of Spades, Bomber, No Sleep 'til Hammersmith and Iron Fist albums plus a string of hit singles to their credit.

In 2014, Eddie went back to his blues roots and released a new studio album through Secret Records.

Clarence Clemons   The E Street Band

Clarence Clemons died aged sixty-nine on the 18th of June

2011 from complications caused by a stroke. He was survived by his wife, Victoria and his sons, Nick, Jarod, Christopher and Charles.

Clarence was born Clarence Anicholas Clemons, Jr. on the 11th of January 1942 in Virginia, USA . When he was nine, his father gave him an alto saxophone as a Christmas present and paid for music lessons. Clarence later switched to baritone saxophone and played in a high school jazz band. His uncle also influenced his early musical development when he bought him his first King Curtis album. and his work with The Coasters in particular, would become a major influence on Clarence and led to him switching to tenor saxophone.

Outside of his work with the E Street Band, Clarence recorded with many other artists and had a number of musical projects on his own. The best known of these are his 1985 vocal duet with Jackson Browne on the Top-20 hit single "You're a Friend of Mine", and his saxophone work on Aretha Franklin's 1985 Top-10 hit single "Freeway of Love".

Kurt Cobain   Nirvana

Kurt Cobain died by suicide aged twenty-seven on the 5th of April 1994 and lay for three days before his body was discovered at his Washington home by a security electrician who saw a shotgun pointing at Kurt's chin. A note was found, addressed to Kurt's childhood imaginary friend Boddah, that stated that Kurt had not "felt the excitement of listening to as well as creating music, along with really writing for too many years now".

When Kurt had been nine years old, his parents divorced. He later said that the divorce had a profound effect on his life, while his mother noted that his personality changed dramatically and Kurt became defiant and withdrawn.

On his 14th birthday in 1981, Kurt's uncle offered him either a bike or a used guitar and he chose the guitar. Soon, he was trying to copy Led Zeppelin's power ballad, "Stairway to Heaven".

Kurt struggled to reconcile the massive success of Nirvana with his underground roots. He also felt persecuted by the media, and began to harbor resentment against people who claimed to be fans of the band, yet refused to acknowledge, or misinterpreted, the band's social and political views. A vocal opponent of sexism, racism and homophobia, he was publicly proud that Nirvana had played at a gay rights benefit.

Eddie Cochran   Solo Artiste

Eddie Cochran died aged twenty-one of severe head injuries on the 17th of April 1960 at St Martin's Hospital, Bath, U.K. after he was involved in a traffic accident in a taxi whilst travelling through Chippenham, Wiltshire, U.K.

A memorial stone commemorating Eddie was placed on the grounds of St Martin's Hospital, in Bath. The stone was restored in 2010 on the 50th anniversary of his death and can be found in the old chapel grounds at the hospital. A memorial plaque was also placed next to the sundial at the back of the old chapel.

Eddie's family moved to California, in 1952 and as his guitar playing improved, he formed a band with two friends from his junior high school. He then dropped out of high school in his first year to become a professional musician. During a show featuring many performers at an American Legion hall, he met Hank Cochran, a songwriter. Although they were not related, they recorded as the Cochran Brothers and began performing together. They recorded a few singles for Ekko Records that were fairly successful and helped to establish them as a performing act. Eddie Cochran also worked as a session musician and began writing songs, making a demo with Jerry Capehart, his future manager.

In July 1956, Eddie Cochran's first solo single was released by Crest Records. It featured "Skinny Jim", now regarded as a rock-and-roll and rockabilly classic. In the spring of 1956, Boris Petroff asked Eddie if he would appear in the musical comedy film The Girl Can't Help It. Eddie agreed and performed the song "Twenty Flight Rock" in the movie. In 1957 Eddie starred in his second film, Untamed Youth, and he had yet another hit, "Sittin' in the Balcony", one of the few songs he recorded that was written by other songwriters, in this case, John D. Loudermilk.

In the Summer of 1957 Liberty Records issued Eddie's only studio album released during his lifetime, Singin' to My Baby. The album included "Sittin' in the Balcony". In 1958, Eddie really found his stride in the teenage anthem "Summertime Blues" , co-written with Jerry Capehart. With this song, Eddie was established as one of the most important influences on rock and roll in the 1950s, both lyrically and musically. Eddie's brief career included a few more hits, including "C'mon, Everybody", "Somethin' Else", "Teenage Heaven" and "Three Steps to Heaven". He remained popular in the United States and the United Kingdom through the late 1950s and early 1960s.

Joe Cocker   Solo Artiste

Joe Cocker died aged seventy from lung cancer on the 22nd of December 2014 whilst in Crawford, Colorado, U.S.A. He was survived by his wife, Pam with whom he had no son or daughters.

Joe was born in Sheffield, UK in 1944 and his main musical influences growing up were Ray Charles and Lonnie Donegan. Joe's first experience singing in public was at age twelve when his elder brother Victor invited him on stage to sing during a gig of his skiffle group. In 1960, along with three friends, Joe formed his first group, the Cavaliers.

Joe left school to become an apprentice gasfitter while simultaneously pursuing a career in music. He developed an interest in blues music and sought out recordings by John Lee Hooker, Muddy Waters, Lightnin' Hopkins and Howlin' Wolf. In 1969, Joe made a cover version of the Beatles' song, "With a Little Help from My Friends" . The record made the number one on the UK Singles Chart.

At the end of 1973, Joe Cocker returned to the studio to record a new album, 'I Can Stand A Little Rain'. The album, released in August 1974, got to number 11 on the US charts and one song from it, a single, a cover of Billy Preston's "You Are So Beautiful," got to number five.

Joe was awarded an OBE in the Queen's 2007 Birthday Honours list for services to music and recording and touring.

Leonard Cohen   Solo Artiste

Leonard Cohen died of cancer, aged eighty-two, on the 7th of November 2016 at his home in Los Angeles, California, U.S.A. He was survived by his son, Adam and his daughter, Lorca. His funeral was held in Montreal, at a cemetery on Mount Royal. As to Leonard's wishes, he was laid to rest with a Jewish rite, in a simple pine casket, on a family plot. Tributes were paid to him by numerous celebrities.

Leonard Cohen was born in 1934 in Montreal, Canada into a middle-class Jewish family. He wrote poetry and fiction throughout much of the 1960s and chose to live in quasi-reclusive circumstances in a house on Hydra, a Greek island in the Saronic Gulf. While living and writing on Hydra, Leonard published the poetry collection and novel The Favourite Game in 1963 and Beautiful Losers in 1966.

In 1967, disenchanted with his poor earnings as an author, Leonard moved to America to pursue a career as a folk music singer and songwriter. In 1970 he toured for the first time, in the U.S., Canada, and Europe, and performed at the Isle of Wight Music Festival in the UK. that year.

Leonard's hit composition, Hallelujah," was first released on his album Various Positions in 1984, and he sang it during his Europe tour in 1985. It has been performed by almost 200 artists in various languages.

Nat King Cole   Solo Artiste

Nat King Cole died aged forty-five on the 15th of February 1965 in following the surgical removal of his cancerous left lung at a Santa Monica hospital. His corpse was interred in Freedom Mausoleum at Forest Lawn Memorial Park, Glendale, California, U.S.A. He was survived by his wife, Maria and daughter, Natalie.

Nat recorded "Sweet Lorraine" in 1940, and it became his first hit.

Throughout the 1950s, Nat continued to have hit records, selling in millions throughout the world. These included "Smile", "Pretend", "A Blossom Fell", and "If I May".

In Los Angeles, Nat looked for work and played piano in nightclubs. When a club owner asked him to form a band, he hired bassist Wesley Prince and guitarist Oscar Moore. They initially called themselves the King Cole Swingsters but changed their name to the King Cole Trio before making radio transcriptions and recording for small labels.

Nat recorded "Sweet Lorraine" in 1940, and it became his first hit but as people heard Nat's vocal talent, they requested more vocal songs, and he obliged. In 1941, the trio recorded "That Ain't Right" for Decca, followed the next year by "All for You" for Excelsior.

Nat appeared in the first Jazz at the Philharmonic concerts in 1944. He also recorded with Illinois Jacquet and Lester Young. In 1946, the trio broadcast King Cole Trio Time, a 15-minute radio program. This was the first radio program to be hosted by a black musician. Between 1946 and 1948, the trio recorded radio transcriptions for Capitol Records Transcription Service.

Nat began recording and performing pop-oriented material in which he was often accompanied by a string orchestra. His stature as a popular star was cemented by hits such as "All for You" in 1943, "The Christmas Song" in 1947, "Route 66", " For Sentimental Reasons" in 1946, "There! I've Said It Again" in 1947 and "Nature Boy" in 1948.

Throughout the 1950s, Nat continued to record hits that sold millions throughout the world, such as "Smile", "Pretend", "A Blossom Fell", and "If I May". His pop hits were collaborations with Nelson Riddle, Gordon Jenkins, and Ralph Carmichael. Riddle arranged several of Nat's 1950s albums, including Nat King Cole Sings for Two in Love in 1953, his first ten inch LP.

 Nat recorded several hit singles during the 1960s, including "Let There Be Love" with George Shearing in 1961, the country-flavored hit "Ramblin' Rose" in August 1962 . He performed in many short films, sitcoms, and television shows and played W. C. Handy in the film St. Louis Blues in 1958.

Nat had one of his last major hits in 1963, two years before his death, with "Those Lazy-Hazy-Crazy Days of Summer", which reached number 6 on the Pop chart. "Unforgettable" was made famous again in 1991 by Nat's daughter Natalie when modern recording technology was used to reunite father and daughter in a duet. The duet version rose to the top of the pop charts, almost forty years after its original popularity.

Natalie Cole   Solo Artiste

Natalie Cole died aged sixty-five on the 31st of December 2015 from Congestive Heart failure at Cedars-Sinai Medical Center, Los Angeles, California, U.S.A. She had cancelled several events in December 2015 due to illness. Natalie's funeral was held on the 11th of January 2016, at a church in Los Angeles.

Natalie grew up listening to a variety of music which

included Aretha Franklin and Janis Joplin. After graduation in 1972 she began singing at small clubs with her
band, Black Magic. With the assistance of a song-writing
and producing duo, she recorded some songs in a studio in
Chicago that was owned by Curtis Mayfield and her demo
tapes led to a contract with Capitol Records, resulting in
the release of her debut album, Inseparable. The media's
billing of Natalie as the "new Aretha Franklin" started a
rivalry between the two singers and a feud which boiled
over at the 1976 Grammy Awards when Natalie beat
Aretha in the Best Female R&B Vocal Performance category, a category in which Aretha had won eight times previously.

Allen Collins   Lynard Skynard

Allen Collins died aged thirty-seven on the twenty-third of
January 1990 from chronic pneumonia while in Jacksonville, Florida, U.S.A., the city of his birth.

Allen Collins joined Skynyrd in Jacksonville, Florida,
just two weeks after its formation by Ronnie Van Zant and
Gary Rossington, along with Bob Burns and Larry Junstrom. Knowing that Allen played guitar and owned his
own equipment, the band decided to approach him about
joining them. Van Zant and Burns both had a reputation
for trouble, and Allen fled on his bicycle and hid up a tree
when he saw them pull up in his driveway. They soon convinced him that they were not there to beat him up and he
agreed to join the band, then known as "The One Percent".

Allen and lead singer Ronnie Van Zant co-wrote many
of the biggest Skynyrd hits, including "Free Bird", "Gimme
Three Steps", and "That Smell". The band received
national success beginning in 1973 while opening for the
Who on their Quadrophenia tour.

On October 20, 1977, an airplane carrying the band
crashed into a forest in Mississippi, killing three band
members, including Van Zant. Allen was seriously injured

in the crash, suffering two broken vertebrae in his neck and severe damage to his right arm. While amputation was recommended, Allen's father refused and he eventually recovered.

During the early 1980s, Allen continued to perform on stage in the Rossington-Allen Band which enjoyed modest success, releasing two albums (Anytime, Anyplace, Anywhere, and This Is the Way), and charting a few singles (notably "Don't Misunderstand Me").

Tragedy struck again just as the Rossington Collins Band was getting off the ground. In 1980, during the first days of the debut concert tour, Allen's wife, Kathy, died suddenly of a hemorrhage during the miscarriage of their third child. This forced the tour's cancellation. With the lingering effects of losing his friends in the plane crash, Kathy's death devastated Allen.

The Rossington-collins Band disbanded in 1982. Allen continued to pursue music, starting the Allen Collins Band, which released one album, Here, There & Back in 1983. The six members included two Skynyrd bandmates – keyboardist Billy Powell and bassist Leon Wilkeson – along with lead singer Jimmy Dougherty, drummer Derek Hess, and guitarists Barry Lee Harwood and Randall Hall. In 1984, Allen tried to resurrect the band, hiring Jacksonville guitarist Mike Owings and bassist Andy Ward King. Later members included guitarist-vocalist Michael Ray FitzGerald and bassist "Filthy Phil" Price.

On the 19th of January, 1986, Allen was driving a new black Ford Thunderbird when he was involved in a car accident that claimed the life of his girlfriend, Debra Jean Watts, and paralyzed him from the waist down, giving limited use of his arms and hands. Allen pleaded no contest to vehicular manslaughter as well as driving under the influence of alcohol but due to his injuries, he would never play guitar on stage again.

Allen' last performance with Lynyrd Skynyrd was at the band's first reunion after the plane crash at the 1979 Volunteer Jam V in Nashville, Tennessee. All remaining members of Lynyrd Skynyrd reunited officially in 1987, but Allen served only as musical director, due to his paralysis. As part of his plea bargain for the 1986 accident, Allen addressed fans at every Skynyrd concert with an explanation of why he could not perform, citing the dangers of drinking and driving, as well as drugs and alcohol. Also because of Allen' accident, the band donated a sizable amount of concert proceeds from the 1987–88 tour to the Miami Project, which is involved in treatment of paralysis. Allen founded Roll For Rock Wheelchair Events and Benefit Concerts in 1988 to raise awareness and to provide opportunities for those living with spinal cord injuries and other physical disabilities.

Brian Connolly   **The Sweet**

Brian Connolly died aged fifty-one on the 9th of February

1997 from renal failure, liver failure and repeated heart attacks after a week in hospital. He was survived by his ex-wife, Marilyn, and his two-year-old son Brian.

At the age of twelve, Brian moved to Harefield, Greater London, where he attended the local secondary modern school. In his mid-teens he joined the Merchant Navy, and got a tiger's head tattooed on his right arm during his Navy service. On his discharge from the Merchant Navy in 1963 he returned to Harefield and played in a number of local bands. The lineup of one featured Brian on vocals, Chris Eldridge and Lee Mordecai on guitars, Mark Conway on bass and drummer Martin Lass.

Tucker and Brian left their band in late 1967 and recruited guitarist Frank Torpey, and bassist Steve Priest, naming their new band The Sweetshop. On the eve of releasing their debut single, Slow Motion, in July 1968, the band shortened their name to The Sweet.

In 1974, Brian was badly beaten after leaving a nightclub in Staines where he received several kicks to his throat resulting in his being unable to sing for some time and permanently losing some of his previously wide vocal range. This incident also meant the band missed out on supporting The Who at Charlton Athletic Football Ground. Several songs on the Sweet Fanny Adams album had to be sung by other members of the band.

Brian developed a significant problem with alcoholism in the mid-1970s and during 1977, when no tours were undertaken and two of Sweet's most successful albums were recorded, the power struggle within the band became increasingly noticeable. Brian's chronic alcohol abuse further compromised his role with the band as his voice began showing the impact in recordings and on stage during Sweet's 1978 US tour. He played his last British show with the classic Sweet line-up at Hammersmith Odeon, London on the 24th of February 1978. Brian's final live performance with the Sweet was in July 1978 in Florida, US, when they supported Alice Cooper. His departure was not made public until March 1979.

In 1981, Brian was admitted to hospital with bloating, and he sustained multiple heart attacks. His health was permanently affected with some paralysis on his left side which would later develop into a nervous system condition.

In January 1983, Brian supported Pat Benatar for three shows in Birmingham, Newcastle and the Hammersmith Odeon, London. Brian's band Encore, included most of the members of Verity, fronted by ex-Argent guitarist John Verity, and Terry Uttley, the bass player from Smokie. Songs played included "Windy City", "Fox on the Run", "Hypnotized" and new numbers, "Sick and Tired", "Red Hair Rage" and "Burning The Candle". The new tracks were made available on a bootleg 7" single and CD.

From early 1984 onward, despite recurrent ill health, Brian toured the UK and Europe with his band The New Sweet. His most successful concerts were annual appearances in West Germany, before and after Germany's reunification. He visited other countries including Denmark, and continued to perform sporadically in the UK.

In 1988, the producer Mike Chapman arranged for Brian and former band members Mick Tucker, Steve Priest and Andy Scott to reunite in Los Angeles, California, and rework studio versions of "Action" and "The Ballroom Blitz". The reunion was with a view to producing a new album for MCA Records, however due to problems with Brian's voice, the project failed and Brian returned to The New Sweet.

Sam Cooke   Solo Artiste

Sam Cooke died aged just thirty-three from a gunshot wound on 11th of December 1964, at a motel, in Los Angeles, California. He was survived by his wife, Barbara and his daughters, Linda and Tracy.

Sam was born Samuel Cooke in Clarksdale, Mississippi, in 1931. Sam's family moved to Chicago in 1933 where he attended high school. He first became known as lead singer with the Highway Q.C.'s when he was a teenager, having joined the group at the age of fourteen.

In 1950, Sam replaced the lead singer of the gospel group the Soul Stirrers, who had signed with Specialty Records. Their first recording under Sam's leadership was the song "Jesus Gave Me Water" in 1951. They also recorded the gospel songs "Peace in the Valley", "How Far Am I from Canaan?", "Jesus Paid the Debt" and "One More River", among many others, some of which Sam wrote. Sam was often credited for bringing gospel music to the attention of a younger crowd of listeners, mainly girls who would rush to the stage when the Soul Stirrers got on the stage just to get a glimpse of Sam.

Sam had 30 U.S. top 40 hits between 1957 and 1964, plus three more posthumously. Major hits like "You Send Me", "A Change Is Gonna Come", "Cupid", "Chain Gang", "Wonderful World", "Another Saturday Night", and "Twistin' the

Night Away" are some of his most popular songs. Twistin' the Night Away was one of his biggest selling albums.

Chick Corea   Solo Artiste

Chic Corea died aged seventy-nine of cancer on the 9th of February, 2021 at his home in Tampa Bay, Florida, United States of America . He was survived by his second wife Gayle and two children, Thaddeus and Liana, from his first marriage.

Chic was born as Armando Corea in Chelsea, Massachusetts and was of southern Italian descent. His father, a jazz trumpeter who led a Dixieland band in Boston in the 1930s and 1940s, introduced him to the piano at the age of four and, hence, Surrounded by jazz, he was influenced by it at an early age.

Chic celebrated his 75th birthday in 2016 by playing with more than twenty different groups during a six-week stand at the Blue Note Jazz Club in Greenwich Village, New York City.

Chris Cornell   Sound Garden

Chris Cornell died by suicide aged fifty-two on the 18th of May 2017. He was survived by his wife, Vicky and his son, Christopher and his daughter, Toni. He was found dead by a bodyguard in the bathroom of a room at the MGM Grand Hotel in Detroit, Michigan, U.S.A. after having performed at a show with Soundgarden at the nearby Fox Theatre during the night before.

Soundgarden was formed in 1984 by Chris who possessed a multi-octave vocal range. Sound Garden's UK chart hits include: "Black Hole Sun" in 1994, "Fell On Black Days" in 1995 and "Pretty Noose" in 1996.

Glen Cornick   Jethro Tull

Glen Cornick died aged sixty-seven at his home in Hawaii, on the 28th of August 2014 due to congestive heart failure.

He is survived by his wife Bridgette, their daughter Molly and their sons Drew and Alex.

Glen toured and recorded with Jethro Tull from late 1967 to late 1970 and played in the three first studio albums of the band. These were, This Was, Stand Up and Benefit in which he played an important role in the arranging of Jethro Tull's music.

Jethro Tull's UK chart hits include: "Love Story" in 1969, "Living In The Past" in 1969, "Sweet Dream" in 1969, "The Witches Promise" in 1970, "Life Is A Long Song" in 1971 and "Ring Out Solstice Bells" in 1976.

Joey Covington   Jefferson Airplane

Joey Covington died aged sixty-seven in an automobile accident in Palm Springs, California, U.S.A. on the 4th of June 2013. He was survived by his wife, Lauren.

Joey became a professional drummer as a young teenager, taking gigs in, among other things, polka bands and strip clubs in his hometown Johnstown, Pennsylvania, USA. He settled in Los Angeles in late 1966.

Joey, whose first recording with Jefferson Airplane was the classic 1969 album Volunteers, appeared on the group's final recordings, writing and singing "Pretty As You Feel" the last hit song for Jefferson Airplane before the band splintered into separate groups, Hot Tuna and Jefferson Starship. Joey's last performance with them was in Palm Springs for a city-sponsored event in June 2013.

Vincent Crane   Atomic Rooster

Vincent Crane, died aged forty-five on the 14th of February 1989 by suicide using a deliberate overdose of Anadin tablets whilst in Westminster, London, United Kingdom. He was survived by his wife, Jean.

Vincent taught himself piano as a teenager before attending Trinity College of Music between 1961 and 1964 and then he took up organ. In late 1966 he formed the Vincent Crane Combo. In 1967 he teamed up with Arthur Brown in The Crazy World of Arthur Brown.

When Arthur Brown temporarily disappeared to a commune, Vincent and drummer Carl Palmer left to form Atomic Rooster, playing their first concert at the Lyceum in London.

Jim Croce   Solo Artiste

Jim Croce died aged aged thirty years in a plane crash on the 20th of September, 1973. He was survived by his wife, Ingrid.

Jim released his first album, Facets, in 1966, with 500 copies pressed. From the mid-1960s to the early 1970s, he performed with Ingrid as a duo. In 1968, the Croces moved to New York City and played small clubs and concerts on the college concert circuit promoting their album "Jim & Ingrid Croce".

David Crosby   The Byrds, Crosby Stills & Nash

David Crosby died aged eighty-one on the 18th of January 2023 after a long illness. He was survived by his wife, Jan, his sons, James and Django and his daughter, Erika.

David had had a liver transplant in 1994 but had suffered hepatitis C, and had type 2 diabetes. In February 2014, at the urging of his doctor, David postponed the final dates of his solo tour to undergo a cardiac catheterization and angiogram, based on the results of a routine cardiac stress test.

David briefly studied drama at Santa Barbara City College before dropping out to pursue a career in music. He performed with singer Terry Callier in Chicago and Greenwich Village, but the duo failed to obtain a recording contract. He also performed with Les Baxter's Balladeers around 1962 and he recorded his first solo session in 1963.

David arrived back in Chicago from New York City and met Jim McGuinn. who later changed his name to Roger McGuinn, and Gene Clark, who were then named the Jet Set. They were augmented by drummer Michael Clarke, at which point David attempted, unsuccessfully, to play bass. Late in 1964, Chris Hillman joined as bassist, and David relieved Gene Clark of rhythm guitar duties. The band obtained a demo acetate disc of Bob Dylan's "Mr. Tambourine Man" and recorded a version of the song, featuring McGuinn's 12-string guitar as well as McGuinn, Crosby, and Clark's vocal harmonizing. The song turned into a massive hit, reaching No. 1 in the charts in the United States and the United Kingdom during 1965.

Around the time of Dave's departure from the Byrds, he met a recently unemployed Stephen Stills at a party at the home of Cass

Elliot in California in March 1968, and the two started meeting informally and jamming together. They were soon joined by Graham Nash, who would leave his commercially successful group the Hollies to play with David and Steve Stills. Their first album, Crosby, Stills & Nash, in 1969, was an immediate hit.

Also in 1969 Neil Young joined the group, and with him, they recorded the album Déjà Vu, which peaked at No. 1 on the Billboard Charts. In December 1969, David appeared with CSNY at the Altamont Free Concert, increasing his visibility after also having performed at Monterey Pop and Woodstock. At the beginning of 1970, he briefly joined with Jerry Garcia, Phil Lesh, and Mickey Hart from Grateful Dead, billed as "David and the Dorks", and making a live recording at the Matrix on December 15, 1970. Following a 1974 tour, Crosby Nash Stills & Young recorded a then-unreleased Dave Crosby song, "Little Blind Fish".

In 1971, Dave released his first solo album, If I Could Only Remember My Name, featuring contributions by Nash, Young, Joni Mitchell, and members of Jefferson Airplane, the Grateful Dead, and Santana.

In January 2014, Dave released his first solo album in 20 years, Croz, recorded in close collaboration with his son James. In September 2017, Dave announced a solo album entitled Sky Trails.

In July 2021 he released what would become his final studio album, For Free. This was followed by the release of the 50th-anniversary expanded version of If I Could Only Remember My Name. It contains remastered songs as well as demos from the original recording sessions. During promotion for the rerelease, Dave said that his second collaborative album with League, Stevens, and Willis was in the works. The result, David Crosby's final release, was a live album recorded during the band's tour, Live at the Capitol Theater, released on 4th October, 2022.

Clem Curtis   The Foundations

Clem Curtis died aged seventy-six on the 27th of March 2017 from cancer. He was survived by his wife, Elena and six sons and a daughter from his previous relationships.

Born in Trinidad as Curtis Clements, Clem arrived in England at the age of fifteen. Clem's mother was a popular singer in Trinidad and Clem claimed that this had contributed to his ear for music.

The Foundations first emerged in January 1967 with Clem as their lead singer and would go on to have worldwide hits with "Baby Now That I've Found You" and "Build Me Up Buttercup".

Charlie Daniels   The Charlie Daniels Band

Daniels died aged eighty three on the 6th of July 2020 from a haemorrhagic stroke in Hermitage, Tennessee, USA. He was survived by his wife, Hazel and his son, Charles.

Already skilled on guitar, fiddle, banjo, and mandolin, Charlie began his music career as a member of the bluegrass band Misty Mountain Boys in the 1950s.

Charlie released his debut album in 1970, and later he formed the Charlie Daniels Band. After the success of "The Devil Went Down to Georgia", a single described as a "a roaring country-disco fusion", Charlie shifted his sound from rock to country music.

Bobby Darin   Solo Artiste

Bobby Darin died at thirty-seven years of age on the 20th of December, 1973 in Cedars of Lebanon Hospital in Los Angeles, California, U.S.A. after a five-man surgical team had worked for over six hours to repair his damaged heart. He was survived by his wife, Andrea and his son, Dodd.

On the 11th of December, Bobby had checked himself into for another round of open-heart surgery to repair the two artificial heart valves he had received in 1971.

Bobby's last wish in his will was that his body be donated to science for medical research. His remains were transferred to the UCLA Medical Centre, later known as Ronald Reagan Medical Centre, shortly after his death.

Miles Davis   Solo Artiste

Miles Davis died aged sixty-five in Santa Monica, California, U.S.A. on the 28th of September 1991 after having had a cerebral haemorrhage, followed by a coma and several days on life support. He was survived by his wife, Betty and his sons, Gregory, Miles and Erin and his daughter, Cheryl.

In 1935, Miles received his first trumpet as a gift from John Eubanks, a friend of his father, and later took weekly lessons. Between 1951 and 1954, Miles released many records on the Prestige record label with varied line-ups

In March and April 1959, Miles recorded what many critics consider his greatest album, 'Kind of Blue' .

In March 1970, Miles began to perform as the opening act for various rock acts, allowing Columbia to market

'Bitches Brew' to a wider audience. By 1985, Miles was a diabetic and required daily insulin injections.

Spencer Davis   The Spencer Davis Group

Spencer Davis died aged eighty-one from pneumonia on the 19th of October, 2020 in Los Angeles, U.S.A. He was survived by his ex-wife, Pauline and their children; daughters Sarah and Lisa and their son Gareth.

In 1963, Spencer went to the Golden Eagle in Birmingham to see the Muff Wood Jazz band, a traditional jazz band featuring Muff Winwood and his younger brother, Steve Winwood. Spencer persuaded them to join him and drummer Pete York as the Rhythm and Blues Quartet. Spencer performed on guitar, vocals and harmonica, Steve Winwood on guitar, organ and vocals, Muff Winwood on bass and Pete York on drums. Reportedly, they adopted the name the Spencer Davis Group because Spencer was the only band member who agreed to press interviews, allowing the other band members to sleep longer.

The group's live reputation attracted the attention of Island Records founder Chris Blackwell who signed them to their first contract and became their manager. They had Number 1 hits in the UK with consecutive single releases in 1966 with"Keep On Running" and "Somebody Help Me". Steve Winwood sang lead vocals on all the Spencer Davis Group's hits up until "I'm a Man" in 1967.

The Spencer Davis Group continued after Steve Winwood left to form Traffic in April 1967 amd they recorded two more albums before splitting in 1969. Various incarnations of the Spencer Davis Group toured in later years under Spencer 's direction.

After the group broke up, Davis moved to California and recorded an acoustic album in mid 1971. He followed it with a solo album, Mousetrap, for United Artists, produced by and featuring Sneaky Pete Kleinow but neither album sold well. Soon after, he moved back to the UK, formed a new Spencer Davis Group and signed with Vertigo Records. In addition, Spencer was an executive at Island Records in the mid-1970s.

In 1993, Spencer formed the supergroup the Class Rock All-Stars but he left the group in 1995 to form World Classic Rockers with former Eagles bassist Randy Meisner, ex Toto singer Bobby Kimball and ex Moody Blues and ex-Wings guitarist Denny Laine.

Doris Day   Solo Artiste

Doris Day died aged ninety-seven on the 19th of May 2019 from pneumonia. She had been divorced from all her four husbands and was survived by her son, Terry.

Doris had seventeen top 30 hits in the United Kingdom, between 1952 and 1964. These were: 'Sugarbush' and 'My Love and Devotion' in 1952, 'Ma Says Pa Says', 'Full Time Job' and 'Lets Walk That-a-way' in 1953, 'Secret Love', 'The Black Hills of Dakota' and 'If I Give My Heart to You' in 1954, 'Ready, Willing and Able', 'Love Me or Leave Me' and 'I'll Never Stop Loving You' in 1955, 'Whatever Will Be Will Be' in 1956, 'A Very Precious Love' and 'Everybody Loves a Lover' in 1958 and 'Move Over Darling' in 1964.

Doris also had her own American radio program, The Doris Doris Day Show, which was broadcast on CBS in 1952 and 1953.

Doris starred in Alfred Hitchcock's suspense film, The Man Who Knew Too Much in 1956 with James Stewart. She sang two songs in the film, "Que Sera, Sera (Whatever Will Be, Will Be)", and "We'll Love Again".

After her retirement from films, Doris lived in Carmel-by-the-Sea, California, U.S.A. where she had many pets and adopted stray animals.

Desmond Decker   The Aces

Desmond Dekker died of a heart attack aged sixty-four on

the 25th of May 2006, at his home in Thornton Heath, London, United Kingdom. Desmond was divorced and was survived by a son and a daughter. At the time he had been preparing to headline a world music festival in Prague.

In 1968 Desmond's single , "Israelites" was released, eventually topping the UK Singles Chart in April 1969 and peaking in the Top Ten of the US Billboard Hot 100 in June 1969.

Desmond Dekker's UK chart hits include: "Israelites" in 1969, "It Miek" in 1969, "You Can Get It If You Really Want" in 1970 and "Sing A Little Song" in 1975.

Dave Dee   Dozy, Beaky, Mick & Tich

Dave Dee died aged sixty-seven of prostate cancer on the 9th of January, 2009 in South West London, U.K. He was survived by his wife, Joanne and his twin sons, Ashley and Elliot and a daughter, Olivia.

Dave Dee became a professional musician in 1962. His first group was called 'Dave Dee and the Bostons', who toured the UK and Germany and and they had a string of hits between 1966 and 1969 as Dave Dee, Dozy, Beaky, Mick & Tich, including one UK number one, Legend of Xanadu, in 1968.

Dave Dee, Dozy, Beaky, Mick & Tich's UK chart hits included: "Hold Tight" in 1966, "Bend It" in 1966, "Save Me" in 1966, "Okay" in 1967, "Zabadak" in 1967 and "Last Night In Soho" in 1968. Dave had continued to perform with his band almost up until his death.

Denis D'Ell   The Honeycombs

Denis D'Ell died aged sixty-one from cancer on the 6th of July 2005 and was survived by his wife, Belinda and by two children from a previous marriage.

Denis was born Denis James Dalziel, in Whitechapel, London, United Kingdom in 1943. After winning a talent contest, he joined a local band called the Sheritons, then the Honeycombs.

"Have I the Right?" was a huge hit and the Honeycombs had further success with "Is It Because?" and made the album 'It's the Honeycombs' in 1964.

Brad Delp   Boston

qBrad Delp died aged fifty-five on the 9th of March 2007 by committing suicide via carbon monoxide poisoning at his home on Academy Avenue in Atkinson, New Hampshire, U.S.A. Two charcoal grills were found to have been lit inside the bathtub causing the room to fill with smoke. A suicide note was paper-clipped to the neck of his T-shirt, which read: "Mr. Brad Delp. 'J'ai une âme solitaire'. I have a lonely soul." He was survived by his ex-wife, Micki and his daughter, Jenna.

Boston's debut album has sold more than 20 million copies, and produced rock standards such as "More Than a Feeling", "Foreplay/Long Time" and "Peace of Mind.

Sandy Denny   Fairport Convention

Sandy Denny died aged just thirty-one years on the 21st of April 1978 from a brain haemorrhage. She was survived by her daughter, Georgia.

Sandy was born, Alexandra Elene MacLean Denny. After briefly working with the Strawbs, Sandy joined Fairport Convention in 1968, remaining with them until 1969. She formed the short-lived band Fotheringay in 1970, before focusing on a solo career. Between 1971 and 1977, Sandy released four solo albums: The North Star Grassman and the Ravens, Sandy, Like an Old Fashioned Waltz and Rendezvous. She also duetted with Robert Plant on "The Battle of Evermore" for Led Zeppelin's album Led Zeppelin IV in 1971.

Sandy's composition "Who Knows Where the Time

Goes?" has been recorded by Judy Collins, Eva Cassidy, and Nina Simone amongst others. Her recorded work has been the subject of numerous reissues, along with a wealth of previously unreleased material which has appeared over the more than forty years since her death, including a 19-CD box set released in November 2010.

Sandy's earliest professional recordings were made later in mid-nineteen sixty-seven for the Saga record label, featuring traditional songs and covers of contemporary folk singers. The folk-rock band, Fairport Convention were auditioning in May 1968 for a replacement singer and Sandy Denny was their choice.

John Denver   Solo Artiste

John Denver died aged fifty-three on the 12th of October 1997 when his small private plane crashed into Monterey Bay in California, USA. He was survived by his wife, Cassandra and his daughter, Jesse Bell.

At the age of eleven, John received an acoustic guitar from his grandmother and he learned to play well enough to perform at local clubs by the time he was in college.

In 1969, John pursued a solo career and released his first album for RCA Records: 'Rhymes & Reasons'.

John Denver's first marriage was to Anne and she was the subject of his hit "Annie's Song," which he composed in only ten minutes as he sat on a Colorado ski lift after the couple had engaged in an argument.

Ronnie James Dio   Rainbow and Heaven & Hell

Ronnie James Dio died of stomach cancer aged sixty-seven on the 16th of May 2010. He was survived by his wife, Wendy and his son, Dan and his daughter, Delilah.

Ronnie's musical career began in 1957, when he and several Cortland, New York, musicians formed the band The

Vegas Kings. The group's lineup consisted of Ronnie on bass guitar, Billy DeWolfe on lead vocals, Nick Pantas on guitar, Tom Rogers on drums and Jack Musci on saxophone. Musci left the band in 1960 and a new guitarist, Dick Botoff, joined the lineup. The band released two singles: The first single was "Conquest"/"Lover" with the A-side being an instrumental track reminiscent of the Ventures and the B-side featuring DeWolfe on lead vocals. The second was "An Angel Is Missing"/"What'd I Say" featuring Ronnie on lead vocals for both tracks.

In late 1967, Ronnie Dio and the Prophets transformed into a new band called the Electric Elves and added a keyboard player. In February 1968, the band was involved in a fatal car accident that killed guitarist Nick Pantas and briefly put Ronnie and the other band members in hospital. Following the accident, the group shortened its name to the Elves and used that name until mid-1972, when it released its first proper album under the name Elf. Over the next few years, the group went on to become a regular opening act for Deep Purple. Elf recorded three albums until the members' involvement in recording the first Rainbow album in early 1975, resulting in Elf disbanding.

In the mid-1970s, Ronnie's vocals caught the ear of Deep Purple guitarist Ritchie Blackmore, who was planning on leaving Deep Purple due to creative differences over the band's new direction. Richie invited Ronnie, along with Gary Driscoll, to record two songs in Tampa, Florida, in December 1974. Being satisfied with the results, Richie decided to recruit more of Elf's musicians and form his own band, initially known as Ritchie Blackmore's Rainbow. They released the self-titled debut album Ritchie Blackmore's Rainbow in early 1975. After that, Ronnie recorded two more studio albums, Rising in 1976 and Long Live Rock 'n' Roll in 1978. During his tenure with Rainbow, Ronnie and Richie were the only constant members. Ronnie is credited on those albums for all lyrical authorship as well as collaboration with Richie on musical arrangement.

Following his departure from Rainbow in 1979, Ronnie joined Black Sabbath, replacing the sacked Ozzy Osbourne. Ronnie had met Black Sabbath guitarist Tony Iommi by chance at the Rainbow on Sunset Strip in Los Angeles in 1979. The two musicians were in similar situations, as Ronnie was seeking a new project and Tony needed a vocalist. Ronnie said of the encounter, "It must have been fate, because we connected so instantly." The pair kept in touch until Ronnie arrived at Tony's Los Angeles house for a relaxed, getting-to-know-you jam session. On that first day, the duo wrote the song "Children of the Sea," which appeared on the Heaven and Hell album, the first the band recorded with Ronnie as its vocalist, released in 1980.

The follow-up album, Mob Rules, in 1981, featured new drummer Vinny Appice but personality conflicts began emerging within the band. In 1982, conflict arose over the mixing of the Live Evil album. Tony asserted that the album's engineer began complaining to him that he would work all day long on a mix, only to have Ronnie return to the studio at night to "do his own mix" in which his vocals were more prominent. This was denied by Ronnie. The conflict led to Ronnie and Appice ultimately quitting the band later that year.

In 1991, Ronnie returned to Black Sabbath to record the Dehumanizer album. The album was a minor hit, reaching the Top 40 in the United Kingdom and number 44 on the US Billboard 200. The single "Time Machine" was featured in the movie Wayne's World, the tenth highest-grossing film of 1992. Close to the end of 1992, Ronnie and Appice again left the band, citing an inability to work with Iommi and Geezer Butler.

Wanting to continue together as a band, Ronnie and Appice formed the eponymous heavy metal band Dio in 1982. Vivian Campbell played guitar and Jimmy Bain played bass, the latter of whom Ronnie had known since his time with Rainbow. Their 1983 debut album, Holy Diver, included the hit singles "Rainbow in the Dark" and "Holy Diver", which have remained the band's signature songs.

The band added keyboardist Claude Schnell and recorded two more full-length studio albums, The Last in Line in 1984 and Sacred Heart in 1985. The band changed members over the years, eventually leaving Ronnie as the only original member in 1990. Except for a few breaks, the band was constantly touring or recording. They released ten albums, with Master of the Moon being the last one, recorded in 2004.

In October 2006, Ronnie joined Black Sabbath members Tony Iommi, Geezer Butler and former Black Sabbath drummer Vinny Appice to tour under the moniker Heaven & Hell, the title of the first Dio-era Black Sabbath album. They chose the name Heaven & Hell as Iommi and Butler were still in Black Sabbath with Osbourne and felt it was best to use a different moniker for the Dio version of the band.

In 2007, the band recorded three new songs under the Black Sabbath name for the compilation album Black Sabbath: The Dio Years. In 2008, the band completed a 98-date world tour and released one album under the Heaven & Hell name, The Devil You Know, to critical and commercial acclaim.

Tommy DiVito   **The Four Seasons**

Tommy DiVito died of Covid 19 aged ninety-two on the 21st of September 2020 in Las Vegas, California, United States of America. He was survived by two children from his first marriage and a daughter from his second marriage.

Tommy's musical career began in the early 1950s when he formed "the Variety Trio" with his brother Nick DeVito and Hank Majewski. This core group performed under various names and changing lineups. The band expanded to a quartet and changed its name to "the Variatones" including the addition in 1954 of singer Francis Castelluccio, later known as Frankie Valli. When they were signed to a recording contract with RCA Victor, in 1956, the quartet had renamed themselves "the Four Lovers". Tommy and Frankie remained the only consistent members of the Four Lovers, as the group released seven singles and one album under the Four Lovers name. Their 1956 debut single, Otis Blackwell's "You're the Apple of My Eye", achieved enough national sales to appear as a minor hit on the Billboard Hot 100 singles chart. The single landed Tommy his first national television appearance, when the Four Lovers appeared on The Ed Sullivan Show in 1956.

After his brother left the group, Tommy continued his musical pursuits, reforming and realigning the group. By 1960 The Four Lovers consisted of Tommy, Valli, Gaudio and vocal arranger Nick Massi, and were mainly used as a backup band for producer Bob Crewe under contract. This is the lineup which adopted the name "The Four Seasons". Released by Vee-Jay Records in July 1962, "Sherry" hit number one in September, the first of three consecutive chart-topping hits by the Four Seasons, the others being "Big Girls Don't Cry" and "Walk Like a Man". In 1963, Tommy and Nick co-founded Vito-Mass Productions, an independent music production business. From 1965 onward, Nick handled most of the day-to-day operations of the company while Tommy remained with the band.

Denny Doherty   Mamas & Papas

Denny Doherty died aged sixty-six at his home in Mississauga, Ontario, Canada on the 19th of January 2007, from kidney failure following surgery for an abdominal aortic aneurysm. He was survived by his Son, John and his daughters, Jessica and Emberly. Denny is interred at the Gate of Heaven Cemetery in Lower Sackville, Nova Scotia.

In 1963, Denny established a friendship with Cass Elliot when she was with a band called the Big 3 and while on tour with the group, Halifax III, Denny met John Phillips and his wife, Michelle.

A few months later, the Halifax III dissolved, and Denny was left without money in Hollywood. Cass Elliot convinced her manager to hire him and, thus, Denny joined the Big 3. Soon, after adding even more band members, they changed their name to the Mugwumps, which soon broke up.

About this time, John Phillips' new band, the New Journeymen, needed a replacement member. Denny, then unemployed, filled the opening. After this, in 1965, Cass Elliot was invited into the formation of a new band, which became the Magic Cyrcle. Six months later the group signed a recording contract with Dunhill Records and changed their name to the Mamas and the Papas. They soon began to record their debut album, If You Can Believe Your Eyes and Ears. Denny sang lead on "California Dreamin", released in December 1965, prior to the release of the debut album early in 1966.

Fats Domino   Solo Artiste

Fats Domino died aged eighty-nine on the 24th of October 2017, at his home in, Louisiana, U.S.A. from natural causes. He was survived by his sons, Antonio, Antoine, Andre and Anatole and his daughters, Antoinette, Anola, Adonica and Andrea.

By age fourteen, Fats was performing in New Orleans bars. In 1947, Billy Diamond, a New Orleans bandleader, accepted an invitation to hear the young pianist perform at a backyard barbecue. Fats played well enough that Diamond asked him to join his band, the Solid Senders, at the Hideaway Club in New Orleans, where he would earn three dollars a week playing the piano.

Fats was signed to the Imperial Records label in 1949, to

be paid royalties based on sales instead of a fee for each song. He and producer Dave Bartholomew wrote "The Fat Man", which had sold a million copies by 1951. Featuring a rolling piano and Fats vocalizing "wah-wah" over a strong backbeat, "The Fat Man" is widely considered the first rock-and-roll record to achieve this level of sales. In 2015. While Fats' own recordings were done for Imperial, he sometimes sat in during that time as a session musician on recordings by other artists for other record labels.

Fats crossed into the pop mainstream with "Ain't That a Shame" which reached the Top Ten. This was the first of his records to appear on the Billboard pop singles chart. Fats eventually had 37 Top 40 singles, but none made it to number 1 on the Pop chart.

Fats's debut album contained several of his recent hits and earlier blues tracks that had not been released as singles, and was issued on the Imperial label in November 1955, and was reissued as Rock and Rollin' with Fats Domino.

His 1956 recording of "Blueberry Hill", reached number two on the Billboard Juke Box chart for two weeks and was number one on the R&B chart for eleven weeks. It was his biggest hit, selling more than five million copies worldwide in 1956 and 1957. Fats had further hit singles between 1956 and 1959, including "When My Dreamboat Comes Home", "I'm Walkin'", "Valley of Tears", "It's You I Love", "Whole Lotta Lovin'" , "I Want to Walk You Home", and "Be My Guest".

Fats had a steady series of hits for Imperial through early 1962, including "Walking to New Orleans" in 1960, and "My Girl Josephine". He toured Europe in 1962 and met the Beatles who would later cite Fats as an inspiration.

Lee Dorsey   Solo Artiste

Lee Dorsey died aged sixty-one from emphysema on the 1st of December 1986, in New Orleans, Louisiana, U.S.A.

Lee was born in New Orleans, Louisiana, and he moved to Portland, Oregon when he was ten years old. His first recording was "Rock Pretty Baby/Lonely Evening" on the Rex label, in 1958. This was followed by "Lottie Mo/Lover of Love", for the small Valiant label in late 1960. In 1960 Lee was discovered by A&R man Marshall Sehorn, who secured him a contract with Fury Records. After meeting songwriter and record producer Allen Toussaint at a party, he recorded "Ya Ya", a song inspired by a group of children chanting nursery rhymes. It went to number seven on the Billboard Hot 100 in 1961, sold over one million copies, and was awarded a gold disc. Although the follow-up "Do-Re-Mi" also made the charts, later releases on Fury were less successful.

Lee was approached again by Toussaint, and recorded Toussaint's song "Ride Your Pony" for the Amy label, a subsidiary of Bell Records. The song reached No. 7 on the R&B chart in late 1965, and he followed it up with "Get Out of My Life, Woman", "Working in the Coal Mine" and "Holy Cow", all of which made the pop charts in both the US and the UK. Lee toured internationally, and also recorded an album, The New Lee Dorsey, in 1966.

Nick Drake   Solo Artiste

Nick Drake died aged twenty-six on the 24th of November 1974 at his home in Warwickshire, UK. from an overdose of an antidepressant drug. He was survived by his wife, Molly.

Nick played piano in the school orchestra, and learned clarinet and saxophone. In 1965, he paid £13 for his first acoustic guitar, and was soon experimenting with open tuning and finger-picking techniques.

Nick recorded his debut album Five Leaves Left in 1968 and had to skip college lectures to travel by train to the sessions in a London recording studio. To provide backing, the producer enlisted contacts from the London folk rock scene, including Fairport Convention guitarist Richard Thompson and Pentangle bassist Danny Thompson.

Post-production difficulties delayed the release by several months, and in July 1968, Melody Maker described Five Leaves Left as "poetic" and "interesting", though NME wrote in October that there was "not nearly enough variety to make it entertaining". It received little radio play outside shows by more progressive BBC DJs including John Peel and Bob Harris.

Ronnie Drew   The Dubliners

Ronnie Drew died aged seventy-three on the 16th of August 2008 in St. Vincent's Hospital, Dublin, Ireland following a long illness. He was survived by his son Phelim and his daughter, Cliodhna.

In the 1950s, Ronnie moved to Spain to teach English and learn Spanish and flamenco guitar. His interest in folk music began at the age of nineteen. When he returned to Ireland, he performed in the Gate Theatre with John Molloy and soon went into the music business full-time.

In 1962, he founded the Ronnie Drew Group with Luke Kelly, Barney McKenna and Ciarán Bourke but they soon changed their name to The Dubliners and quickly became one of the best known Irish folk groups.

Ronnie left the Dubliners in 1974 then he rejoined in 1979, but then left for good in 1995, though he did reunite with the group in 2002 for a 40th anniversary celebration. From 1995 onwards, Ronnie pursued a solo career and also recorded with many other artists, including Christy Moore, The Pogues, Antonio Breschi, Dropkick Murphys, Eleanor Shanley.

In August 2006, Ronnie was honoured in a ceremony where his hand prints were added to the "Walk of Fame" outside Dublin's Gaiety Theatre.

Spencer Dryden   Jefferson Airplane

Spencer Dryden died aged sixty-six from colon cancer on the 11th of January 2005. He was survived by his three sons, Jeffrey, Jesse, and Jackson, and six grandchildren, and his mother.

In mid-1966 Spencer was recruited as the drummer in leading San Francisco psychedelic band Jefferson Airplane. During this time, he had an affair with their lead singer, Grace Slick.

Spencer left the music business for a short period, but returned to drumming as a member of the New Riders of the Purple Sage.

John Ducann   Atomic Rooster

John Du Cann died of a heart attack aged sixty-five on at his home in Norfolkshire, United Kingdom, on the 21st of September 2011.

John's early bands included the Wiltshire-based The Sonics and London-based The Attack. He went on to lead a psychedelic, progressive, hard rock band called Andromeda, before being asked to join Atomic Rooster, featuring re-recorded guitar parts and vocals for their 1970 self-titled debut album, and the albums 'Death Walks Behind You' in 1970 and 'In Hearing of Atomic Rooster' in 1971. John wrote "Devil's Answer", Atomic Rooster's biggest hit, which reached number four in the UK singles charts in July 1971.

Judith Durham   The Seekers

Judith Durham died aged seventy-nine on the 5th of August 2022 from chronic lung disease. She was given a state memorial service by the Australian state of Victoria on the net day and was interred with her late husband at Springvale Botanical Cemetery.

Judith was born in July 1943 in Victoria, Australia. She at first planned to be a pianist and gained the qualification of Associate in Music, in classical piano at the University of Melbourne Conservatorium. She had some professional engagements playing piano and had classical vocal training as a soprano, and performed blues, gospel and jazz pieces. Her singing career began one night at the age of eighteen when she asked the leader of the Melbourne University Jazz Band, whether she could sing with his band. In 1963, she began performing at the same club with Frank Traynor's Jazz Preachers, using her mother's maiden name of Judith Durham.

The Seekers consisted of Judith Durham, Athol Guy, Bruce Woodley and Keith Potger. W&G Records signed the Seekers for an album, Introducing the Seekers, in 1963.

In early 1964, the Seekers sailed to the United Kingdom on SS Fairsky on which the group provided the musical entertainment. During November, 1964, at EMI's Abbey Road Studios, the Seekers recorded "I'll Never Find Another You" and in February 1965, the song reached number one in the record charts of the UK and Australia. The group had further Top ten hits with "A World of Our Own", "Morningtown Ride" and "Someday, One Day", "Georgy Girl" and "The Carnival Is Over".

On a tour of New Zealand in February 1968, Judith advised the group that she was leaving the Seekers and left in July 1968. Judith returned to Australia in 1968. During her solo career, she released albums titled For Christmas with Love, Gift of Song and Climb Ev'ry Mountain. In 1970, she made the television special Meet Judith Durham in London, ending with her rendition of "When You Come to the End of a Perfect Day".

In 2003, Judith toured the UK in "The Diamond Tour" celebrating her 60th birthday. The tour included the Royal Festival Hall and a CD and DVD of the concert were issued.

On the 21st of November 1969, Judith Durham married her musical director, British pianist Ron Edgeworth but they made the choice not to have children.

Ian Dury   The Blockheads

Ian Dury died aged fifty-seven of metastatic colorectal cancer on the 27th of March 2000. He was survived by his sons Baxter, Albert and Billy and by his daughter, Jemima.

Ian formed Kilburn and the High Roads in 1971, and they played their first gig at Croydon School of Art during December 1971. Ian was vocalist and lyricist, co-writing with pianist Russell Hardy.

They soon found favour on London's pub rock circuit and signed to Dawn Records in 1974. Ian then formed The Blockheads and the single "Sex & Drugs & Rock & Roll", released in August 1977, marked Ian's Stiff Records debut. Although it was banned by the BBC, it was named Single of the Week by NME on its release. The single was soon followed, that September, by the album New Boots and Panties! which achieved platinum status. Ian Dury and the Blockheads quickly gained a reputation as one of the top live acts of new wave music.

The band worked solidly over the eighteen months between the release of "Rhythm Stick" and their next single, "Reasons to Be Cheerful, Part 3", which returned them to the charts, making the UK Top ten.

The Blockheads toured the UK and Europe throughout 1981, sometimes augmented by jazz trumpeter Don Cherry, ending the year with their only tour of Australia. The Blockheads disbanded in early 1982, after Ian secured a new recording deal with Polydor Records through A&R man Frank Neilson. Choosing to work with a group of young musicians which he named the Music Students, he recorded the album Four Thousand Weeks' Holiday.

In the early 1990s, Ian appeared with English band Curve on the benefit compilation album Peace Together.

Ian and Curve singer Toni Halliday shared vocals on a cover of the Blockheads' track "What a Waste".

Ian Dury & the Blockheads' last public performance was a charity concert in aid of Cancer BACUP on the 6th of February 2000 at the London Palladium.

Dennis Edwards   The Temptations

Dennis Edwards died from meningitis aged seventy-four on the 1st of February 2018 in a Chicago hospital. He was survived by his wife, Brenda.

Dennis had been briefly married to Ruth Pointer, whom he wed in Las Vegas in 1977 and the couple had a daughter, Issa Pointer, who became a member of her mother's vocal group, The Pointer Sisters.

The Temptations officially introduced Dennis in July 1968 on stage in Valley Forge, Pennsylvania after which he led the group through its psychedelic, funk, and disco periods, singing on hits such as "Cloud Nine".

The Temptations UK chart hits include: "I'm Gonna Make You Love Me" in 1969, "Get Ready" in 1969, "Ball of Confusion" in 1970, "Just My Imagination" in 1971 and "Papa Was A Rollin' Stone in 1973.

Mama Cass Elliot   The Mamas & Papas

Mama Cass Elliott died of heart failure aged thirty-two on the 29th of July 1974 in Mayfair, London, U.K. She was survived by her daughter, Owen and was buried in Mount Sinai Memorial Park Cemetery in Los Angeles, U.S.A.

Cass was known for her sense of humor and optimism, and was considered by some to be the most charismatic member of the Mamas & Papas, her powerful, distinctive voice being a major factor in their success. She is best remembered for her vocals on the group's hits "California Dreamin'", "Monday, Monday", "Words of Love", and the solo "Dream a Little Dream of Me", recorded in 1968.

After the breakup of The Mamas & the Papas, Cass embarked on a solo singing career. Her most successful recording during this period was 1968's "Dream a Little Dream of Me" from her solo album.

Cass was married twice, the first time in 1963 to James Hendricks which reportedly was never consummated and was annulled in 1968. In 1971, Cass married journalist Donald von Wiedenman, heir to a Bavarian barony but their marriage ended in divorce after a few months.

Cass gave birth to her daughter Owen in 1967 but never publicly identified the father.

Keith Emerson   Emerson Lake & Palmer

Keith Emerson died aged seventy-one on the 11th of March 2016 in Santa Monica, California, U.S.A. of a self-inflicted gunshot wound to his head and his death was ruled a suicide. He was survived by his ex-wife, Elinor and his sons, Damon and Aaron.

In 1967, Keith formed the band, The Nice to back soul singer P. P. Arnold and then the group set out without her, quickly developing a strong live following. The group's sound was centred on Keith's Hammond organ showmanship and their radical rearrangements of classical music themes known as "symphonic rock".

In 1970, Keith left the Nice and formed Emerson, Lake & Palmer (ELP) with bassist Greg Lake from King Crimson and drummer Carl Palmer from Atomic Rooster. Within a few months, the band played its first shows and recorded its first album, having quickly obtained a record deal with Atlantic Records.

Following ELP's 1974 tour, the members agreed to put the band on temporary hiatus and pursue individual solo projects. During this time, Keith composed his "Piano

Concerto No. 1" and recorded it with the London Philharmonic Orchestra.

In the 1980s, Keith began to write and perform music for
films, as his orchestral and classical style was more suited
for film work than for the then current pop and rock market.

John Entwistle   The Who

John Entwistle died aged fifty-seven on the 27th of June
2002 from a heart attack at the Hard Rock Hotel and
Casino in Las Vegas, USA, one day before the scheduled
first show of the Who's 2002 United States tour. He was
survived by his ex-wife, Maxene and his son, Christopher.

John had gone to bed that night with a groupie who
woke to find John cold and unresponsive. The medical
examiner determined that his death was due to a heart
attack induced by a cocaine overdose.

In the 1960's, the Who considered several changes of
name, and finally settling on the name the Who, but temporarily performed as the High Numbers for four months
in 1964.

John was the only member of the Who to have had formal musical training. In addition to the bass guitar, he
contributed backing vocals and performed on the French
horn, trumpet, bugle, and Jew's harp, and on some occasions he sang the lead vocals on his own compositions.

While John Entwistle was known for being the quietest
member of the Who, he was the first member of the band
to wear a Union Jack waistcoat, a piece of clothing which
later became one of Pete Townshend's signature gar-
ments.

Tom Evans   Badfinger

Tom Evans died aged thirty-six on the 10th of November
1983 when he hanged himself to death in his garden following an argument with guitarist Joey Molland about the

royalties for the song "Without You". He was survived by his wife Marianne and his son, Stephen.

Badfinger enjoyed major successes in the early 1970s with singles such as "No Matter What," "Day After Day," and "Baby Blue". Each featured some of Tom's vocals; background harmony or dual lead. Tom's high-career moment was with his composition "Without You," a song co-written with bandmate Pete Ham. The song became a Number one hit worldwide for Harry Nilsson and has since become a standard in the music industry.

Badfinger's UK chart hits include: "Come And Get It" in 1970, "No Matter What" in 1971, and "Day After Day" in 1972.

Phil Everly   The Everly Brothers

Phil Everly died aged seventy-four of lung disease on the 3rd of January 2014 of lung disease at a medical centre in Burbank, California, U.S.A. He was survived by his wife Patti and his sons, Jason and Chris.

Phil and Don Everly had UK chart hits including: "Bye Bye Love" in 1957, "Wake Up Little Susie" in 1957, "All I Have to Do is Dream" in 1958, "Bird Dog" in 1958, "Cathy's Clown" in 1960 and "The Price of Love" in 1965.

Don Everly   The Everly Brothers

Don Everly's died aged eighty-four of undisclosed causes on the 21st of August 2021 in Nashville Tennessee, USA. He was survived by his wife, Adela and his son, Edan and his daughters, Stacey and Erin.

The brothers Everly were raised in a musical family, first appearing on radio singing along with their father Ike Everly and mother Margaret Everly as "The Everly Family" in the 1940s. When the brothers were still in high school, they gained the attention of prominent Nashville musicians including Chet Atkins, who began to promote them for national attention.

They began writing and recording their own music in 1956, and their first hit song came in 1957, with "Bye Bye Love". which hit Number one in the spring of 1957, and additional hits followed through 1958, including "Wake Up Little Susie", "All I Have to Do Is Dream", and "Problems". In 1960, they signed with Warner Bros. Records and recorded "Cathy's Clown", written by themselves, which was their biggest selling single. Additional hit singles continued through 1962, with "That's Old Fashioned" being their last top-10 hit.

Adam Faith   Solo Artiste

Adam Faith died aged sixty-two of a heart attack on the 8th of March 2003, at a Staffordshire hospital in the United Kingdom. He was survived by his wife, Jackie and his daughter, Katya.

Adam became one of Britain's most significant early pop stars. He began his musical career in 1957, while working as a film cutter in London in the hope of becoming an actor and also singing with and managing a skiffle group called the Worried Men. The group played in Soho coffee bars and became a resident band where they appeared on a BBC Television live music programme. The producer was impressed by Adam and arranged a solo recording contract with HMV followed by another recording contract with Parlophone. His next record in 1959, "What Do You Want?" became his first number one hit in the UK Singles Chart, and his pronunciation of the word 'baby' as 'bay-beh' became a catchphrase.

Adam's next release was a double A-side single, "Made You" backed with "When Johnny Comes Marching Home", which made the top ten. His début album Adam was released on in November 1960 to critical acclaim.

Adam made six further albums and thirty-five singles and he managed to lodge twenty consecutive single releases on the UK Singles Chart, starting with "What Do You Want?" in November 1959 and culminating with "I Love Being in Love with You" in mid-1964. Adam's last top ten hit in the UK, in October 1963, was "The First Time".

Ella Fitzgerald   Solo Artiste

Ella Fitzgerald died aged seventy-nine from a stroke at home in Beverly Hills, Los Angeles, Califfornia, U.S.A. on the 15th of June 1996. She had suffered from diabetes for several years of her later life, which had led to numerous complications.

Ella made her most important debut at the age of seventeen in 1934, in one of the earliest Amateur Nights at the Apollo Theater, New York. She sang "Judy" and "The Object of My Affection" and won first prize.

In January 1935, Ella won the chance to perform for a week with a band at the Harlem Opera House.

Ella recorded several hit songs, including "Love and Kisses" and "(If You Can't Sing It) You'll Have to Swing It (Mr. Paganini)". But it was her 1938 version of the nursery rhyme, "A-Tisket, A-Tasket", a song she co-wrote, that brought her public acclaim. "A-Tisket, A-Tasket" became a major hit on the radio and was also one of the biggest-selling records of the decade.

Ella recorded nearly one hundred and fifty songs with Chic Webb's orchestra between 1935 and 1942. In addition to this work, she performed and recorded with the Benny Goodman Orchestra and had her own side project, too, known as Ella Fitzgerald and Her Savoy Eight.

Andy Fletcher   Depeche Mode

Andy Fletcher died aged sixty from an aortic dissection on the 26th of May 2022. He was survived by his wife, Grainne, their son Joe and daughter Megan.

Andy and friends Vince Clarke and Martin Gore were in their mid-teens when punk rock became popular on the music scene. Andy and Vince formed the short-lived band No Romance in China, in which Andy played bass guitar. In 1980, Andy, Vince and Martin formed another group called Composition of Sound. Vince served as chief songwriter and also provided lead vocals until singer Dave Gahan was recruited into the band later in 1980, after which they adopted the name Depeche. Vince left the group in late 1981, shortly after the release of their debut album Speak & Spell. Their 1982 follow-up album, A Broken Frame, was recorded as a trio, with Martin taking over primary song-writing duties. Musician and producer Alan Wilder joined the band in late 1982 and the group continued as a quartet.

In 1989, while the band was working on the album, Violator, Andy suffered from anxiety and depression and he had a relapse in 1993 during the recording of Songs of Faith and Devotion. One year later, he had to leave the Exotic Tour/Summer Tour '94 due to a nervous break-down, and the band played without him in South America and the United States.

After Alan Wilder left Depeche Mode in 1995, the band's core trio of Dave, Martin, and Andy remained active up to the release of their 2017 album, Spirit, and the ensuing world tour.

Keith Flint   The Prodigy

Keith Flint died aged forty-nine from suicide by hanging on the 4th of March 2019 at his home in Essex, United Kingdom. He was survived by his Japanese wife Mayumi.

Keith was born Keith Charles Flint in Redbridge, London. He was expelled from school at the age of fifteen and then worked as a roofer and later enthusiastically embraced the acid-house music scene of the late 1980's.

In 1996, just before the release of the Prodigy's third album, Keith moved from being a dancer for the group to being its vocalist. When he performed vocals on the hit single "Firestarter", the accompanying video showcased Keith's new iconic punk look. The Prodigy album 'Invaders Must Die' was released in February 2009 and featured vocals by Keith Flint on many of the tracks.

Dan Fogelberg   Solo Artiste

Dan Fogelberg died of prostate cancer aged fifty-six on the 16th of December 2007 at his home in Colorado, U.S.A. He was survived by his wife, Jean.

Dan's widow announced that a song written and recorded by Dan for her, for Valentine's Day 2005, "Sometimes a Song", would be sold on the Internet and that all proceeds would go to the Prostate Cancer Foundation. The song was released on

Valentine's Day 2008 and was also included on a CD released in September 2009 entitled Love in Time, a collection of eleven previously unpublished songs.

Tom Fogerty   Creedence Clearwater Revival

Tom Fogerty died of Tuberculosis aged forty-eight on the 6th of September 1990 in Scottsdale, Arizona, U.S.A. where he lived. He was survived by his second wife Tricia and six children.

Tom started singing rock and roll when in high school, however, Tom and his younger brother, John, had separate groups. Tom's band, Spider Webb and the Insects, signed a recording contract with Del-Fi Records but broke up in 1959 before releasing any records. The Blue Velvets, a group led by John, began backing Tom. Eventually Tom joined the band, and the group recorded three singles, with Tom on lead vocals, for Orchestra Records in 1961 and 1962. By the mid nineteen sixties, the band had been renamed 'The Golliwogs' and were recording with Fantasy Records. In nineteen sixty-eight the band was again renamed to 'Creedence Clearwater Revival' by which time John Fogerty had become the full-time lead singer and main songwriter.

During the few years of the life of Creedence Clearwater Revival, Tom sang backing vocals and wrote songs, but only one of his songs ("Walking on the Water") was put on a record.

After leaving Creedence Clearwater Revival, Tom began performing and recording as a solo artist. He had minor hits with "Goodbye Media Man" and others and remained with Fantasy Records. His nineteen seventy-one solo debut album, 'Tom Fogerty', reached number seventy-eight on the Billboard Hot 200 chart.

Throughout the remainder of the nineteen seventies and nineteen eighties, Tom continued to record and claimed all royalties.

Wayne Fontana   The Mindbenders

Wayne Fontana died aged seventy-four from cancer on the 6th of August 2020. He was survived by his ex-wife, Suzanne and his daughter and two sons.

Wayne was born in Levenshulme, Manchester, Lancashire, UK. In June 1963 he formed his backing group, the Mindbenders, and secured a recording contract with, Fontana Records. With the band, Wayne released his biggest single "The Game of Love" and after several less successful singles, including "It's Just a Little Bit Too Late" and "She Needs Love" he left the band in October 1965.

Wayne remained under contract to the record label after parting with the Mindbenders and continued alone, using musicians working under the name of the Opposition. Sometimes the band was billed as the Mindbenders, sometimes just as the Wayne Fontana Band. Struggling to achieve chart success, Wayne recorded a number of songs by outside writers with flip-sides being mostly his own compositions. Wayne's biggest solo single, "Pamela, Pamela", written by Graham Gouldman, reached number eleven on the UK singles chart in early 1967 and was his last single to chart in the UK. The later singles included another Gouldman composition, "The Impossible Years". In 1970 he was one of the first performers at the Glastonbury Festival.

Dean Ford   Marmalade

Dean Ford died aged seventy-two from Parkinson's Disease on the 31st of December 2018. He was survived by his daughter, Tracey.

Dean first began singing in public accompanying a jazz ensemble at his local parish church dance hall. He formed his first musical group The Tonebeats at age thirteen, one of several he hooked up with during his teenage years. By the time he left high school at age fifteen, he had been gaining some exposure as a featured singer. His break came after a performance with the Monarchs at the Barrowland Ballroom in Glasgow in 1963, where he was seen by members of the popular east Glasgow band The Gaylords and was subsequently invited to join them as their singer. The Gaylords were re-named Dean Ford and the Gaylords and with hopes of achieving more commercial success, Dean and the band relocated to London in 1965.

Three years later, having changed their name to Marmalade, they became the first Scottish band to score a number one hit on the UK Singles Chart. In addition to his lead vocals, Dean co-wrote the songs "Reflections of My Life", "Rainbow", "My Little One", and "I See The Rain" and added instrumental support on harmonica and tambourine.

After several lineup changes, Marmalade was reduced to three band members by 1973, with Dean being the lone founding member.

With the dissolution of the original Marmalade, Dean embarked on a solo career and released a self-titled LP in 1975. After his solo album failed to chart, Dean was released by his record company and, battling alcoholism, he moved to Los Angeles in 1979. Virtually unknown as a recording artist in the U.S.A, he was unable to cash in on his earlier success with Marmalade. However, with the help of Alcoholics Anonymous, Dean got sober by 1986 and he turned to music again by appearing in small clubs and open-mic venues whilst his royalties from his song; "Reflections of My Life" kept him financially afloat.

Robbie France

Robbie France died aged fifty-two of a ruptured aorta on the 14th of January 2012 whilst in Spain.

In 1990 Robbie joined Wishbone Ash, with whom he toured and commenced the recording of the album 'Strange Affair'. However, friction occurred between Robbie and Wishbone Ash bassist Martin Turner, resulting in Robbie's dismissal from the band.

In 1994, Robbie became a founder member of Skunk Anansie and recorded and co-produced their debut album 'Paranoid & Sunburnt'. He co-wrote the hit track "Weak", which was covered by Rod Stewart. He also recorded the B-side, "Army of Me", with Björk.

Robbie left Skunk Anansie in 1995, joining the German group Alphaville the next day. He toured and recorded with Alphaville until an accident in which he severed his Achilles tendon. He lived in Poland for over two years, hosting his own radio programme, and appeared on various television shows. In 1998, he moved to Mazarrón, Spain, to concentrate on writing his first novel, Six Degrees South, which was published on 7th December 2011.

Aretha Franklin

Aretha Franklin died on the 16th of August 2018 aged seventy-six from a pancreatic neuroendocrine tumour at her home in Michigan, U.S.A. She as survived by her sons, Clarence, Edward and Ted and Kecalf.

Numerous celebrities in the entertainment industry and politicians paid tribute to her, including former U.S. president Barack Obama who said she "helped define the American experience".

As a young gospel singer, Aretha spent summers on the circuit in Chicago. After turning eighteen Aretha confided to her father that she aspired to follow Sam Cooke in recording pop music and moved to New York. Serving as her manager, he agreed to the move and helped to produce a two-song demo that soon was brought to the attention of Columbia Records, who agreed to sign her in 1960. During this period, Aretha would be coached by a choreographer to prepare for her pop performances.

Before signing with Columbia, Sam Cooke tried to persuade Aretha's father to have his label, RCA, sign Aretha. He had also been courted by local record label owner Berry Gordy to sign Aretha and her elder sister Erma to his Tamla label. Aretha's father felt the label was not established enough yet. Aretha's first Columbia single, "Today I Sing the Blues", was issued in September 1960 and later reached the top ten of the Hot Rhythm & Blues chart.

In January 1961, Columbia Records issued Aretha's first secular album, Aretha: With The Ray Bryant Combo. The album featured her first single to chart the American Billboard Hot 100, "Won't Be Long", which also peaked at number seven on the Rythm & Blues chart. Before the year was out, Aretha scored her first top forty single with her rendition of the standard, "Rock-a-Bye Your Baby with a Dixie Melody", which also included the Rythm & Blues hit, "Operation Heartbreak", on its flip side. "Rock-a-Bye" became her first international hit, reaching the top 40 in Australia and Canada. By the end of 1961, Aretha was named as a "new-star female vocalist" in DownBeat magazine. In 1962, Columbia Records issued two more albums.

By 1964, Aretha began recording more pop music, reaching the top ten on the Rythm & Blues chart with the ballad "Runnin' Out of Fools" in early 1965. By the mid-1960s, Aretha was netting one hundred thousand dollars from countless performances in nightclubs and theatres. Also during that period, she appeared on rock and roll shows such as Hollywood A Go-Go and Shindig!.

In November 1966, after six years with Columbia Records, Aretha chose not to renew her contract with the company and signed to Atlantic Records. In January 1967, she travelled to Muscle Shoals, Alabama, to record at FAME Studios and recorded the song, "I Never Loved a Man (The Way I Love You)", backed by the Muscle Shoals Rhythm Section. The song was released the following month and reached number one on the Rythm & Blues chart, while also peaking at number nine on the Billboard Hot 100, giving Aretha Franklin her first top-ten pop single.

That April, Atlantic issued Aretha's version of Otis Redding's "Respect", which shot to number one on both the Rythm & Blues and pop charts. "Respect" became her signature song and was later hailed as a civil rights and feminist anthem.

Aretha's debut Atlantic album, I Never Loved a Man the Way I Love You, also became commercially successful, later going gold. Aretha scored two more top-ten singles in 1967, including "Baby I Love You" and "(You Make Me Feel Like) A Natural Woman". In 1968, she issued the top-selling albums Lady Soul and Aretha Now, which included some of her most popular hit singles, including "Chain of Fools", "Ain't No Way", "Think" and "I Say a Little Prayer".

Aretha toured outside the US for the first time in May 1968, including an appearance in Amsterdam where she played to a near hysterical audience who covered the stage with flower petals. She also appeared on the cover of Time magazine in June 1968.

Andy Fraser   Free

Andy Fraser died aged sixty-two on 16th of March 2015 at his home in California of a heart attack caused by Atherosclerosis. He is survived by his daughters Hannah and Jasmine Fraser.

Andy Fraser was born in the Paddington area of Central London, UK and started playing the piano at the age of five. He was trained classically until twelve, when he switched to guitar. By age thirteen he was playing in West

Indian clubs and after being expelled from school, in 1968 at the age of 15, he enrolled at Hammersmith College of Further Education. There, another student, Sappho Korner, introduced him to her father, pioneering blues musician and radio broadcaster Alexis Korner, who became a father figure to him. Shortly thereafter, upon receiving a telephone call from bandleader John Mayall who was looking for a bass player, Alexis Korner suggested Andy.

Alexis was also integral to Andy's next move, to the blues /rock band Free. Andy produced and co-wrote the song "All Right Now" with singer, Paul Rodgers, which became a worldwide number one hit.

Marie Fredricsson   Roxette

Marie Fredriksson died from a brain tumor aged sixty-one on the 9th of December 2019 in Sweden. She was survived by her husband, Mikael Bolyos, her daughter, Inez Josefin and son, Oscar.

Marie was born in Sweden in 1958 and had five sisters and brothers. After graduating from music school in 1977, Marie moved to Halmstad, where she worked in theatre before becoming involved in the local indie music scene.

Marie had a successful career in Sweden prior to forming Roxette. She was a member of punk group Strul, a band which created their own music festival in 1979. Strul's dissolution led to the creation of her next project, the short-lived MaMas Barn, after which she began releasing solo work. Her first album, Het vind, was issued in 1984, followed by Den sjunde vågen in 1986 and .. Efter stormen in 1987. Roxette's international breakthrough coincided with a quiet period for Marie as a solo artist. Further solo albums included Den ständiga resan in 1992 and I en tid som vår in 1996.

In 2002, after fainting at home, Marie was diagnosed with a brain tumour. During her rehabilitation, she continued to record music as a solo artist, resulting in The Change in 2004 and Min bäste vän in 2006, as well as the single "Där du andas" in 2008 which was her first and only solo number one single in Sweden. Marie and Gessle later reunited to record more albums as Roxette and the pair embarked on a worldwide concert tour.

Glen Frey   The Eagles

Glen Frey died on the 18th of January 2016 at age sixty-seven from complications of rheumatoid arthritis, acute ulcerative colitis, and pneumonia. He was survived by his wife Cindy, their daughter Taylor and sons Deacon and Otis.

Glen met drummer Don Henley in 1970 when they were signed to the same label, Amos Records. When Linda Ronstadt needed a backup band for an upcoming tour, her manager hired Glen because they needed someone who could play rhythm guitar and sing. Glen was approached to join Linda Ronstadt and Randy Meisner and Bernie Leadon were also hired. While on the tour, Glen and Henley decided to form a band together and they were joined by Randy Meisner on bass and Bernie Leadon on guitar, banjo, steel guitar, mandolin and dobro, forming the Eagles. Glen played guitar and keyboards and Don Henley playing drums. The Eagles went on to become one of the world's bestselling bands. Glen wrote or co-wrote, often with Don, many of the group's songs and sang the lead vocals on a number of its hits including "Take It Easy", "Peaceful Easy Feeling", "Already Gone", "Tequila Sunrise", "Lyin' Eyes", "New Kid in Town", "Heartache Tonight" and "How Long".

The Eagles broke up in 1980 and reunited in 1994, when they released a new album, Hell Freezes Over. The album had live tracks and four new songs and a supporting tour followed.

The Eagles released the album Long Road Out of Eden

in 2007, and Glen participated in the Eagles' Long Road Out of Eden Tour from 2008 through to 2011.

Billy Fury   Solo Artiste

Billy Fury died of a heart attack aged forty-two on the 28th of January, 1983 at his home in London, UK. He was survived by his wife, Lisa.

Billy Fury was born Ronald Wycherley in Liverpool, UK in 1940. He began music lessons on a piano during his pre-teen years and aquired his first guitar by the age of fourteen. Billy fronted his own group in 1955 and also worked on a tugboat and later as a docker. At this time, he entered and won a talent competition and by 1958 had started composing his own songs.

Billy released his first hit single for Decca, "Maybe Tomorrow", in 1959. In 1960 he reached Number nine in the UK Singles Chart with his own composition "Colette", followed by "That's Love" and his first long-playing-record The Sound of Fury.

Billy then concentrated less on rock and roll and more on mainstream ballads, including "Halfway to Paradise" which reached Number three in the UK Singles Chart in 1961.

Eddie Gagliardi   Foreigner

Ed Gagliardi died aged sixty-two from cancer on the 11th of May, 2014 in New York, USA. He was survived by his wife, Loretta and his daughter, Nicole.

Ed was was a member of Foreigner from the beginning in 1976 and played a red Rickenbacker bass guitar, left-handed, even though he was naturally right-handed.

In 1977, Foreigner released its self-titled debut album and they peaked at number four on the US album chart and got in the top 10 in Canada and Australia, while yielding two top ten single hits in North America, "Feels Like the First Time" and "Cold as Ice". Their 1978 follow-up, Double Vision, was even more successful peaking at number three in North America with two hit singles, "Hot Blooded" and Double Vision. This album had Rick Wills replacing Ed Gagliardi on bass guitar.

Steve Gaines   Lynard Skynard

Steve Gaines died aged twenty-eight on the 20th of October, 1977 in an air crash which also killed his sister, Cassie and bandmate, Ronnie Van Zant. He was survived by his wife, Teresa and his daughter, Corrina.

When Steve was fifteen years old, he saw the Beatles performing live in Kansas City and after being driven home from the concert, he persuaded his father to buy him his first guitar.

In December 1975, Steve's older sister, Cassie, became a member of Lynyrd Skynyrd's female backup singers, the band who had been seeking a replacement for one of three lead guitarists in its line-up. Cassie recommended Steve.

Rory Gallagher   Taste

Rory Gallagher died aged forty-seven on the 14th of June, 1995 from complications following a liver transplant. He was survived by his wife, Nicola and his son, Seanie and his daughter, Lucy.

Rory was buried in a cemetery near Cork City, Ireland. The grave's headstone is in the image of an award he received in 1972 for International Guitarist of the Year. Rory played a worn sunburst 1961 Fender Stratocaster for some years.

After winning a cash prize in a talent contest when he was twelve Rory began performing in his adolescence with both his acoustic guitar, and an electric guitar. While still in school, playing songs by Buddy Holly and Eddie Cochran, he discovered his greatest influence in Muddy

Waters and began experimenting with folk, blues, and rock music.

Rory formed Taste, a blues rock and R&B power trio, in 1966. Performing extensively in the UK, the group played regularly at London's Marquee Club and supported both Cream at their Royal Albert Hall farewell concert, and the supergroup Blind Faith on a tour of the USA.

Jerry Garcia   The Grateful Dead

Jerry Garcia died aged fifty-three from a heart attack on the 9th of August 1995 in Marin County, California, U.S.A. He was survived by his wife, Deborah and his daughters, Heather, Annabelle and Theresa.

Jerry served as lead guitarist, as well as one of the principal vocalists and song-writers of the Grateful Dead until he died. He composed songs including "Dark Star", "Franklin's Tower", and "Scarlet Begonias", amongt many others.

Jerry was also well remembered onstage for his extended guitar improvisations with the Grateful Dead.

Freddie Garrity   Freddie & The Dreamers

Freddie Garrity died aged sixty-nine in Bangor, North Wales, U.K. on the 19th of May 2006 after being taken ill while on holiday there. Freddie was cremated in Stoke-on-Trent, Staffordshire, U.K. where his ashes are interred. He was survived by his wife Christine and one son and three daughters.

Freddy had continued to perform until 2001, when he was diagnosed with emphysema after collapsing during a flight; this forcing him into retirement. With his health in decline, Freddie had settled in a bungalow in Newcastle-under-Lyme, Staffordshire, U.K.

Freddie's trademark was his comic dancing and his habit of leaping up and down during performances. This, combined with his almost skeletal appearance and horn-rimmed glasses, made him an eccentric figure in the UK pop scene of the early 1960s.

Freddie continued to perform up until 2001, when he was diagnosed with emphysema after collapsing during a flight, which forced him into retirement.

Stephen Gately   Boyzone

Stephen Gately died aged thirty-three on the 10th of October 2009 at his home in Port d'Andratx, Mallorca, Spain. He was survived by his mother, Margaret and his brothers, Tony, Alan and Mark; and his sister, Michele. His death was caused by a pulmonary oedema resulting from an undiagnosed heart condition.

Stephen joined Boyzone upon their formation in 1993. Boyzone's first success outside of Ireland was when the song "Love Me for a Reason" reached number two in the UK Singles Chart in 1995. The group split suddenly following a string of performances in Dublin's Point Theatre in 2000. By this time, they had achieved six number ones on the UK Singles Chart.

After success with Boyzone, the band decided in 2000 to move on to solo projects. Stephen Gately was the first, with his debut solo single, "New Beginning", released during May 2000 which reached number three in the UK charts.

Stephen came out as gay in 1999 after discovering that an acquaintance was about to sell the details of his sexuality to the media. He was subsequently described as a "champion of gay rights, although, a reluctant one".

Marvin Gaye   Solo Artiste

Marvin Gaye died of a gunshot wound aged forty-four on the 1st of April 1984 after his father shot him in the heart and then in his left shoulder. Marvin had intervened in a fight between his parents, an action which sparked the altercation with his father, resulting in his death. He was survived by his father, Marvin Snr and his mother, Alberta and his brothers, Frankie and Antwaun and his sisters, Jeanne and Zeola and his sons, Marvin and Frankie and his daughter, Nona.

After Marvin's funeral, his body was cremated at Forest Lawn Memorial Park at the Hollywood Hills and his ashes were scattered into the Pacific Ocean.

Marvin began singing in church when he was four years old with his father often accompanying him on piano. Marvin and his family were part of a Pentecostal church known as the House of God. Marvin Gaye was encouraged to pursue a professional music career after a performance at a school play at eleven singing Mario Lanza's "Be My Love".

In 1956, seventeen-year-old Marvin dropped out of high school and enlisted in the United States Air Force as a basic airman but, discouraged by having to perform menial tasks, he pretended to have mental illness and was discharged soon afterwards.

Following his return, Marvin and a friend formed the vocal quartet The Marquees which performed in the Washington area and soon began working with Bo Diddley, who assigned the group to Columbia subsidiary OKeh Records but this did not last.

The Marquees changed its name to Harvey and the New Moonglows, and relocated to Chicago. The group recorded several sides for Chess in 1959, including the song "Mama Loocie", which was Marvin Gaye's first lead vocal recording.

In 1960, the group disbanded and Marvin performed at Motown president Berry Gordy's house. Shortly afterwards, Marvin signed with the Motown subsidiary, Tamla. He released his first single, "Let Your Conscience Be Your Guide", in May 1961, and his album, 'The Soulful Moods of Marvin Gaye', followed one month later.

Marvin's first solo hit, *"Stubborn Kind of Fellow"*, was

later released that September, reaching number eight on the American R&B chart and number forty-six on the Billboard Hot 100.

In 1964, Marvin Gaye recorded a successful duet album with singer Mary Wells titled "Together", which reached number forty-two the American pop album chart. Marvin's next solo hit, "How Sweet It Is (To Be Loved By You)", which Holland-Dozier-Holland wrote for him, reached number six on the US Hot Hundred and reached the top fifty in the UK.

After scoring a hit duet, "It Takes Two" with Kim Weston, Marvin

began working with Tammi Terrell on a series of duets, including "Ain't No Mountain High Enough", "Your Precious Love", "Ain't Nothing Like the Real Thing" and "You're All I Need to Get By".

"I Heard It through the Grapevine" was recorded by Marvin in April 1967 which became a number one hit in the UK and in late 1968, it became Marvin's first recording to reach number one on the Billboard Hot 100.

In 1973, Marvin released the 'Let's Get It On album' and its title track became his second number one single on the Hot 100, the album subsequently staying in the charts for two years and selling over three million copies.

Lowell George   Little Feat

Lowell George died aged thirty-four on the 29th of June 1979 of a heart attack in a hotel room. He was survived by his daughter Forrest, his first wife, Pattie, their son, Luke, a daughter, Inara.

In November 1968, Lowell joined Zappa's Mothers of Invention as rhythm guitarist and nominal lead vocalist and he can be heard on the Weasels Ripped My Flesh album.

After leaving the Mothers of Invention, Lowell invited fellow musicians bassist Roy Estrada, keyboardist Bill

Payne and drummer Richie Hayward to form a new band, which they named Little Feat. Lowell usually played lead guitar and focused on slide guitar. Lowell had begun his slide playing using the casing of a spark plug socket wrench, rather than the traditional glass or steel finger tube.

Robin Gibb   The BeeGees

Robin Gibb died aged sixty on the 20th of May 2012 from liver and kidney failure whilst in London, U.K. He was survived by his wife, Dwina and his sons, Robin Jnr. and Spencer and his daughter, Melissa. He was buried at the Church of St Mary the Virgin, near his home in Thame, Oxfordshire, UK.

Born on the Isle of Man during the late 1940s, the Gibb brothers moved to their father's home town Chorlton-cum-Hardy, Manchester, England where, in 1955 they formed a skiffle/rock-and-roll group called the Rattlesnakes, with Barry on guitar and vocals, Robin and Maurice on vocals, and friends on drums and a tea-chest bass. In May 1958, however, the Rattlesnakes disbanded when their two friends left.

In August 1958, the Gibb family, including older sister Lesley and infant brother Andy, emigrated to Australia and settled in Redcliffe, Queensland, just north-east of Brisbane. The Gibb brothers began performing music to raise pocket money and a Speedway promoter who had hired them to entertain the crowd at the Redcliffe Speedway in 1960, introduced them to Brisbane radio-presenter.

During the next few years, they began working regularly at resorts on the Queensland coast and through his songwriting, Barry sparked the interest of someone who helped them get a recording deal in 1963 with Festival Records as the Bee Gees. They then released some single records and in 1962 they were chosen as the supporting act for Chubby Checker's concert at the Sydney Stadium. A minor pop hit in 1965 called "Wine and Women" led to the group's first album.

The BeeGees began their return journey to England in January 1967. Before their departure demos had been sent to Brian Epstein, who managed the Beatles. After an audition in February 1967, the Bee Gees signed a five-year contract whereby Polydor Records would release their records in the UK, and Atco Records would do so in the US. Work quickly began on the group's first international album.

The 45 rpm single, "New York Mining Disaster 1941", sung by Robin, their second British single, was issued to radio stations. The Bee Gees' next single, "To Love Somebody", soon went into the US Top 20. Originally written for Otis Redding, "To Love Somebody", a soulful ballad sung by Barry, has since become a pop standard covered by many artists.

Maurice Gibb   The BeeGees

Maurice Gibb died aged fifty-three at Mount Sini Medical Center in Miami Beach, Florida, U.S.A. on the 12th of January 2003, due to complications with a twisted intestine. He was survived by his second wife, Yvonne and his son, Adam and his daughter, Samantha.

In April 1970 Maurice released his first solo single, "Railroad". In May 1970 the album Sing a Rude Song was released in the UK with Maurice singing lead vocals on the three songs on the album.

The Bee Gees reunited during August 1970 and Maurice began taking a few lead vocals on a Bee Gees tracks including "Lay It on Me", "Country Woman", "On Time" and "You Know It's For You". In 1981, Maurice recorded some instrumental tracks for his unreleased instrumental album Strings and Things, including "Image of Samantha".

In September 1986, the Bee Gees began writing and recording songs for their upcoming album ESP on which

Maurice sang lead vocal on the song "Overnight". Maurice composed and recorded the instrumental "The Supernaturals" in July 1985 which was later dubbed on the film of the same name . During April 2001, The Bee Gees released their 23rd and final studio album named "This Is Where I Came In" which included Maurice's compositions, "Walking on Air" and "Man in the Middle".

Andy Gibb   Solo Artiste

Andy Gibb died aged thirty on the 10th of March 1988 as a result of myocarditis, an inflammation of the heart muscle caused by a recent viral infection. He was survived by his daughter, Peta.

Andy's body was taken to America where he was interred at Forest Lawn Memorial Park in Hollywood Hills, Los Angeles.

Andy quit school at the age of thirteen, and with an acoustic guitar given to him by his elder brother Barry, he began playing at tourist clubs around Ibiza in Spain after his parents moved there, and later on the Isle of Man, where his parents later moved.

In June 1974, Andy formed his first group called Melody Fayre which included Isle of Man musicians on guitar, bass and drums. The group was managed by Andy's mother, Barbara, and had regular bookings on the small island's hotel circuit. Andy's first recording, in August 1973, was a Maurice Gibb composition, "My Father Was a Rebel", which Maurice also produced and played on.

Andy returned to Australia in 1974 partly because he believed that Australia had been a good training ground for the Bee Gees, it would also help him.

Andy later joined the band Zenta, consisting of himself on vocals, Rick Alford on guitar, Paddy Lelliot on bass, Glen Greenhalgh on vocals, and Trevor Norton on drums. Zenta supported international artists Sweet and the Bay City Rollers on the Sydney leg of their Australian tours.

Andy's pop chart hits in the UK included, "I Just Wanna be Your Everything, in 1977, "Shadow Dancing" and "An Ever Lasting Love" in 1978 and "Don't Throw It All Away" in 1979.

Andrew Gold   Solo Artiste

Andrew Gold died aged fifty-nine on the 3rd of June 2011 from heart failure whilst in Los Angeles, USA. He was survived by his second wife Leslie, his first wife Vanessa and three daughters: Emily, Victoria, and Olivia.

By the early 1970s, Andrew was working full-time as a musician, songwriter and record producer. In 1975, he debuted as a solo artist, with the self titled album, 'Andrew Gold'. He released four studio albums during the 1970s and over twelve after. The second of his 1970s studio albums, released in 1976, was titled "What's Wrong With This Picture?" and. from it, he released his hit single "Lonely Boy," which reached number seven on the American Billboard Hot 100 chart in June 1977 and was included in a number of film soundtracks, including Boogie Nights in 1997 and Adam Sandler's 1998 movie The Waterboy.

Andrew's UK chart hits included "Lonely Boy" in 1977, and "Never Let Her Slip Away" in 1978 and "How Can This Be Love" in 1978 and "Thank You For Being A Friend" in 1978.

Ric Gretch   Family & Blind Faith

Ric Grech died aged of forty-three on the 17th of March 1990 of renal failure as a result of alcoholism. He had retired from music in 1977 and had moved back to Leicester in Leicestershire, U.K.

Ric originally gained notice in the United Kingdom as the bass guitar player for the progressive rock group Family which he joined when it was a largely blues-based live act in Leicester known as the Farinas. Family released their first single, "Scene Through The Eye of a Lens," in September 1967 on the Liberty label in the UK, which got the band signed to Reprise Records. The group's 1968 debut album 'Music in a Doll's House' was an underground hit that highlighted the songwriting talents of Roger Chapman and John "Charlie" Whitney as well as Chapman's piercing voice, but Ric Grech also stood out with his rhythmic, thundering bass work on songs such as "Old Songs New Songs" and "See Through Windows," along with his adeptness on cello and violin.

In the spring of 1969, former Cream guitarist Eric Clapton and former Traffic frontman Steve Winwood formed the supergroup Blind Faith and, in need of a bassist, they recruited Ric.

Blind Faith's debut gig was in front of one hundred thousand people on a warm day in London's Hyde Park on the 7th of June, 1969.

Peter Green   **Fleetwood Mac**

Peter Green died peacefully in his sleep, aged seventy three on the 25th of July 2020. He was survived by his ex-wife Jane and their daughter; Rosebud.

In 1966, Peter and some other members of Peter B's Looners formed a further act called Shotgun Express, a Motown-style soul band which also included Rod Stewart, but Peter left this group after just a few months and from July 1966 he filled in as a member of John Mayall's Bluesbreakers.

In 1967, Peter decided to form his own blues band, Fleetwood Mac, and he then left the Bluesbreakers at that point.

Peter's new band, with Mick Fleetwood on drums and Jeremy Spencer on guitar, was initially called "Peter Green's Fleetwood Mac". They scored a hit with Peter's song "Black Magic Woman", later covered by Santana, followed by the guitar instrumental "Albatross" in 1969, which reached number one in the British singles charts .

Beginning with the melancholy lyric of "Man of the World", Peter's bandmates began to notice changes in Peter's state of mind. He took large doses of LSD, grew a beard and began to wear robes and a crucifix. While touring Europe in March 1970, Peter took LSD at a party at a commune near Munich, an incident cited by the then Fleetwood Mac manager as the crucial point in his mental decline into schizophrenia. After a final performance on the 20th of May 1970, Peter left Fleetwood Mac.

Dave Greenfield   The Stranglers

Dave Greenfield died aged seventy-one on the 3rd of May 2020 from Coronavirus. He was survived by his wife, Pamela.

Dave joined The Stranglers after auditioning in 1975 and played with them until his death. The Strangler's UK chart hits included: "Peaches" in 1977, "No More Heroes" in 1977, "Golden Brown" in 1982 and "Strange Little Girl" in 1982. Dave and Jean-Jacques Burnel released an album together in 1983, Fire & Water (Ecoutez Vos Murs), which was used as the soundtrack for the movie 'Ecoutez vos murs', directed by Vincent Coudanne .

Jimmy Greenspoon   Three Dog Night

Jimmy Greenspoon died aged sixty-seven from cancer on the eleventh of March 2015 in North Potomac, Maryland,U.S.A. He was survived by his wife, Susie and a daughter, Heather, and two granddaughters. In 2014, Jimmy had been diagnosed with metastatic melanoma, and at that time stopped touring with Three Dog Night .

Three Dog Night's UK chart hits included, "Mama Told Me Not to Come" in 1970 and "Joy To The World" in 1971.

John Gustafson   Roxy Music & Quatermass

John Gustafson died of cancer aged seventy-two on the twelfth of September 2014. He was survived by his wife Anne, his sons; John, Lee, Joe and daughters; Alice and Lucy.

John is probably best known for playing bass guitar for several re-incarnations of the Ian Gillan Band and for his earlier participation in the progressive rock band, Quatermass . John was a member of Roxy Music for four years and performed on three of their studio albums.

Bill Haley   The Comets

Bill Haley died of a brain tumour aged fifty-five on the 9th of February 1981 in his home town of Harlingen, Texas. U.S.A. He was survived by his wife, Martha and some sons and daughters.

Bill had made his final performances in South Africa in 1980 . He was posthumously inducted into the Rock and Roll Hall of Fame in 1987 when his son Pedro represented him at the ceremony.

Bill is credited by many with first popularizing rock and roll music in the early 1950s with his group Bill Haley & His Comets and million-selling hits such as "Rock Around the Clock", "See You Later, Alligator", "Shake, Rattle and Roll", "Rocket 88", "Skinny Minnie", and "Razzle Dazzle". He sold over twenty-five million records worldwide.

Terry Hall   The Specials

Terry Hall died aged sixty-three from pancreatic cancer on the 18th of December 2022. He was survived by his second wife, Lindy and his sons, Felix, Leo and Orson.

Terry became an active member of the burgeoning Coventry music scene of the late 1970s, playing in a local punk band called Squad and being credited as a composer on their "Red Alert" single.

Initially the frontman of Automatics which became the Specials in early 1979, Terry first came to prominence in the UK when BBC Radio 1 disc jockey John Peel played the Special's debut single "Gangsters" on his show.

The single "Ghost Town", released in June 1981, spent three weeks at number one and ten weeks in the top 40 of the UK Singles Chart.

Pete Ham   Badfinger

Pete Ham died by suicide aged twenty-seven on the 24th of April 1975 when he hung himself. He was survived by his pregnant wife and her son.

Pete Ham was born in Swansea, Wales, U.K. He formed a local rock group called The Panthers in 1961. This group would undergo several name and lineup changes before it became The Iveys in 1965.

The Iveys changed their name to Badfinger with the single release of "Come and Get It", a composition written by Paul McCartney, and it became a worldwide Top Ten hit. Pete's "No Matter What" composition became another Top Ten worldwide hit after its release in late 1970.

Pete Ham's greatest songwriting success came with his co-written composition "Without You" – a worldwide number One when it was later covered by Harry Nilsson and released in 1972. The song has since become a ballad standard and is covered by hundreds of singers from many genres.

Paul Hammond   Atomic Rooster

Paul Hammond died aged thirty-nine in 1992 in London U.K. from an accidental drug overdose.

When Atomic Rooster drummer Carl Palmer left the group to form Emerson, Lake & Palmer in the summer of 1970, he was replaced a few months later by Paul Hammond, joining vocalist & guitarist John Cann and key-board player Vincent Crane. The band subsequently recorded the 'Death Walks Behind You' album in September of that year, followed by the hit singles "Tomorrow Night" and "Devil's Answer".

Sarah Harding   Girls Aloud

Sarah Harding died from Cancer aged thirty-nine on the 5th of September 2021.

Sarah's professional career began in 2002 when she successfully auditioned for the ITV reality series Popstars: The Rivals, during which she won a place in the girl group Girls Aloud. The group achieved twenty consecutive top ten singles (including four number ones) in the UK, six albums that were certified platinum by the British Phonographic Industry (BPI), two of which went to number one in the UK, and accumulated a total of five BRIT Award nominations. In 2009, Girls Aloud won "Best Single" with their song "The Promise".

Jet Harris   The Shadows

Jet Harris died aged seventy-one from cancer on the 18th of March 2011 at the home of his partner Janet in Winchester, Hampshire, U.K. It was two years after Jet, who had been a heavy smoker, had been diagnosed with cancer. Jet was survived by five sons and one daughter.

In 2012 the UK Heritage Foundation erected a blue plaque in his memory at the Kingswood Centre, Honeypot Lane, Kingsbury, London NW9 on the site of the former Willesden Maternity Hospital where he was born. At the luncheon that followed the unveiling of the plaque, various musicians took part in a performance in Jet's memory.

George Harrison died of cancer aged fifty-eight on the 29th of November 2001. He was survived by his wife, Olivia and his son, Dhani. George was cremated at Hollywood Forever Cemetery and his funeral was held at the Self-Realization Fellowship Lake Shrine in Pacific Palisades, California. His ashes were then scattered in the Ganges and Yamuna rivers near Varanasi, India.

George's earliest musical influences included George Formby, Cab Calloway, Django Reinhardt and Hoagy Carmichael, and by the 1950s, Carl Perkins and Lonnie Donegan were significant influences. In early 1956 he had an epiphany: while riding his bicycle, he heard Elvis Presley's "Heartbreak Hotel" playing from a nearby house, and the song piqued his interest in rock and roll. At school, he often sat at the back of the class drawing guitars in his schoolbooks.

George became part of the Beatles when they were still a skiffle group called the Quarrymen, with Paul McCartney and John Lennon as members. Led by primary songwriters John Lennon and Paul McCartney, the Beatles evolved from John Lennon's previous group, the Quarrymen, and built their reputation playing clubs in Liverpool and Hamburg over the three years from 1960, initially with Stuart Sutcliffe playing bass. The core trio of Lennon, McCartney and Harrison, together since 1958, went through a succession of drummers before asking Ringo Starr to join them in 1962. Manager Brian Epstein moulded them into a professional act, and producer George Martin guided and developed their recordings, greatly expanding their domestic success after signing to EMI Records and achieving their first hit, "Love Me Do", in late 1962. As their popularity grew into the intense fan frenzy dubbed "Beatlemania", the band acquired the nickname "the Fab Four".

By early 1964, the Beatles were international stars and

had achieved unprecedented levels of critical and commercial success. They became a leading force in Britain's cultural resurgence, ushering in the British Invasion of the United States pop market, and soon made their film debut with A Hard Day's Night, in 1964. A growing desire to refine their studio efforts, coupled with the untenable nature of their concert tours, led to the band's retirement from live performances in 1966. At this time, they produced records of greater sophistication, including the albums Rubber Soul, in 1965, Revolver in 1966 and Sgt. Pepper's Lonely Hearts Club Band in 1967, and enjoyed further commercial success with "The Beatles", also known as "the White Album", in 1968 and Abbey Road in 1969.

Mike Harrison   Spooky Tooth

Mike Harrison died aged seventy-two on the 25th of March 2018 . Mike's main fame came as a lead singer of Spooky Tooth, a band that he initially co-founded, with Mike Kellie, Luther Grosvenor and Greg Ridley and which Gary Wright then joined. Mike Harrison, Grosvenor, Ridley and Kellie had previously been in a Carlisle-based band called The V.I.P.s, which also included Keith Emerson.

When Keith Emerson left in early 1967 to co-found The Nice, the remaining band members changed the band's name to Art and released one album in late 1967 on Island Records. Label owner Chris Blackwell took an interest in the band, encouraging them to work with Gary Wright and arranged for Jimmy Miller to be the band's producer. With the addition of Gary Wright, the band became known as Spooky Tooth, releasing four albums between 1968 and 1970 and three more albums during a 1972-1974 period.

Keef Hartley   The Keef Hartley Big Band

Keef Hartley died aged sixty-seven on the 26th of November 2011 in Preston, Lancashire, U.K.

Keef Hartley was born in Preston, Lancashire, U.K. and studied drumming under Lloyd Ryan, who also taught Phil Collins the drum rudiments. His career began as the replacement for Ringo Starr as a drummer for Rory Storm and the Hurricanes, a Liverpool-based band, after Ringo joined The Beatles. Subsequently he played and recorded with The Artwoods, then achieved some notability as John Mayall's drummer, including his role as the only musician, other than Mayall, to play on Mayall's 1967 "solo" record 'The Blues Alone'. He then formed The Keef Hartley Big Band, mixing elements of jazz, blues, and rock and roll. The group played at Woodstock in 1969 and they released five albums, including Halfbreed and The Battle of North West Six.

Alex Harvey   The Sensational Alex Harvey Band

Alex Harvey died aged forty-six of a heart attack on the 4th of February 1982. He was survived by his second wife, Trudy, and two sons, Alex and Tyro.

The Sensational Alex Harvey Band were voted the fifth greatest Scottish band of all time in a 2005 survey.

In 1972, Alex formed the Sensational Alex Harvey Band, often shortened to SAHB, with guitarist Zal Cleminson, bassist Chris Glen, and cousins Hugh and Ted McKenna on keyboards and drums respectively.

SAHB produced a succession of highly regarded albums and tours throughout the 1970s. The Sensational Alex Harvey Band had top 40 hits in Britain with the single "Delilah", a cover version of the Tom Jones hit, which reached number seven in 1975, and also with "The Boston Tea Party" in June 1976.

After Alex left the group in 1976, the other members

continued as SAHB without him, producing the album Fourplay. Alex re-joined the group for 1978's Rock Drill. SAHB with Alex Harvey toured the UK in Autumn 1981 with the last gig at Workington's Carnegie Theatre on the 1st of November that year.

Bobby Hatfield   The Righteous Brothers

Bobby Hatfield died aged sixty-three on the 5th of November 2003 at the Radisson Hotel in downtown Kalamazoo, Michigan, U.S.A. He was found by an employee at the hotel after he apparently died in his sleep, hours before a scheduled Righteous Brothers concert.

Three months later an autopsy and toxicology report concluded that an overdose of cocaine had precipitated a fatal heart attack and that Bobby had advanced coronary disease.

Graduating in 1958. Bobby had briefly considered signing as a professional baseball player, but his passion for music led him to pursue a singing career and he eventually encountered his singing partner, Bill Medley, while attending California State University.

Their first number one hit was "You've Lost That Lovin' Feelin'," produced by Phil Spector in 1964.

Richie Havens   Solo Artiste

Richie Havens died aged seventy-two of a heart attack at his home in Jersey City, New Jersey, U.S.A. on the 22nd of April 2013.

As to Richie's request, his remains were cremated and his ashes were scattered from the air over the original site of the Woodstock Festival. He was survived by his wife Nancy, three children, five grandchildren, and two great-grandchildren.

Richie Havens' live performances earned widespread notice. His Woodstock appearance in 1969 catapulted him into stardom and was a major turning point in his career. As the festival's first performer, he held the crowd for nearly three hours.

Taylor Hawkins   Foo Fighters

Taylor Hawkins died aged fifty on the 25th of March, 2022. He was survived by his wife, Alison, his son, Shane and daughters Annabelle and Everleigh.

On March 25, 2022, emergency services were called to the Four Seasons Casa Medina hotel in Bogotá, Colombia, where Taylor was suffering from chest pain in his hotel room. Health personnel arrived and found hims unresponsive, however, they performed CPR, but he was declared dead at the scene. No cause of death was given.

The following day, Colombian authorities announced that a preliminary urine toxicology test indicated that Taylor had ten substances in his system at the time of his death, including opioids, benzodiazepines, tricyclic antidepressants, and THC. .

Taylor's final performance with the Foo Fighters before his death was at the Lollapalooza Argentina festival on March 20, 2022.

The Foo fighters had the following UK hit singles: "This Is A Call" in 1995, I'll Stick Around in 1995, For All The Cows" in 1995, "Big Me" in 1996, "Monkey Wrench" in 1997, "Everlong" in 1997, "My Hero" in 1998, and "Walking After You:Beacon Light" in 1998.

Isaac Hayes   Solo Artiste

Isaac Hayes died aged sixty-five on the 10th of August 2008 from a stroke. He was buried at Memorial Park Cemetery in Memphis, Tennessee, USA. He was survived by his sons, Isaac, Darius, Vincent and Nano Kwadjo and his daughters, Heather, Felicia, Veronica, Lili, Melanie and Nikki.

Isaac Hayes was born in 1942 and after his mother died young and his father abandoned the family, Isaac was raised by his maternal grandparents.

At age five Isaac began singing at his local church and taught himself to play the piano, the Hammond organ, the flute, and the saxophone.

Isaac began his recording career in the early 1960s, as a session player for various acts of the Memphis-based Stax Records. He later wrote a string of hit songs with songwriting partner David Porter, including "You Don't Know Like I Know", "Soul Man", "When Something Is Wrong with My Baby" and "Hold On, I'm Comin'".

In early 1971, Isaac composed music for the soundtrack of the successful movie 'Shaft. The title theme, with its wah-wah guitar and multi-layered symphonic arrangement, would become a world-wide hit single, and spent two weeks at number one in the American Billboard Hot Hundred.

Isaac's UK chart hits were: "Theme From Shaft" in 1971, "Disco Connection" in 1976 and "Chocolate Salty Balls" in 1998.

Richie Hayward   Little Feat

Richie Hayward died aged sixty-four from pneumonia on the 12th of August 2010. He was survived by wife, Shauna and his son, Severin.

Richie had taken his first steps into the world of drumming by banging out rhythms on an orange crate and by the time he was ten, he was developing his own style. Later on, having acquired a set of real drums, he played his first gig at the Moose Lodge in Nevada, Iowa, on New Year's Eve 1959. He later bought a plane ticket to Los Angeles and after a stint with the Rebels, he answered an advertisement in the LA Free Press in 1966 which read "Drummer Wanted, Must Be Freaky", and was recruited into the Factory, an offshoot from Frank Zappa's Mothers of

Invention. However, the Factory's guiding light, the singer, songwriter and guitarist Lowell George, had ambitions to build a new band, and set about forming what would become Little Feat.

Richie played his final live performance in July, 2010 when he played drums with Little Feat at the Vancouver Island Music Festival in Canada.

Robert Heaton   New Model Army

Robert Heaton died aged forty-three on the 4th of November 2004 from pancreatic cancer. He was survived by his wife, Robin and his son, Marlon.

Robert Heaton was born in Knutsford, Cheshire, United Kingdom but lived in Canada and Belgium as a child. He was musically gifted, eventually mastering the guitar and harmonica as well as the drums, for which he is better-known, and also played keyboards and violin. Robert began playing guitar plus drummed along to his father's collection of traditional jazz recordings and developed a very eclectic musical taste. He took in obvious rock influences including Led Zeppelin and ZZ Top but also but also the country music of Johnny Cash and classical composers including Beethoven, Mozart, Tchaikovsky and Vivaldi.

Robert Heaton's arrival marked the beginning of New Model Army's professional years. Robert brought professional experience to the band's touring life and was responsible for the hiring of their long-term tour manager 'Tommy T' Walker. Together with frontman Justin Sullivan, Robert was the core of the band, originally alongside Stuart Morrow on bass and then later with Jason 'Moose' Harris. Robert's wide-ranging musical interests are manifested in the music for the anthemic song "Green and Grey".

Dick Heckstall-Smith   Colosseum

Saxophonist Dick Heckstall-Smith died aged seventy on the 17th of December 2004 from acute liver failure. He was survived by his ex-wife Gaby and by their son, Arthur.

Dick completed his education at Dartington Hall School, before reading agriculture and co-leading the university jazz band at Sidney Sussex College, Cambridge in 1953. Aged fifteen, Dick had taken up the soprano saxophone after being captivated by the sound of Sidney Bechet.

Dick was an active member of the London jazz scene from the late 1950s He joined Blues Incorporated, Alexis Korner's groundbreaking blues group, in 1962, recording the album "R&B from the Marquee". The following year, he was a founding member of that band's breakaway unit, The Graham Bond Organisation.

In 1967, Dick became a member of guitarist-vocalist John Mayall's blues rock band, Bluesbreakers who released the album 'Bare Wires' in 1968. From 1968 to 1971, Dick was a member of the pioneering UK jazz-rock band Colosseum, a band affording Dick an opportunity to showcase his writing and instrumental virtuosity, playing two saxophones simultaneously. After leaving Colosseum, Dick recorded solo albums and fronted and played in several other fusion units.

Jimi Hendrix   The Jimi Hendrix Experience

Jimi Hendrix died from asphyxia aged twenty-seven on the 18th of September 1970. He had been found unconscious and unresponsive after which paramedics took him to St Mary Abbot's Hospital in London, U.K. where he was pronounced dead.

Monika, his girlfriend, said that they had conversed until around seven a.m before she went to sleep, then, when she awoke around four hours later, she found Jimi still breathing but unresponsive, then, alarmed, she called for an ambulance. To determine the cause of death, the

138

coroner Gavin ordered a post-mortem examination on Jimi's body, by a forensic pathologist who completed the inquest and concluded that Jimi had aspirated his own vomit and died of asphyxia while intoxicated with barbiturates. Monika later revealed that Jimi had taken nine of her prescribed Vesparax sleeping tablets.

After Jimi's body had been embalmed it was flown to Seattle, Washington and interred at Greenwood Cemetery in Renton, Washington, near his mother's gravesite.

In mid-1958, at age fifteen, Jimi acquired his first acoustic guitar and earnestly applied himself, playing the instrument for several hours daily, watching others and getting tips from more experienced guitarists, and listening to blues artists such as Muddy Waters, B.B. King, Howlin' Wolf, and Robert Johnson.

Soon after, Jimi formed his first band, the Velvetones, but, without an electric guitar, he could barely be heard over the sound of the group. Jimi then realized that he needed an electric guitar in order to continue and in mid-1959, his father bought him a white Supro Ozark. Jimi's first gig was with an unnamed band in the basement of a synagogue but he later joined the Rocking Kings, which played professionally at venues such as the Birdland club. When someone stole his guitar after he left it backstage overnight, he acquired a red Silvertone Danelectro.

Following's arrival in London, his manager, Chas Chandler, began recruiting members for a band in order to highlight Jimi's talents.

By 1969, Jimi Hendrix was one of the world's highest-paid rock musicians and that August, he headlined the Woodstock Music and Art Fair that showcased many of the most popular bands of the era.

Jon Hiseman   Colosseum

Jon Hiseman died from a brain tumour on the 12th of June 2018 in Sutton, UK, aged seventy-three. He was survived by his wife Barbara and their son Marcus and daughter Anna and four grandchildren.

In the mid-1960s Jon played in sessions such as the early Arthur Brown single, "Devil's Grip". In 1966 he replaced Ginger Baker in the Graham Bond Organisation and also played for a brief spell with Georgie Fame and the Blue Flames. He then joined John Mayall's Bluesbreakers in 1968 and played on their album, Bare Wires. In April 1968 he left John Mayall to form the jazz rock band, Colosseum, which disbanded in November 1971, although Jon later formed Colosseum II in 1975.

Jon subsequently played in jazz groups, notably with his wife, saxophonist Barbara Thompson, with whom he recorded and produced over fifteen albums. Andrew Lloyd Webber, searching for a "sound" for an album to feature his brother Julian on cello, stumbled upon Colosseum II by accident and imported the whole band into his "Variations" project. This was the start of a ten-year relationship with Jon Hiseman, whose drumming features on recordings, TV specials and musicals.

In 1982 Jon built what was at the time a state-of-the-art recording studio next to his home, and together with the compositional skills of Barbara Thompson produced many recordings for film and television soundtracks.

Colosseum reunited in June 1994 with the same line-up of musicians as when they broke up twenty-three years earlier and they played the Freiburg Zelt Musik Festival in Germany.

Bob Hite   Canned Heat

Bob Hite died aged thirty-eight on the 5th of April 1981 from a drugs overdose. During a break between sets at The Palomino Club in North Hollywood, California, U.S.A., he was handed a drug vial by a fan. Thinking it contained cocaine, Bob Hite stuck a straw into the vial and snorted it but the drug was heroin and Bob turned blue and collapsed and soon died.

Bob, as a young man, was introduced to guitarist Al Wilson and, in 1965, he formed a band with Al which Henry Vestine joined soon after and the trio formed the core of Canned Heat. They were eventually joined by Larry Taylor on bass guitar and Frank Cook on drums. Bob performed with Canned Heat at Woodstock in August 1969 and the performances were included in the 1994 "Director's Cut" version of the movie, Woodstock.

Jim Hodder   Steely Dan

Jim Hodder died aged forty-two on the 5th of June 1990 when he drowned in the swimming pool of his home in California.

As drummer and lead vocalist, Jim joined the Boston-based psychedelic rock group, The Bead Game, which built a local following and, in 1972, he accepted an invitation from guitarist Jeff "Skunk" Baxter to relocate to Los Angeles and join Steely Dan. They then were a new group built around songwriters Donald Fagen and Walter Becker with whom the two were working.

Jim acted as the group's drummer, but was also given occasional lead vocal duties.

Chas Hodges   Chas & Dave

Chas Hodges died of pneumonia aged seventy-four on the 22nd of September 2018 in England, U.K. He was survived by his wife, Joan and his son, Nicholas and his daughters, Juliet and Kate.

Chas first became interested in Rock 'n' Roll music after listening to Little Richard on Radio Luxembourg in around 1956. He was then inspired by Lonnie Donegan to learn to play the guitar when he was twelve, and joined a skiffle band a year later in 1957. In May 1958, he went to a Jerry Lee Lewis concert and got interested in learning to play piano. Chas, however, became a professional musician by the age of sixteen, playing bass guitar with various local bands.

Chas met Dave Peacock in 1963 when a friend of Dave gave Chas a lift home and found they had similar taste in music.

In 1972, Chas and Dave considered forming a band together, singing in their own accent about things they knew and they began to perform as the duo Chas & Dave. Chas, although originally a bass player, played the piano and guitar while Dave played bass.

Chas and Dave recorded their first album as Chas & Dave in 1974, an album called "One Fing Anuvver" and was released in 1975.

Dave Holland   Judas Priest

Dave Holland died aged sixty-nine from liver cancer, on the 16th of January 2018.

Dave began piano lessons at the age of six, but soon developed a passion for drums and asked his parents to let him have a set.

After his first appearance as a stand-in for a local band, Dave realised he wanted to be a musician. When he was fourteen years old, he supplemented his pocket money by playing with another local band titled The Drumbeats, and selling furniture and carpet.

When still young Dave listened to traditional jazz. He cited his first rock influence as Johnny Kidd and the Pirates. Later, he became interested in funk music in the vein of Booker T & the MG's, blues rock of Free and progressive—psychedelic music of Traffic.

Dave joined Judas Priest in August 1979 and played drums on many of their platinum albums, including British Steel, Scream for Vengeance, Defenders of Faith, and Turbo and Ram.

Michael Holliday — Solo Artiste

Michael Holliday died from a drugs overdose, aged thirty-eight, on the 29th of October 1963 in Croydon, Surrey, UK. He was survived by his estranged wife, Margaret. His grave can be found at Anfield Cemetery, Priory Road, Liverpool, UK.

Michael had battled for years with stage fright and had a mental breakdown in nineteen-sixty-one. He was born in Liverpool, U.K. and his career in music began after winning an amateur talent contest. In 1951 he secured two summer seasons of work as a vocalist with Dick Denny's band at a Butlin's Holiday Camp.

In March nineteen-fifty-three Michael joined the Eric Winstone Band, another Butlin's contracted band that toured when the summer season's work was over. They also broadcast occasionally on BBC Radio. In December nineteen-fifty-four, Michael wrote to the BBC requesting a television audition. His audition came in April 1955 and he made his first TV appearance that year, a performance seen by the head of A&R for EMI's Columbia record label, who signed Michael toa solo record deal.

Mark Hollis — Talk Talk

Mark Hollis died aged sixty-four on the 25th of February 2019 after a short illness from which he never recovered. He was survived by his wife, Felicity and two sons.

Between school and the launch of his music career, Mark worked in factories and as a laboratory technician. Reflecting on this period in his life, he later said that he could never wait to get home and start writing songs and lyrics and all day long he'd be jotting ideas down on bits of paper and just waiting for the moment when he could put it all down on tape.

Ed Hollis, Mark's older brother, mentored Mark and introduced him to the music industry. With Ed's encouragement and assistance, Mark formed his first band, The Reaction. Emerging in the post-punk era, the Reaction's sound reflected Mark's interest in early garage rock.

Mark was best known for being the lead singer and primary songwriter of the band Talk Talk between 1981 and 1991, when they disbanded. In 1998, Mark released an self-titled solo album.

Buddy Holly   Buddy Holly & the Crickets

Buddy Holly died aged twenty-two on the 3rd of February 1959, when his plane crashed, shortly after take-off in Iowa, U.S.A. His body, along with those of other entertainers were all ejected from the plane on impact. He was survived by his wife, Maria.

Buddy's body was interred in the City of Lubbock Cemetery, Texas, USA. His headstone carries the original spelling of his surname (Holley) and a carving of his Fender Stratocaster guitar.

By 1955, after graduating from high school, Buddy had decided to pursue a full-time career in music and was further encouraged after seeing Elvis Presley performing live in Lubbock.

Buddy and his band were signed to Decca Records in 1956. In the contract, Decca misspelled Buddy's last name as "Holly"; and from then on, he was known as Buddy Holly, instead of Holley.

"That'll Be the Day" was released in May 1957 and it topped the US "Best Sellers in Stores" chart that September and was number one on the UK Singles Chart for three weeks during November. In September Coral released "Peggy Sue", backed with "Everyday", with Buddy Holly credited as the performer. By October, "Peggy Sue" had reached number three on Billboard's pop chart and number two on the Rythm&Blues chart; it peaked at number six on the UK Singles chart. As the success of the song grew, it brought more attention to Buddy Holly, with the band at the time being billed as "Buddy Holly and the Crickets".

Hugh Hopper   Soft Machine

Hugh Hopper died of Leukaemia on the 7th of June 2009 aged sixty-four. He is survived by his wife Christine whom he had married just two days before his death.

In 1964 Hugh formed The Wilde Flowers, a pop music group, in Canterbury. Hugh's role with Soft Machine was initially as the group's road manager but in 1969 he was recruited to be their bassist for their second album, Volume Two. Hugh continued with Soft Machine, playing bass and contributing numerous compositions until 1973. During his tenure the group evolved from a psychedelic pop group to an instrumental jazz-rock fusion band.

After leaving Soft Machine, through the end of the 1970s, Hugh worked with groups including Stomu Yamashta's East Wind, Isotope, Gilgamesh, and the Carla Bley Band. He also played in a couple of cooperative bands alongside former Soft Machine saxophonist Elton Dean.

Hugh also recorded two solo albums and worked with Japanese musician and composer Yumi Hara Cawkwell as a duo called HUMI.

Michael Hossack   The Doobie Brothers

Michael Hossack died from cancer aged sixty-five on the 12th of March 2012. He was survived by his son, Mike.Jnr and his daughter, Erica.

Michael started playing drums in the Little Falls Cadets, a Boy Scout drum and bugle corps. His discipline to play alongside other drummers came from the teachings of his instructors, all to whom he gave much credit.

After graduating from high school, Michael served for four years in the United States Navy during the Vietnam War era. After being honorably discharged in 1969, he returned home to New Jersey to pursue a career in law enforcement. However, a close friend talked him into auditioning for a California-based band called Mourning Reign. After playing in upstate New York, the band relocated to the San Francisco bay area and signed with a production company that had also signed the newly formed rock band, the Doobie Brothers.

Although Mourning Reign was short-lived, Michael Hossack's abilities gained considerable exposure and he was invited to join with the Doobie Brothers in 1971.

Aaliyah Dana Houghton   Solo Artiste

Aaliyah Dana Haughton died aged twenty-two on the 25th of August 2001 when she with members of her record company boarded a light aircraft at the Marsh Harbour Airport in Abaco Islands, the Bahamas, to travel to the Opa-locka Airport in Florida. They had a flight scheduled the following day, but with filming finishing early, Aaliyah and her entourage were eager to return to the United States and made the decision to leave immediately. The designated airplane was smaller than the one on which they had originally arrived, but the whole party and all of the equipment were accommodated on board. The plane crashed shortly after takeoff, about sixty metres from the end of the runway and exploded. Aaliyah and the eight others on board were all killed.

Aaliyah's body was set in a silver-plated copper-deposit casket, which was carried in a glass horse-drawn hearse. An estimated 800 mourners attended the procession. After the service, twenty two white doves were released to symbolize each year of Aaliyah's life.

Aaliyah's debut album, Age Ain't Nothing but a Number, was released in May 1994 and sold seventy four thousand copies in its first week. Aaliyah's UK chart hits include: "Back And Forth" in 1994, "You Are Love" in 1994, "Age Ain't Nothing But A Number" in 1995, "Down With The

Clique" in 1995, "The Thing I Like" in 1995, "I Need You Tonight" in 1996, "If Your Girl Only Knew" in 1996, "Got To Give It Up" in 1996, "Four Page Letter" in 1997, "The One I Gave My Heart To" in 1997, "Journey To The Past" in 1998 and "Are You That Somebody? In 1998.

Whitney Houston   Solo Artiste

Whitney Houston died aged forty-eight on the 11th of February 2012 at the Beverly Hilton Hotel in Los Angeles, California, U.S.A. Whitney had reportedly appeared "disheveled" and "erratic" in the days just before her death. She was buried in Fairview Cemetery, Westfield, New Jersey, next to her father.

On the 22nd of March 2012, the Los Angeles County Coroner's Office reported that Whitney's death was caused by drowning and the effects of atherosclerotic heart disease and cocaine use and the office stated that the amount of cocaine found in Whitney's body indicated that she used the substance shortly before her death. The manner of death was listed as an accident.

Whitney's UK chart hits include: "Saving All My Love for You" in 1985, "Greatest Love of All" in 1986, "I Wanna Dance with Somebody" in 1987, "So Emotional" in 1987, "One Moment in Time" in 1988 and "I Will Always Love You" in 1992.

Brian Howe   Bad Company

Brian Howe died aged sixty-six on the 6th of May 2020 of cardiac arrest whilst he was en route to a hospital in Florida, United States of America. Brian was survived by his sister Sandie, his three children, and three grandchildren.

After a call from Mick Jones of Foreigner, whom Brian had tried to work with earlier in his career, he was introduced to Mick Ralphs and Simon Kirke of Bad Company.

In 1986, Mick Ralphs and Simon Kirke decided to

regroup for a new project. Their label, Atlantic Records, however, insisted they resume with the Bad Company name. Paul Rodgers was already engaged with a new group called The Firm. With Paul gone, the remaining two members partnered with Brian as the new lead singer. Brian's vocal style brought more of a pop-rock sound to the band. They hired producer Keith Olsen to produce the new line-up's initial album, 'Fame and Fortune' in 1986.

Bad Company's next album, Holy Water, was written mostly by Brian and Terry and was released in June 1990. Brian released his first solo album, Tangled in Blue, in 1997.

Alan Hull   Lindisfarne

Alan Hull died aged fifty on the 17th of November 1995 of a heart thrombosis . He was survived by wife Patricia and their three daughters.

Alan had been working on a new album called Statues & Liberties. After his funeral, Alan's ashes were scattered at the mouth of the River Tyne in Newcastle, U.K. In 2012 an Alan Hull memorial plaque was unveiled on the front of Newcastle City Hall, at a ceremony attended by hundreds of fans, and video broadcasted by Sky and ITV Tyne Tees.

Michael Hutchence   INXS

Michael Hutchence died aged thirty-seven on the 22nd of November 1997 at the Ritz-Carlton hotel in Double Bay, Sydney, Australia. His death was reported by the New South Wales Coroner to be the result of suicide by hanging. Actress Kym Wilson was the last person to see Michael alive when she visited him in his hotel room the previous evening.

In July 1996, Michael and English television presenter Paula Yates had a daughter they named Tiger Lily.

Scott Hutchison died aged thirty-six of suicide on the 10th of May 2018, in Edinburgh, Scotland, U.K.

Scott was reported missing by Scottish police and the members of Frightened Rabbit on the 9th of May 2018 and was last seen leaving a hotel in the South Queensferry district of the city.

Initially considering himself solely a guitarist, Scott began singing at the age of nineteen, stating that up until that point he was just a guitar player and that he didn't know he could sing and that he had been told that he could not. In 2003, Scott began performing under the name Frightened Rabbit, a name given to him by his mother to describe his once shy nature, and he began recording and performing with his brother. The following year, the duo recorded the band's debut album, "Sing the Greys".

DEAD STARS I - L

Niel Innes

Bonzo Dog Doo-dah Band

Niel Innes died of heart attack aged seventy-five on the 29th of December 2019. He was survived by his wife, Yvonne and their three sons, Miles, Luke, and Barney.

While at College Niel started a band with other students that was originally named The Bonzo Dog Dada Band after the art movement Dada, which they renamed the Bonzo Dog Doo-Dah Band. Niel Innes had met Vivian Stanshall at the Central School of Art, where both studied drawing. Together they wrote most of the band's songs, including "I'm the Urban Spaceman", their one-and-only U.K. hit single . Niel Innes won an Ivor Novello Award for Best Novelty Song in 1968 for "I'm the Urban Spaceman".

Marvin Isley

The Isley Brothers

Marvin Isley died aged fifty-six on the 6th of June, 2010, from complications of diabetes in a hospital in Chicago, Illinois, U.S.A. He was survived by his wife, Sheila, his son, Cory, his daughters Sydney and Jalen and his brothers Ronald, Ernie and Rudolph.

Marvin began playing bass guitar while in high school and by the end of the decade was being tutored and mentored by his elder brothers. In 1971, Marvin began performing bass guitar on The Isley Brothers' album, Givin' It Back and within two years, he became an official member of the group. In addition to playing bass, Marvin also provided percussion and also wrote or co-wrote some of the group's hits including "Fight the Power", "The Pride" and "Between the Sheets".

Rudolph Isley

The Isley Brothers

Rudolph Isley died at home aged eighty-four from a heart

attack on the 11th of October, 2023. He was survived by his wife, Elaine and his daughters, Elizabeth, Valerie and Elaine and his son, Rudolph Jnr and his brothers, Ronald and Ernie.

Rudolph was born in April, 1939 and raised in Cincinnati, Ohio, USA where he began singing in church at a young age. By his teen years, Rudolph was singing as member of The Isley Brothers with Kelly, Ronnie and Vernon. In 1957, following Vernon's death, the remaining three elder Isleys moved to New York to seek a recording deal, later recording for smaller labels until landing a deal with RCA Records in 1959 where they wrote, recorded and released their first successful recording, a song called "Shout". By the summer of 1957, the Isley family had moved from Cincinnati to a new home in Englewood, New Jersey.

Following "Shout", the brothers recorded for other labels with modest success with exceptions including the top 40 hit, "Twist & Shout" and the Motown hit, "This Old Heart of Mine". In the 1960s, Rudy and his brothers founded the T-Neck Records label to promote their recordings. Following their split with Motown, they reactivated the label and scored a Grammy-winning smash with "It's Your Thing" in 1969. While Ronald Isley was the prominent lead singer of the group, Rudolph did record a few lead vocals on some Isley Brothers songs, following the reactivation of T-Neck. After the group reorganized into a band following the inclusion of younger brothers Ernie and Marvin and in-law Chris Jasper, Rudolph would share lead vocals with his brothers Ron and Kelly on hits such as "Fight the Power" and "Livin' in the Life". He also sang full lead on other tunes such as "You Still Feel the Need" from the album, Harvest for the World, and their 1979 hit, "It's a Disco Night (Rock Don't Stop)". In 1986, his eldest brother Kelly suddenly died of a heart attack in his sleep. Kelly's death devastated Rudolph as the brothers had been close. After recording the albums Smooth Sailin' and Spend the Night in 1989, Rudolph left the group and the music industry for good to follow a lifelong goal of being a Christian minister. Rudy had been known for wearing hats and fur-attired clothing and was also known for carrying a cane. He was inducted as member of the Isleys to the Rock and Roll Hall of Fame in 1992. Rudolph had married his wife Elaine in 1958. At first, he and his family settled at a house he bought in Teaneck, New Jersey, where they lived for ten years. By the mid-1970s, he was living in Haworth, New Jersey. Though having had health issues following his exit from the Isleys, his wife Elaine has stated that his health was good and Rudy was watching what he was eating. Rudolph briefly reunited with Ronald & Ernie in 2004 where the brothers were honored with a lifetime achievement award at the BET Awards. He and his wife were long-term residents of Otisville, New York before moving to Olympia Fields near Chicago in 2013, where they bought R. Kelly's former house to be near their children and grandchildren.

O'Kelly Isley Jnr   The Isley Brothers

O'Kelly Isley Jnr died aged forty-eight of a Heart Attack on the 31st of March 1986 at his home in Alpine, New Jersey, U.S.A. He was survived by his two sons, Frank and Doug.

O'Kelly was the eldest of the Isley Brothers soul band and began singing with his brothers at church. When he was sixteen, O'Kelly and his three younger brothers, Rudy, Ronnie and Vernon, formed The Isley Brothers and toured the gospel circuit. Following the death of Vernon Isley from a road accident, the brothers decided to try their hand at doo-wop and moved to New York to find a recording deal and in 1959, they signed with RCA Records.

Michael Jackson died aged fifty from Cardiac Arrest on the 25th of June 2009 in Los Angeles, California, U.S.A. His memorial was held on the following 7th of July after which a private family service was held at the Forest Lawn Memorial Park's Hall of Liberty in Los Angeles.

Michael grew up with three sisters, Rebbie, La Toya, and Janet, and five brothers Jackie, Tito, Jermaine, Marlon, and Randy).

Michael had a troubled relationship with his father. In 2003, Joe Jackson acknowledged that he regularly whipped Michael as a boy. Joe was also said to have verbally abused his son, often saying that he had a "fat nose". Michael Jackson stated that he was physically and emotionally abused during incessant rehearsals, though he credited his father's strict discipline with playing a large role in his success.

Michael's fifth solo album, Off the Wall, , established Michael as a solo performer. The album helped his transition from the bubblegum pop of his youth to the more complex sounds he would create as an adult. Off the Wall was the first solo album to generate four top ten hits in the United States: "Off the Wall", "She's Out of My Life", and the chart-topping singles "Don't Stop 'Til You Get Enough" and "Rock with You". The album reached number three on the Billboard 200 and eventually sold over twenty million copies worldwide.

More success came with Michael's sixth album, 'Thriller', released in late 1982. The album earned Michael seven more Grammys and eight American Music Awards, including the Award of Merit, the youngest artist to win it. It was the best-selling album worldwide in 1983 and became the best-selling album of all time in the United States and the best-selling album of all time worldwide, selling an estimated sixty-five million copies.

Pervis Jackson   The Spinners

Pervis Jackson died aged seventy from cancer on the 18th of August, 2008 in Detroit, Michigan, U.S.A. He was survived by his wife Claudreen and two sons and two daughters.

Originating from the New Orleans area, Pervis was one of the original five members of the Spinners, which started out in the late 1950s singing doo-wop in Detroit. They worked under the Motown label in the 1960s but shot to stardom after moving to Atlantic Records in the 1970s. With songs including "Mighty Love," "I'll Be Around," "One of a Kind" and "Then Came You," the Spinners were a constant on the American R&B and pop charts of the 1970s. Pervis Jackson last performed on the 19th of July 2008 in California.

Tony Jackson   The Searchers

Tony Jackson died aged sixty-five on the 18th of August 2003 in a Nottingham hospital. He had been suffering from diabetes, heart disease and cirrhosis of the liver after a lifetime of heavy alcohol consumption.

Tony Jackson was born in Liverpool, United Kingdom and after leaving school he trained as an electrician. Tony was inspired by the skiffle sound of Lonnie Donegan, and then by Buddy Holly and other U.S. rock and rollers and he founded the skiffle group the Martinis before joining the then guitar duo, the Searchers.

Tony was lead singer and played bass on the band's first two the United Kingdom hits, "Sweets for My Sweet" and "Sugar and Spice and he was featured on both "Don't Throw Your Love Away" and "Love Potion No. 9".

Etta James   Solo Artiste

Etta James died aged seventy-three from leukaemia on the 20th of January 2012 in hospital in California, U.S.A. The singers Stevie Wonder and Christina Aguilera each gave a musical tribute at her funeral before she was entombed at Inglewood Park Cemetery in Los Angeles.

In early 1961, Etta released what was to become her signature song, "At Last", which reached number two on the R&B chart and number 47 on the American Billboard Hot 100.

On her 2004 release, 'Blue Gardenia', she returned to a jazz style. Her final album for Private Music, 'Let's Roll', released in 2005, won the Grammy Award for Best Contemporary Blues Album.

Etta performed at the top jazz festivals in the world, including the Montreux Jazz Festival. She also often performed at free summer arts festivals throughout the United States.

Al Jarreau   Solo Artiste

Al Jarreau died aged seventy-six of respiratory failure on the 12th of February 2017 and is interred in the Forest Lawn Memorial Park in Hollywood Hills, California, U.S.A. He was survived by his wife, Susan, and their son, Ryan.

One of Al Jarreau's most commercially successful albums is Breakin' Away from 1981, which includes the hit song "We're in This Love Together". He won the 1982 Grammy Award for Best Male Pop Vocal Performance for Breakin' Away.

Paul Jeffries   Cockney Rebel

Paul Jeffreys died aged thirty-six, along with his wife , Rachel on 21st of December, 1988 when their Pan Am Flight 103 on the way to their honeymoon exploded, the wreckage falling over the town of Lockerbie, Scotland.

Paul was born on the 13th of February 1952 and was an English rock musician, playing bass guitar in Cockney

Rebel between 1972 and 1974, working on the group's first two albums and later working with other British bands, including Be-Bop Deluxe from 1974 to 1980 and Electric Eels until 1981.

General Johnson   Chairman of the Board

General Johnson died aged sixty-nine, apparently from lung cancer, on the 13th of October, 2010, in Atlanta, Georgia, United States of America. He was survived by his wife, Julia and his sister, Barbara and his sons, Norman and Antonio and his daughter, Sonya

General made an early start in music when he began singing in his church choir at the age of six. His recording debut came six years later on Atlantic Records, who recorded his group the Humdingers, although the tracks remain unreleased.

General Johnson attempted an abortive solo career before joining the then new Invictus label in Detroit, Michigan and steered by Holland-Dozier-Holland, General created Chairmen of the Board. Their debut single, "Give Me Just a Little More Time", rose to number 3 in the US Billboard R&B chart in 1970. Further hits followed including "(You've Got Me) Dangling on a String" and "Everything's Tuesday."

Wilco johnson   Dr Feelgood

Wilco Johnson died aged seventy-five from pancreatic cancer on the 21st of November 2022, at his home in Westcliff-on-Sea, UK. He was survived by his sons, Matthew and Simon.

After graduating from university, Wilco travelled to India before returning to Essex to play with the Pigboy Charlie Band. The band evolved into Dr. Feelgood – a mainstay of the 1970s pub rock movement.

Wilco developed his own image, coupling jerky movements on stage, his so-called "duck walk", with a choppy guitar style, occasionally raising his guitar to his shoulder like a gun.

His style formed the essential driving force behind Dr. Feelgood during their initial years, including the band's first four albums, Down by the Jetty, Malpractice, Stupidity, and Sneakin' Suspicion, all released between 1975 and 1977.

Brian Jones   The Rolling Stones

Brian Jones died aged twenty-seven on the 2nd of July 1969. He was discovered motionless at the bottom of his swimming pool at Cotchford Farm in the village of Hartfield in East Sussex, U.K. His

Swedish girlfriend, Anna, was convinced Brian was alive when he was taken out of the pool, insisting he still had a pulse. However, by the time the doctors arrived it was too late and he was pronounced dead. The coroner's report stated "death by misadventure" and noted his liver and heart were heavily enlarged by drug and alcohol abuse.

The Rolling Stones performed at a free concert in Hyde Park two days after Brian's death. The concert had been scheduled as an opportunity to present the Stones' new guitarist, Mick Taylor. The Stones decided to dedicate the concert to Brian.

Brian listened to classical music as a child, but preferred blues, particularly Elmore James and Robert Johnson and he began performing at local blues and jazz clubs, while busking and working odd jobs. Brian left his hometown, Cheltenham, in Gloucestershire and moved to London where he became friends with fellow musicians including Alexis Korner.

Brian put an advertisement in a Soho club information sheet in May 1962, inviting musicians to audition for a new R&B group at the Bricklayer's Arms pub. Piano player Ian Stewart was the first to respond and later singer Mick Jagger joined this band.

The Rolling Stones played their first gig in July 1962 in the Marquee Club in London. In June 1969, however, Brian was visited by Mick Jagger, Keith Richards, and Charlie Watts and was told that the group he had formed would continue without him, perhaps an unintended prelude to his death.

Davey Jones   The Monkees

Davey Jones died of a heart attack aged sixty-six on the 29th of February 2012. He was survived by his wife, Jessica and daughters, Talia, Sarah, Jessica and Annabel. Davey had gone to tend his fourteen horses at a farm in Indiantown, Florida and after riding one of his favourite horses around the track, he had complained of chest pains and had difficulty breathing. On Wednesday, the 7th of March 2012 a private funeral service was held at Holy Cross Catholic parish in Indiantown, Florida. The three surviving Monkees, Peter Tork, Micky Dolenz and Michael Nesmith, attended memorial services in New York City as well as organising their own private memorial in Los Angeles along with Davey's family and close friends. He was survived by his third wife, Jessica and his daughters, Talia, Sarah, Jessica and Annabel.

Davey was born David Thomas Jones in Manchester, Lancashire, U.K. in 1945. His television acting debut was on the British television soap opera Coronation Street and he also appeared in the 1960's BBC police tv series Z-Cars. Moreover, he took the role as the Artful Dodger in a production of Oliver! in London's West End, a move which changed his life forever. Davey played the role in London and then on Broadway and was nominated for a Tony Award. On 9th February 1964, Davey appeared in the U.S.A. on The Ed Sullivan Show.

From 1966 to 1971, Davey was a member of the Monkees, a pop beat group formed expressly for a television show of the same name. Davey sang lead vocals on many of the Monkees' re-cordings, including "I Wanna Be Free" and "Daydream Believer".

After the Monkees officially disbanded in 1971, Davey kept himself busy by establishing a New York City-style street market in Los Angeles, called "The Street".

Janis Joplin   Solo Artiste

Janis Joplin died of a heroin overdose aged twenty-seven on the 4th of October 1970 at the at a Landmark hotel in California, U.S.A.

Janis had cultivated a rebellious manner and styled herself partly after her female blues heroines and partly after the Beat poets. Her first song, 'What Good Can Drinkin' Do', was recorded on tape in December 1962 at the home of a fellow University of Texas student.

Janis left Texas in January 1963 and moved to San Francisco. Just prior to joining Big Brother and the Holding Company, she recorded seven studio tracks in 1965. In 1966, Janis' bluesy vocal style attracted the attention of the psychedelic rock band Big Brother and the Holding Company, a band that had gained some renown among the nascent hippie community in Haight-Ashbury. Janis joined Big Brother on June 1966 and her first public performance with them was at the Avalon Ballroom in San Francisco.

The band's debut studio album, 'Big Brother & the Holding Company', was released by Mainstream Records in August 1967, shortly after the group's breakthrough appearance in June at the Monterey Pop Festival.

For her first major studio recording, Janis Joplin played a major role in the arrangement and production of the songs that would comprise Big Brother and the Holding Company's second album, 'Cheap Thrills'.

After splitting from Big Brother and the Holding Company, Janis formed a new backup group, the Kozmic Blues Band. Janis appeared at the Woodstock Festival coming on stage at approximately 2 a.m., on Sunday, 17th August 1969.

Larry Junstrom Lynard Skynard

Larry Junstrom died aged seventy on the 6th of October 2019, in Jacksonville, Florida, U.S.A. He was survived by his wife Thania.

Larry, a founding member of Lynyrd Skynyrd and long-time bassist for the band .38 Special, was born in 1949 in Pittsburgh, Pennsylvania, U.S.A. Larry began his musical career in the mid-1960s playing in early versions of Lynyrd Skynyrd, alternately known as My Backyard, the Noble Five and the One Percent, alongside Ronnie Van Zant, Garry Rossington, Bob Burns and Allen Collins. They eventually chose their more familiar name as a sarcastic homage to their Jacksonville high school gym teacher, Leonard Skinner, who was notorious for checking the length of the boy's hair.

Paul Kantner Jefferson Airplane

Paul Kantner died aged seventy-four on 28th of January 2016 in San Francisco, California, U.S.A. from multiple organ failure and septic shock. He was survived by his two sons, Gareth and Alexander and his daughter, China.

Paul attended high school, completing three years of college education before dropping out to focus on the music scene. During the summer of 1965, singer Marty Balin saw Paul perform at a San Francisco folk club, and invited him to co-found a new band, which became Jefferson Airplane.

Paul was the only musician to appear on all albums recorded by Jefferson Airplane as well as Jefferson Starship. Paul's song-writing often featured lyrics with science-fiction or fantasy themes.

Although the band retained a relatively egalitarian songwriting structure, Paul became Jefferson Airplane's dominant creative force from 1967's 'After Bathing at Baxter's' onward, writing the chart hits "The Ballad of

You and Me and Pooneil", "Watch Her Ride" and "Crown of Creation".

On the album, Blows Against the Empire, Paul and Grace Slick sang about a group of people escaping Earth in a hijacked starship.

Paul had been in love with Grace Slick for some time, but she was involved in a relationship with the band's drummer, Spencer Dryden. After their two-year affair ended, he finally had a chance with Grace. In 1969, they began living together publicly as a couple. Grace Slick became pregnant, and a song about their child's impending birth, "A Child Is Coming," appeared on Blows Against the Empire. Paul and Grace's daughter China Wing Kantner was born in 1971.

Mick Karn   Japan

Mick Karn died of cancer aged fifty-two at his home in London on the 4th of January 2011. He was survived by his wife, Kyoko and his son, Metis.

The band, Japan, began as a group of friends, who all studied at Catford Boys' School in South East London, UK.

As the band started to achieve commercial success with the release of Tin Drum, and "Ghosts", which reached the top five in 1982, tensions and personality conflicts between band members arose. Mick was principally the bassist within Japan, but also played all the wind instruments, including the saxophone. On the album, Tin Drum, he played the Chinese suona for the authentic oriental sound. Mick's use of the fretless bass guitar, a relatively unusual instrument in modern popular music, produces a distinctive sound and playing style, which makes his playing instantly recognisable.

Japan's UK chart hits include, "Quiet Life" in 1981, "Ghosts" in 1982, "Cantonese Boy" in 1982 and "I Second That Emotion" in 1982.

Terry Kath Chicago

Terry Kath **Chicago**

Terry Kath died from an accidental gunshot aged thirty-one on the 23rd of January 1978 in Woodland Hills, California, United States of America. He was survived by his ex-wife Pamela and his daughter, Michelle.

Chicago's members were devastated over losing Terry and strongly considered disbanding, but were later persuaded that they should continue without him.

Unlike several other Chicago members who received formal music training, Terry was mostly self-taught and enjoyed jamming.

Terry joined his first semi-professional band, The Mystics, in 1963, moving to Jimmy Rice and the Gentlemen in 1965. He then played bass in a road band called Jimmy Ford and the Executives.

Terry was regarded as Chicago's bandleader and best soloist; and his vocal, jazz and hard rock influences are regarded as integral to the band's early sound.

Terry Kath sang lead vocals on several of Chicago's early songs, including "I'm a Man", "Colour My World" and "Make Me Smile".

Eddie Kendricks The Temptations

Eddie Kendricks died aged fifty-two on the 5th of October 1992 from lung cancer. He was survived by his three children, Parris, Aika, and Paul. Eddie was buried in Elmwood Cemetery, Birmingham, Alabama, U.S.A.

In 1955, Eddie and friends formed a doo-wop group called The Cavaliers, and began performing around Birmingham, Alabama. The group decided to move for better opportunities in their musical careers, and in 1957 they moved to Cleveland, Ohio where they met manager Milton Jenkins, and soon moved with him to Detroit, Michigan, where the group renamed themselves "The Primes." Under Jenkins' management, the Primes were successful in the Detroit area. In 1961 the Primes disbanded and Eddie joined a band which later changed their name to "The Temptations" and signed to Tamla Motown.

The Temptations began singing background for Mary Wells and, after an initial dry period, They quickly became one of the most successful male vocal group of the 1960s. Technically Eddie was first tenor in the group's harmony, although he predominately sang in a falsetto voice.

The Temptations UK chart hits include: "My Girl" in 1965, "I'm Gonna Make You Love Me" in 1969, "Get Ready" in 1969, "Cloud Nine" in 1969, "I Can't Get Next to You" in 1970, "Ball Of Confusion" in 1970, "Just My Imagination" in 1971 and "Papa Was A Rollin' Stone" in 1973.

Johnny Kidd   The Pirates

Johnny Kidd died aged thirty in a car crash on the 7th of October 1966 and was cremated at Golders Green Crematorium in North London, United Kingdom. He was survived by his wife, Jean.

In 1959 Johnny and his band were given a recording test for their first single called, "Please Don't Touch". A contract with HMV quickly followed and the group were then informed their group's name would be changed to Johnny Kidd & the Pirates.

Johnny's UK chart hits include: "Please Don't Touch" in 1959, "Shakin' All Over" in 1960 and "I'll Never Get Over You" in 1963.

Lemmy Kilminster   Motorhead & Hawkwind

Lemmy died aged seventy on the 28th of December 2015 from prostate cancer, congestive heart failure, and cardiac arrhythmia at his apartment in Los Angeles, California, U.S.A. He was survived by his son, Paul.

In 1971 Lemmy joined the space rock band Hawkwind as a bassist and vocalist. He had no previous experience as a bass guitarist, and was cajoled into joining immediately before a benefit gig in Notting Hill. He quickly developed a distinctive style that was strongly shaped by his early experience as a rhythm guitarist, often using double stops and chords rather than the single note lines preferred by most bassists. His bass work was a fundamental part of the Hawkwind sound during his tenure, perhaps best documented on 'Space Ritual'. He also provided the lead vocals on several songs, including the band's biggest UK chart single, "Silver Machine", which reached Number three in the UK charts in 1972.

B.B. King   Solo Artiste

B.B.King died aged eighty-nine on the 14th of May 2015 in Las Vegas, Nevada, U.S.A. An autopsy revealed B.B.King's death was due to complications of Alzheimer's disease and congestive heart failure. He was survived by his son, Robert as well as other sons and daughters.

B.B.King's body was laid out in a purple satin vest and a floral tuxedo jacket over a white tuxedo shirt and flanked by two black Gibson guitars, at the B.B. King Museum and Delta Interpretive Center, in Indianola. Fans lined up to view his open casket.

B.B.King gained visibility among rock audiences as an opening act on the Rolling Stones' 1969 American Tour. He won a 1970 Grammy Award for the song "The Thrill Is Gone"; his version became a hit on both the pop and R&B charts.

B.B.King was inducted into the Blues Hall of Fame in 1980, the Rock and Roll Hall of Fame in 1987, and the Official Rhythm & Blues Music Hall of Fame in 2014. In 2004, he was awarded the international Polar Music Prize, given in recognition of exceptional achievements in the creation and advancement of music.

Ben E King died aged seventy-six on the 13th of April 2015 at the Hackensack University Medical Center in New Jersey, U.S.A. He was survived by his wife Betty and three children and six grand-children.

In 1958, Ben joined a doo-wop group called the Five Crowns. Later that year, the Drifters' manager George Treadwell fired the members of the original Drifters, and replaced them with the members of the Five Crowns.

Ben had a string of Rythm & Blues hits with the group on Atlantic Records. He co-wrote and sang lead on the first Atlantic hit by the new version of the Drifters, "There Goes My Baby" in 1959.

In May 1960, Ben left the Drifters in preparation for a solo career. Remaining with Atlantic Records on its Atco imprint, Ben scored his first solo hit with the ballad "Spanish Harlem".

His next single, "Stand by Me", written with Jerry Leiber and Mike Stoller, ultimately would be voted as one of the Songs of the Century by the Recording Industry Association of America.

Ed King   Lynard Skynard

Ed King died of cancer aged sixty-eight at home in Nashville, Tennessee, U.S.A on the 22nd of August 2018.

Ed was one of the founding members of the band Strawberry Alarm Clock, formed in Los Angeles in the mid-1960s. The band's largest success was with the single "Incense and Peppermints", which reached number 1 on the American Billboard Hot 100. While with the band he played both electric 6-string guitar and bass guitar.

Ed met the members of Jacksonville, Florida-based Southern rock band Lynyrd Skynyrd when the band opened for Strawberry Alarm Clock on a few shows in early 1968. It wasn't until 1972 that he joined them, replacing someone else who had left the band.

His guitar playing and songwriting skills were an essential element on Lynyrd Skynyrd's first three albums: 'Lynyrd Skynyrd', 'Second Helping' and 'Nuthin' Fancy', Moreover, Ed co-wrote the song, "Sweet Home Alabama".

Ed decided to leave Lynyrd Skynyrd in 1975 during the "Torture Tour" and he was replaced the following year by Steve Gaines, who, incidentally, shared Ed's birthdate.

Solomon King   Solo Artiste

Solomon King died of cancer aged seventy-three on the 21st of January 2005 in Oklahoma, U.S.A. He was survived by his third wife and by four offspring.

Solomon first began singing professionally in 1952 and his chart success in the UK began with "She Wears My Ring", which was a top three hit in 1968, and was also a hit in forty other countries, but failed to reach the American Billboard Hot Hundred chart. Solomon continued singing in clubs in the U.S.A. after returning there in 1980.

Soloman's UK chart hits include: "She Wears My Ring" in 1968 and "When We Were Young" in 1968.

Kathy Kirby   Solo Artiste

Kathy Kirby died aged seventy-two of a suspected heart attack on the 19th of May 2011 In London, U.K. She was survived by her sister Pat and her brother Douglas.   .

Kathy had been diagnosed with schizophrenia and was in poor physical and mental health for much of her life. After her retirement she lived in a series of apartments and hotels in West London, settling in a flat in South Kensington. She then survived on state benefits and some royalties while living mostly in seclusion.

Kathy was married briefly to writer and former London policeman Fred Pye in the 1970s, then, following her bankruptcy in 1975 and a court case following an arrest over an unpaid hotel bill, she was referred to London's St Luke's psychiatric hospital in 1979.

Kathy's vocal talent became apparent early in her life and she took singing lessons with a view to becoming an opera singer. However, she became a professional singer after meeting bandleader Bert Ambrose at the Ilford Palais in 1956 and remained with Ambrose's band for three years. He was her manager, mentor and lover until his death in 1971.

In 1962 Kathy signed a contract with Decca Records, for whom her first single was " Big Man" in October 1962. She had her first hit, "Dance On!", which peaked at number eleven in the UK chart and number one in Australia. Its follow-up was an upbeat reworking of the Doris Day classic "Secret Love" which peaked at number four on the British chart and stayed there for about five months.

In December 1983 Kathy gave one last concert in Blackpool, UK, then retired from show business altogether. Kathy's UK chart hits include: "Dance On" in 1963, "Secret Love" in 1963, "Let Me Go Lover" in 1964, "You're The One" in 1964, and "I Belong" in 1965.

Danny Kirwin   Fleetwood Mac

Danny Kirwan died of pneumonia aged sixty-eight on the 8th of June 2018. He was survived by his son Dominic and his ex-wife, Clare.

Danny was only seventeen when he came to the attention of established British blues band Fleetwood Mac, while he was playing in London with his first band Boilerhouse.

Drummer Mick Fleetwood, previously a member of John Mayall & the Bluesbreakers, suggested to Peter Green that Danny could join Fleetwood Mac, and Mick Fleetwood asked Danny to join the band in August 1968. Danny played his first gig with the Fleetwood Mac during that August at the Nag's Head Blue Horizon Club in Battersea, South London.

Danny's first recorded work with Fleetwood Mac was his guitar contribution to the instrumental hit single "Albatross". Danny's skills came further to the forefront on the 1969 album Then Play On where he split the songwriting and lead vocal duties almost equally with Peter Green, with many of the performances featuring their dual lead guitars.

In the late 1970s Danny Kirwan's mental health deteriorated significantly and since then he played no further part in the music industry and during the 1980s and 1990s, he suffered a period of homelessness while living in London.

Keith Knudsen   The Doobie Brothers

Keith Knudsen died from pneumonia aged fifty-six on the 8th of February, 2005. He was survived by his wife, Kate, and his daughter Dayna.

Keith's big break came in 1974 when he was invited to join The Doobie Brothers and joined the band during the recording of the 1974 Top 10 platinum album, "What Were Once Vices Are Now Habits".

Keith did not get behind the drum kit in the recording studio until the album "Stampede" in 1975. However, his contribution to the group's vocal harmonies in the studio and in concert was as crucial as his drumming.

The Doobie Brother's UK chart hits include: "Listen To The Music" in 1974, "Take Me In Your Arms" in 1975, "Minute By Minute" in 1979 and "Long Train Running" in 1993.

Alexis Korner   Blues Incorporated, CCS

Alexis Korner died aged fifty-five from lung cancer on the 1st of January 1984 in London, United Kingdom. He was survived by his wife, Roberta and his daughter, Sappho and his sons Nicholas and Damien.

In 1961, Alexis and Cyril Davies formed Blues Incorporated, initially a loose-knit group of musicians with a shared love of electric blues and R&B music. The group included, at various times, Charlie Watts, Jack Bruce, Ginger Baker, Long John Baldry, Graham Bond, Danny Thompson and Dick Heckstall-Smith.

In 1970, Alexis formed a big-band ensemble called CCS (short for "The Collective Consciousness Society") which had several hit singles. UK chart hits by CCS include: "Whole Lotta Love" in 1970, "Walkin" in 1971, "Tap Turns On The Water" in 1971, "Brother" in 1972 and "Band Played The Boogie" in 1973.

Paul Kossoff   Free

Paul Kossoff died aged twenty-five of a pulmonary embolism on the 19th of March 1976. He was cremated and interred at the Golders Green Crematorium, London, U.K. and his epitaph reads "All Right Now". Paul was survived by his father, David.

Paul Kossoff started playing the guitar in the mid-1960s. In April 1968, he teamed up with vocalist, Paul Rodgers and bassist, Andy Fraser to form Free. They toured for two years, during which they recorded two albums: Tons of Sobs in 1968 and Free in 1969.

Greater success came in 1970 when their third album, Fire and Water , spawned the hit single, "All Right Now".

Frankie Laine   Solo Artiste

Frankie Laine died aged ninety-three of heart failure on the 6th of February, 2007, at Scripps Mercy Hospital in San Diego, California, United States of America. He was survived by his wife, Marcia and a brother, Philip and his stepdaughters, Pamela and Jan.

An album of western classics established Frankie as "a cowboy singer" for many young fans who grew up in the

1960s. The tracks include stereo remakes of some of his biggest hits including: "The Cry of the Wild Goose", "Mule Train", "Gunfight at O.K. Corral", and "The 3:10 to Yuma".

Frankie's UK chart hits include: "High Noon" in 1952, "I Believe" in 1953, "Where The Wind Blows" in 1953, "Answer Me" in 1953, "Granada" in 1954, "Cool Water" in 1955, "Sixteen Tons" in 1956, "A Woman In Love" in 1956, and "Rawhide" in 1960.

Greg Lake   King Crimson, ELP

Greg Lake died from Cancer on the 7th of December 2016 aged sixty-nine while in London, United Kingdom. He was survived by his wife, Regina and his daughter, Natasha.

Greg discovered rock and roll in 1957 when he bought Little Richard's record "Lucille" then at the age of twelve he first learned to play the guitar and wrote his first song, "Lucky Man", which he merely committed to memory. He recalled his mother, a pianist, as his initial musical influence. She bought Greg a second hand guitar to learn on and then he took guitar lessons.

Greg joined his first band, Unit Four, as their singer and guitarist, playing cover songs through 1965. Following their split, Greg and Unit Four bassist Dave Genes formed another covers group, the Time Checks, until 1966. Gregg then became a member of The Shame, where he is featured on their single, "Don't Go Away Little Girl", written by Janis Ian.

Greg formed a friendship with future King Crimson co-founder and guitarist Robert Fripp, who formed King Crimson and their record company suggested getting a proper lead singer. He chose Greg for this role, but asked him to play bass instead of guitar to avoid having to get a bass player into the group. This marked Greg's first time playing bass.

'King Crimson' supported their album, 'In the Court of the Crimson King', with a tour of the UK and the USA.

Some of the shows featured rock band the Nice as the opening act. During this, Greg struck up a friendship with Nice keyboardist Keith Emerson. When King Crimson returned to the UK in early 1970, Greg agreed to sing on the band's second album, In the Wake of Poseidon, and appear on the music television show Top of the Pops with them, performing the song "Cat Food".

In April 1970, Greg left King Crimson and united with Keith Emerson, along with drummer Carl Palmer to form the progressive rock supergroup, Emerson, Lake & Palmer.

In 1975, while still a member of ELP, Greg achieved solo chart success when his single, "I Believe in Father Christmas", reached number two on the UK Singles Chart and it has since become a Yuletide perennial.

Bobby Lakind   The Doobie Brothers

Bobby Lakind died aged forty-seven from colon cancer on the 24th of December 1992. He was survived by his sons Nicky and Cutter.

Bobby was a conga player, vocalist, songwriter and occasional backup drummer with The Doobie Brothers. Originally a lighting roadie for the band, he was invited to join as a sideman for studio sessions after band members noticed his talent when he played around on the congas after a concert.

Bobby was a session man with the Doobie Brothers from 1976 and, moreover, he joined them onstage.

The Doobie Brothers' UK chart hits include: "Listen To The Music" in 1974, "Take Me In Your Arms" in 1975, "What A Fool Believes" in 1979 and "Long Train Running" in 1993.

Ronnie Lane   The Small Faces, Slim Chance

Ronnie Lane died aged fifty-one from pneumonia, on the 4th of June 1997 and was buried in the Masonic Cemetery,

Trinidad, Colorado, U.S.A. He was survived by his wife, Susan.

After leaving school at the age of sixteen, Ronnie met Kenney Jones at a local pub, and they formed a group they named The Outcasts. After starting with playing lead guitar, Ronnie quickly switched to bass and when shopping for a Harmony bass guitar he visited the J60 Music Bar in Manor Park, London where he met singer Steve Marriott, who was working there. Ronnie bought his new bass, then went to Steve's house after work where he was introduced to Steve's Motown and Stax collection of records.

Ronnie and Steve soon set out to form a band, recruiting friends Kenney Jones and Jimmy Winston.

The Small Faces initially had Ronnie Lane on bass guitar, Steve Marriott as guitarist and lead vocalist, Kenney Jones as drummer, and Jimmy Winston on keyboards. However, they made their debut in 1965, with Ian McLagan replacing Jimmy Winston on organ.

Ronnie and Steve began writing hit songs consistently, including "Itchycoo Park" and "All or Nothing".

After leaving the Faces, Ronnie formed his own band, Slim Chance, who recorded the singles "How Come" and "The Poacher" and the album "Anymore for Anymore".

Honey Lantree   The Honeycombes

Honey Lantree died aged seventy-five from Breast Cancer at her home in Great Bardfield, Essex, United Kingdom on the 23rd of December 2018. She was survived by her husband, David and sons Matthew and Simon and five grandchildren.

Honey was born Anne Margot Lantree and after attending school in Highams Park, Essex, United Kingdom, she began to focus on a career as a hairdresser, training in a salon in Hackney, East London. The owner of the salon also led an amateur group called the Sheratons and its members would sometimes leave their instruments at his house. One day, in 1963, Anne picked up the drumsticks and found that she had a natural talent.

Moreover, the owner of the salon showed Anne's brother, John, how to play the bass, and subsequently, the Sheratons evolved. They were given a residency in a pub in North London, and became so popular that the landlord offered them work five nights a week.

From there they secured an audition with the record producer Joe Meek, who had his own studio in the nearby Holloway Road. When Joe Meek saw the band had a female drummer, he recognised a good selling point fast.

At that stage the group were performing various pop hits but then got new material from songwriters, Ken Howard and Alan Blaikley, also floor managers at the BBC. They heard the Honeycombes and offered them the song, "Have I the Right", which subsequently spent fourteen weeks in the UK charts.

UK chart hits by the Honeycombes include: "Have I the Right" in 1964, "Is It Because" in 1964, "Something Better Beginning" in 1965 and "That's The Way" in 1965

Mario Lanza   Solo Artiste

Mario Lanza died of a Pulmonary embolism aged thirty eight on the 7th of October 1959 in Rome, Italy. He was survived by his wife, Betty and his sons, Marc and Damon and his daughters, Colleen and Ellisa.

Born Alfredo Arnold Cocozza in Philadelphia, USA he was exposed to classical singing at an early age by his Italian parents and by age 16, his vocal talent had become apparent.

Mario's budding operatic career was interrupted in World War II when he was assigned to Special Services in the U.S. Army Air Corps.

He resumed his singing career with a concert in Atlantic City, New Jersey with the NBC Symphony Orchestra in September 1945.

In 1951, Mario portrayed Enrico Caruso in The Great Caruso, which was the MGM film company's biggest success of the year.

Mario moved to Rome in May 1957, where he worked on the film Seven Hills of Rome, and returned to performing live in November of that year, singing in England for Queen Elizabeth II at the Royal Variety Show at the London Palladium.

Mario Lanza's UK chart hits include: "Because You're Mine" in 1952, "Drinking Song" in 1955, "I'll Walk With God" in 1955 and "Serenade" in 1955.

Derek Leckenby   Herman's Hermits

Derek Leckenby died aged fifty-one of Blood Cancer on the 4th of June, 1994. He was survived by his wife, Leonie and his daughters, Kara and Abigail.

Derek was part of a Manchester band when music manager Harvey Lisberg recruited him to join Herman's Hermits.

An accomplished lead guitarist and musician, Derek played on many of the Hermit's early hits and composed songs with bandmates Keith Hopwood, Peter Noone and Karl Green.

Derek is credited with arranging Herman Hermit's first big hit, "I'm into Something Good". His skills on guitar and dobro are heard on releases such as the LP 'A Whale of a Tale' and the later singles, such as "Ginny Go Softly" and "Heart Get Ready for Love".

Hermans Hermits UK chart hits include: "I'm Into Something Good" in 1964, "Silhouettes" in 1965, "Wonderful World" in 1965, "Just A Little Bit Better" in 1965, "A Must To Avoid" in 1965, "No Milk Today" in 1966, "There's A Kind Of Hush" in 1967, "Sunshine Girl" in 1968, "Something's Happening" in 1968, "My Sentimental Friend" in 1969 and "Years May Come, Years May Go" in 1970.

Alvin Lee died aged sixty-eight on the 6th of March 2013 whilst in Estepona, Spain. He was survived by his wife, Evi and his daughter, Jasmine.

In 1960, Alvin, along with bassist Leo Lyons, formed the core of the band Ten Years After after being influenced by his parents' collection of jazz and blues records and the advent of rock and roll music.

Alvin's performance at the Woodstock Festival in 1969 at Max Yasgur's dairy farm in Bethel, New York, United States, was captured on film in the documentary of the event, and his 'lightning-fast' playing helped catapult him to stardom. The film brought Alvin's music to a worldwide audience, although he later lamented that he missed the lost freedom and spiritual dedication of earlier audiences.

Ten Years After went on to release ten albums. Their sole UK singles chart hit was "Love Like A Man" in 1970.

Arthur Lee   Love

Arthur Lee died aged sixty-one on the 3rd of August 2006 from complications of Leukaemia whilst in Memphis, Tennessee, U.S.A. He was survived by his wife, Dianne.

Arthur Lee's first musical instrument was an accordion, which he took lessons for from a teacher. While he was never formally taught about musical theory and composition, Arthur was able to mimic musicians from records and compose his own songs and eventually he persuaded his parents to buy him an organ and a harmonica.

As a songwriter, Arthur composed the surf songs "White Caps" and "Ski Surfin' Sanctuary". "My Diary" was the first Arthur Lee composition that came near to becoming a hit. It was written when Arthur was a teenager, about his teenage sweetheart Anita.

Love released three albums with core members Arthur Lee, Johnny Echols, Bryan MacLean, and Ken Forssi.

Love's music has been described as a mixture of folk-rock, psychedelic rock, baroque pop, Spanish-tinged pop, R&B, garage rock, and even proto-punk.

Peggy Lee   Solo Artiste

Peggy Lee died of a heart attack aged eighty-one on the 21st of January 2002 in Bel Air, Los Angeles, California, U.S.A. She was survived by her daughter, Nicki.

Peggy first sang professionally over KOVC radio in Valley City, North Dakota. She later had her own series on a radio show sponsored by a local restaurant that paid her a salary in food. Both during and after her high school years, Peggy Lee sang for small sums on local radio stations.

In 1942 Peggy had her first American number one hit, "Somebody Else Is Taking My Place", followed by "Why Don't You Do Right?" in 1943 which sold over one million copies and made her famous. She also sang with Benny Goodman's orchestra in two 1943 films, "Stage Door Canteen" and "The Powers Girl".

Peggy recorded a popular version of the song "Fever" written by Eddie Cooley and John Davenport, to which she added her uncopyrighted lyrics ("Romeo loved Juliet," "Captain Smith and Pocahontas"). Peggy continued to perform into the 1990s, sometimes confined to a wheelchair.

Peggy Lee's UK chart hits include: "Mr Wonderful" in 1957, ""Fever" in 1958 and "Till There Was You" in 1961.

John Lennon   The Beatles

John Lennon died aged forty whilst in New York, U.S.A. on the 8th of December 1980 after a crazed gunman named Mark Chapman shot him in the back four times while John and Yoko were returning to their New York apartment after being at the Record Plant. He was survived by his first wife, Cynthia and his then wife, Yoko and his sons, Sean and Julian and his stepdaughter, Kyoko.

John was rushed in a police cruiser to the emergency room of nearby Roosevelt Hospital, where he was pronounced DOA. Earlier that evening, John had willingly autographed a copy of his album "Double Fantasy" for his killer.

John's corpse was cremated at Ferncliff Cemetery in New York and Yoko scattered his ashes in Central Park, where the Strawberry Fields memorial was later created.

As a child, after passing his eleven-plus exam, John attended Quarry Bank School in Liverpool from September 1952 to 1957, and was described at the time as a happy-go-lucky, good-humoured, easy going, lively boy.

John failed all his GCE O-level examinations, but was accepted into the Liverpool College of Art, but only after his aunt and headmaster spoke up for him.

At age fifteen, John formed a skiffle group called the Quarrymen. John first met Paul McCartney at the Quarrymen's second performance, which was held at a garden fête after which he asked Paul to join his band. Paul recommended his friend George Harrison as the lead guitarist. In August 1960, the Beatles engaged for a forty-eight night residency in Hamburg, Germany and were seriously in need of a drummer and they asked Pete Best to join them. Later, however, Pete Best was replaced with drummer Ringo Starr which completed the four-piece line-up that would endure until the group's break-up in 1970. The band's first single, "Love Me Do", was released in October 1962 and reached number seventeen on the British charts and they recorded their debut album, 'Please Please Me' in February 1963 and achieved mainstream success.

After the Beatles' final concert on the 29th of August 1966, John filmed the anti-war black comedy "How I Won the War", his only appearance in a non-Beatles feature film, before rejoining his bandmates for an extended period of recording. In 1967 they released the number one single, "Strawberry Fields Forever" and their iconic album, Sgt. Pepper's Lonely Hearts Club Band.

In June 1967, the Beatles performed John's "All You Need Is Love" as Britain's contribution to the Our World satellite broadcast, before an international audience estimated at up to four hundred million people.

John married Yoko Ono on the 20th of March 1969 and soon released a series of 14 lithographs called "Bag One" depicting scenes from their honeymoon. John's creative focus continued to move beyond the Beatles, and between 1968 and 1969 he and Yoko recorded three albums of experimental music together: Unfinished Music No. 1: Two Virgins (known more for its cover than for its music), Unfinished Music No. 2: Life with the Lions and Wedding Album. In 1969, they formed the Plastic Ono Band, releasing Live Peace in Toronto 1969. Between 1969 and 1970, John released the singles "Give Peace a Chance", which was widely adopted as an anti-Vietnam War anthem, "Cold Turkey", which documented his withdrawal symptoms after he had became addicted to heroin, and "Instant Karma!".

John left the Beatles in September 1969, but agreed not to inform the media while the group renegotiated their recording contract.

Linda Lewis   Solo Artiste

Linda Lewis died of Natural Causes aged seventy-two at her home in Waltham Abbey on the 3rd of May 2023. She was survived by her husband, Neil and her son, Jesse.

Linda's parents were of British-Guyanese and Jamaican heritage and she was raised primarily by her mother, who was a jazz singer. Linda attended stage school and was regularly cast in non-speaking television and film roles such as A Taste of Honey in 1961 and she also appeared as a screaming fan in the first Beatles' film, A Hard Day's Night in 1964.

Linda signed with Polydor Records and in 1967 recorded the single "You Turned My Bitter into Sweet", which is now a collectable Northern Soul record. During 1967, Linda formed White Rabbit and she also recorded the album Ferris Wheel in 1970 and the single "Can't Stop Now". On 19th September 1970, Linda appeared at the first Glastonbury Festival. After a chance meeting with a Warner Bros. Records executive, Linda signed to the label's imprint Reprise and also worked as a session vocalist in this period.

Linda's first hit single "Rock-a-Doodle-Doo" reached number fifteen in the UK Singles Chart in the summer of 1973, and it was followed by the album Fathoms Deep. This album established her as one of Britain's most promising young female singer-songwriters and was critically acclaimed. Several appearances on the BBC TV show Top of the Pops raised her profile, and an extensive world tour with Cat Stevens followed. On her return to the studio, she signed to Arista Records and recorded what would become her breakthrough album "Not a Little Girl Anymore" in 1975.

On the 5th of July 1975, Linda opened the Knebworth Festival. Three more albums followed over the next few years. In 1986 and 1987, she recorded with her sisters Dee and Shirley as Lewis, then as Lewis Sisters.

During the next decade, Linda retreated from public life and moved to Los Angeles. Although, in 1984, she again appeared at the Glastonbury Festival, as well as recording for Electricity Records.

On the 3rd of February 2007, BBC Four featured performances by Linda in a sixty-minute recording of a Barbican show with the Soul Britannia All Stars.

Tony Lewis   **The Outfield**

Tony Lewis died aged sixty-two of unknown causes on the 19th of October 2020 at home near London, UK. He was survived by his wife, Carol.

Tony was born in the East End of London and grew up

in a tough, working-class neighbourhood where music served as a bright spot in his life, and his love for music began early. The radio was always on in Lewis' home, and his first influences were classics of the 1960s. He became a fan of the Beatles, T. Rex, David Bowie, the Rolling Stones, and various glam rock bands of the 1970's.

Tony became lead singer and the bass guitar player of The Outfield who toured extensively and the band released their second album called 'Bangin' in 1987 and a third album, Voices of Babylon, in 1989. Throughout the late 1980's the band continued to tour throughout the USA.

Gordon Lightfoot   Solo Artiste

Gordon Lightfoot died aged eighty-four of natural causes at Sunnybrook Health Sciences Centre in Toronto, Canada, on the 1st of May, 2023. He was survived by his wife, Kim, his sons, Fred, Gaylen, Miles and Eric, and his daughters Ingrid and Meredith.

Gordon was born in Canada in 1938 and was of Scottish descent. His mother recognized Gordon's musical talent early on and schooled him to become a successful child performer. At the age of twelve, after winning a competition, he made his first appearance at Massey Hall in Toronto, a venue he would ultimately play over 170 more times throughout his career.

As a teenager, Gordon learned piano and taught himself to play drums and percussion. He performed extensively throughout high school and taught himself to play folk guitar. He moved to Los Angeles in 1958 to study jazz composition and orchestration for two years at Westlake College of Music but he missed Toronto and returned there in 1960, living in Canada thereafter, though he did much work in the United States.

Gordon's UK chart hits include: "If You Could Read My Mind" in 1971, "Sundown" in 1974, "The Wreck of the Edmund FitzGerald"in 1977 and "Daylight Katy" in 1978.

Alan Longmuir died aged seventy on the 2nd of July 2018 at Forth Valley Royal Hospital in Larbert, Scotland. He was survived by his wife, Eileen and his son, Jordan and his sisters, Betty and Alice and his brother, Derek.

Being a member of a musical family, Alan formed his first band at the age of seventeen who changed their name and line-up to later become the Bay City Rollers. Until his career took off, Alan worked as a plumber.

In 1976, at the height of the band's popularity, Alan left and was replaced by rhythm guitarist Ian Mitchell. Alan, however, returned to the group in 1978 and thereafter switched between bass guitar, rhythm guitar and keyboards.

Bay City Rollers' UK chart hits include: "Keep On Dancing" in 1971, "Shang-A-Lang" in 1974, "Bye Bye Baby" in 1975, "Give A Little Love" in 1975 and "I Only Wanna Be With You" in 1976.

Lisa (Left Eye) Lopez   Solo Artiste

Lisa 'Left-Eye' Lopes died aged thirty on the 25th of April 2002 in La Celba, Honduras after she was caught up in a traffic collision. She was later interred at Hillandale Memorial Gardens, Lithonia, Georgia, U.S.A. Lisa was survived by her mother, Wanda.

By age ten Lisa had formed the musical trio The Lopes Kids with her siblings, with whom she sang gospel songs at local events and churches. She attended the Philadelphia High School for Girls.

At the age of nineteen, having heard of an open casting call for a new girl group through her then-boyfriend, Lisa moved to Atlanta to audition. Originally starting as a female trio called 2nd Nature, the group had been renamed TLC, derived from the first initials of its members at the time.

After the release of 'FanMail', Lisa began to expand her solo career. She became a featured rapper on several singles, including Spice Girl Melanie C's "Never Be the Same Again", which topped the charts in 35 countries, including the United Kingdom. She was also featured on "U Know What's Up", the first single from Donell Jones' second album, Where I Wanna Be, and she rapped a verse in "Space Cowboy" with NSYNC on their 2000 album, No Strings Attached.

Trini Lopez   Solo Artiste

Trini Lopez died aged eighty-three on the 11th of August, 2020, in Palm Springs, California, United States of America from some complications of COVID-19.

Trini formed formed a band in Wichita Falls, Texas, USA, when aged fifteen. In 1957 Trini and his group "The Big Beats" went to New Mexico and got a record contract with Columbia Records, which released two instrumental singles. Trini left the group and made his first solo recording, his own composition "The Right To Rock", for the Dallas-based Volk Records, and then signed with King Records in 1959, recording more than a dozen singles for that label.

Near the end of 1962, after the King contract had expired, Trini landed a steady engagement at a nightclub called PJ's, where his audience grew quite fast. He was heard there by Frank Sinatra, who had started his own label, Reprise Records, and who subsequently signed Trini to it.   .

Trini's debut live album, "Trini Lopez at PJ's" was released in 1963 and the album included a version of Pete Seeger's "If I Had a Hammer", which reached number one in thirty-six countries and it sold over one million copies to be awarded a gold disc. He also performed his own version of the traditional Mexican song "La Bamba" on the album and his recording of the tune was later reissued as a single in 1966.

Trini was still recording and appearing live in the years leading up to his death. He took part in a benefit concert to raise money for the victims of the 2004 Indian Ocean earthquake and tsunami and appeared as a guest performer in a number of shows held in Maastricht in the Netherlands with the Dutch violinist and composer André Rieu. He continued to record and 'El Inmortal' was released in 2010 plus in the following year he released his 65th album, "Into The Future".

John Lord   Deep Purple

Jon Lord died aged seventy-one from a pulmonary embolism on the 16th of July 2012 at a London clinic. He was survived by his second wife Vickie and his daughters Sara and Amy.

Jon's father was an amateur saxophonist and encouraged Jon in music from an early age. Jon studied classical piano from the age of five, with a local teacher and a focus on classical music gave a grounding to his work, in composition, arranging and instrumental solos on piano, organ and electronic keyboards.

Jon moved to London when twenty-six intending to pursue an acting career. He enrolled at the Central School of Speech and Drama. Minor acting jobs followed, however, he continued playing the piano and organ in nightclubs and did session musician work to earn a living. Jon began a career in bands in 1960 with the jazz ensemble 'The Bill Ashton Combo'.

In 1967 Jon met businessman Tony Edwards who was looking to invest in the music business. Session guitarist Ritchie Blackmore was called in and he met Jon for the first time. Tony was impressed enough by Jon to ask him to form a band.

Jon continued to focus on his classical aspirations alongside his Deep Purple rock career. The BBC, commissioned him to write a piece resulting in "Gemini Suite" being performed by Deep Purple and the Light Music Society under Malcolm Arnold at the Royal Festival Hall in September

1970. This piece became the basis for his first solo album called Gemini Suite and released in November nineteen 1972.

Jon Lord's first band line-up after Deep Purple was Paice Ashton Lord which lasted only one year but created one album called 'Malice in Wonderland'.

In July 2011, Jon performed his last live concert appearance, the Sunflower Jam at the Royal Albert Hall, where he premiered a joint composition with Rick Wakeman.

Jon Lord's Concerto for Group and Orchestra was recorded in Liverpool and at Abbey Road Studios, London throughout 2011.

Billy Lyall   Pilot

Billy Lyall died aged thirty-six on the 1st of December 1989 of AIDS-related causes.

Billy was singer, keyboard-player and flautist with Pilot. The 1974 Pilot single "Magic" was a Number Eleven UK hit and Number Five in America. It sold over one million copies, and was awarded a gold disc by the R.I.A.A.

The song "January" gave them their greatest success in the UK, securing the number one spot in the UK Singles Chart on 1st February 1975. It stayed at number one for three weeks and also went to number one in Australia where it stayed up top for eight weeks.

Phil Lynott   Thin Lizzy

Phil Lynott died aged thirty-six on the 4th of January 1986 in a hospital's intensive care unit from pneumonia, heart failure and septicaemia. He was survived by a wife, Caroline and daughters

Sarah and Cathleen. He was buried in St Fintan's Cemetery, Sutton, Dublin.

Towards the end of 1969, Phil Lynott with Brian Downey and Eric Bell. formed Thin Lizzy whose first top ten hit was in 1973, a rock version of the traditional Irish song "Whiskey in the Jar".

However, it was not until the recruitment of guitarists Scott Gorham and Brian Robertson, and the release of Jailbreak in 1976, that Thin Lizzy became international superstars on the strength of the album's biggest hit, "The Boys Are Back in Town". The song reached the top 10 in the UK, number one in Ireland and was a hit in the US and Canada.

In 1978, Phil Lynott had began to work on projects outside of Thin Lizzy. He was featured in Jeff Wayne's Musical Version of The War of the Worlds, singing and speaking the role of Parson Nathaniel on "The Spirit of Man". He performed sessions for a number of artists, including singing backing vocals with Bob Geldof.

In 1980, though Thin Lizzy were still enjoying considerable success, Phil Lynott launched a solo career with the album, Solo in Soho which was a Top 30 UK album and yielded two hit singles that year; these were: "Dear Miss Lonelyhearts" and "King's Call".

Phil Lynott's final single, "Nineteen", co-written by Laurence Archer and Phil Lynott was released a few weeks before his death

Kirsty MacColl   Solo Artiste

Kirsty MacColl died aged forty-one in a boating accident in Cozumel, Mexico on the 18th of December 2000. She was survived by her partner, James and her sons, Louis and Jamie.

Kirsty's corpse was repatriated to the United Kingdom, and was cremated after a humanist funeral at Mortlake Crematorium in South-West London.

Kirsty came to notice when Chiswick Records released an EP by local punk rock band the Drug Addix with Kirsty on backing vocals under the pseudonym, Mandy Doubt. Stiff Records executives were not impressed with the band, but liked Kirsty and subsequently signed her to a solo deal.

Her debut solo single "They Don't Know", released in 1979, peaked at number two on the Music Week airplay chart.

Kirsty moved to Polydor Records in 1981 and had a UK number fourteen hit with "There's a Guy Works Down the Chip Shop Swears He's Elvis", taken from her critically acclaimed debut album 'Desperate Character'. In 1983 she returned to Stiff Records, where a cover of Billy Bragg's "A New England" in 1985 got to number seven in the UK charts.

In the U.S.A. Kirsty was most known as the writer of "They Don't Know". Kirsty re-emerged in the British charts in December 1987, reaching Number two with The Pogues on "Fairytale of New York", a duet with Shane MacGowan. This led to her accompanying The Pogues on their British and European tour in 1988, an experience which she said helped her temporarily overcome her stage fright.

Ray Manzarek died aged seventy-four on the 20th of May 2013, at a hospital in Rosenheim, Germany from bile duct cancer. He was survived by his wife Dorothy, their son, Pablo, and his three grandchildren. For the last decade of his life, Ray and his wife had lived in a refurbished farmhouse near Vichy Springs, California in the Napa Valley, USA.

Ray, of Polish descent, took private piano lessons when growing up. In 1961, he enrolled at the University of California, Los Angeles School of Law. Unable to acclimate to the curriculum, he transferred to the Department of Motion Pictures, Television and Radio as a graduate student before dropping out altogether after breaking up with a girlfriend. Although he attempted to enlist in the Army Signal Corps as a camera operator on a drunken lark during a visit to New York City, he was instead assigned to the highly selective Army Security Agency as a prospective intelligence analyst in Okinawa and then Laos. While in the Army, Ray Manzarek played in various musical ensembles and first smoked and grew cannabis.

Following his return to the United States, Ray re-enrolled in UCLA's graduate film program in 1962, where he received a M.F.A. in cinematography in 1965. During this period, he met future wife Dorothy and undergraduate film student Jim Morrison. At the time, Ray was in a band called Rick & the Ravens with his brothers Rick and Jim. Forty days after finishing film school, thinking they had gone their separate ways, Ray and Jim Morrison met by chance on Venice Beach in Los Angeles. When Jim sang rough versions of songs he had written, Ray liked them and co-founded The Doors with Jim at that moment. During this period, Ray also met guitarist Robby Krieger and drummer John Densmore at a Transcendental Meditation lecture and recruited them for the incipient band.

The Doors lacked a bass guitarist, except during recording sessions, so at live performances Ray played the bass parts on a Fender Rhodes Piano Bass. His signature sound was that of the Vox Continental combo organ, an instrument used by many other psychedelic rock bands of the era.

In 2006, Ray collaborated with composer and trumpeter Bal. The album that resulted, Atonal Head, is an exploration in the realm of electronica. The two musicians integrated jazz, rock, ethnic and classical music into their computer-based creations.

In his last years Ray often sat in with local bands in the Napa County, California area, where he relocated in the early 2000s. In May 2010, he recorded with slide guitarist Roy Rogers an album called Translucent Blues and in February 2012, he recorded "Breakn' a Sweat" with DJ Skrillex and his fellow Doors members Robby Krieger and John Densmore.

Bob Marley   The Wailers

Bob Marley died aged thirty-six on the 11th of May 1981 at Cedars of Lebanon Hospital in Miami, Florida, U.S.A. due to the spread of melanoma to his lungs and brain. He was survived by his wife, Rita and his twelve offspring.

Bob Marley received a state funeral in Jamaica on 21st of May 1981, which combined elements of Ethiopian Orthodoxy and Rastafari tradition. He was buried in a chapel near his birthplace.

Bob's album 'Uprising' had been released in May 1980 and his band completed a major tour of Europe, where it played its biggest concert to 100,000 people in Milan. After the tour Bob went to America, where he performed two shows at Madison Square Garden in New York City as part of the Uprising Tour.

Bob's last concert occurred at the Stanley Theatre (now called The Benedum Center For The Performing Arts) in Pittsburgh, Pennsylvania, U.S.A. on the 23rd of September 1980.

The Wailers' first album for Island, 'Catch a Fire', was released worldwide in April nineteen-seventy-three, packaged like a rock record with a unique Zippo lighter lift-top. Initially selling 14,000 units, it didn't make Bob Marley a star, but received a positive critical reception. It was followed later that year by the album Burnin' which included the song "I Shot the Sheriff".

Bob had his international breakthrough with his first hit outside Jamaica, "No Woman, No Cry", from the Natty Dread album. This was followed by his breakthrough album in the United States, "Rastaman Vibration", which reached the Top 50 of the Billboard Soul Charts.

Bob Marley's UK chart hits include: "No Woman No Cry" in 1975, "Exodus" in 1977, "Jamming" in 1977, "Is This Love" in 1978, "Could You Be Loved" in 1980, "Buffalo Soldier" in 1983, "One Love" in 1984 and "Iron Lion Zion" in 1992.

Steve Marriott   The Small Faces

Steve Marriott died aged forty-four on the 20th of April 1991 in a house-fire in Essex, U.K. He was survived by his third wife Toni, his son, Toby and his daughters: Lesley, Tanya and Mollie Mae. The Small Faces song "All or Nothing" was played as the requiem at Steve Marriott's funeral held on the 30th of April 1991. Amongst the mourners, noted attendees included ex-Small Faces drummer Kenney Jones, as well as Peter Frampton, Joe Brown, PP Arnold, Terence Stamp, Jerry Shirley and Greg Ridley.

In 1959 at the age of twelve, Steve formed his first band with school friends which was called 'The Wheels', later the 'Coronation Kids', and finally 'Mississippi Five'. They would play the local coffee bars in East Ham and perform Saturday morning gigs at the Essoldo Cinema in Manor Park, London. Steve was a cheeky, hyperactive child, according to his mother Kay, and well known by his neighbours in Strone Road for playing pranks and practical jokes.

In 1961 Steve auditioned and was accepted as a student at the Italia Conti Academy of Theatre Arts in London. After his enrolment he quickly gained acting roles, working consistently in film, television and radio, often typecast as the energetic Cockney kid. Later Steve lost interest in acting and reversed his attention to his first love, music.

In July 1964, Steve first saw his future Small Faces partners, Ronnie Lane and 16-year-old drummer Kenney Jones performing at the Albion in Rainham, with their bands. Ronnie and Steve met again by chance in a music shop where Steve was working. Ronnie came in looking to buy a bass guitar, and afterwards was invited to Steve's home to listen to his extensive collection of American R&B records. With their shared love of Rythm & Blues they were soon firm friends. Steve was invited by Ronnie and Kenny Jones to perform at their band's regular gig in South London. They then decided to form their own group which was later joined by Ian McLagan on organ. The Small Faces were signed to Don Arden within six weeks of forming and quickly became a successful Mod band well regarded by the Mod followers when their debut single, "Whatcha Gonna Do About It" got into the UK singles chart.

Steve Marriott co-wrote most of Small Faces' hit singles and he wrote the rock-ballad "Tin Soldier" to woo model Jenny Rylance whom he eventually married.

Bernie Marsden   Whitesnake

Bernie Marsden died aged seventy-two of Bacterial Meningitis on the 24th of August 2023. He was survived by his wife, Frances and his daughters, Charlotte and Olivia.

After playing with local Buckingham based groups, including Clockwork Mousetrap, Bernie formed Skinny Cat at the age of seventeen. He got his first professional gig with UFO in 1972 and next played with Glenn Cornick's Wild Turkey in 1973, before joining drummer Cozy Powell's band, Hammer. He then joined Babe Ruth in 1975 and played on two albums; these were: Stealin' Home in 1975 and Kid's Stuff in 1976.

In 1978, Bernie formed a new band with former Deep Purple vocalist David Coverdale and guitarist Micky Moody. The band started as David Coverdale's Whitesnake, which then became Whitesnake. Bernie played on the first EP, first five albums and a live album: Snakebite, in 1978, Trouble in 1978, Lovehunter in 1979, Ready & Willing in 1980, Live In The Heart Of The City in 1980, Come An' Get It in 1981 and Saints & Sinners in 1982.

After his departure from Whitesnake, Gerry formed a short-lived band called Bernie Marsden's SOS and shortly after, he formed the band Alaska with Robert Hawthorne on vocals and Richard Bailey on keyboards. Alaska released two melodic rock albums in two years, Heart of the Storm in 1984 and The Pack in 1985 before breaking up. In 1986, Bernie put together MGM with former Whitesnake members Neil Murray and Mel Galley.

In 1989, Bernie reunited with Whitesnake guitarist Moody to form The Moody Marsden band, recording an acoustic live album in Norway called Live In Hell and an electric live album recorded in England called "Never Turn Our Back on the Blues" that featured Ringo Starr's son Zak Starkey on drums. Marsden & Moody toured throughout Europe and recorded one studio album called Real Faith in 1994. They later formed a new band called "The Snakes" with Norwegian vocalist Jørn Lande focused on only playing songs from their time in Whitesnake, releasing a studio abum called "Once Bitten" and a live record, Live in Europe, both in 1998.

Bernie released two solo albums during his time in Whitesnake. No more solo albums appeared until the release of his Green and Blues in 1994. Bernie played guitar with Elkie Brooks and a personal highlight of his long career was playing guitar in the Ringo Starr Band; with shows in Monaco and in the UK. In 2021, Bernie teamed up with Conquest Music to release his next solo album, "Kings", a tribute to the Blues giants, Albert King, Freddie King and BB King.

Gerry Marsden   The Pacemakers

Gerry Marsden died of a heart infection aged seventy-eight on the 3rd of January 2021 in a Merseyside hospital. He was survived by his wife, Pauline, and his two daughters, Yvette and Victoria.

Gerry and the Pacemakers formed in 1959 and they were the second group signed by manager Brian Epstein, the first being the Beatles. Gerry's first single was "How Do You Do It?" in 1963 which was a number one hit which was recorded at Abbey Road Studios and released on EMI's Columbia label.

Gerry and the Pacemakers second number one was "I Like It", followed by "You'll Never Walk Alone", both released later in 1963. The group's other singles included "It's Gonna Be Alright", "I'm the One", "Don't Let the Sun Catch You Crying", and "Ferry Cross the Mersey", all released in 1964.

Al Martino   Solo Artiste

Al Martino died aged eighty-two from a heart attack on the 13th of October 2009, in Springfield, Pennsylvania, U.S.A. He was survived by his wife, Judi and his daughters, Debbie, Alison and Alana and his son, Alfred.

While growing up, Al worked alongside his brothers, Pasquale and Frank as a bricklayer. He aspired to become a singer, emulating artists such as Al Jolson and Perry Como, and by the success of a family friend, Alfredo Cocozza, who had changed his name to Mario Lanza.

After serving with the United States Navy in World War II, during which he was part of, and injured in, the Iwo Jima invasion, Al began his singing career. Encouraged by

Mario Lanza, he adopted the stage name Al Martino and began singing in local nightclubs. In 1948, he moved to New York City, recorded some songs for the Jubilee label, and in 1952, won first place on a Talent Scouts television program with a performance of the hit song "If".

As a result, he won a recording contract with the Philadelphia-based independent record label BBS, where he recorded "Here in My Heart". The song spent three weeks at number one on the US pop charts in June 1952, earning Al Martino a gold disc, and later in the year it also reached the top of the UK charts, the first UK Singles chart, published by the New Musical Express on 14th November 1952.

His popularity allowed him to continue to perform and record successfully in the UK, headlining at the London Palladium and having six further British chart hits in the period up to 1955, including "Now" and "Wanted".

In 1963, he had his biggest U.S. chart success with "I Love You Because", a cover of Leon Payne's 1950 country music hit.

Al had four other U.S. top 10 hits in 1963 and 1964 - "Painted, Tainted Rose" , "I Love You More and More Every Day", "Tears and Roses", and "Silver Bells" . One of his biggest hits was "Spanish Eyes", achieving several gold and platinum discs for sales. Recorded in 1965, the song reached number five on the UK Singles chart when reissued in 1973.

Al played the role of Johnny Fontane in the 1972 film The Godfather, as well as singing the film's theme, "Speak Softly Love".

John Martyn   Solo Artiste

John Martyn died aged sixty of acute respiratory distress syndrome on the 29th of January 2009, in hospital in Thomastown, County Kilkenny, Ireland. He was survived by his partner, Teresa, and his son, Spencer and his daughter, Mhairi.

John began his professional musical career when he was seventeen, playing a fusion of blues and folk resulting in a distinctive style which made him a key figure in the British folk scene during the mid 1960s. He signed to Island Records in 1967 and released his first album, London Conversation, the following year, soon followed by 'The Tumbler'. By 1970 John had developed a wholly original and idiosyncratic sound, first apparent on 'Stormbringer!' in 1970.

In 1973, John released one of the defining British albums of the 1970s, 'Solid Air', the title song a tribute to deceased singer-songwriter Nick Drake.

John's marriage broke down at the end of the 1970s and out of this dark period came the album 'Grace and Danger' released in October 1980.

Barrie Masters   The Hot Rods

Barrie Masters died of a drug overdose, aged sixty-three, on the 2nd of October, 2019 in Essex, United kingdom. He was survived by a son and a daughter.

Barrie formed Eddie and the Hot Rods in Canvey Island, Essex, U.K. during 1975 with guitarist Dave Higgs, drummer Steve Nicol and bassist Rob Steele. In November 1975, after positive press reviews of their live shows, they were signed by Island Records. They first appeared in the UK Singles Chart in 1976 with their 'Live at the Marquee' EP and their single "Teenage Depression".

Their biggest hit came with the song "Do Anything You Wanna Do" in the summer of 1977, using their shorter, snappier name, The Rods. This single made the British Top 10 at number nine in August 1977 . They appeared at the Reading Festival held in August 1977 and also in that year, as the Hot Rods, they toured the United States with the Ramones and Talking Heads.

Phil May died aged seventy-five on the 15th of May 2020, in a hospital in King's Lynn, Norfolk, United Kingdom, from complications following hip surgery after a cycling accident. He was survived by his son, Paris and his daughter, Sorrel and by his partner Colin.

Phil formed the Pretty Things at Sidcup Art College in 1963 with guitarist Dick Taylor, who had recently left the fledgling Rolling Stones. With Phil May as lead singer, the band became part of the British blues rock scene and quickly gained a recording contract. They became popular and had hit singles including the UK Top Ten hit, "Don't Bring Me Down".

In the late 1960's, The Pretty Things started to branch out into psychedelia and Phil May became a prominent counterculture figure, known for his claim of having "the longest hair in Britain" - also for drug-taking and bisexuality. The Pretty Thing's 1968 album "S.F. Sorrow", often regarded as the first rock opera, had songs and lyrics based on stories written by Phil May, which were often written whilst the album was being recorded. Phil later admitted that his usage of LSD had a major impact on the album, saying that it was like a sharpening of the imagination for him and that he did not think S.F. Sorrow would have been possible without LSD.

The Pretty Things' UK chart hits include: "Don't Bring Me Down" in 1964, "Honey I Need" in 1965 and "Come See Me" in 1966.

John Mayhew   Genesis

John Mayhew died aged sixty-two on the 26th of March 2009 of a heart condition in Glasgow, Scotland. He was survived by his brother Paul.

John inherited his love of music from his mother, and played with bands in the Ipswich area, including 'The

Clique' and 'The Epics'. He moved to London in the late 1960's where he joined a band called 'Milton's Finger', and recorded a few songs.

John joined Genesis in the summer of 1969 to replace a departing drummer. John said in an interview that he was contacted by Mike Rutherford who had found his phone number. The band was impressed by John's long-haired appearance and skill and because he had brought his own drums with him. John stayed with Genesis until July 1970 after which he was replaced by Phil Collins.

In 1982, John moved to Australia, where he found work as a carpenter. In 1989, he briefly returned to England and in 2006, he attended a Genesis convention in London and played drums for a tribute band called ReGenesis.

Henry McCullough   The Grease Band, Wings

Henry McCullough died of a heart attack aged seventy-two on the 14th of June 2016, at his home at Ballywindelland, Ballymoney, Northern Ireland. He was survived by his wife Josie and son Jesse.

Henry first came to prominence in the early 1960s as the teenage lead guitarist with the Skyrockets, an Irish show-band from Enniskillen.

In 1967 Henry moved to Belfast where he joined bass guitar player Chris Stewart, vocalist Ernie Graham and drummer Dave Lutton to form a psychedelic rock band called the People. Later that year they all moved to London and were signed to Chas Chandler's management, who changed their name to Éire Apparent.

Henry returned to London in 1969 to work with Joe Cocker as a member of the Grease Band with whom he toured America, performing at the Woodstock Festival, and he later played on the Grease Band's eponymous album.

During his time with the Grease Band he appeared as lead guitarist on the studio album of Andrew Lloyd Webber and Tim Rice's rock opera Jesus Christ Superstar in 1970 and on the progressive Spooky Tooth album The Last Puff in 1970.

In January 1972 Paul McCartney asked Henry to join his then new band, Wings, with an eye toward starting a tour of British universities. Henry's first recording with Wings was the February 1972 protest single, "Give Ireland Back to the Irish". He spent more than a year in Wings, playing lead guitar on several singles, including "Hi, Hi, Hi", "Live and Let Die" and "My Love", as well as on the album Red Rose Speedway. However, Henry left Wings just before the Band on the Run sessions in August 1973.

In 1975 Henry joined the Frankie Miller Band with bassist Chris Stewart, keyboard player Mick Weaver and drummer Stu Perry and they recorded the album, The Rock with Miller. Later that year, Henry released a solo album called "Mind Your Own Business" on George Harrison's Dark Horse label.

Henry played concerts as a session musician with Roy Harper, Frankie Miller, Eric Burdon, Marianne Faithfull, Ronnie Lane and Donovan and in 1977 he temporarily joined Dr. Feelgood, following the departure of Wilko Johnson.

Jimmy McCulloch   Thunderclap Newman, Wings

Jimmy McCulloch died aged twenty-six on the 27th of September 1979. An autopsy found that he had died of heart failure due to morphine and alcohol poisoning. He was survived by his wife, Linda.

Jimmy got inspiration to play guitar from Django Reinhardt records and began to play at the age of eleven and he first rose to fame in 1969 when he joined the band Thunderclap Newman who had a UK Number One hit with "Something in the Air" that year.

In October 1971, Jimmy played guitar in concert with John Mayall's Bluesbreakers in England and Germany and also his band Bent Frame made its performance debut in London, subsequently renaming itself the Jimmy McCulloch Band. They toured England and Scotland in February 1972.

In June 1972, Jimmy joined the blues rock band 'Stone the Crows' to replace their guitarist who had been electrocuted on stage. However, Stone the Crows broke up in June 1973.

Jimmy joined Paul McCartney's Wings in August 1974 with his debut track with them being. "Junior's Farm". In September 1977, Jimmy left Wings to join the reformed Small Faces during the latter band's nine date tour of England that month. He played guitar on the Small Faces' album, '78 in the Shade'. In 1979, Jimmy joined another band called the Dukes and his last recorded song, "Heartbreaker", appeared on their only album, 'The Dukes'.

Ian McDonald   King Crimson, Foreigner

Ian McDonald died aged seventy-five from colon cancer on the 9th of February 2022 in New York City, USA. He was survived by his son, Ian and his ex-wife, Laura.

Ian grew up in a musical family, regularly listening to records, and taught himself the guitar. His music interests ranged from classical orchestra to dance bands to rock. At ge fifteen he left school and began a five-year stint in the British Army as a bandsman. In 1963 he enrolled at the Royal Military School of Music, where he took clarinet and learned to read music. Ian later learned piano, flute and saxophone and taught himself music theory. His experience of playing with army bands gave him great musical adaptability as he had to learn many different musical styles such as show tunes, classical, jazz, and military marches.

After leaving the army, Ian moved back to London and was introduced to Robert Fripp and Michael Giles which led to the formation of King Crimson.

Three months after their first gig, they supported the Rolling Stones at a free concert in Hyde Park to great applause. Ian's saxophone solo was a high point on their track "21st Century Schizoid Man", and he went on to play this on their first album In the Court of the Crimson King. He also played harpsichord, piano, organ, clarinet, zither, flute, and Mellotron, which he used extensively on the album.

Ian and the drummer left the King Crimson due to growing friction. They formed a duo that released one album entitled McDonald and Giles. Ian moved to New York City in the mid 1970's and became a founding member of the band Foreigner in 1976. For them he played guitar as well as his woodwinds and keyboards and he helped record three albums which made Foreigner a big success.

In 1996, Ian toured with former Genesis guitarist Steve Hackett. He also contributed saxophone and flute to several tracks on Judy Dyble's 2009 release "Talking With Strangers".

Ted McKenna   Sensational Alex Harvey Band

Ted McKenna died aged sixty eight on the 19th of January 2019, of a haemorrhage during a routine operation for a hernia. He was survived by his son, Casey and his daughter, Laura.

Ted was the drummer of The Sensational Alex Harvey Band from 1972 to 1978, and then worked with artists including Rory Gallagher, 1978–1981; Greg Lake & Gary Moore in The Greg Lake Band, 1981–83; the Michael Schenker Group (MSG), 1981–84; Bugatti & Musker, 1982; Ian Gillan; and worked on a solo album for Nazareth singer Dan McCafferty in 1975.

Ted had his own band called Ted McKenna's Gold; formed at the end of 1986. In 1992, Ted and Zal Cleminson formed The Party Boys, an idea Ted had in Australia whilst working with Womack and Womack. They recruited keyboardist Ronnie Leahy from Stone The Crows, and invited well-known rock singers including Stevie Doherty, Fish, and Dan McCafferty.

In 2004, Ted reformed Sensational Alex Harvey Band with remaining members Zal Cleminson, Hugh McKenna, and Chris Glen, but this time introduced vocalist Max Maxwell, formerly of The Shamen. Around this time they released the live album Zalvation, which was the band's first official release since Rock Drill in 1977.

Although primarily known as a rock musician, Ted worked with jazz guitarist John Etheridge, Juno Award-winning American/Canadian blues guitarist Amos Garrett, American soul duo, Womack & Womack, Paul Rose, Gwyn Ashton, The Rhumboogie Orchestra, Frank O'Hagan, and Fish. He toured with Rory Gallagher bassist Gerry McAvoy and Dutch guitar virtuoso Marcel Scherpenzeel in "Band of Friends".

Scott McKenzie   **Solo Artiste**

Scott McKenzie died aged seventy-three on the 18th of August 2012 in Los Angeles, California, U.S.A. after suffering from Guillain–Barré syndrome from 2010. He was survived by two ex-wives, Anzy and Alana.

Scott grew up in North Carolina and Virginia, where he became friends with the son of one of his mother's friends, John Phillips. In the mid-1950s, he sang briefly with Tim Rose in a high school group called The Singing Strings, and later with John Phillips, Mike Boran, and Bill Cleary formed a doo wop band called, The Abstracts.

In 1961 John Phillips and Scott McKenzie met Dick Weissman and formed the folk group, The Journeymen and they recorded three albums and seven singles for Capitol Records.

Scott once declined an opportunity to join the Mamas & the Papas. John Phillips wrote and co-produced "San Francisco (Be Sure to Wear Flowers in Your Hair)" for

Scott and played guitar on the recording . It was released in May 1967 in the United States and was an instant hit, reaching number one in the UK, number four on the Billboard Hot 100 and number two in the Canadian RPM Magazine charts and sold over seven million copies globally.

Ron McKernan   The Grateful Dead

Ron "Pigpen" McKernan died aged twenty-seven on the 8th of March 1973, of gastro-intestinal hemorrhage at his home in Corte Madera, California, U.S.A. He was survived by his wife, Donna.

Ron grew up with African American friends and enjoyed black music and culture. As a youth, he taught himself blues piano, guitar and harmonica and developed a biker culture image. Ron moved to Palo Alto, California, with his family, where he became friends with musician Jerry Garcia at the age of fourteen.

Ron began spending time around coffeehouses and music stores, and worked at Dana Morgan's Music Store in Palo Alto with Jerry. who, one night invited him on stage to play harmonica and sing the blues. Jerry Garcia was impressed and Ron became the blues singer in local jam sessions. He was initially nicknamed "Blue Ron" before settling on "Pigpen". While a member of the Grateful Dead, Ron sang and played blues-influenced organ and harmonica.

In the early years of the Grateful Dead, Ron McKernan was easily recognisable by his biker image, making him a minor celebrity. In 1969, the band's record company, Warner Bros., ran a "Pigpen Look-Alike Contest".

Ian McLagan   The Small Faces

Ian McLagan died aged sixty-nine from a stroke on the 3rd of December 2014 at University Medical Center Brackenridge in Austin, Texas. U.S.A. He was survived by his ex-wife, Sandy and his son Lee.

Ian first started playing in bands in the early 1960s, initially using the Hohner Cembalet before switching to the Hammond Organ and Wurlitzer electric piano, as well as occasional guitar. In 1965 he was hired to join The Small Faces and played his debut gig with them at London's Lyceum Theatre on the 2nd of November that year.

After the Faces split up in 1975, Ian worked as a sideman for the Rolling Stones, both in the studio and on tour and on various Ronnie Wood projects. In addition, his session work has backed artists including Jackson Browne, Joe Cocker, Bob Dylan, Melissa Etheridge, Bonnie Raitt, Paul Westerberg, Izzy Stradlin, John Hiatt, Frank Black, Nikki Sudden, John Mayer, Bruce Springsteen, Tony Scalzo, Carla Olson and Mick Taylor.

Christine McVie   Fleetwood Mac

Christine McVie died of a stroke and cancer, aged seventy-nine, on the 13th of November 2022.

Christine was introduced to the piano when she was four years old, but did not study music seriously until the age of eleven. She continued classical training to the age of fifteen, but shifted her musical focus to rock and roll when her brother acquired a Fats Domino songbook. Other early influences included the Everly Brothers.

Christine studied sculpture at Moseley School of Art in Birmingham, UK for five years with the aim of becoming an art teacher. While at art school, she met budding musicians in Britain's blues scene. Her introduction to performing music came when she met guitarist Stan Webb and bass player Andy Silvester, who were in a band called Sounds of Blue. Knowing that Christine had musical talent, they invited her to join them.

In 1967, then performing under the name Christine Perfect, Christine heard that Silvester and Webb were forming a blues band, to be called Chicken Shack, and were looking for a pianist. She contacted them and was invited to join them as pianist, keyboard player and backing vocalist. Chicken Shack's debut release was "It's Okay with Me Baby", which was written by and featured Christine. Chicken Shack also had a hit with a cover of Ellington Jordan's "I'd Rather Go Blind", which featured Christine on lead vocals. Christine received a Melody Maker award for UK's best female vocalist in 1969 and another in 1970. She left Chicken Shack in 1969, having married Fleetwood Mac bassist John McVie a year earlier, feeling that she would not see her husband if they were in different bands.

Christine was a fan of Fleetwood Mac, and while she was touring with Chicken Shack the two bands would often meet. Both bands were signed to the Blue Horizon label, and Christine played piano as a session musician on Peter Green's songs on Fleetwood Mac's second studio album, Mr. Wonderful. She was invited to join Fleetwood Mac as a keyboard player in 1970 after the departure of founding member Peter Green.

Christine became an integral member of Fleetwood Mac as keyboard player, songwriter and female lead vocalist. The first studio album on which she played as a full band member was Future Games in 1971.

Christine moved with the rest of Fleetwood Mac to California in 1974, where Bob Welch left and Stevie Nicks and Lindsey Buckingham joined.

In 1976, Christine began an on-the-road affair with the band's lighting director which inspired her to write "You Make Loving Fun", a top-10 hit from their next album, Rumours, one of the best-selling albums of all time.

Tony McPhee   **The Groundhogs**

Tony McPhee died aged seventy-nine on the 6th of June 2023 from complications from a fall he had the previous year. He was survived by his ex-wives, Christine and Susan, and by his sons, Conan and Vincent and his sister, Olive.

Tony was a guitarist and singer and was the founder of the British blues and rock band the Groundhogs. He was given the name "T.S." — standing for "Tough Shit" in 1966.

The Groundhogs backed Champion Jack Dupree and John Lee Hooker on UK concerts in the mid-1960s. The band evolved into a blues-rock trio that produced three UK Top 10 albums in the UK in the early 1970s. Although they have continued to play in various line-ups to the present, Tony officially retired from the band in 2015.

Clyde McPhatter   The Drifters

Clyde McPhatter died aged thirty-nine of the complications of heart, liver, and kidney disease on the 13th of June 1972 in The Bronx, New York, U.S.A. He was survived by his widow, Lena and his son Patrick.

Starting at the age of five, Clyde sang in his father's church gospel choir along with his three brothers and three sisters and when he was ten, he was the soprano-voiced soloist for the choir.

In 1945 the family relocated to New York City, where Clyde formed a gospel group, the Mount Lebanon Singers.

In 1950, after winning the coveted Amateur Night at Harlem's Apollo Theater contest, Clyde returned to his job as a store manager but was later recruited by Billy Ward and his Dominoes and was present for the recording of "Sixty Minute Man" for Federal Records.

Clyde was then signed to Atlantic on the condition that he form his own group and he promptly assembled a group and called them the Drifters. They recorded a few tracks in June 1953, including a song called "Lucille," written by Clyde himself. This group, however, did not have the sound Atlantic executives were looking for and Clyde was prompted to assemble another group of singers. His revised lineup recorded and released hits including "Money Honey," "Such a Night," "Honey Love," "White Christmas" and "Whatcha Gonna Do," with the record label displaying the group name as "Clyde McPhatter & the Drifters".

Clyde's 1956 recording "Treasure of Love" was his first number one hit on the Rythm&Blues charts as a solo artist and spent one week in the UK Singles Chart. It reached number sixteen on the U.S. pop charts, sold over two million copies in the United States alone, and was awarded a gold disc by the RIAA.

Tony Meehan   The Shadows

Tony Meehan died aged sixty-two on the 28th of November 2005 at St Mary's Hospital, Paddington, London, U.K. as a result of head injuries, following a fall down the main staircase at his flat in Maida Vale, West London. He was survived by his wife, Sue and five sons and two daughters.

As the drummer with the Shadows, Tony helped to lay the foundations for British rock'n'roll, both backing Cliff Richard and on a long string of instrumental hits recorded under the group's own name. As the first backing band to emerge as stars in their own right, they were early trail-blazers for the beat-group boom that eclipsed them.

Tony left the Shadows in October 1961 to work as an arranger/producer and session drummer for Joe Meek and from early 1962. He teamed again with Jet Harris and as a duo had success with the instrumental "Diamonds" which also included Jimmy Page on acoustic rhythm guitar. "Diamonds" was a number one hit in the UK. Harris and Tony Meehan had two further hit singles together – "Scarlett O'Hara" and "Applejack".

Tony Meehan quit the music industry in the 1990s for a major career change as a psychologist, as a result of his lifelong hobby and interest. He worked in London at a local college lecturing in psychology until his death.

Randy Meisner died aged seventy-seven due to com-plications associated with chronic obstructive pulmonary disease (COPD) in Los Angeles, USA on the 26th of July 2023. He was survived by his son, Eric and his daughters, Dana and Heather.

Randy played bass and sang with a local band named The Dynamics from 1961 to 1965. Their first paying job was in the dance hall in Torrington, Wyoming, in 1961.

In August 1965, The Dynamics signed a record deal with Sully Records of Amarillo, Texas. They recorded three songs, with Randy singing lead on two: "One Of These Days" and "So Fine".

In the summer of 1967, The Poor was booked for two weeks at the Salvation Club in New York City, opening for The Jimi Hendrix Experience. Rev-Ola released a CD of The Poor's music in 2003, which included one song written by Randy, "Come Back Baby".

In May 1968, after auditioning, Randy joined Poco and appeared on the group's first album, Pickin' Up the Pieces.

In September 1971, Randy, with Don Henley, Glenn Frey, and Bernie Leadon, formed the Eagles and they released their eponymous debut album in 1972. While he usually played the bass and sang backing vocals for the Eagles, he wrote, co-wrote, and/or sang lead on songs on each of the group's first five albums, most notably "Take It to the Limit", the band's first million-selling single, and the third song released from One of These Nights. Other songs he wrote and sang lead on include "Try and Love Again," "Is it True?," "Take the Devil," and "Tryin'." He also wrote "Certain Kind of Fool" with Frey and Henley and sang lead.

During the 1976/1977 tour in support of the album Hotel California, Randy suffered from ill health and exhaustion while the band toured frequently for over eleven months.

Randy decided to leave the Eagles after the final date of the tour and returned to Nebraska to be with his family. His last performance was in East Troy, Wisconsin, on the 3rd of September 1977.

Following his departure from the Eagles, Randy went on to release solo albums in 1978 and 1980. Throughout the early 1980s, he toured with his band, Meisner & the Silverados. In 1985, Randy became part of an all-star band, Black Tie, whose cover of Buddy Holly's "Learning the Game" became a hit on U.S. country radio. They released one album together in 1990. From 1987 to 1989, Randy formed a band and toured with former Firefall singer-songwriter Rick Roberts, called the Roberts-Meisner Band.

Randy reunited with the Drivin' Dynamics for a performance in 2000, when the band and Randy as a solo performer was inducted into the Nebraska Music Hall of Fame. In the 2000s he performed as a part of the World Classic Rockers touring group. After suffering severe chest pains and being hospitalized in August 2004, Randy cut back on his touring schedule. His last known public performance was in 2008 in Naples, Florida.

Harold Melvin   The Blue Notes

Harold Melvin died aged fifty-seven on the 24th of March 1997 of a stroke whilst in Philadelphia, Pennsylvania, U.S.A. He was survived by his wife Ovelia and five children.

The young Harold sang doo-wop on street corners with his childhood friends. They took up the name Harold Melvin & the Blue Notes and released the "If You Love Me" single on the local Josie label in 1956. The group played the local club scene, recording intermittently for small labels. The Blue Notes constantly changed line-up but were very much Harold's group, though he didn't always appear on stage with them. Rather, he choreographed their routines as well as arranging and composing some of ·

their material, though they mostly sung standards and show tunes when performing in supper clubs.

By 1970, Harold Melvin was the only original member left, and Teddy Pendergrass, who had joined from the Cadillacs, had stepped

out from behind the drumkit to take up lead vocals in a line-up which also comprised Lloyd Parkes, Lawrence Brown and Bernard Wilson. Harold Melvin & the Blue Notes joined a roster which would soon include the O'Jays, Billy Paul and the Three Degrees and take over from Tamla Motown as the sound of mid-Seventies America.

Harold Melvin's UK chart hits include: "If You Don't Know Me By Now" in 1973, "The Love I Lost" in 1974 and "Don't Leave Me This Way" in 1977. .

Freddie Mercury   Queen

Freddie Mercury died aged forty-five on the 24th of November 1991 at his home in Kensington, London, U.K. just over twenty-four hours after issuing a statement that he had AIDs. The official cause of death was bronchial pneumonia resulting from AIDS.

Freddie Mercury was born in Zanzibar, East Africa. His parents were Parsis from the Gujarat region of the province of Bombay in India. The family surname is derived from the town of Bulsar (now known as Valsad) in southern Gujarat. As Parsis, Freddie Mercury and his family practised the Zoroastrian religion. The Bulsara family had moved to Zanzibar so that Freddie's father could continue his job as a cashier at the British Colonial Office. Freddie had a younger sister, Kashmira.

Freddie Mercury spent most of his childhood in India and began taking piano lessons at the age of seven. In 1954, at the age of eight, Freddie Mercury was sent to study at St. Peter's School, a British-style boarding school for boys, in Panchgani near Mumbai). At the age of twelve he formed a school band, The Hectics, and covered rock and roll artists such as Cliff Richard and Little Richard. It has been said that one of his formative musical influences at the time was Bollywood singer Lata Mangeshkar.

At the age of seventeen, Freddie and his family fled from Zanzibar for safety reasons due to the 1964 Zanzibar Revolution. The family moved into a small house in Feltham, Middlesex, UK. Freddie enrolled at Isleworth Polytechnic in West London where he studied art. He ultimately earned a diploma in Art and Graphic Design at Ealing Art College. A British citizen at birth, Freddie remained so for the rest of his life.

Following graduation, Freddie joined a series of bands and sold second-hand clothes in the Kensington Market in London.

In April 1970 Freddie joined guitarist Brian May and drummer Roger Taylor who had previously been in a band called Smile. In 1971 they found their bass player John Deacon who was to stay with the band until 1997. Despite reservations of the other members and Trident Studios, the band's initial management, Freddie chose the name "Queen" for the new band. At about the same time, he changed his family surname, Bulsara, to Mercury. Freddie designed Queen's logo.

Although Freddie's speaking voice naturally fell in the baritone range, he delivered most songs in the tenor range. His known vocal range extended from bass low F to soprano high F.

A research team undertook a study in 2016 to understand the appeal behind Mercury's voice. Led by Professor Christian Herbst, the team noted his notably faster vibrato and use of subharmonics, particularly in comparison to opera singers. The research team studied vocal samples from 23 commercially available Queen recordings, his solo work, and a series of interviews of the late artist.

Over the course of his career, Freddie Mercury performed an estimated seven hundred concerts in countries around the world with Queen.

Alan Merrill Merrill died aged sixty-nine in Manhattan, New York, USA on the 20th of March 2020 from complications arising from COVID-19.

In 1969, Alan auditioned for the New York City band, the Left Banke. The audition was successful, but the band dissolved. Shortly thereafter, he left to reside in Japan, where his mother was living, and began his professional career there by joining the band The Lead, who were contracted to RCA Victor Records. The Lead had some chart success, but the project soon fell apart when two of the American members of the group were deported.

Merrill subsequently signed a solo management deal with Watanabe Productions, who contracted him to Atlantic Records, and changed his professional surname from Sachs (pronounced sax) to Merrill, apparently because "Merrill" sounded less lascivious and was more commercially viable when spoken by young Japanese pop music fans. He recorded one album with Atlantic, Alone in Tokyo (February 1971) which yielded a single, "Namida" (Teardrops).

In 1974, in London, Alan formed the band Arrows (as lead singer and bass guitarist), with drummer Paul Varley and guitarist Jake Hooker and they signed with Mickie Most's RAK Records. In March 1974, the Arrows were in the top 10 in the UK charts with the song "Touch Too Much". The Arrows became a popular band with teens.

The Arrows had another hit single with "My Last Night With You" which reached the UK top 30 in 1975.

With the Arrows, Alan sang three chart hit records as the band's lead singer, all produced by Mickie Most, "Touch Too Much" , "Toughen Up" and "My Last Night With You". They made one more single that would be an important one. "I Love Rock 'n' Roll" in 1975 whch was composed by Alan but with a co-writer credit going to Arrows bandmate Jake Hooker.

The recording was later flipped to A-side status, and the band made one television performance with the song. The show's producer Muriel Young was so impressed with the Arrows that she made a pitch to Granada ITV for them to have their own television series. The Arrows then got their own weekly TV series Arrows in 1976, taking over from the Bay City Rollers Granada TV series

Shang-a-Lang. The Arrows signed with MAM Management.

In 1983, Alan recorded a solo album for Polydor Records, simply entitled Alan Merrill, a collection of self-composed tracks. Some friends contributing to this record were Steve Winwood, Mick Taylor and Dallas Taylor. It was released in 1985 and received critical acclaim.

The Arrows 1974 top 10 UK hit "Touch Too Much", featuring lead vocals by Alan appears on the soundtrack of the feature film The Look Of Love. The Arrows' songs "We Can Make It Together" and "Moving Next Door To You" (composed by Alan Merrill and Jake Hooker) were used on the BBC1 TV show Homes Under The Hammer.

George Michael   Wham

George Michael died aged fifty-three on the 25th of December 2016, at his home in Goring-on-Thames, near London, U.K. A senior coroner in Oxfordshire attributed the death to natural causes as the result of a dilated cardiomyopathy with myocarditis and a fatty liver. George was born in London, UK and at school he befriended his future Wham! partner Andrew Ridgeley. The two had the same career ambition of being musicians. George formed the duo Wham! with Andrew in 1981. Their first album 'Fantastic' reached number one in the UK in 1983 and produced a series of top ten singles including "Young Guns", "Wham Rap!" and "Club Tropicana". Their second album, 'Make It Big', reached number one on the charts in the US. Singles from that album included "Wake Me Up Before You Go-

Go", "Freedom", "Everything She Wants", and "Careless Whisper" which reached number one in nearly 25 countries, including the UK and US, and was George's first solo effort as a single.

The beginning of George's solo career, during early 1987, was a duet with Aretha Franklin. The recording of "I Knew You Were Waiting" was a one-off project that helped George Michael achieve an ambition by singing with one of his favourite artists. It scored number one on both the UK Singles Chart and the US Billboard Hot 100 upon its release. For George Michael, it became his third consecutive solo number one in the UK from three releases, after 1984's "Careless Whisper" and 1986's "A Different Corner".

In late 1987, George Michael released his debut solo album, 'Faith'. The first single released from the album was "I Want Your Sex", in mid-1987. The song was banned by many radio stations in the UK and US, due to its sexually suggestive lyrics.

Sales of Faith are more than 25 million units and the album was highly acclaimed by music critics.

In 1996, George Michael was voted Best British Male, at the MTV Europe Music Awards and the Brit Awards; and at the British Academy's Ivor Novello Awards, he was awarded the title of 'Songwriter of The Year' for the third time. George Michael performed a concert at Three Mills Studios, London, for MTV Unplugged.

'Ladies & Gentlemen:The Best of George Michael' was George Michael's first solo greatest hits collection released in 1998.

'Ladies & Gentlemen' was a success, peaking at number one on the UK Albums Chart for eight weeks. It has spent over two hundred weeks in the UK Charts, and is the thirty-eighth best-selling album of all time in the UK.

'Twenty Five' was George Michael's second greatest hits album, celebrating the 25th anniversary of his music career. Released in November 2006 by Sony BMG, it debuted at number-one in the UK. The album contains songs chiefly from George Michael's solo career but also from his earlier days in Wham.

In October 2011, George Michael was announced as one of the final nominees for the Songwriter's Hall of Fame. In November, he had to cancel the remainder of the tour as he became severely ill with pneumonia in Vienna, Austria.

In February 2012, two months after leaving hospital, George Michael made a surprise appearance at the 2012 Brit Awards at London's O2 Arena, where he received a standing ovation, and presented Adele the award for Best British Album.

Roger Miller   Solo Artiste

Roger Miller died aged fifty-six of lung and throat cancer on the 25th of October 1992. He was survived by his wife, Mary, his son, Dean and daughter Shannon Elizabeth.

Roger listened to the Grand Ole Opry on a Fort Worth station when growing up. At seventeen, he stole a guitar out of desperation to write songs; however, he turned himself in the next day and he chose to enlist in the United States Army to avoid jail.

On leaving the Army, Roger travelled to Nashville to begin his musical career. He met with Chet Atkins, who asked to hear him sing, loaning him a guitar since Roger Miller did not own one. Roger Miller found work as a bellhop at Nashville's Andrew Jackson Hotel, and he was soon known as the "singing bellhop." He was finally hired by Minnie Pearl to play the fiddle in her band. He then met George Jones, who introduced him to music executives from the Starday Records label who scheduled an audition. Impressed, the executives set up a recording session with Jones in Houston. Jones and Roger Miller collaborated to write "Tall, Tall Trees" and "Happy Child."

Roger became a member of his Cherokee Cowboys and returned to Nashville and wrote "Invitation to the Blues," which was covered by Rex Allen and later by Ray Price, whose recording was a number three hit on country charts. Roger then signed with Tree Publishing on a salary of fifty dollars per week.

Roger signed a recording deal with Decca Records in 1958. He was paired with singer Donny Lytle, who later gained fame under the name Johnny Paycheck, to perform the Roger Miller-written song "A Man Like Me," and later "The Wrong Kind of Girl."

Mitch Mitchell   **The Jimi Hendrix Experience**

Mitch Mitchell died aged sixty-one of Natural Causes on the 12th of November 2008 in a hotel room in Portland, Oregon, U.S.A. He was survived by his wife, Dee, a daughter and two grandchildren.

Mitch had became a musician through working at a drum shop on Saturdays while still at school. One of his first bands was the Soul Messengers. Early in his career, he gained considerable musical experience as a touring and session musician and In 1965, he temporarily was the drummer in the Pretty Things.

From December 1965 until October 1966, Mitch was the drummer of Georgie Fame and the Blue Flames, appearing on their 1966 album, Sweet Things.

Mitch auditioned for Jimi Hendrix's band in October 1966, edging out drummer Aynsley Dunbar on the flip of a coin. Mitch's fast, driving, jazz influenced playing meshed well with Hendrix's open-ended, revolutionary approach to the electric guitar.

Mitch came from a jazz background, and like many of his contemporaries in the London scene, was influenced by Elvin Jones, Max Roach, and Joe Morello. He played in Jimi Hendrix's Experience

from October 1966 up until mid-1969.

After Jimi Hendrix's death, Mitch finished production work with engineer Eddie Kramer on incomplete Jimi

Hendrix recordings, resulting in the album releases "The Cry of Love" and "Rainbow Bridge".

Francis Monkman   Curved Air, Sky

Francis Monkman died aged seventy-three from cancer on the 12th of May 2023. He was survived by his partner, Christine.

Francis was a pupil at Westminster School where he studied organ and harpsichord, later studying at the Royal Academy of Music, winning the Raymond Russell prize for virtuosity on the harpsichord and becoming a member of the Academy of St. Martin in the Fields.

Wanting to experiment with more spontaneous music forms, Francis learned how to play guitar and began to associate himself with rock music. In the late 1960s he founded the rock band Sisyphus, which evolved into the pioneering band Curved Air. He played on their first three albums, doubling on keyboards and guitar and exploring his interest in jamming, overtones, natural harmonies and freer aspects of musicality. With group violinist Darryl Way, Monkman also contributed the bulk of the band's composing, although he and Way rarely collaborated. Differences of opinion with Way ultimately led to Monkman's departure from the band following the release of Phantasmagoria in 1972.

After leaving Curved Air, Monkman contributed to the Renaissance album Prologue in 1972, worked with Al Stewart including contributing to the album Past, Present and Future in 1973 as well as Lynsey de Paul on her Surprise album and toured with The Shadows on their 20 Golden Greats Tour in 1977.

In 1978, Francis became a member of classical/rock music fusion band Sky alongside guitarists John Williams and Kevin Peek, bass player Herbie Flowers and drummer /percussionist Tristan Fry. His keyboard work with Sky included extensive classical or classically-inspired harpsichord playing (highlighted on the band's electric version of Bach's "Toccata", which reached number five in the UK Singles Chart, and secured Sky a Top of the Pops appearance. For their debut album, he wrote the non-hit single "Cannonball" and the twenty-minute long second-side composition "Where Opposites Meet".

During his time with Sky, Francis had continued to release solo recordings which mingled original composition with film and television soundtracks and library music. His 1978 album Energism included the electronic "Achievements of Man", from which extracts were used as the theme to the BBC programme Think Again. He also composed the piece "Current Affairs", used by Channel 4 as the introduction to Engineering Announcements, provided by the IBA. He would also become known as a synthesizer demonstrator on programs such as the BBC's Tomorrow's World.

In 1980, Francis 's soundtrack to the British film The Long Good Friday was so successful that he opted to amicably leave Sky in order to concentrate on television and soundtrack work.

In 1981, Francis released a rock album called Dweller on the Threshold. This was the first album on which he had sung lead vocals.

After a twenty year break, Francis started to release further albums.

Francis played guitar as well as keyboards in Curved Air, switching between them when playing live. According to the sleeve notes for the second Sky album, Sky 2 he also played additional guitar parts on his composition "FIFO", alongside John Williams and Kevin Peek.

Keith Moon   The Who

Keith Moon died aged thirty-two, of drug overdose on the 7th of September 1978 and was found dead in bed at his flat in London. He was survived by his wife, Kim and a daughter, Amanda.

Keith joined his local Sea Cadet Corps band at the age of twelve on the bugle, but found the instrument too difficult to learn and decided to take up drums instead. He was also interested in practical jokes and home science kits, with a particular fondness for explosions.

In December nineteen-sixty-two he joined the Beachcombers, a semi-professional London cover band playing hits by groups including the Shadows. During his time in the group Keith Moon incorporated theatrical tricks into his act, including "shooting" the group's lead singer with a starter pistol. The Beachcombers all had day jobs but Keith, who worked in the sales department at British Gypsum, had the keenest interest in turning professional. In April 1964, at age seventeen, he auditioned for the Who.

Keith Moon's style of drumming was considered unique by his bandmates, although they sometimes found his unconventional playing frustrating; Jon Entwistle noted that he tended to play faster or slower according to his mood and wouldn't play across his kit. He later added that he'd play zig-zag and that was why he had two sets of tom-toms. Roger Daltrey has said that Keith Moon just instinctively put drum rolls in places that other people would never have thought of putting them.

Keith played a four, then a five-piece drum kit during his early career. His nineteen-sixty-five set consisted of Ludwig drums and Zildjian cymbals. By nineteen-sixty-six, feeling limited by this setup and inspired by Ginger Baker's double bass drum, he switched to a larger Premier kit. This setup did not have a hi-hat, since Keith Moon used crash and ride cymbals instead. He remained a loyal customer of Premier.

Keith led a destructive lifestyle. During the Who's early days he began taking amphetamines, and in a New Musical Express interview said his favourite food was "French Blues." He spent his share of the band's income quickly, and was a regular at London clubs such as the Speakeasy and the Bag O' Nails; the combination of pills and alcohol escalating into alcoholism and drug addiction later in his life.

Johnny Moore   The Drifters

Johnny Moore died aged sixty-four from pneumonia on the 13th of December, 1998 in London, United Kingdom. He was survived by his wife Jennifer, and their three sons.

Born John Darrel Moore in 1934 in Selma, Alabama, United States of America, Johnny Moore began as lead of the Cleveland based group the Hornets, before being discovered by the Drifters whom he joined aged twenty-one as lead vocalist in New York in 1955.

Johnny was drafted into the US Army for national service and upon returning he recorded as a soloist under the name "Johnny Darrow". He then rejoined the Drifters, then with four new members, and became the lead singer in 1964, after the death of Rudy Lewis, who was due to record "Under the Boardwalk" the next day, and Johnny Moore then did instead. Subsequently, he became permanent lead and had a string of hits with the Drifters in the 1960s, most notably "Saturday Night At The Movies", "Come On Over To My Place", "At The Club" and "Up In The Streets Of Harlem". He remained with the Drifters touring the United Kingdom from early 1970 to 1998, establishing him as the Drifter's longest-serving member. In 1982, exhausted, he left the Drifters and then launched his own group based in London.

Gary Moore   Skid Row, Thin Lizzy

Gary Moore died aged fifty-eight of a heart attack on the 6th of February 2011 while on holiday with his girlfriend at a hotel in Spain. According to newspaper reports, Gary's fatal heart attack was brought on by a massive amount of alcohol he had consumed the evening of his death. He was survived by his ex-wife, Kerry, his sons Jack and Gus and his daughters, Lily and Saoirse. Gary's eldest son Jack and Gary's brother, Cliff, performed the traditional song "Danny Boy" at Gary's funeral. This was reported in a Belfast newspaper as a flawless tribute at which some mourners in the church wept openly.

Gary got his first quality guitar, a Fender Telecaster, at the age of fourteen, and learned to play the right-handed instrument in the standard way, despite being left-handed. In 1968, after performing with a number of Belfast-based bands he was "headhunted" as the replacement guitarist in the Dublin-based band Skid Row and he moved to Dublin. Gary's greatest influence in the early days was English guitarist Peter Green of Fleetwood Mac who was a mentor to Gary Moore when performing in Dublin.

Skid Row then went on to play shows across Europe and the USA, opening for a number of high-profile bands. It was with this group that Gary Moore earned a reputation in the music industry, and his association with Phil Lynott began. Gary Moore left Skid row in December 1971.

In 1970, Gary Moore moved to England and remained there, apart from two short periods in the United States. In 1973, under the name "The Gary Moore Band", he released his first solo album, Grinding Stone.

In 1974 he re-joined Phil Lynott, when he first joined Thin Lizzy after the departure of founding member Eric Bell.From 1975 to August 1978, he was a member of Colosseum II and in 1977 he re-joined Thin Lizzy.

Between late 1977 and early 1978 while moving from Colosseum II and a future return to the ranks of Thin Lizzy, Gary recorded the album Back on the Streets, featuring the hit single "Parisienne Walkways" which reached the Top Ten in the UK singles Chart in April 1979. While Back on the Streets was climbing the charts, Gary had joined Thin Lizzy on a more permanent basis. Recording the album Black Rose which reached number two in the UK album chart.

In July 1979, he left Thin Lizzy permanently to focus on a solo career, but went on to form the short lived band G-Force recording an album for Jet Records. A couple of other albums were made at this time, but not released until after Gary had signed to, and found some success with Virgin Records in 1982, and had released the album Corridors of Power.

Gary experimented with many musical genres, including rock, jazz, blues, country, electric blues, hard rock, and heavy metal.

Jim Morrison   The Doors

Jim Morrison died aged twenty-seven on the 3rd of July 1971 in France at a rented Paris apartment. The official cause of death was listed as heart failure. He was found by his girlfriend Pamela Courson in a bathtub at his apartment.

In 1957, Jim attended Alameda High School in Alameda, California for his freshman and first semester of his sophomore year. He finished high school in Alexandria, Virginia, graduating from George Washington High School in June 1961.

In January 1964, Jim moved to Los Angeles to attend the University of California and enrolled in a class on Antonin Artaud in the Comparative Literature program within the UCLA English Department.

In the summer of 1965, after graduating with a bachelor's degree from the UCLA film school, Jim led a bohemian lifestyle in Venice Beach and wrote the lyrics of many of the early songs the Doors would later perform live and record on albums. Jim and fellow UCLA student, Ray Manzarek, were the first two members of the Doors, forming the group during that summer. They had met months earlier as cinematography students.

The Doors achieved national recognition after signing with Elektra Records in 1967. The single "Light My Fire" spent three weeks at number one on the Billboard Hot 100 chart in July and August 1967.

By the release of their second album, 'Strange Days', the Doors had become one of the most popular rock bands in the United States.

Jim spoke fondly of his Irish and Scottish ancestry and was inspired by Celtic mythology in his poetry and songs.

The Door's UK chart hits include: "Light My Fire" in 1967, "Hello I Love You" in 1968 and "Riders On The Storm" in 1971.

Matt Munro   Solo Artiste

Matt Munro died aged fifty-four on the 7th of February 1985 from liver cancer at a hospital in Kensington, London. He was survived by his widow, Mickie, and his sons, Mitchell and Matthew and his daughter, Michelle.

Matt's singing was first noticed while serving in the British armed forces in Hong Kong. By 1956, Matt Monro had become a featured vocalist with the BBC Show Band. An important influence on his early career was the pianist Winifred Atwell, who became his mentor, provided him with his stage name, and helped him sign with Decca Records.

In 1957 Matt Monro released Blue and Sentimental, a collection of standard songs. Despite the album's critical acclaim, Matt Monro languished among the numerous young male singers trying to break through at the end of the 1950s, many of them emulating Frankie Vaughan by recording cover versions of American hits. A short recording contract with Fontana Records followed.

Matt had a hit with the Beatles' "Yesterday" in 1965, releasing the first 45rpm single of the most recorded song of all time. The following year, Matt sang the Oscar-winning title song for the film, Born Free, which became his signature tune.

Dee Murray   The Elton John Band

Dee Murray died aged forty-five on the 15th of January 1992 from a stroke whilst in Tennessee, U.S.A. He was survived by his wife, Anett, his son, Ashley and daughters Jenna and Didi.

Before joining Elton John as his touring sideman in 1970, Dee was a member of the Spencer Davis Group. Dee played on Elton John's hit albums, including the milestone album Goodbye Yellow Brick Road, singles, and world tours for several years. In 1975, after recording Captain Fantastic and the Brown Dirt Cowboy, Dee Murray was released from the band because Elton wanted to achieve a different sound. He said at the time "The band always rattled along. I want it to chug".

Between 1978 and 1979, Dee Murray worked as part of Alice Cooper's backing band. In the 1980s, Dee played on numerous Nashville sessions for artists including Michael Brown, Lewis Storey, Beth Nielsen Chapman and John Prine.

Johnny Nash   Solo Artiste

Johnny Nash died aged eighty on the 6th of October, 2020, of natural causes at home in Houston, Texas, United States of America after a period of declining health. He was survived by his wife, Carli and his daughter, Monica and his son, Johnny Jnr.

After signing with record label ABC-Paramount, Johnny made his recording debut in 1957 with the single "A Teenager Sings the Blues" and had his first chart hit in early 1958 with a cover of Doris Day's "A Very Special Love". Promoted as a rival to Johnny Mathis, Johnny Nash also found success as an actor early in his career, appearing in the screen version of playwright Louis S. Peterson's 'Take a Giant Step' in nineteen fifty-nine. He continued releasing singles on a variety of labels such as Groove, Chess, Argo, and Warner Bros.

Johnny Nash's nineteen seventy-two reggae-influenced single "I Can See Clearly Now" sold over one million copies, and in November nineteen seventy-two. "I Can See Clearly Now" reached number one on the Billboard Hot 100 and remained atop the chart for four weeks, spending the same four weeks atop the adult contemporary chart. "There Are More Questions Than Answers" was a third hit single taken from his album.

Johnny Nash's UK chart hits include: "Hold Me Tight" in 1968, "Cupid" in 1969, "I Can See Clearly Now" in 1972 and "Tears On My Pillow in 1975.

Prince Rogers Nelson   Solo Artiste

'Prince' Rogers Nelson died from a drug overdose aged fifty-seven at his home in Paisley Park, California, U.S.A. on the 21st of April 2016 and his cremated remains were placed into a custom, 3D printed urn shaped like his Paisley Park estate.

'Prince's father was a pianist and songwriter, and his mother a jazz singer. In 1975 the husband of 'Prince's cousin, formed the band '94 East' and wrote the songs, and 'Prince contributed guitar tracks.

In 1976, Prince created a demo tape with producer Chris Moon, in Moon's Minneapolis studio. Unable to secure a recording contract, Moon brought the tape to Owen Husney, a Minneapolis businessman, who signed 'Prince' age seventeen years old, to a management contract, and helped him create a demo at Sound 80 Studios in Minneapolis with a producer.

In 1980, 'Prince' released the album 'Dirty Mind', which contained sexually explicit material. Recorded in 'Prince' Rogers Nelson's own studio, this album was certified gold, and the single Uptown reached Number five on the Billboard Dance chart and Number five on the Hot Soul Singles charts.

In 1981, 'Prince' formed a side project band called the

Time. The band released four albums between 1981 and 1990, with 'Prince' writing and performing most of the instrumentation and backing vocals and with lead vocals by Morris Day. In late 1982, 'Prince' released a double album, '1999', which sold over three million copies. A lead single from Purple Rain, When Doves Cry, became a signature song of 'Prince.

1991 marked the debut of 'Prince's new band, the New Power Generation. With significant input from his band members, Diamonds and Pearls was released on October 1st 1991. Reaching Number three on the Billboard 200 album chart, Diamonds and Pearls saw four hit singles released in the United States.

In 1992, 'Prince' Rogers Nelson and The New Power Generation released his twelfth album, 'Love Symbol Album', bearing only an unpronounceable symbol on the cover. The album peaked at Number five on the Billboard 200.

In 1994, 'Prince' began to release albums in quick succession. 'Chaos and Disorder', released in 1996, was Prince's final album of new material for Warner Bros., as well as one of his least commercially successful releases. 'Prince released 'Crystal Ball', a five-CD collection of unreleased material, in 1998. In 1999, Prince once again signed with a major label, Arista Records, to release a new record, Rave Un2 the Joy Fantastic. In an attempt to make his new album a success, he gave more interviews than at any other point in his career. In April 2004, Prince released 'Musicology' through a one-album agreement with Columbia Records. The album rose as high as the top five on some international charts, including the US, UK, Germany, and Australia. In late 2005, Prince signed with Universal Records to release his album, '3121'. Prince played twenty-one concerts in London during mid-2007.

Ricky Nelson died in a plane crash, aged forty-five on the 31st of December 1985. He was survived by his wife, Kristin, his daughter ,Tracy and sons Gunnar, Sam, Eric and Matthew.

Ricky played clarinet and drums in his teens, learned the rudimentary guitar chords, and vocally imitated his favorite Sun Records rockabilly artists in the bathroom at home or in the showers at the Los Angeles Tennis Club. He was strongly influenced by the music of Carl Perkins.

At age sixteen, Rickie wanted to impress his girlfriend of two years, Diana, who was an Elvis Presley fan and, although he had no record contract at the time, told her that he, too, was going to make a record. With his father's help, he secured a one-record deal with Verve Records, an important jazz label looking for a young and popular personality who could sing or be taught to sing. In March 1957, he recorded the Fats Domino standard "I'm Walkin'" and "A Teenager's Romance" which was released in late April 1957 as his first single.

"I'm Walkin'" reached number four on Billboard's Best Sellers in Stores chart, and its flip side, "A Teenager's Romance", hit number two. When the television series went on summer break in 1957, Ricky made his first road trip and played four state and county fairs in Ohio and Wisconsin with the Four Preps, who opened and closed for him.

In 1958, Ricky Nelson recorded seventeen-year-old Sharon Sheeley's "Poor Little Fool" for his second album. On 4th August 1958, "Poor Little Fool" became the number one single on the American Billboard's newly instituted Hot 100 singles chart and sold over two million copies.

During 1958 and 1959, Ricky placed twelve hits on the charts in comparison with Elvis Presley's eleven. In the summer of 1958, Ricky conducted his first full-scale tour.

By 1960, the Ricky Nelson International Fan Club had 9,000 chapters around the world.

From 1957 to 1962, Ricky had thirty Top-40 hits, more than any other artist except Elvis Presley, who had fifty-three. Many of Ricky Nelson's early records were double hits with both the A and B sides hitting the American Billboard charts.

Andy Newman   Thunderclap Newman

Andy Newman died aged seventy-three on the 29th of March 2016. He was survived by his brother, Robin.

Andy's first musical efforts were on his great-grand-mother's old wooden-framed piano, later replaced by an iron-framed upright model. His father would play Victorian ballads and short classical pieces, but Andy's tastes inclined towards New Orleans jazz and dance bands from the 1920s and 1930s. After leaving secondary school he joined the G.P.O as a trainee engineer.

The band that would become Thunderclap Newman was formed in late 1968 at the instigation of the Who's Pete Townshend, and comprised Andy Newman alongside a drummer and vocalist.

During recording sessions at IBC Studios in Portland Place, central London, around Christmas in 1968, with Pete Townshend producing and playing the bass under the pseudonym Bijou Drains, they recorded basic tracks for Something in the Air. At the time, Andy Newman was a telephone engineer for the General Post Office, but subsequently quit to be in the group.

Something in the Air was released as a single in May 1969. The song rose to the top of the UK charts and stayed there for three weeks.

Olivia Newton John   Solo Artiste

Olivia Newton John died aged seventy-three from cancer on the 8th of August 2022 in Santa Barbara, California,

USA. She was survived by her husband, John and her daughter, Chloe.

Tributes were paid by John Travolta, Barbra Streisand, Anthony Albanese and many other celebrities. As a mark of respect, Melbourne and Sydney lit up many of their landmarks. In September 2022, Olivia's family held a "small and very private" memorial service in California for the singer, who asked to be cremated and have her ashes scattered in Byron Bay.

After relocating from Britain to America in 1974, Olivia set up residence in Malibu, California, where for forty years she owned several properties, including a horse ranch and beach houses.

In 1978, Olivia starred in the musical film Grease, which was the highest-grossing musical film at the time and whose soundtrack remains one of the world's best-selling albums. It features two major hit duets with co-star John Travolta: "You're the One That I Want", which is one of the best-selling singles of all time, and "Summer Nights".

With global sales of more than one hundred million records, Olivia established herself as one of the best-selling music artists of all time.

Harry Nilson   **Solo Artiste**

Harry Nilsson died aged fifty-two of heart failure on the 15th of January 1994 whilst in his California home. He is interred in Pierce Brothers Valley Oaks Memorial Park in Westlake Village, California, U.S.A. Harry was survived by his wife, Una, his sons; Zak, Kief, Ben, Beau and Oscar and his daughters Annie and Olivia.

By 1958, Harry was intrigued by emerging forms of popular music, especially rhythm and blues artists like Ray Charles. He had made early attempts at performing while he was working at the Paramount, forming a vocal duo with his friend Jerry Smith.

In 1963, Harry began to have some early success as a

songwriter, working on a song for Little Richard. Upon hearing Harry Nilsson sing, Little Richard reportedly remarked: "My! You sing good for a white boy!"

In 1964, Harry worked with Phil Spector, writing three songs with him. He also established a relationship with songwriter and publisher Perry Botkin, Jr., who began to find a market for Harry's songs.

Harry signed with RCA Victor 1966 and released an album the following year, Pandemonium Shadow Show, which was a critical, if not commercial, success. Music industry insiders were impressed both with the song-writing and with Harry's pure-toned, multi-octave vocals.

Pandemonium Shadow Show was followed in 1968 by Aerial Ballet, an album that included Harry's rendition of Fred Neil's song "Everybody's Talkin'". A minor US hit at the time of release (and a top 40 hit in Canada), the song would become more popular a year later when it was featured in the film Midnight Cowboy, and it would earn Harry his first Grammy Award. The song would also become Harry's first US top 10 hit, reaching number 6, and his first Canadian number one.

Harry's next album, Harry in 1969, was his first to hit the charts, and also provided a Top 40 single with "I Guess the Lord Must Be in New York City" (written as a contender for the theme to Midnight Cowboy), used in the Sophia Loren movie La Mortadella. While the album still presented Harry Nilsson as primarily a songwriter, his astute choice of cover material included, this time, a song by then-little-known composer Randy Newman, "Simon Smith and the Amazing Dancing Bear". Harry Nilsson was so impressed with Newman's talent that he devoted his entire next album to Newman compositions.

In 1973 Harry was back in California, and when John Lennon moved there during his separation from Yoko Ono, the two musicians rekindled their earlier friendship. John Lennon was intent upon producing Harry's next album, much to Harry's delight.

Ric Ocasek died aged seventy-five from hypertensive and atherosclerotic cardiovascular diseases at his townhouse in New York City, U.S.A. on the 15th of September, 2019. He was survived by his wife, Paulina and sons, Jonathan and Oliver.

Ric met future Cars bassist Benjamin Orr in Cleveland, Ohio in 1965 after Ric saw Benjamin performing with his band the Grasshoppers. He reconnected with Benjamin a few years later in Columbus, Ohio, and the two began booking bands together. They formed a band called ID Nirvana in 1968 and performed in and around Ohio State University.

Ric and Orr were in various bands in Columbus and Ann Arbor, Michigan, before relocating to Boston in the early 1970s. In Boston, they formed a folk rock band called Milkwood. They released one album, How's the Weather, on Paramount Records in early 1973 but it failed to chart. Future Cars keyboardist Greg Hawkes played on Milkwood's album. After Milkwood, Ric formed the group Richard and the Rabbits and some of the songs they played became the early Cars songs.

Ric was a founding member of the Cars, recording numerous hit songs from 1978 to 1988. He played rhythm guitar and sang lead vocals for a majority of songs After splitting writing duty with Ben Orr in the 1970s, Ric Ocasek became the principal songwriter of the band, and wrote nearly all of the Cars' material, sharing credit on only a few songs with bandmate Greg Hawkes as co-writer. In 2010, Ric Ocasek reunited with the surviving original members of the Cars to record their first album in 24 years, titled Move Like This.

Sinéad O'Connor   Solo Artiste

Sinéad O'Connor died aged fifty-six from undisclosed causes on the 26th of July 2023 at her flat in Herne Hill,

South London. She was survived by her son, Jake and her daughters, Roisin and Yeshua.

In the early 2000s, Sinéad revealed that she suffered from fibromyalgia and the pain and fatigue she experienced had caused her to take a break from music between 2003 and 2005. She was also diagnosed with complex post-traumatic stress disorder and borderline personality disorder.

In August 2015, Sinéad announced that she was to undergo a hysterectomy after suffering gynaecological problems for over three years. She would later blame the hospital's refusal to administer hormonal replacement therapy after the operation as the main reason for her mental health issues in the subsequent years.

Sinéad was born in the Cascia House Nursing Home in Dublin, on the 8th of December 1966, the third of five children.

During February 1985, when Sinéad was eighteen, her mother died in a car accident, aged 45, after losing control of her car on an icy road and crashing into a bus.

Sinéad met the sister of Paul Byrne, drummer for the band In Tua Nua, who heard Sinéad singing "Evergreen" by Barbra Streisand. She recorded a song with them called "Take My Hand" but they felt that at fifteen, she was too young to join the band. Through an ad, however, she placed in Hot Press in mid-1984, she met Colm Farrelly. Together they recruited a few other members and formed a band called Ton Ton Macoute. The band moved to Waterford briefly while Sinéad attended Newtown School, but she soon dropped out of school and followed them to Dublin, where their performances received positive reviews.

Sinéad's time as singer for Ton Ton Macoute brought her to the attention of the music industry, and she was eventually signed by Ensign Records. She also acquired an experienced manager, Fachtna Ó Ceallaigh, former head of U2's Mother Records.

Her first album "The Lion and the Cobra" was released in 1987 on Chrysalis Records, and it reached gold record status, earning a Best Female Rock Vocal Performance Grammy nomination. The single "Mandinka" was a big college radio hit in the United States, and "I Want Your Hands on Me" received both college and urban play in a remixed form that featured rapper MC Lyte. In her first U.S. network television appearance, Sinéad sang "Mandinka" on Late Night with David Letterman in 1988. The song "Troy" was also released as a single in the UK, Ireland, and the Netherlands, where it reached number five on the Dutch Top 40 chart.

Sinéad named Bob Dylan, David Bowie, Bob Marley, Siouxsie and the Banshees, and the Pretenders as the artists who influenced her most on her debut album.

Sinéad's second album in 1990, entitled, I Do Not Want What I Haven't Got, gained considerable attention and mostly positive reviews: it was rated "second best album of the year" by the NME. She was praised for her voice and original songs, while being noted for her appearance: trademark shaved head, often angry expression, and sometimes shapeless or unusual clothing. The album, most notably, contained her international breakthrough hit "Nothing Compares 2 U", a song written by Prince.

During 1990, Sinéad was criticised after she stated that she would not perform if the United States national anthem was played before one of her concerts; Frank Sinatra threatened to "kick her in the ass". After receiving four Grammy Award nominations, she withdrew her name from consideration. Although nominated for the Brit Award for International Female Solo Artist, which she won, she did not attend the awards ceremony, but did accept the Irish IRMA in February 1991.

The 1993 soundtrack to the film In the Name of the Father featured Sinéad's "You Made Me the Thief of Your Heart". Her more conventional Universal Mother album, in 1994, spawned two music videos for the first and second

singles, "Fire on Babylon" and "Famine", that were nominated for a Grammy Award for Best Short Form Music
Video. She toured with Lollapalooza in 1995, but dropped
out when she became pregnant with her second child.

In 1994, Sinéad appeared in A Celebration: The Music of
Pete Townshend and The Who, also known as Daltrey Sings
Townshend. This was a two-night concert at Carnegie Hall
produced by Roger Daltrey of the Who in celebration of his
50th birthday. A CD and a VHS video of the concert were
issued in 1994, followed by a DVD in 1998.

Faith and Courage was released in 2000, including the
single "No Man's Woman", and featured contributions
from Wyclef Jean of the Fugees and Dave Stewart of Eury-
thmics. Her 2002 album, Sean-Nós Nua, marked a departure in that Sinéad interpreted or, in her own words,
"sexed up" traditional Irish folk songs, including several in
the Irish language. In Sean-Nós Nua, she covered a well-
known Canadian folk song, "Peggy Gordon", interpreted
as a song of lesbian, rather than heterosexual, love.

In 2003, Sinéad contributed a track to the Dolly Parton
tribute album Just Because I'm a Woman, a cover of Parton's "Dagger Through the Heart". That same year, she
also featured on three songs of Massive Attack's album
100th Window before releasing her double album, She
Who Dwells in the Secret Place of the Most High Shall
Abide Under the Shadow of the Almighty. This compilation contained one disc of demos and previously unreleased tracks and one disc of a live concert recording.
Directly after the album's release, Sinéad announced that
she was retiring from music. However, Collaborations, a
compilation album of guest appearances, was released in
2005 featuring tracks recorded with Peter Gabriel.

Sinéad released two songs from her album Theology to
download for free from her official website: "If You Had a
Vineyard" and "Jeremiah". The album, a collection of covered and original Rastafari spiritual songs, was released in
June 2007. The first single from the album, the Tim Rice and

Andrew Lloyd Webber classic "I Don't Know How to Love Him", was released in April 2007. To promote the album, Sinéad toured extensively in Europe and North America.

In 2011, Sinéad worked on recording a new album, titled Home, to be released in the beginning of 2012. She planned an extensive tour in support of the album but suffered a serious breakdown between December 2011 and March 2012, resulting in the tour and all other musical activities for the rest of 2012 being cancelled. Sinéad resumed touring in 2013 with The Crazy Baldhead Tour. The second single "4th and Vine" was released in February 2013.

In February 2014, it was revealed that Sinéad had been recording a new album of original material, titled The Vishnu Room, consisting of romantic love songs. In early June 2014, the new album was retitled I'm Not Bossy, I'm the Boss, with an 11th of August release date. The title derives from the Ban Bossy campaign that took place earlier the same year. The album's first single is entitled "Take Me to Church".

In October 2020, Sinéad released a cover of Mahalia Jackson's Trouble of the World, with proceeds from the single to benefit Black Lives Matter charities. On the 4th of June 2021, Sinéad announced her immediate retirement from the music industry. While her final studio album, No Veteran Dies Alone, was due to be released in 2022, Sinéad stated that she would not be touring or promoting it.

In January 2022, Sinéad's son, Shane, died by suicide at the age of seventeen. She subsequently decided to cancel her 2022 tour and her album "No Veteran Dies Alone" was postponed indefinitely.

Roy Orbison   **Solo Artiste**

Roy Orbison died aged fifty-two of a heart attack on the 6th of December 1988. He was survived by his wife Barbara and his sons Roy Jnr, Wesley and Alex.

Roy used thick corrective glasses from an early age. He

was not confident about his appearance and began dyeing his nearly-white hair black when he was still quite young. He was readily available to sing, however, and often became the focus of attention when he did.

On Roy's sixth birthday, his father gave him a guitar. He later recalled that by the age of seven music would be his life. His major musical influence as a youth was country music. When, later in life, he later joined the supergroup, The Traveling Wilburys, he adopted the name of 'Lefty' Wilbury for his character.

Roy was one of the first recording artists to popularize the "Nashville sound", doing so with a group of session musicians known as the A-Team.

His composition, 'Only The Lonely' transformed Roy into an overnight star. He appeared on American Bandstand and toured the U.S.A. for three months non-stop with Patsy Cline. When Elvis Presley heard "Only the Lonely" for the first time, he bought a box of copies to pass to his friends.

Roy's dark and brooding persona, combined with his tremulous voice in lovelorn ballads marketed to teenagers, made Roy into a superstar during the early 1960s. He had a string of hits in 1963 with "In Dreams", "Falling" , and "Mean Woman Blues" coupled with "Blue Bayou". Roy finished the year with a Christmas song written by Willie Nelson titled "Pretty Paper".

Roy was the only American artist to twice have a number-one single in Britain with 'It's Over' on June 25th 1964, and 'Oh, Pretty Woman' on October 8th 1964.

It was in 1987 that Roy began collaborating with Electric Light Orchestra lead vocalist and bandleader Jeff Lynne on a new album. Concurrently, Lynne was completing production work on George Harrison's Cloud Nine album, and all three individuals ate lunch together one day when Roy accepted an invitation to sing on a song of George's. They subsequently contacted Bob Dylan, who, in turn, allowed them to use a recording studio in his home. Along the way,

George made a quick visit to Tom Petty's residence to obtain his guitar. By that evening, the group had written "Handle with Care", which led to the concept of recording an entire album. They called themselves the Travelling Wilburys, representing themselves as half-brothers with the same father. They gave themselves stage names; Roy calling himself "Lefty Wilbury".

Roy was in high demand for concerts and interviews once again, and was seemingly ecstatic about it. He began writing songs and collaborating with many musicians from his past and newer fans, to develop a solo album, 'Mystery Girl'.

In April 1989 Roy became the first deceased musician since Elvis Presley to have two albums in the USA Top Five at the same time.

Delores O'Riordan   The Cranberries

Delores O'Riordan died aged forty-six at the Hilton hotel in Mayfair, London, UK on the 15th of January 2018. The coroner's office ruled that she died as a result of accidental drowning due to alcohol intoxication. She was survived by her husband, Don and their children, Taylor, Molley and Dakota.

On 23rd January Delores was buried after a service at a church in Ballybricken, County Limerick, Ireland after which the Cranberries' song "When You're Gone" was played.

In 1989, brothers Mike and Noel Hogan formed The Cranberry Saw Us in Limerick, Ireland and the next year they placed an advertisement for a female singer and Delores O'Riordan responded and auditioned by writing lyrics and melodies to some existing demos. When she returned with a rough version of "Linger", she was hired, and they recorded Nothing Left At All and the group changed their name to "The Cranberries".

Their demo earned the attention of both the UK press

and record industry and sparked a bidding war between major British record labels. Eventually, the group signed with Island Records. As part of The Cranberries Delores released five albums.

In 2006, Delores O'Riordan was listed among the ten richest women in Ireland.

Benjamin Orr   The Cars

Benjamin Orr died aged fifty three of Pancreatic Cancer on the 4th of October 2000 at his home in Atlanta. Benjamin was survived by his son, Ben.

Benjamin's final public appearance was on the 27th of September, 2000, in a Big People concert in Anchorage, Alaska, U.S.A.

Ben grew up in Ohio, and attended a high school before joining local band the Grasshoppers as lead singer and guitarist in 1964. In 1965, the Grasshoppers released two singles on the Sunburst label: "Mod Socks" and "Pink Champagne" the latter written by Ben Orr.

The Grasshoppers dissolved in 1966, when two of the band members were drafted into the U.S. Army, after which Ben joined the band Mixed Emotions, and later the Colours.

Later, Ben was drafted as well, although he received a deferment after approximately a year and a half in the Army.

Benjamin first met Ric Ocasek in Cleveland, Ohio in the 1960s after Ric saw Benjamin performing with the Grasshoppers. A few years later, Benjamin moved to Columbus, Ohio, where he and Ric formed a musical partnership that would continue in various incarnations, until the break up of the Cars in 1988.

As a member of the Cars, Benjamin sang lead vocal on some of the band's best known songs, including their first top forty hit "Just What I Needed", "Let's Go," and "Drive", their highest charting single in America.

The Car's UK chart hits include: "My Best Friends Girl" in 1978, "Just What I Needed" in 1979, "Since You've Been Gone" in 1982 and "Drive" in 1984.

Robert Palmer   Solo Artiste

Robert Palmer died aged fifty-four in a Paris hotel room from a heart attack on the 26th of September 2003. He was survived by his parents; two sons and a daughter from his first marriage: ; a son and daughter from his second marriage, and his brother, Mark.

Robert had met his future wife Sue in 1968 and had two children, Jim and Jane. The family moved to New York in the mid-1970s and then to the Bahamas a few years later. In 1993, Robert relocated to Lugano, Switzerland and he divorced Sue the same year.

In 1970 Robert joined the twelve-piece jazz-rock fusion band Dada, which featured singer Elkie Brooks. After a year they formed soul/rock band Vinegar Joe. Robert played rhythm guitar in the band, and shared lead vocals with Elkie Brooks. Signed to the Island Records label, they released three albums: Vinegar Joe in 1972, Rock 'n' Roll Gypsies in 1972 and Six Star General in 1973, before disbanding in March 1974.

Island Records signed Robert Palmer to a solo deal in 1974. His first solo album 'Sneakin' Sally Through the Alley' was recorded in New Orleans, Louisiana, in 1974.

In 1995, Robert released a greatest hits album, which reached number four in the UK. In 1995 he reunited with other members of Power Station to record a second album. Robert Palmer and the band completed the album Living in Fear in 1996.

Rick Parfitt   Status Quo

Rick Parfitt died from Sepsis aged sixty-eight on the 24th of December 2016 in Spain in a Marbella hospital. He was survived by his wife, Lyndsay and their twins Tommy and Lily and also by his first wife, Marietta and their son, Richard and also his second wife Patty and their son, Harry.

In August 2014, while on a European tour with Status Quo, Rick was hospitalised in Pula, Croatia, forcing the cancellation of six shows on the tour. He had suffered a heart attack while on his tour bus after performing a concert in Austria, and had a stent inserted.

In 1967, Rics band Traffic Jam changed their name to The Status Quo beginning Rick's almost 50-year career in the band. Early successes came with the Rossi-penned hit "Pictures of Matchstick Men".

The band's more popular songs during the early 1970's include "Paper Plane", "Caroline", "Down Down", "Rain", "Rockin' All Over the World" and "Whatever You Want".

Jaco Pastorious   Weather Report

Jaco Pastorious died of a brain haemorrhage aged thirty-five on the 21st of September 1987. He was survived by his sons Felix and Julius.

Jaco had visited the Midnight Bottle Club in Wilton Manors, Florida and kicked in a glass door after being refused entrance to the club. He was then engaged in a violent confrontation with the club's bouncer, who had a black belt in karate. As a result Jaco was hospitalized then fell into a coma, then died.

As a boy, Jaco was energetic and spent much of his time shirtless on the beach, climbing trees, running through the woods, and swimming in the ocean. He was intensely competitive and excelled at baseball, basketball, and football.

Jaco played drums until he injured his wrist playing football when he was thirteen. The damage was severe enough to warrant corrective surgery which also inhibited his ability to play the drums.

At the age of seventeen , Jaco had begun to appreciate

jazz and had saved enough money to buy an upright bass. Its deep, mellow tone appealed to him, though it strained his finances. He had difficulty maintaining the instrument, which he attributed to the humidity in Florida. When he woke one day to find it had cracked, he traded it for a 1962 Fender Jazz Bass.

In the early 1970s, Jaco taught bass at the University of Miami, where he befriended jazz guitarist Pat Metheny, who was also on the faculty.

Jaco attended a concert in Miami by the jazz fusion band Weather Report. After their bassist left Weather Report, Jaco was asked to join the band and he made his band debut on the album Black Market in 1976, in which he shared the bass playing. Jaco was fully established as bass player for the recording of Heavy Weather in 1977, which contained the Grammy-nominated hit "Birdland".

In 1982, Jaco toured with Word of Mouth as a twenty-one piece big band. While in Japan, to the alarm of his band members, he shaved his head, painted his face black, and threw his bass guitar into Hiroshima Bay. Jaco was diagnosed with bipolar disorder in late 1982 after the tour.

Dennis Payton   The Dave Clark Five

Dennis Payton died aged sixty-three of cancer on the 17th of December 2006 in Bournemouth, Hampshire, United Kingdom. He was survived by his partner, Lindsay, and two sons and two stepsons.

Dennis Payton was born in East London, United Kingdom and as a child he learned to play guitar, saxophone and other wind instruments. As a teenager he played in a jazz band while studying to become an electrician. Through his band membership, he made acquaintance with members of other bands. Being a competent musician, he was often invited to join them, and he moved from one band to another. One of his acquaintances was Dave Clark, the leader of the group 'Dave Clark Five.

Apart from saxophone, Dennis Payton occasionally played guitar and harmonica (he played the harmonica solo on the group's hit single "Catch Us If You Can" and played the sousaphone on "The Red Balloon"), and sang background vocals. Dennis Payton also co-wrote over two dozen songs with Dave Clark for the group, two of which he sang lead vocals: "I Miss You" and "Man in the Pin Striped Suit."

In 1970, the group disbanded. Dennis became an estate agent in Bournemouth, but he continued to play in a few amateur bands in his spare time.

The Dave Clark Five's UK chart hits include: "Glad All Over" in 1963, "Bits And Pieces" in 1964, "Catch Us If You Can" in 1965, "Everybody Knows" in 1967, Red Baloon" in 1968, "Good Old Rock 'n' Roll" in 1969 and "Everybody Get Together" in 1970.

Laurence Payton   **The Four Tops**

Lawrence Payton died aged fifty-nine from Liver Cancer on the 20th of June 1997 in Southfield, Michigan, U.S.A. He was survived by his wife, Yone and his sons, Sonny, Larry and Roquel and his daughter, Kimberly.

Lawrence and Renaldo Benson both attended Northern High School in Detroit and met Levi Stubbs and Abdul Fakir at a school birthday party. The four teenagers began singing in 1953 as The Four Aims but later changed their name to the Four Tops.

Although successful in the local area as a performance group, recording success eluded them until signing with the newly established Tamla Motown label in 1963.

They then became one of the biggest recording acts of the sixties, charting more than two dozen hits through to the early eighties.

The original Four Tops enjoyed continued success as a headline performance act and remained together for forty-three years until Lawrence Payton's death.

Neil Peart died aged sixty-seven of brain cancer on the 7th of January, 2020 in Santa Monica, California, U.S.A.

Neil's first exposure to musical training came in the form of piano lessons, which he later said in his instructional video A Work in Progress did not have much impact on him. He had a penchant for drumming on various objects around the house with a pair of chopsticks, so for his thirteenth birthday his parents bought him a pair of drum sticks, a practice drum, and some lessons, with the promise that if he stuck with it for a year they would buy him a kit.

His parents bought him a drum kit for his fourteenth birthday and he began taking lessons at the Peninsula Conservatory of Music. His stage debut took place that year at the school's Christmas pageant. His next appearance was at Lakeport High School with his first group, The Eternal Triangle. At this show he performed his first solo.

By his late teens, Neil had played in local bands such as Mumblin' Sumpthin', and the Majority. These bands practiced in basement recreation rooms and garages and played church halls, high schools, and skating rinks.

At eighteen years old after struggling to achieve success as a drummer in Canada, Neil travelled to London, England, hoping to further his career as a professional musician. Despite playing in several bands and picking up occasional session work, he was forced to support himself by selling jewelry at a shop called The Great Frog on Carnaby Street.

After eighteen months Peart became disillusioned by his lack of progress in the music business; he placed his aspiration of becoming a professional musician on hold and returned to Canada and was recruited to play drums for a St. Catharines band known as J R Flood, who played on the Southern Ontario bar circuit. Soon after, a mutual acquaintance convinced Neil to audition for the Toronto-based band Rush, which needed a replacement for its original drummer.

Neil officially joined the band on July 29, 1974, two weeks before the group's first US tour. He soon settled into his new position, also becoming the band's primary lyricist. Before joining Rush he had written a few songs, but, with the other members largely uninterested in writing lyrics, Neil's previously under-utilized writing became as noticed as his musicianship. The band were working hard to establish themselves as a recording act, and Neil, along with the rest of the band, began to undertake extensive touring.

Teddy Pendergrass   The Blue Notes

Teddy Pendergrass died aged fifty-nine from respiratory failure on the 13th of June 2010 Pennsylvania, U.S.A. He was survived by his wife Joan, his sons Tamon and Teddy and his daughters Ladonna and Tisha. His body was interred at the West Laurel Hill Cemetery in Bala Cynwyd, Pennsylvania.

Teddy grew up in Philadelphia and often sang at church. He dreamed of being a pastor and got his wish when, at ten, he was ordained a minister. Teddy also took up drums during this time and was a junior deacon of his church.

At high school Teddy sang with the Edison Mastersingers. He dropped out in the eleventh grade to enter the music business and recorded his first song, "Angel With Muddy Feet".

Teddy played drums for several local Philadelphia bands, eventually becoming the drummer of The Cadillacs. In 1970, he was spotted by the Blue Notes' founder, Harold Melvin , who convinced Teddy to play drums in the group. However, during a performance, Teddy began singing along, and Melvin, impressed by his vocals, made him the lead singer. Before Teddy joined the group, the Blue Notes had struggled to find success. That all changed when they landed a recording deal with Philadelphia International Records in 1971, thus beginning Teddy Pendergrass's successful collaboration with label founders Kenny Gamble and Leon Huff.

In 1977, released his self-titled album, which went platinum on the strength of the disco hit "I Don't Love You Anymore", Its follow-up single, "The Whole Town's Laughing At Me", became a top twenty Rhythm & Blues hit.

Teddy Pendergrass' popularity became massive at the end of 1978. With sold-out audiences packing his shows, his manager who was known for his innovative approaches to publicizing his artists - soon noticed that a huge number of his audience consisted of women of all races. Gordon devised a plan for Teddy Pendergrass' next tour to play to just female audiences, starting a trend that continues today called "women-only concerts." With four platinum albums and two gold albums, Teddy Pendergrass was on his way to being what the media called "the black Elvis," not only in terms of his crossover popularity but also due to him buying a mansion akin to Elvis' Graceland, located just outside his hometown of Philadelphia. By early 1982, Teddy Pendergrass was perhaps the leading Rythm&Blues male artist of his day.

Richard Penniman   Little Richard

Richard Penniman died aged eighty-seven from bone cancer on the 9th of May, 2020 at his home in Tullahoma, Tennessee, United States of America after a two-month illness. He was survived by his brother, sister, and son who were all with him at the moment of his death.

In childhood, he was nicknamed Lil' Richard by his family because of his small and skinny frame. A mischievous child who played pranks on neighbors, Little Richard began singing in church at a young age. Possibly as a result of complications at birth, he had a slight deformity that left one of his legs shorter than the other. This produced an unusual gait, and he was mocked for his said effeminate appearance.

Richard's family were very religious and joined various A.M.E., Baptist, and Pentecostal churches, with some family members becoming ministers. Little Richard enjoyed the Pentecostal churches the most, because of their feelingful worship and live music. He later recalled that people in his neighbourhood sang gospel songs throughout the day during segregation to keep a positive outlook, because there was so much poverty and so much prejudice in those days. He had observed that people sang to feel their connection with God and to wash their trials and burdens away. Gifted with a loud singing voice, Richard recalled that he was always changing the key upwards and that they once stopped him from singing in church for and hollering so loud.

Richard attended Macon's Hudson High School, where he eventually learned to play alto saxophone, joining his school's marching band in fifth grade. While in high school, he got a part-time job at Macon City Auditorium for local secular and gospel concert promoter Clint Brantley. He sold Coca-Cola to crowds during concerts of star performers of the day such as Cab Calloway, Lucky Millinder, and his favorite singer, Sister Rosetta Tharpe.

It was in October 1947 that Sister Rosetta Tharpe overheard fourteen year-old Richard singing her songs before a performance at the Macon City Auditorium and she invited him to open her show. After that show, Rosetta paid him, inspiring him to become a professional performer. Little Richard stated that he was inspired to play the piano after he heard Ike Turner's piano intro on Rocket 88.

Richard joined his first musical band, Buster Brown's Orchestra, where Brown gave him the name Little Richard. Performing in the minstrel show circuit, Richard, in and out of drag, performed for various vaudeville acts such as Sugarfoot Sam from Alabam, the Tidy Jolly Steppers, the King Brothers Circus and Broadway Follies. Having settled in Atlanta, Georgia, at this point, Richard began listening to rhythm and blues and was further influenced by Brown's and Wright's flashy style of showmanship. Inspired by Brown and Wright, Little Richard decided to become a rhythm-and-blues singer and after befriending Wright, began to learn how to be an entertainer from him.

Moving to Houston, he formed a band called the Tempo Toppers, performing as part of blues package tours in Southern clubs such as Club Tijuana in New Orleans and Club Matinee in Houston. Richard signed with Don Robey's Peacock Records in February 1953, recording eight sides, including four with Johnny Otis and his band.

Disillusioned by the record business, Richard returned to Macon in 1954 and struggling with poverty settled for work as a dishwasher for Greyhound Lines. That year, he disbanded the gospel-flavored Tempo Toppers and formed a hard-driving rhythm and blues band, the Upsetters, which included drummer Charles Connor and saxophonist Wilbert Lee Diamond Smith then began to tour successfully, even without a bass guitarist. Around this time, Little Richard signed a contract to tour with fellow R&B singer Little Johnny Taylor.

Recorded in three takes in September 1955, Tutti Frutti was released as a single that November & became an instant hit, reaching number two on the American Billboard magazine's

Rhythm and Blues Best-Sellers chart and crossing over to the pop charts in both the United States and in the United Kingdom.

Richard's next hit single, Long Tall Sally in 1956, hit number one on the R & B chart and number thirteen on the Top hundred while reaching the top ten in Britain. Like Tutti Frutti it sold over a million copies. In 1957, Little Richard was given a singing role in the film, The Girl Can't

Help It. That year, he scored more hit success with songs including Jenny, Jenny and Keep A-Knockin'.

Richard's first album, "Here's Little Richard", was released by Specialty Records in May 1957 and peaked at number thirteen on the American Billboard Top LPs chart. In 1994, Little Richard sang the theme song to the award-winning PBS Kids and TLC animated television series 'The Magic School Bus', which was based on the book series created by Joanna Cole and Bruce Degen and published by Scholastic Corporation.

Throughout the first decade of the 21st century, Little Richard kept up a stringent touring schedule, performing primarily in the United States and Europe but sciatic nerve pain in his left leg and then replacement of the involved hip began affecting the frequency of his performances by 2010. Despite his health problems, Little Richard continued to perform to receptive audiences and critics.

Carl Perkins   Solo Artiste

Carl Perkins died aged sixty-five from throat cancer on the 19th of January 1998 in hospital in Tennessee, U.S.A. He was survived by his wife Valda, his daughter, Debbie and his three sons, Stan, Greg, and Steve.

Carl grew up hearing southern gospel music sung by white friends in church and by Afro-American field workers when he worked in the cotton fields. With his first guitar, he taught himself parts of Acuff's "Great Speckled Bird" and "The Wabash Cannonball", having heard them played on the radio.

At age fourteen, using the I-IV-V chord progression common in country music of the day, Carl wrote a song that came to be known around Jackson as "Let Me Take You to the Movie, Magg" This song later persuaded Sam Phillips to sign Carl Perkins to his Sun Records label.

Carl began performing regularly on WTJS in Jackson during the late 1940s as a sometime member of the Tennessee Ramblers. He also appeared on Hayloft Frolic, on which he performed two songs, sometimes including "Talking Blues" as done by Robert Lunn on the Grand Ole Opry.

In the autumn of 1955, Carl wrote "Blue Suede Shoes" after seeing a dancer get angry with his date for scuffing up his shoes. Several weeks later, in December 1955, Carl and his band recorded the song during a session at Sun Studio in Memphis. Released in January 1956, "Blue Suede Shoes" was a massive chart success. In the United Kingdom, the song became a Top Ten hit, reaching number ten on the British charts. It was the first record by a Sun artist to sell a million copies. The flip side, "Honey Don't", was covered by the Beatles. In 1959, Carl wrote the country-and-western song "The Ballad of Boot Hill" for Johnny Cash, who recorded it on an EP for Columbia Records. In the same year, Carl was cast in a Filipino movie produced by People's Pictures, Hawaiian Boy, in which he sang "Blue Suede Shoes".

In 1981 Carl recorded the song "Get It" with Paul McCartney, providing vocals and playing guitar with Paul.

Carl's last album, Go Cat Go!, released by the independent label Dinosaur Records in 1996, features Carl singing duets with Bono, Johnny Cash, John Fogerty, George Harrison, Paul McCartney, Willie Nelson, Tom Petty, Paul Simon, and Ringo Starr. His last major concert performance was the Music for Montserrat all-star charity concert at London's Royal Albert Hall on the 15th of September 1997.

Tom Petty   The Heartbreakers, The Travelling Wilburys

Tom Petty died of cardiac arrest aged sixty-six on the 2nd of October 2017. He was survived by his wife, Dana and daughters Adria and Anna Kim.

During the summer of 1961, Tom's uncle had been working on the set of the Elvis film 'Follow That Dream' in nearby Ocala. He invited his nephew to drop in and watch the film-shoot. Tom became an instant Elvis fan and when twelve years old his parents gifted him his first acoustic guitar as a Christmas present.

Tom started a rock band known as the Epics which later evolved into Mudcrutch. During September of 1979, Tom Petty and the Heartbreakers performed at a Musicians United for Safe Energy concert at Madison Square Garden in New York. Their rendition of "Cry To Me" was featured on the resulting album called 'No Nukes'.

In 1988, Tom Petty joined the Travelling Wilburys, which included George Harrison, Bob Dylan, Roy Orbison, and Jeff Lynne. The group decided to record a full album, Travelling Wilburys Vol. 1. The second Wilburys album, entitled Travelling Wilburys Vol. 3 and recorded without the then deceased Roy Orbison, followed in 1990.

John Philips   The Mamas & Papas

John Phillips died aged sixty-five on the 18th of March 2001 from heart failure whilst in Palm Springs, Los Angeles, California, U.S.A. He was survived by his fourth wife, Farnaz, his son, Jeffrey and his daughters, Mackenzie, Bijou and Chynna. John was interred at Forest Lawn Cemetery which is nearby.

John was born in South Carolina and attended Linton Hall Military School in Bristow, Virginia. He formed a group of teenage boys, who sang doo-wop songs.

John longed to have success in the music industry and travelled to New York to find a record contract in the early 1960s. His first band, The Journeymen, was a folk trio, with Scott McKenzie and Dick Weissman. They were fairly successful, putting out three albums and several appearances on the 1960s TV show, Hootenanny.

John further developed his craft in Greenwich Village, during the American folk music revival, and met future Mamas & the Papas group vocalists Denny Doherty and Cass Elliot there around that time.

John was the primary songwriter and musical arranger of The Mamas & the Papas. After being signed to Dunhill, they had several Billboard Top Ten hits, including "California Dreamin'", "Monday, Monday", "I Saw Her Again", "Creeque Alley", and "12:30 ". John also wrote "San Francisco (Be Sure to Wear Flowers in Your Hair)" in 1967 for former bandmate Scott McKenzie which was a massive hit in the UK.

Wilson Pickett   Solo Artiste

Wilson Pickett died aged sixty-four of a heart attack on the 19th of January 2006, in Reston, Virginia, U.S.A. He was laid to rest in a mausoleum at Evergreen Cemetery in Louisville, Kentucky. Wilson was was survived by his ex-wife Bonnie, his sons, Lynderrick and Michael, and his daughters, Veda and Saphan .

Wilson spent the twilight of his career playing dozens of concert dates every year until 2004, when he began suffering from health problems. While in the hospital, he returned to his spiritual roots and told his sister that he wanted to record a gospel album, but he never recovered.

Wilson Picket's forceful, passionate style of singing was developed in the church and on the streets of Detroit, under the influence of recording stars such as Little Richard.

In 1955, Wilson joined a gospel group called the Violinaires. They played with a second gospel group on concert tour in America. After singing for four years in the popular gospel-harmony group, Wilson, lured by the success of gospel singers who had moved to the lucrative secular music market, joined the Falcons in 1959.

The Falcons were an early vocal group bringing gospel into a popular context, thus paving the way for soul music. The group featured notable members who became major solo artists; when Wilson Picket joined the group, Eddie Floyd and Mack Rice were members. Wilson's biggest success with the Falcons was "I Found a Love", co-written by Wilson Picket and featuring his lead vocals. While only a minor hit for the Falcons, it paved the way for Wilson to embark on a solo career. Wilson later had a solo hit with a re-recorded two-part version of the song, included on his 1967 album The Sound of Wilson Picket.

Soon after recording "I Found a Love", Wilson cut his first solo recordings, including "I'm Gonna Cry", in collaboration with Don Covay. He also recorded a demo for a song he co-wrote, "If You Need Me", a slow-burning soul ballad featuring a spoken sermon and sent the demo to Jerry Wexler, a producer at Atlantic Records. Wexler gave it to the label's recording artist Solomon Burke, Atlantic's biggest star at the time.

Wilson's first significant success as a solo artist came with "It's Too Late," an original composition. Entering the charts in July of 1963, it peaked at number seven on the Rythm&Blues chart ; the same title was used for his debut album, released in the same year.

Wilson's breakthrough came at Stax Records' studio in Memphis, Tennessee, where he recorded his third Atlantic single, "In the Midnight Hour" in 1965. This song was Wilson's first big hit. It sold over one million copies, and was awarded a gold disc.

Other big hits from this era in Wilson's career included two covers: Mack Rice's "Mustang Sally" and Dyke & the Blazers' "Funky Broadway". Both tracks were million sellers.

Late 1969 found Wilson at Criteria Studios in Miami. Hit covers of the Supremes' "You Keep Me Hangin' On" and The Archies' "Sugar Sugar" and the Picket original "She Said Yes" came from these sessions. Wilson then teamed up with established Philadelphia-based hit-makers Gamble and Huff for the 1970 album in Philadelphia, which featured his next two hit singles, "Engine No. 9" and "Don't Let the Green Grass Fool You", the latter selling one million copies.

Fayette Pinkney   The Three Degrees

Fayette Pinkney died aged sixty-one of acute respiratory failure on the 27th of June 2009 in Lansdale, Pennsylvania, U.S.A.

Fayette was one of three young teenagers brought together by manager Richard Barrett to form The Three Degrees in 1963. She was a part of the group until she was sacked by Barrett from the group in 1976, and was with them through their great years and sang on many of their greatest hits, such as "When Will I See You Again" and "Take Good Care of Yourself".

Fayette travelled to London in January 1979 to record her only solo album, One Degree, which she did in just two weeks. She later worked as a counsellor and vocal coach and, in addition to singing with her church's inspirational choir, she travelled with a group called the Intermezzo Choir Ministry.

Gene Pitney   Solo Artiste

Gene Pitney died of a heart attack aged sixty-six on the 5th of April 2006 whilst touring the UK. He was survived by his wife Lynne and their three sons Todd, Chris, and David. His final show at Cardiff's St David's Hall, Wales, had earned him a standing ovation.

Gene attended high school where he formed his first band, Gene & the Genials. He scored his first chart single, which made the Top 40, the self-penned "(I Wanna) Love My Life Away," on which he played several instruments and multi-tracked the vocals. He followed that same year with his first Top 20 single Town Without Pity in1961 which won a Golden Globe Award and was nominated for an Academy Award for Best Song, but lost the award to "Moon River".

Gene's popularity in the UK market was ensured by the breakthrough success of "Twenty Four Hours from Tulsa," a Bacharach and David song, which peaked at number five in Britain at the start of 1964. It was only Gene Pitney's third single release in the UK to reach the singles chart, and the first to break into the Top Twenty there; it was also a hit in the U.S.A., peaking at number seventeen on the Hot 100.

Gene Pitney's UK chart hits include: "Twenty Four Hours From Tulsa" in 1963, "I'm Gonna Be Strong" in 1964, "Looking Through The Eyes of Love" in 1965, "Nobody Needs Your Love" in 1966 and "Somethings Gotten Hold of My Heart" in 1967.

Bonnie Pointer   The Pointer Sisters

Bonnie Pointer died of cardiac arrest aged sixty-nine on the 8th of June 2020. She was survived by her sister, June and her ex-husband, Jeffrey.

Bonnie and younger sister June began singing together in their father's West Oakland Church of God in Oakland, California. They formed the Pointers in 1969 and after Anita joined the duo that same year, they changed their name to the Pointer Sisters and recorded several singles for Atlantic Records between 1971 and 1972. In December 1972, they recruited older sister Ruth and released their debut album as the Pointer Sisters in 1973. Their self-titled debut yielded the hit "Yes We Can Can".

Bonnie also released three solo albums, including two self-titled albums for Motown, before retiring from the studio. At the beginning of 2008, she embarked on a European tour, and worked on her autobiography.

The Pointer Sister's UK chart hits include: "Slowhand" in 1981, "Automatic" in 1984 and "Jump For My Love" in 1984.

Rudy Pompilli   The Comets

Rudy Pompilli died aged fifty-one from lung cancer on the 5th of February, 1976, in Philadelphia, Pennsylvania, United States of America.

Rudy was skilled at playing both saxophone and clarinet, and spent the beginning of his career playing in jazz bands. Rudy was invited to join the Comets in September 1955, after Bill Haley's previous sax player quit.

Within a few months of joining The Comets, Rudy had become the band's most visible member, aside from Bill Haley himself, becoming the focus of "Rudy's Rock", a show-stopping instrumental co-written by Rudy Pompilli and Bill Haley that debuted in the 1956 movie 'Rock Around the Clock'. When released as a single, "Rudy's Rock" reached number 34 on the American Billboard singles chart and making it the first instrumental record of the rock and roll era to chart.

Cozy Powell   Rainbow, Whitesnake

Cozy Powell died aged fifty on the 5th of April 1998 due to a a motor accident near Bristol, U.K. He was ejected through a windscreen and died at the scene.

Cozy started playing drums aged twelve in the school orchestra, thereafter playing along in his spare time to popular singles of the day. The first band he was in, called the Corals, played each week at the youth club in Cirencester. At the age of fifteen, Cozy had already worked out an impressive drum solo. His band, The Sorcerers became Youngblood, and a series of singles were released in late 1968–69.

Cozy also played with swamp rocker Tony Joe White at the Isle of Wight Festival in 1970. He then landed the then highly prestigious drumming job with Jeff Beck's. Their first project was to record an album of Motown covers in the USA. After the recording of two albums, Rough and Ready in October 1971 and Jeff Beck Group in July 1972, the band fell apart.

Cozy formed Cozy Powell's Hammer in April 1974. In 1975 Cozy joined Rainbow. Cozy and Ritchie Blackmore were the only constants in the band's line-up over the next five years, as Blackmore evolved the sound of the band from a neo-classical hard rock-heavy metal to a more commercial AOR sound. Rainbow's 1979 Down to Earth LP, from which singles "Since You Been Gone" and "All Night Long" are taken, proved to be the band's most successful album thus far. However, Cozy was concerned over the overtly commercial sound and decided to leave Rainbow, although not before they headlined the first ever Monsters of Rock show at Castle Donington, England, on 16th August 1980. The festival was Cozy Powell's last show with Rainbow.

After he left Rainbow he worked with vocalist Graham Bonnet, he too an ex-Rainbow member, on Bonnet's new project called Graham Bonnet & The Hooligans.

Dave Prater   Sam & Dave

Dave Prater died aged fifty on the 9th of April 1988 in a car crash in Sycamore, Georgia, U.S.A. He was survived by his second wife, Judith and five children from his first marriage.

Dave grew up singing gospel music in the church choir, and was a veteran of the gospel group the Sensational Hummingbirds, in which he sang with his older brother. Dave met his future partner, Sam Moore, in the King of Hearts Club in Miami in 1961, signing to Roulette Records shortly thereafter. Sam & Dave released six singles for Roulette, including two songs that Dave co-wrote with Sam.

They were signed in late 1964 by Jerry Wexler to Atlantic Records, with an agreement that allowed them to record in Memphis with Stax Records. Their first two singles failed to chart, but the duo's November 1965 single, "You Don't Know Like I Know," started a series of ten straight top twenty Billboard Rythm&Blues hits, including "Hold On, I'm Comin'" and "You Got Me Hummin'" in 1966 , "When Something Is Wrong with My Baby" and

"Soul Man" in 1967, and "I Thank You" in 1968. Dave sang the tenor lead first verse on their only ballad to become a hit single, "When Something Is Wrong with My Baby", demonstrating an impressive vocal range in the upper register.

All of their biggest hits were written and produced by Isaac Hayes and David Porter, who worked as songwriters for Stax. Sam & Dave's Stax records also benefited greatly from the backing of the Stax house band, Booker T. & the M.G.'s, and the Stax horn section, the Mar-Keys. These highly regarded musicians co-wrote and contributed greatly to the recordings. Sam & Dave's Stax recordings through nineteen sixty-seven were engineered by Stax founder and co-owner Jim Stewart, who created the "Memphis sound" at Stax by recording sessions essentially live in a single take.

Dave. Their last performance together was on 31st December 1981, at the Old Waldorf in San Francisco, California, U.S.A.

In 1982, Dave Prater, Jnr started touring with Sam Daniels. This duo was also billed as Sam & Dave.

Steve Priest   **The Sweet**

Steve Priest died of failing health aged seventy-two on 4th of June, 2020 in La Cañada Flintridge, California, United States of America. Steve was survived by his wife Maureen and their three daughters, Lisa, Danielle and Maggie.

Steve began playing in Hayes local bands as a young teenager, after being influenced by artists including Jet Harris of the Shadows, the Rolling Stones and the Who.

In nineteen sixty-eight, Steve was invited to form a four-piece band with vocalist Brian Connolly, drummer Mick Tucker, and guitarist Frank Torpey, the band that was to become The Sweet. The Sweet was a band that went through many ups and downs but success started in 1971, after they teamed up with songwriters Nicky Chinn and

Mike Chapman . they did, however, pen a number of their own hits.

Steve Priest often directly backed up Brian Connolly's vocals and took distinctive short high pitched vocal leads which was a key to their musical style at that time. He adopted a camp image, wearing heavy make-up and outrageous costumes.

After Brian Connolly left The Sweet in early 1979, Steve Priest became the main singer. This continued until 1982, when the original Sweet disbanded. By this time, Steve Priest had divorced his first wife, Pat, and moved to New York City. On 18th of June 1981, he married his second wife Maureen, who was then the East Coast Director of Publicity and Artist Relations of Capitol/EMI Records in New York. While in New York, Steve formed a band called the Allies with guitarist Marco Delmar and drummer Steve Missal. Success was elusive, although their composition "Talk To Me" was featured in the movie, Fast Food.

In January 2008, Steve Priest formed a new version of the Sweet which played mainly festivals and venues in the U.S.A. and Canada and in early 2009. They released a live CD, recorded in August 2008 at the Morongo Casino in Cabazon, California.

Reg Presley   **The Troggs**

Reg Presley died aged seventy-one on the 4th of February 2013 from cancer and a succession of strokes. He was survived by his wife, Brenda and by his son, Jason and his daughter, Karen. Reg was cremated at Basingstoke Crematorium, Hampshire, U.K. A blue plaque in his memory was unveiled in Andover High Street marking the building where The Troggs originally rehearsed.

Reg was the lead singer with the 1960s beat band The Troggs, whose hits included "Wild Thing" and "With a Girl Like You." He also wrote the song "Love Is All Around", which was later featured in both the movies "Four Weddings and a Funeral" and "Love Actually".

Elvis Presley   Solo Artiste

Elvis Presley died of suspected drug misuse aged forty-two on the 16th of August 1977 in Memphis, Tennessee, U.S.A.

Elvis's funeral was held two days later at Graceland. Approximately eighty thousand people lined the processional route to Forest Hill Cemetery, where Elvis was buried next to his mother. Within a few days, "Way Down" topped the country and UK pop charts.

In September 1941, Elvis entered first grade at school where his instructors regarded him as "average". He was encouraged to enter a singing contest after impressing his schoolteacher with a rendition of Red Foley's country song "Old Shep" during morning prayers.

The contest, held at the Mississippi-Alabama Fair and Dairy Show in October nineteen-forty-five, was Elvis's first public performance. Dressed as a cowboy, the ten-year-old Elvis stood on a chair to reach the microphone and sang "Old Shep". He recalled getting fifth place. A few months later, Elvis received his first guitar on his birthday. Over the following year, he received basic guitar lessons from two of his uncles and the new pastor at the family's church.

When Elvis was twelve years old, someone scheduled him for two on-air performances. Elvis Presley was overcome by stage fright the first time, but succeeded in performing the following week. Elvis, who never received formal music training or learned to read music, studied and played by ear.

In January nineteen-fifty-four, Elvis cut a second acetate at Sun Records—"I'll Never Stand In Your Way" and "It Wouldn't Be the Same Without You". That April, Elvis began working for the Crown Electric company as a truck driver.

A combination of Elvis Presley's strong response to

rhythm and nervousness at playing before a large crowd led Elvis to shake his legs as he performed and his wide-cut pants emphasized his movements, provoking young women in the audience to begin screaming.

From August through October, nineteen-fifty-four they played frequently at the Eagle's Nest club and returned to Sun Studio for more recording sessions, and Elvis quickly gained confidence on stage.

Elvis made what would be his only appearance on Nashville's Grand Ole Opry on October 2nd nineteen-fifty-four. Two weeks later, Elvis was booked on Louisiana Hayride, the Opry's chief rival.

By early nineteen-fifty-five, Elvis Presley's regular Hayride appearances, constant touring, and well-received record releases had made him a regional star, from Tennessee to West Texas. That January, the manager signed a formal management contract with Elvis Presley and brought him to the attention of Colonel Tom Parker, whom he considered the best promoter in the music business. Having successfully managed top country star Eddy Arnold, Colonel Tom Parker was now working with the new number-one country singer, Hank Snow. Colonel Parker booked Elvis Presley on Snow's February tour. When the tour reached Odessa in Texas, a nineteen year-old Roy Orbison saw Elvis Presley for the first time and has been known to say that Elvis's energy was incredible and that Elvis Presley's instinct was just amazing and he just didn't know what to make of it and that there was just no reference point in the current culture to compare it. Elvis made his television debut on March 3rd nineteen-fifty-five on the KSLA-TV broadcast of Louisiana Hayride. By August, nineteen-fifty-five, Sun Records had released ten sides credited to " Elvis Presley, Scotty and Bill".

At the Country Disc Jockey Convention in early November, nineteen-fifty-five, Elvis was voted the year's most promising male artist. Several record companies had by now shown interest in signing him. After three major labels made offers of up to twenty-five thousand dollars, Colonel Tom Parker and Phillips struck a deal with RCA Victor on November 21st nineteen-fifty-five to acquire Elvis Presley's Sun contract for an unprecedented forty-thousand dollars. Elvis Presley, at twenty years , was still a minor, so his father signed the contract.

By December, RCA had begun to heavily promote its new singer, and before the month's end had reissued many of Elvis Presley's Sun recordings.

In January 1956 Elvis made his first recordings for RCA in Nashville. The session produced the moody, unusual "Heartbreak Hotel", released as a single in January 1956. Colonel Tom Parker finally brought Elvis Presley to national television, booking him on CBS's Stage Show for six appearances over two months. The program, produced in New York, was hosted on alternate weeks by big band leaders and brothers Tommy and Jimmy Dorsey. After Elvis Presley's first appearance, on January 28th nineteen-fifty-six introduced by disc jockey Bill Randle, Elvis Presley stayed in town to record at RCA's New York studio. The sessions yielded eight songs, including a cover of Carl Perkins' rockabilly anthem "Blue Suede Shoes". In February, Elvis Presley's "I Forgot to Remember to Forget", a Sun recording initially released the previous August, reached the top of the Billboard country chart.

Twelve weeks after its original release, "Heartbreak Hotel" became Elvis's first number-one pop hit. In late April, nineteen-fifty-six Elvis began a two-week residency at the New Frontier Hotel and Casino on the Las Vegas Strip. Amid his Vegas tenure, Elvis, who had serious acting ambitions, signed a seven-year contract with Paramount Pictures. He began a tour of the Midwest in mid-May, taking in fifteen cities in as many days.

After a show in La Crosse, Wisconsin, an urgent message on the letterhead of the local Catholic diocese's newspaper was sent to FBI director J. Edgar Hoover. It warned that "Elvis Presley is a definite danger to the security of the

United States. Elvis Presley's actions and motions were such as to rouse the sexual passions of teenaged youth. After the show, more than 1,000 teenagers tried to gang into Elvis Presley's room at the auditorium. Indications of the harm Elvis Presley did just in La Crosse were two high school girls whose abdomen and thigh had Elvis Presley's autograph.

Elvis recorded "Hound Dog", along with "Any Way You Want Me" and "Don't Be Cruel". The Jordanaires sang harmony, as they had on The Steve Allen Show; they would work with Elvis Presley through the nineteen-six-ties.

Accompanying Elvis Presley's rise to fame, a cultural shift was taking place that he both he both inspired and came to symbolize. Igniting the biggest pop craze since Glenn Miller and Frank Sinatra, Elvis Presley brought rock'n'roll into the mainstream of popular culture. As Elvis Presley set the artistic pace that other artists followed and more than anyone else, gave the young a belief in themselves as a distinct and somehow unified generation; he was first in America ever to feel the power of an integrated youth culture.

Elvis undertook three brief tours during 1957 continuing to generate a crazed audience response.

In March 1958, Elvis was conscripted into the U.S. Army as a private at Fort Chaffee, near Fort Smith, Arkansas. His arrival was a major media event. Hundreds of people descended on Elvis as he stepped from the bus; photographers then accompanied him into the fort. Elvis announced that he was looking forward to his military stint, saying he did not want to be treated any differently from anyone else. But then, during a two-week leave in early June, Elvis Presley recorded five songs in Nashville. After training, Elvis joined the 3rd Armored Division in Friedberg, Germany, in 1958. Introduced to amphetamines by a sergeant while on maneuvers, he became "practically evangelical about their benefits"—not only for energy, but for "strength" and weight loss, as well—and many of his friends in the outfit joined him in indulging.

While in Friedberg, Elvis met fourteen-year-old Priscilla Beaulieu. They would eventually marry after a seven-and-a-half-year courtship.

Elvis returned to the United States in March 1960, and was honorably discharged with the rank of sergeant. The train that carried him from New Jersey to Tennessee was mobbed all the way, and Elvis Presley was called upon to appear at scheduled stops to please his fans. On a night in March 1960 he entered RCA's Nashville studio to cut tracks for a new long-playing-record along with a single, "Stuck on You", which was rushed into release and swiftly became a number one hit.

Colonel Tom Parker pushed Elvis into a heavy film making schedule, focused on formulaic, modestly budgeted musical comedies. Elvis at first insisted on pursuing more serious roles, but when two films in a more dramatic vein, Flaming Star in 1960 and Wild in the Country in 1961, were less commercially successful, he reverted to the formula. Among the twenty-seven films Elvis made during the nineteen-sixties, there were few further exceptions.

In the first half of the 1960's, three of Elvis's soundtrack long-playing-records hit number one on the pop charts, and a few of his most popular songs came from his films, such as "Can't Help Falling in Love" in nineteen sixty-one and "Return to Sender" in nineteen sixty-two. "Viva Las Vegas", the title track to the nineteen-sixty-four film, was a minor hit as a B-side, and became truly popular only later.

Shortly before Christmas nineteen-sixty-six, more than seven years since they first met, Elvis Presley proposed to Priscilla Beaulieu. They were married on May 1st nineteen-sixty-seven, in a brief ceremony in their suite at the Aladdin Hotel in Las Vegas. The flow of formulaic films and assembly-line soundtracks rolled on.

The International Hotel in Las Vegas, boasting the

largest showroom in the city, announced that it had booked Elvis Presley, scheduling him to perform fifty-seven shows over four weeks in 1969.

Elvis assembled new, top-notch accompaniment, led by guitarist James Burton and including two gospel groups, The Imperials and The Sweet Inspirations. He recruited Bill Belew to design variants of karate kassgis for him; these, in jumpsuit form, would be his "stage uniforms" in his later years.

Billy Preston   Solo Artiste

Billy Preston died from Pericarditis and Coma aged fifty-nine on the 6th of June 2006 whilst in Scottsdale, Arizona, U.S.A. He was survived by his sister, Gwen.

Billy Preston was was a committed Christian throughout his life and he openly expressed his faith in works such as his 1970s hit "That's the Way God Planned It".

Although the details did not become fully known to the general public until after his death, Billy Preston struggled throughout his life to cope with his homosexuality, and the lasting effects of the traumatic sexual abuse he suffered as a boy. Although his sexual orientation became known to friends and associates in the music world Billy did not publicly come out as gay until just before he died.

Billy Preston was born in Houston, Texas, U.S.A. and when he was three, the family moved to Los Angeles, and Billy began playing piano while sitting on his mother Robbie's lap. Noted as a child prodigy, Billy Preston was entirely self-taught and never had a music lesson. By the age of ten, he was playing organ onstage backing gospel singers and at age eleven he appeared on an episode of Nat King Cole's NBC network TV show singing the Fats Domino hit "Blueberry Hill" with Nat Cole.

Billy Preston first met the Beatles as a sixteen-year-old in 1962, while part of Little Richard's touring band, when their manager Brian Epstein organized a Liverpool show, at which the Beatles opened. Billy Preston is one of several people referred to as the "Fifth Beatle". At one point during the Get Back sessions, John Lennon proposed the idea of having him join the band, to which Paul McCartney countered that it was difficult enough reaching agreements with four members.

Billy accompanied the Beatles on electric piano for its rooftop concert, the group's final public appearance. In April 1969, their single "Get Back" was credited to "The Beatles with Billy Billy Preston".

Charlie Pride   Solo Artiste

Charlie Pride died aged eighty-six on the 12th of December, 2020 in Dallas, Texas, United States of America due to medical complications which were related to COVID-19. He was survived by his wife Rozene, their two sons, Kraig and Dion, their daughter, Angela and five grand-children and two great-grand-children.

Charlie performed his music solo at clubs and with a four-piece combo called the Night Hawks during a time he lived in Montana but his break came when Chet Atkins at RCA Victor heard a demonstration tape and got Charlie a contract. In 1966, Charlie released his first RCA Victor single, "The Snakes Crawl at Night" and Nashville manager and agent Jack D. Johnson signed him to a contract.

In 1967, he became the first black performer to appear at the Grand Ole Opry since founding member DeFord Bailey, who had last appeared in 1941. Between 1969 and 1971, Charlie Pride had eight singles that reached number one on the US Country Hit Parade and also charted on the Billboard Hot 100: "All I Have to Offer You (Is Me)", "(I'm So) Afraid of Losing You Again", "I Can't Believe That You've Stopped Loving Me", "I'd Rather Love You", "Is Anybody Goin' to San Antone", "Wonder Could I Live There Anymore", "I'm Just Me", and "Kiss an Angel Good Mornin'". The pop success of these songs reflected the country/pop crossover sound that was reaching country music in the 1960s and early 1970s, known as "Country-politan". In 1969, his compilation album, The Best of Charley Pride, sold more than one million copies, and was awarded a gold disc.

In 1971, Charlie released what would become his biggest hit, "Kiss an Angel Good Mornin", a million-selling cross-over single.

John Prine   **Solo Artiste**

John Prine died aged seventy-three on the 7th of April, 2020 in Nashville, Tennessee, U.S.A. after experiencing COVID-19 symptoms. He was survived by his wife, Fiona and sons Jack and Tommy.

In the late 1960s, while John was delivering mail, he began to sing songs he had written at open-microphone evenings in Chicago. The bar was a gathering spot for nearby Old Town School of Folk Music teachers and students. After his first open mic, he was offered paying gigs. After a review was published, John's popularity grew and he became a central figure in the Chicago folk revival. John's self-titled debut album was released in 1971.

John's second album, Diamonds in the Rough in 1972, was a surprise for many after the critical success of his first LP; it was an uncommercial, stripped-down affair that reflected John's fondness for bluegrass music. His subsequent albums from the 1970s include Sweet Revenge in 1973, and "Christmas in Prison", and Common Sense in 1975.

In 1991, John released the Grammy Award-winning The Missing Years, his first collaboration with producer and Heartbreakers bassist Howie Epstein. The title song records Prine's humorous take on what Jesus did in the unrecorded years between his childhood and ministry. On February 8, 2018, John announced his first new album of original material in 13 years, titled The Tree of Forgiveness, would be released.

DEAD STARS Q – S

Pete Quaife   The Kinks

Pete Quaife, died aged sixty-six of kidney failure on the 23rd of June 2010. Pete founded a group known as The Ravens in 1963 with brothers Ray and Dave Davies. In late 1963 or early 1964, they changed their name to The Kinks, and hired Mick Avory as a drummer. The group scored major international hit records throughout the 1960s. Their early singles, including "You Really Got Me" and "All Day and All of the Night", have been cited as an early influence on the hard rock and heavy metal genres. In the band's early days, Pete Quaife, who was generally regarded as the best-looking member, was often their spokesman.

After retiring from the music business, Pete Quaife resided in Denmark throughout the 1970s. He relocated to Belleville, Ontario in 1980, where he worked as a cartoonist and artist but moved back to Denmark in 2005.

Gerry Rafferty   Stealers Wheel

Gerry Rafferty died aged sixty-three of liver failure on the 4th of January 2011 whilst in Stroud, Gloucestershire, U.K. He was survived by his wife, Carla and his daughter, Martha.

Gerry learned both Irish and Scottish folk songs as a boy. He recalled that growing up in Paisley he was hearing all these songs when he was two or three, songs like "She Moves Through the Fair", which his mother sang beautifully and Irish traditional songs and Scots traditional songs". Heavily influenced by folk music and the music of the Beatles and Bob Dylan, Gerry Rafferty started to write his own material.

In 1969 Gerry Rafferty became the third member of a folk-pop group, The Humblebums, composed of comedian

Billy Connolly and Tam Harvey. Harvey left shortly afterwards, and Gerry Rafferty and Connolly continued as a duo, recording two albums for Transatlantic Records.

In 1971, Transatlantic owner Nathan Joseph signed Gerry Rafferty as a solo performer. Gerry Rafferty recorded his first solo album, 'Can I Have My Money Back?', with Hugh Murphy, a staff producer working for the label.

In 1972, Gerry joined Egan to form Stealers Wheel and recorded three albums with the American songwriters and producers Leiber & Stoller. After the disputes were resolved in 1978, he recorded his second solo album, 'City to City', with producer Hugh Murphy, which included the song with which he remains most identified, "Baker Street". The single reached number three in the UK and number two in the USA. The album sold over 5.5 million copies. Gerry considered this his first proper taste of success.

'Baker Street' featured a distinctive saxophone solo played by Raphael Ravenscroft, although the origins of the solo have been disputed. As Gerry recalled in a 1988 interview; when he wrote the song he saw that bit as an instrumental part but he didn't know what for. They tried electric guitar but it sounded weak, and they tried other things and he thought it was Hugh Murphy's suggestion that they tried saxophone.

Gerry's next album, Night Owl, also did well. Guitarist Richard Thompson helped by performing on the track "Take The Money and Run", and the title track was a UK Number five hit in 1979. "Days Gone Down" reached Number seventeen in the USA. The follow-up single "Get It Right Next Time" made the UK and US Top forty.

In 2008, Gerry Rafferty moved away from California and briefly rented a home in Ireland, where his drinking soon became a problem. In July that year, he flew to London, where he stayed in the five-star Westbury Hotel in Mayfair and began a four-day drinking session that left his room extensively damaged.

Johnnie Ray died aged sixty-three of hepatic encephalopathy resulting from liver failure at Cedars-Sinai Medical Centre, LA, California on the 24ᵗʰ of February 1990 . In early 1990, poor health had forced Johnnie to check into Cedars-Sinai near his home in Los Angeles, California, U.S.A. He is buried at Hopewell Cemetery near Hopewell, Oregon, in a grave plot alongside his mother, father, and sister.

Johnnie Ray suffered from alcoholism throughout his life, though during the 1950s at the height of his fame, newspaper and magazine pieces about him did not disclose the extent of his drinking problem. On 2nd September 1952, Johnnie was arrested in Boston for public intoxication, but was released four hours later.

In nineteen-sixty-nine, shortly after Johnnie returned to the United States from a European tour with Judy Garland, an American doctor informed him that he was well enough to drink an occasional glass of wine. He resumed drinking heavily and his health began to decline again.

During nineteen-fifty-one, prior to Johnnie's fame, he was arrested in Detroit for accosting and soliciting an undercover vice squad police officer for sex in the restroom of the Stone Theatre, a burlesque house. When he appeared in court, he pleaded guilty to the charges, paid a fine, and was released.

Due to his obscurity at the time, Detroit newspapers did not report the story. After his rise to fame the following year, rumors about his sexuality began to spread as a result of the incident.

Despite her knowledge of the solicitation arrest, Marilyn Morrison, daughter of the owner of West Hollywood's Mocambo nightclub, married Johnnie Ray at the peak of his American fame. The wedding ceremony took place in New York a short time after he gave his first New York concert, which was at the Copacabana. The New York

Daily News made the wedding its cover story for May 26th, 1952.

Aware of Johnnie's sexuality, his new wife told a friend she would "straighten it out." However, the couple separated in nineteen-fifty-three and divorced in 1954.

In nineteen-sixty-nine, Johnnie headlined a European concert tour with Judy Garland. He served as the best man at her wedding to her last husband, nightclub manager Mickey Deans, in London on 15th March nineteen-sixty-nine. Denmark and Sweden were among the countries where Johnnie and Judy Garland performed together.

In nineteen-eighty-one, Johnnie hired Alan Eichler as his manager and resumed performing with an instrumental trio rather than with the large orchestras he and his audiences had been accustomed to for the first twenty-five years of his career.

In nineteen-eighty-six, Johnnie Ray appeared as a Los Angeles taxicab driver in Billy Idol's "Don't Need a Gun" video and is name-checked in the lyrics of the song.

Johnnie's first record, the self-penned R&B number for Okeh Records, "Whiskey and Gin," was a minor hit in nineteen-fifty-one. The following year he dominated the charts with the double-sided hit single of "Cry" and "The Little White Cloud That Cried." Selling over two million copies of the 78rpm single, Johnnie Ray's delivery struck a chord with teenagers and he quickly became a teen idol.

Otis Redding   Solo Artiste

Otis Redding died in a plane crash aged twenty-six on the 10th of December 1967. He was survived by his wife Zelma and his sons, Otis III and Dexter and daughter Karla. Otis was entombed at his ranch in Round Oak, about twenty miles north of Macon, Georgia, U.S.A.

At an early age, Otis Redding sang in the Vineville Baptist Church choir and learned guitar and piano. From age ten, he took drum and singing lessons. At Ballard-Hudson High School, he sang in the school band. His passion was singing, and he often cited Little Richard and Sam Cooke as influences.

At age fifteen, Otis left school to help financially support his family; his father had contracted tuberculosis and was often hospitalized, leaving his mother as the family's primary income earner. He worked as a well digger, as a gasoline station attendant and occasionally as a musician.

Otis's breakthrough came in 1958 on disc jockey Hamp Swain's "The Teenage Party," a talent contest at the local Roxy and Douglass Theatres. Johnny Jenkins, a locally prominent guitarist, was in the audience and, finding Otis's backing band lacking in musical skills, offered to accompany him. Jenkins later worked as lead guitarist and played with Otis during several later gigs. Otis was then hired by the Upsetters. Otis Redding was well paid, making about twenty-five dollars per gig.

In mid 1960, Otis moved to Los Angeles where he wrote his first songs, including "She's Allright," "Tuff Enuff," "I'm Gettin' Hip" and "Gamma Lamma". Otis signed with Confederate and recorded his second single, "Shout Bamalama" (a rewrite of "Gamma Lamma") and "Fat Girl", together with his band Otis and the Shooters. Around this time he and the Pinetoppers attended a "Battle of the Bands" show in Lakeside Park.

Otis made "These Arms of Mine", with "Hey Hey Baby" on the B-side. The single was released by Volt in October 1962 and charted in March the following year."These Arms of Mine" and other songs from the 1962–nineteen-sixty-three sessions were included on Otis's debut album, Pain in My Heart. "That's What My Heart Needs" and "Mary's Little Lamb" were recorded in June nineteen-sixty-three. The title track, recorded in September nineteen-sixty-three, sparked copyright issues, as it sounded like Irma Thomas's "Ruler of My Heart". Despite this, Pain in My Heart was released on January 1st 1964, and peaked at number twenty on the Rythm&Blues chart and at number eighty-five on the Billboard Hot 100.

In November 1963, Otis travelled to New York to perform at the Apollo Theater for the recording of a live album for Atlantic Records.

Most of Otis Redding's songs after "Security", from his first album, had a slow tempo. Disc jockeys accordingly labeled him "Mr. Pitiful", and subsequently Cropper and Otis wrote the eponymous song. That and top 100 singles "Chained and Bound", "Come to Me" and "That's How Strong My Love Is" were included on Otis Redding's second studio album, 'The Great Otis Redding Sings Soul Ballads', released in March nineteen sixty-five. Jenkins began working independently from the group out of fear Galkin, Walden and Cropper would plagiarize his playing style, and so Cropper became Otis Redding's leading guitarist. Around nineteen sixty-five, Otis co-wrote "I've Been Loving You Too Long".

Otis was one of the first soul artists to perform for rock audiences in the western United States. His performance received critical acclaim, including positive press in the Los Angeles Times, and he penetrated mainstream popular culture. Bob Dylan attended the performance and offered Otis Redding an altered version of one of his songs, "Just Like a Woman".

In late nineteen sixty-six, Otis Redding returned to the Stax studio and recorded several tracks, including "Try a Little Tenderness".

In nineteen-sixty-seven, Otis Redding performed at the influential Monterey Pop Festival as the closing act on Saturday night, the second day of the festival. Until that point, Otis was still performing mainly for black audiences. His act, which included his own song "Respect" and a version of the Rolling Stones' "Satisfaction", was well received by the audience. In early December 1967, Otis again recorded at Stax. One new song was " Dock of the Bay", which was written with Steve Cropper while they were staying with their friend, Earl "Speedo" Simms, on a houseboat in Sausalito.

Noel Redding   **The Jimi Hendrix Experience**

Noel Redding died of haemorraging aged fifty-seven at his home in Ireland on the 11th of May 2003. He was survived by a brother, a sister and a son. In the village of Ardfield, local people erected a plaque to his memory.

Noel's first band was The Lonely Ones which made a privately pressed EP at the Hayton Manor Studio in Stanford, Kent, in 1963.

At age seventeen, Noel went professional and toured clubs in Scotland and Germany with Neil Landon and the Burnettes, which were formed in late 1962, and The Loving Kind, formed in November 1965. In addition, The Lonely Ones reunited in September 1964, and Noel Redding remained with them a year before taking his leave.

Noel Redding switched from guitar to bass on joining the Jimi Hendrix Experience and he helped create the three landmark albums Are You Experienced, Axis: Bold as Love, and Electric Ladyland, as well as performing in some of Jimi Hendrix's most celebrated concerts.

In 1968, Noel formed the group Fat Mattress and provided guitar and vocals. Hendrix's manager, Michael Jeffery, attempted to reunite the Jimi Hendrix Experience months after the Woodstock event. The three were interviewed by Rolling Stone magazine, but no shows or recordings resulted. Noel Redding soon went on to other projects. While living in Los Angeles he formed Road, a three-piece in the same psychedelic hard rock vein as the Experience, with Rod Richards on guitar and Les Sampson on drums, and Noel Redding himself switching back to bass. They released one album, Road in 1972, with the three members taking turns on lead vocals.

In 1997, Fender produced the Noel Redding Signature Jazz bass in a signed limited edition of 1000.

Noel's last performance was in Clonakilty at De Barras pub, where he had held the Friday night residency for nearly twenty years, performing with some of the local musicians who appeared on his last album.

Helen Reddy   Solo Artiste

Helen Reddy died aged seventy-eight on the 29th of September, 2020, in Los Angeles, California, USA. She had suffered from Addison's disease and dementia for some time but no actual cause of death was released. She was survived by her daughter, Traci and her son, Jordan.

Helen had Irish, Scottish, and English ancestry and at age four, she joined her parents on the Australian vaudeville circuit, singing and dancing. She sang on radio and television, eventually winning a talent contest on the Australian pop music TV show Bandstand, the prize ostensibly being a trip to New York City to cut a single for Mercury Records. After arriving in New York in 1966, she was informed by Mercury that her prize was only the chance to "audition" for the label and that Mercury considered the Bandstand footage to constitute her audition, which was deemed unsuccessful. However, she decided to remain in the United States with her three year-old daughter, -Traci and pursue a singing career.

While in Chicago, Helen gained a reputation singing in local lounges, including Mister Kelly's, and in 1968, she landed a deal with Fontana Records, a division of major label Chicago-based Mercury Records. Her first single, "One Way Ticket", on Fontana was not an American hit, but it did give Helen her first appearance on any chart, as it peaked at number 83 in her native Australia.

Helen's stardom was solidified when her single "I Am Woman" reached number one on the Billboard Hot 100 in December 1972.

Over the next five years following her first success, Helen had more than a dozen U.S. top-40 hits, including two more number-one hits. On 23rd July 1974, Helen received a star on the Hollywood Walk of Fame for her work in the music industry.

Helen was most successful on the Easy Listening chart, scoring eight number-one hits there over a three-year span, from "Delta Dawn" in 1973 to "I Can't Hear You No More" in 1976.

Of Helen's eight subsequent single releases on Capitol, five reached the Easy Listening top fifty, including, "Candle on the Water",: "The Happy Girls" , and "I Am Woman", Helen's only chart item that she co-wrote. Also the disco tracks "Ready or Not" and "Make Love to Me" , the latter a cover of an Australian hit by Kelly Marie, which gave Helen Reddy a lone R&B chart ranking at number fifty-nine. Helen Reddy also made it to number ninety-eight on the Country chart with "Laissez les bon Temps Rouler", the B-side to "The Happy Girls".'

In 1990, Helen issued 'Feel So Young' on her own label – an album that includes remakes of her repertoire favourites. Meanwhile, her one recording in the interim had been the 1987 dance maxi-single "Mysterious Kind", on which Helen had vocally supported Jessica Williams. The 1997 release of 'Centre Stage' was an album of show tunes that Helen Reddy recorded for Varèse Sarabande; the track "Surrender" – originating in Sunset Boulevard – was remixed for release as a dance maxi-single. Helen Reddy's final album was the 2000 seasonal release 'The Best Christmas Ever'. In April 2015, Helen Reddy released a cover of The Beatles' "All You Need Is Love" for the album 'Keep Calm and Salute The Beatles' on the Purple Pyramid label.

In the mid-1980s, Helen embarked on a new career in the theatre. She mostly worked in musicals, including Anything Goes, Call Me Madam, The Mystery of Edwin Drood, and – both on Broadway and the West End – Blood Brothers. She also appeared in four productions of the one-woman show Shirley Valentine.

Helen announced her retirement from performing in 2002, giving her farewell performance with the Edmonton Symphony Orchestra. The same year, she moved from her long-time residence in Santa Monica, California, back to her native Australia to spend time with her family, living first on Norfolk Island before taking up residence in Sydney.

Lou Reed   The Velvet Underground

Lou Reed died from liver disease aged seventy-one on the 27th of October 2013 at his home in Southampton, New York, U.S.A. He was ssurvived by his wife, Laurie.

Having learned to play the guitar from the radio, Lou developed an early interest in rock and roll and rhythm and blues, and during high school played in several bands. Lou began experimenting with drugs at the age of sixteen. His first recording was as a member of a doo-wop-style group called the Jades. His love for playing music and his desire to play gigs brought him into confrontation with his anxious and unaccommodating parents.

Many of Lou's guitar techniques, such as the guitar-drum roll, were inspired by jazz saxophonists, such as Ornette Coleman.

Lou graduated with honors from Syracuse University's College of Arts and Sciences with a B.A. in English in June 1964.

In 1964, Lou moved to New York City and began working as an in-house songwriter for Pickwick Records. He wrote and recorded the single "The Ostrich", a parody of popular dance songs of the time, which included lines such as "put your head on the floor and have somebody step on it". His employers felt that the song had hit potential, and assembled a supporting band to help promote the recording. The ad hoc group, called "The Primitives", included Welsh musician John Cale who was impressed by Lou's early repertoire and a partnership began to evolve.

Lou and John Cale lived together on the Lower East Side, and invited Lou's college acquaintance guitarist Sterling Morrison and Cale's neighbour drummer Angus MacLise to join the group, thus forming the Velvet Underground.

The group soon caught the attention of artist Andy Warhol. One of Warhol's first contributions was to integrate them into the Exploding Plastic Inevitable. Warhol's associates inspired many of Lou's songs as he fell into a thriving, multifaceted artistic scene. Lou Reed rarely gave an interview without paying homage to Warhol as a mentor.

In 1971, Lou signed a recording contract with RCA Records and recorded his first solo album in London with top session musicians including Steve Howe and Rick Wakeman, members of the progressive rock group Yes. The album, 'Lou Reed', contained smoothly produced versions of unreleased Velvet Underground songs.

Lou's breakthrough album, 'Transformer', was released in November 1972 and it introduced Lou to a wider audience, especially in the UK. The hit single "Walk on the Wild Side" was an ironic yet affectionate salute to the misfits and hustlers who once surrounded Andy Warhol.

Lou followed 'Transformer' with the darker 'Berlin', a concept album about two junkies in love in the city. The songs variously concern domestic violence, drug addiction, adultery and prostitution, and suicide.

In 1990, following a twenty-year hiatus, the Velvet Underground reformed for a Fondation Cartier benefit in France. Lou released his sixteenth solo record, 'Magic and Loss', in 1992, an album about mortality, inspired by the death of two close friends from cancer. In 1993, the Velvet Underground again reunited and toured throughout Europe.

Lou's 1996 album, 'Set the Twilight Reeling', and 2000's 'Ecstasy', both produced by Hal Willner, drew praise from most critics. In May 2000, Lou Reed performed before

Pope John Paul II at the Great Jubilee Concert in Rome. In 2001, Lou made a cameo appearance in the movie adaptation of Prozac Nation.

In April 2003, Lou embarked on a new world tour supporting both new and released material, with a band including cellist Jane Scarpantoni and singer Anohni. In 2011, the American heavy metal band Metallica recorded a full-length collaboration album with Lou entitled 'Lulu', released on November 1st in North America and October 31st everywhere else. In September 2013 Lou was interviewed, in Soho, London by Mark Beaumont of the New Musical Express about the photobook Transformers. It was to be Lou Reed's last interview.

Jim Reeves   Solo Artiste

Jim Reeves died aged forty on the 31st of July 1964 in an air crash while flying over Brentwood, Tennessee, USA. He was survived by his wife, Mary. Thousands of people travelled to pay their last respects at his funeral two days later. The coffin, draped in flowers from fans, was driven through the streets of Nashville and then to Reeves' final resting place near Carthage, Texas.

Jim's rich voice brought millions of new fans to country music from every corner of the world. Although the crash of his private airplane took his life, posterity will keep his name alive because people will remember him as one of country music's most important performers.

Keith Relf   The Yardbirds

Keith Relf died aged thirty-three on the 12th of May 1976 from electrocution in his home and was buried in Richmond Cemetery in South West London, UK. He was survived by his wife, Annie and his sons Danny and Jason.

Keith Relf started playing in bands around the summer of 1956 as a singer, guitarist, and harmonica player. His blues harp was a key part of the Yardbirds' sound and success and he co-wrote many of the original Yardbirds songs including "Shapes of Things", "I Ain't Done Wrong", "Over Under Sideways Down", "Happenings Ten Years Time Ago". He also sang an early version of "Dazed and Confused" in live Yardbirds concerts, a song later recorded by the band's successor group Led Zeppelin. After the Yardbirds broke up in July 1968, Keith formed the acoustic duo Together, with fellow Yardbird Jim McCarty, followed immediately by Renaissance (which also featured his sister Jane Relf). After leaving Renaissance in 1970, Keith started producing other artists: Steamhammer, folk-rock band Hunter Muskett, the acoustic world music group Amber, psychedelic band Saturnalia, and blues-rock band Medicine Head. In 1974, he formed progressive/rock group Armageddon. Their self-titled debut, 'Armageddon', was recorded in England and released in the United States on A&M Records.

Charlie Rich   Solo Artiste

Charlie Rich died aged sixty-two of a pulmonary embolism on the 25th of July 1995 in a motel in Hammond, Louisiana, U.S.A. He was survived by his wife, Margaret, his sons Allan and Jack and his daughters Renee and Laurie. He was buried in the Memorial Park Cemetery in Memphis, Tennessee, U.S.A.

Charlie enrolled at Arkansas State College on a football scholarship and then transferred to the University of Arkansas as a music major after a football injury. He left after one semester to join the United States Air Force in 1953. While stationed in Enid, Oklahoma, U.S.A. he formed "the Velvetones," playing jazz and blues.

Upon leaving the military in 1956 he began performing in clubs around the Memphis area, playing both jazz and R&B. During this time, he began writing his own songs. After recording some demonstration songs for Sam

Phillips at Sun Records that Phillips considered not commercial enough and "too jazzy". Charlie Rich became a regular session musician for Sun Records, playing on a variety of records by Lewis, Johnny Cash, Bill Justis, Warren Smith, Billy Lee Riley, Carl Mann, and Ray Smith.

Charlie's third single for the Sun subsidiary, Phillips International Records, was the 1960 Top 30 hit, "Lonely Weekends" and it sold more than one million copies and was awarded a gold disc by the Recording Industry Association of America.

Charlie's career then stalled and he left the struggling Sun label in 1963, signing with a subsidiary of RCA Victor, Groove. His first single for Groove, "Big Boss Man", was a minor hit, but again, his Chet Atkins-produced follow-ups all failed to be big. Charlie Rich moved to Smash Records early in 1965. Charlie's new producer, Jerry Kennedy, encouraged Charlie to emphasize his country and rock n' roll leanings, although Charlie Rich considered himself a jazz pianist and had not paid so much attention to the country music scene since his childhood. The first single for Smash was "Mohair Sam", an R&B-inflected novelty-rock number written by Dallas Frazier, and it became a top 30 pop hit.

Epic Records signed Charlie Rich in 1967, mainly on the recommendation of producer Billy Sherrill. Sherrill helped Charlie Rich refashion himself as a Nashville Sound balladeer during an era when old rock 'n' roll artists like Jerry Lee Lewis and Conway Twitty were finding a new musical home in the country and western format. The new Charlie Rich sound paid off in the summer of 1972, when "I Take It on Home" went to number six on the country charts. The title track from his 1973 album Behind Closed Doors became a number-one country hit early in that year, then crossing over into the top 20 on the pop charts. This time, his follow-up single did not disappoint, as "The Most Beautiful Girl" spent three weeks at the top of the country charts and two weeks at the top of the pop charts. Now that he was established as a country music star, Behind Closed Doors won three awards from the Country Music Association that year: Best Male Vocalist, Album of the Year, and Single of the Year. The album was also certified gold. Charlie Rich won a Grammy Award for Best Male Country Vocal Performance, and he took home four Academy of Country Music awards.

After "The Most Beautiful Girl," number-one hits came quickly, as five songs topped the country charts in 1974 and crossed over to the pop charts. The songs were "There Won't Be Anymore", "A Very Special Love Song", "I Don't See Me In Your Eyes Anymore", "I Love My Friend", and "She Called Me Baby".

Bill Rieflin   REM

Bill Rieflin died aged fifty-nine from cancer on the 24th of March, 2020. He was survived by his mother and his brothers, Richard and Fritz and daughters Mayda and Alex and sister, Tracy.

Bill began his professional career in his hometown of Seattle and in 1975. He played drums for The Blackouts starting in 1979.

Bill appeared on all KMFDM records released from 1995 to 2003 as a drummer, programmer, vocalist and keyboardist. He toured with the band as a bassist in 2002 in support of its comeback album, Attak. and performed on the 2011 KMFDM album, WTF?!. Eventually Peter Buck offered Bill the opportunity to sit in with R.E.M., who were missing a permanent drummer since the 1997 departure of Bill Berry. The band gave him the live drummer slot in its 2003 tour. They later announced that Bill would fill the role indefinitely.

Bill formed an experimental ensemble under the name 'Slow Music' in 2005 (including Fripp and Buck) in which he played synthesizers rather than drums. The group played a small handful of live dates in 2005 and 2006 and became inactive for several years. He was also involved in a music collaboration project entitled The Humans, which consisted of him, Chris Wong, Robert Fripp and Toyah Willcox. The band performed a series of live dates in Estonia in Autumn 2007 and 2009, and released their debut album We are the Humans in 2009. In 2012, Bill performed on drums for Robbie Williams's album 'Take the Crown'.

Lyn Ripley   Twinkle

Twinkle died from cancer aged sixty-six on the 21st of May 2015 on the Isle of Wight, U.K. She is survived by her husband Graham and their son, Michael and their daughter, Amber.

Twinkle owed her early entrance to recording studios at the age of sixteen to her boyfriend, Dec Cluskey, of the hit pop group The Bachelors, who was introduced to her by her sister, a music journalist, and who passed on to his manager a demo that Twinkle's father played to him. Her song "Terry" was a teenage tragedy song about the death of a boyfriend in a motorcycle crash which conjured up a dark mood with its doleful backing vocals, spooky organ, 12-string guitar and slow, emphatic rhythm. The follow-up, "Golden Lights", was also self-written . Twinkle made few live appearances but performed "Terry" at the annual New Musical Express hit concerts.

Minnie Ripperton   Solo Artiste

Minnie Riperton died of cancer aged thirty-one on the 12th of July, 1979 in Los Angeles, California, U.S.A. she was survived by her husband, Richard and their son, Marc and their daughter, Maya.

Minnie was interred in the Westwood Village Memorial Park Cemetery in Los Angeles where her epitaph is the opening line of her most famous song: "Lovin' you is easy 'cause you're beautiful." .

Minnie received operatic vocal training when young Minnie but was becoming interested in soul, rhythm and blues, and rock music.

Minnie's first professional singing engagement was with The Gems, when she was fifteen. The Gems had relatively limited commercial success, but proved to be a good outlet for Minnie's talent.

While a part of Studio Three, Minnie met her mentor, producer Billy Davis, who wrote her first local hit, "Lonely Girl", as well as "You Gave Me Soul" and in honor of him she used the pseudonym Andrea Davis for the release of those two singles. Some months after her Andrea Davis singles got on radio, Minnie joined Rotary Connection, a funky rock-soul group creation of Marshall Chess, the son of Chess Records founder Leonard Chess.

In 1973, Minnie Riperton signed with Epic Records, and the family moved to Los Angeles, California. The subsequent record, 'Perfect Angel', turned out to be one of Minnie's best-selling albums. Included were the rock-soul anthem "Reasons"; the second single, "Take a Little Trip" (written by Stevie Wonder, who also coproduced the album). With the fourth single, "Lovin' You", the album caught on, and in April 1975, the song went to the top of the charts in the U.S. and 24 other countries. The song reached no. 2 in the UK Singles Chart, and number three on the U.S. R&B charts. It sold more than one million copies, and was awarded a gold disc by the RIAA in April 1975.

After Perfect Angel, Minnie started on her third album, 'Adventures in Paradise' released in 1975.

Marty Robbins   Solo Artiste

Marty Robbins died aged fifty-seven on the 8th of December 1982, at St. Thomas Hospital in Nashville, Tennessee, U.S.A. Marty had a history of cardiovascular disease and after his third heart attack, he underwent quadruple coronary bypass surgery from which he did not recover and died six days later. He was survived by his wife Marizona, his son Ronny and daughter Janet.

At seventeen, Marty left his troubled home to serve in the United States Navy as an LCT coxswain during World War II. He was stationed in the Solomon Islands in the Pacific Ocean.

To pass the time during the war, he learned to play the guitar, started writing songs, and came to love Hawaiian music.

After his discharge from the military in 1947, he began to play at local venues in Phoenix, then moved on to host his own show on KTYL and then his own television show on KPHO-TV in Phoenix and got a record deal with Columbia Records. Marty also became known for his appearances at the Grand Ole Opry in Nashville, Tennessee.

Although by 1960 Marty Robbins' output was largely country music, his initial hits like "Singing the Blues", "Knee Deep in the Blues", "The Story of My Life", "She Was Only Seventeen", and "A White Sport Coat and a Pink Carnation" were generally regarded as more pop/teen idol material than his hits from 1960 onwards ("El Paso" etc.). His 1957 recording of "A White Sport Coat and a Pink Carnation" sold over one million copies, and was awarded a gold record.

In 1961, Marty wrote the words and music and recorded "I Told the Brook," a ballad later recorded by Billy Thorpe.

He won the Grammy Award for the Best Country & Western Recording 1961 for his follow-up album More Gunfighter Ballads and Trail Songs, and was awarded the Grammy Award for Best Country Song in 1970, for "My Woman, My Woman, My Wife".

Robbie Robertson   The Band

Robbie Robertson died aged eighty in Los Angeles on the 9th of August 2023, after a year-long battle with prostate cancer. He was survived by his wife, Janet and his son, Sebastian and his daughters, Alexandra and Delphine.

The Band began performing regularly in spring 1969, with their first live dates as the Band taking place at the Winterland Ballroom in San Francisco. Their most notable performances that year were at the 1969 Woodstock Festival and the UK Isle of Wight Festival with Bob Dylan that August. The Band's eponymous album was released in September 1969, and became a critical and commercial success.

The song from that album that had the strongest cultural influence was "The Night They Drove Old Dixie Down", a song exploring a Confederate man's life after defeat of the South following the American Civil War.

The Band rented The Woodstock Playhouse in Woodstock, New York with the intent of recording a new live album there, but the city council voted against it, so they recorded on location, but without an audience. Robbie handled most of the songwriting duties as before. Robbie brought in Todd Rundgren to engineer the album which was recorded in two weeks'. These sessions became their third album.

The Band's next album, Cahoots, was recorded at Albert Grossman's newly built Bearsville Studios and was released in October 1971. That album received mixed reviews.

The Band continued to tour throughout 1970 and 1971. A live album recorded at a series of shows at the Academy of Music in New York City was released in 1972 as the double album Rock Of Ages.

In October 1973, the Band released an album of cover songs entitled Moondog Matinee. In February 1973, Bob Dylan relocated from Woodstock, New York to Malibu, California and Robbie moved to Malibu in the summer of 1973.

The 1974 tour began at the Chicago Stadium in January, 1974, and ended at The Forum in Inglewood, California in

February. The shows began with more songs from the new Planet Waves album and with covers that Dylan and the Band liked, but as the tour went on, they moved toward playing older and more familiar material, only keeping "Forever Young" from the Planet Waves album in the set list. Dylan and the Band played a number of tracks from the controversial 1965–1966 World Tour, this time to wildly enthusiastic response from the audience where there had been mixed reaction and boos nine years previously.

Following the 1974 reunion tour with Bob Dylan, rock manager Elliot Roberts booked the Band with the recently reunited Crosby, Stills, Nash, and Young. On the 4th of September, both artists played Wembley Stadium in London, appearing with Jesse Colin Young and Joni Mitchell.

After moving to Malibu in 1973, Robbie and the Band had discovered a ranch in Malibu near Zuma Beach called "Shangri-La", and decided to lease the property.

The album release of The Basement Tapes, credited to Bob Dylan and the Band, was the first album production that took place in the new studio. The album, produced by Robbie, featured a selection of tapes from the original 1967 Basement Tapes sessions with Dylan, as well as demos for tracks eventually recorded for the Music From Big Pink album. Robbie cleaned up the tracks, and the album was released in July 1975.

Shangri-La Studios proved to be a return to a clubhouse atmosphere that the Band had enjoyed previously at Big Pink, and in the spring of 1975, the group began work on Northern Lights – Southern Cross, their first release of original material in four years. One of the best known tracks on the album is "Acadian Driftwood", the first song with specifically Canadian subject material.

Jim Rodford   Argent

Jim Rodford died aged seventy-six after a fall down the stairs at his home on the 20th of January 2018. He is survived by his wife Jean, his sons Steve and Russell and daughter, Paula.

Jim was born in St Albans, Hertfordshire, UK. and in the late 1950s and early 1960s he was a member of the Bluetones, the biggest band in St Albans at the time. Although he did not become a band member at this stage, Jim was instrumental in helping his younger cousin Rod Argent form the Zombies in 1964. Jim later joined the Mike Cotton Sound as a bass guitarist.

Along with Rod Argent, Jim was one of the founding members of Argent. When Rod Argent quit the band, the remaining three members Jim Rodford, Bob Henrit, and John Verity formed the short-lived band Phoenix. Eventually, Jim joined the Kinks as a bass guitarist in 1978 and played with them until their final dissolution in 1996.

Kenny Rogers   The 1st Edition

Kenny Rodgers died aged eighty-one under hospice care on the 20th of March 2020 in Sandy Springs, Georgia, U.S.A. He was survived by his fifth wife, Wanda, and sons, Kenny Jnr, Christopher, Justin and Jordan and his daughter, Carole.

Kenny Rodgers was born in Houston, Texas, U.S.A. the fourth of eight children and was of both Irish and Native American ancestry. In a recording career dating back to the 1950s, Kenny moved from teenage rock'n'roll through psychedelic rock to become a country-pop crossover artist of the 1970s and 1980s. He had a minor solo hit in 1957 called "That Crazy Feeling". After sales slowed down, Kenny joined a jazz group called The Bobby Doyle Three, who got a lot of work in clubs thanks to a reasonable fan following. The group recorded for Columbia Records but they disbanded in 1965. Kenny also worked as a producer, writer and session musician for other performers, including country artists Mickey Gilley and Eddy Arnold. In 1966 he joined the New Christy Minstrels as a singer and double bass player.

After feeling that the Minstrels were not offering the success he wanted, Kenny and fellow members left the group and then formed The First Edition in 1967 and they chalked up a string of hits on both the pop and country charts, including "Just Dropped In (To See What Condition My Condition Was In)", "But You Know I Love You", "Ruby, Don't Take Your Love to Town", "Tell It All, Brother", "Reuben James", and "Something's Burning".

When the First Edition broke up in 1976, Kenny launched his solo career and soon developed a more middle-of-the-road sound that sold to both pop and country audiences. He has charted more than sixty top 40 hit singles in the U.S.A. including two number ones; "Lady" and "Islands in the Stream". His music has also been featured in top-selling movie soundtracks, including 'Convoy', 'Urban Cowboy', and 'The Big Lebowski'.

After leaving his backing band in 1976, after almost a decade with the group, Kenny signed a solo deal with United Artists. The single "Lucille" in 1977 was a major hit, reaching number one on the pop charts in twelve countries, selling over five million copies, and firmly establishing Kenny's post First Edition career.

"Islands in the Stream", Kenny Rodgers' duet with Dolly Parton, was the first single to be released from 'Eyes That See in the Dark' in the United States, and it quickly went to number one in the Billboard Hot 100, as well as topping Billboard's country and adult contemporary singles charts; it was certified Platinum by the Recording Industry Association of America for shipping two million copies in the United States.

In 2013, Kenny recorded a new album with the name 'You Can't Make Old Friends'. This album included the title track, a new duet with Dolly Parton, which was his first single released in six years. In 2015, Kenny Rodgers announced his farewell tour, titled 'The Gambler's Last Deal'.

Kenny Rodgers' final concert in Nashville took place on the 25th of October, 2017 at the Bridgestone Arena where he was joined by an array of guest artists.

Mick Ronson   Spiders from Mars

Mick Ronson died aged forty-six of liver cancer on the 29th of April 1993. He was survived by his wife, Suzanne, his sons Nicholas and Joakim and his daughter, Lisa. In his memory, the Mick Ronson Memorial Stage was constructed in Queen's Gardens, Hull.

As a child, Mick was trained classically to play piano, recorder, violin, and the harmonium. He initially wanted to be a cellist, but moved to guitar upon discovering the music of Duane Eddy, whose sound on the bass notes of his guitar sounded to Mick similar to that of the cello. He joined his first band, The Mariners, in November 1963, when he was seventeen. His stage debut with The Mariners was in support of the Keith Herd Band at Brough Village Hall. While Mick was working with The Mariners, another local Hull group – The Crestas – recruited him on the advice of The Mariners' bassist.

In 1965, Mick left The Crestas, moving to London to seek work. He took a part-time job as a mechanic, and joined a band called The Voice. After playing a few dates with the group, Mick returned from a weekend in Hull to find their gear piled at his flat and a note explaining that the rest of the group had gone to The Bahamas. Mick stayed in London and teamed up briefly with a soul band called The Wanted, before eventually returning to Hull. In 1966, he joined Hull's top local band, The Rats.

In 1967 The Rats recorded the one-off psychedelic track, "The Rise and Fall of Bernie Gripplestone". In March 1970, during the recording sessions for Elton John's album Tumbleweed Connection, Mick played guitar on the track "Madman Across the Water".

Early in 1970, John Cambridge came to Hull in search

for Mick, intent upon recruiting him for a new David Bowie backing band called The Hype. He found Mick marking out a rugby pitch, one of his duties as a Parks Department gardener for Hull City Council. Having failed in his earlier attempts in London, Mick was reluctant, but eventually agreed to accompany Cambridge to a meeting with David Bowie. Two days later, Mick made his debut with David Bowie on John Peel's national BBC Radio 1 show.

Mick's guitar and arranging during the Spiders from Mars era provided much of the underpinning for later punk rock musicians. His guitar work was next heard on David Bowie's Aladdin Sane and 1973 covers album Pin Ups. After leaving David Bowie's entourage after the "Farewell Concert" in 1973 , Mick released three solo albums. His solo debut Slaughter on 10th Avenue, featured a version of Elvis Presley's "Love Me Tender", as well as his most famous solo track, "Only After Dark".

Mick had a short-lived stint with Mott the Hoople then he became a long-time collaborator with Mott's former leader Ian Hunter, commencing with the album 'Ian Hunter' and featuring the UK Singles Chart Number fourteen hit "Once Bitten, Twice Shy", including a spell touring as the Hunter-Ronson Band.

Mick was also a member of Bob Dylan's "Rolling Thunder Revue" live band, and can be seen both on and off-stage in the film of the tour. He made a connection with Roger McGuinn during this time, which led to his producing and contributing guitar and arrangements to McGuinn's 1976 solo album 'Cardiff Rose'.

Tim Rose   **Solo Artiste**

Tim Rose died aged sixty-two at a London hospital of a heart attack on the 24th of September 2002. He was buried in Brompton Cemetery in South-West London. He had no decendents.

Tim learned to play the banjo and guitar, and won the top music award in high school. Tim's first band was The Singing Strings, which included his friend Scott McKenzie, who later joined with John Phillips (eventually of The Mamas & the Papas) in a local group called The Abstracts, later The Smoothies and eventually The Journeymen. In 1962, Tim teamed up with ex-Smoothie Michael Boran as Michael and Timothy. Jake Holmes, Rich Husson and Tim formed a group called The Feldmans, later known as Tim Rose and the Thorns.

In 1962 Tim met singer Cass Elliot at a party in Georgetown and formed a folk trio with her and singer John Brown called The Triumvirate. Later they changed the name to The Big 3. They soon landed a job at The Bitter End, a folk club in New York's Greenwich Village.

Their success grew, with appearances on national television programs, and they recorded two albums: The Big 3 in 1963 and The Big 3 Live at the Recording Studio in 1964. Songs included "Grandfather's Clock", and an anti-war dirge written by Fred Hellerman and Fran Minkoff, "Come Away Melinda", a re-recorded version of which was one of Tim Rose's most successful solo singles several years later.

After The Big 3, Tim went solo, and by 1966, his prospects had improved. In November of that year, he played two gigs at the Fillmore Auditorium in San Francisco; headlining were the Grateful Dead and Jefferson Airplane. CBS Records signed Tim to a multi-album record deal; the first album, Tim Rose, came out in 1967. It featured a new version of "Come Away Melinda" and "Long Time Man", which was also previously recorded with The Big 3 as well as his versions of two songs that would become standards: Billy Roberts' "Hey Joe" and Bonnie Dobson's "Morning Dew". Both were released as singles, and would be further covered by many artists, from the Grateful Dead to Clannad. Backed up by a trio that included William Lewis Wexler on keyboards and flute.

Tim recorded The Gambler in 1977, with a group that included guitarist Andy Summers, only to find that the record company refused to release it. He returned to New York for a number of years, living in Hell's Kitchen on Restaurant Row, and then much later Lincoln Square near Central Park. Having lost his contacts in the music industry, he was forced to work as a construction labourer until an opportunity arose to sing jingles for TV commercials in early 1980.

By the late 1980s, Tim had reached the lowest point in his career. After his marriage broke up, he gave up drinking. In 1986, Nick Cave included "Long Time Man", a version very close to Tim Rose's, on the album Your Funeral, My Trial. Cave went on to assist Tim in recovering his career, and encouraged him to play live shows again. By the late 1990s to early 2000s, most of his back catalogue had been re-released.

Gary Rossington   Lynard Skynard

Gary Rossngton died aged seventy-one of un-revealed causes, at his home in Milton, Georgia, USA on the 5th of March 2023. He was survived by his wife, Dale and a daughter, Mary Elizabeth.

Gary suffered a heart attack in October 2015, after which two Lynyrd Skynyrd concerts had to be cancelled. In July 2021, he underwent emergency heart surgery.

Gary is best known as a founding member of rock band Lynyrd Skynyrd, in which he played lead and rhythm guitar and he was the longest-surviving founding member.

It was Gary's love of baseball that indirectly led to the formation of Lynyrd Skynyrd in the summer of 1964 when he became acquainted with Ronnie Van Zant and Bob Burns while playing on rival Jacksonville baseball teams and the trio decided to jam together one afternoon.

Gary's instrument of choice was a 1959 Gibson Les Paul which he had purchased from a woman whose boyfriend had left her and left behind his guitar. He named it "Berniece" in honor of his mother, whom he was extremely close to after the death of his father. Gary Rossngton played lead guitar on "Tuesday's Gone" and the slide guitar for "Free Bird". Along with Collins, Gary Rossngton also provided the guitar work for "Simple Man". Besides the Les Paul, he used various other Gibson Guitars including Gibson SGs. Gibson also released a Gary Rossngton SG/Les Paul in their Custom Shop.

Andy Rourke   The Smiths

Andy Rourke died aged fifty-nine from pancreatic cancer on the 19th of May 2023 at a cancer treatment center in New York City. He was survived by his wife, Francesca.

Andy joined the Smiths after their first gig, having known guitarist Johnny Marr since secondary school, and played on their entire discography. After the group broke up in 1987, he performed on some of lead vocalist Morrissey's early solo releases. Andy recorded with Sinéad O'Connor and the Pretenders in the early 1990s, and was a member of the supergroup Freebass and the band D.A.R.K. He organised the Versus Cancer concerts from 2006 to 2009.

Andy was born in Manchester in 1964. When he left school he passed through a series of menial jobs, playing guitar and bass in various rock bands, as well as in the short-lived funk band Freak Party, with Marr.

Marr later teamed up with Morrissey to form the Smiths and Andy joined the band after its first gig in 1982, when Marr fired original bass player Dale Hibbert. The band's second studio album, Meat Is Murder, featured the track "Barbarism Begins at Home", a seven-minute funk-inspired track regarded by several critics as one of Andy's greatest contributions.

Then having heroin addiction, Andy was arrested for drug possession and sacked from the band in early 1986, via a handwritten note left on his car windscreen by Morrissey. A session musician was brought in as a replacement and found Andy Rourke's compositions difficult to learn and he was relieved when Andy was restored two weeks later, having being cleared to tour the United States. Just after Andy's restoration, the Smiths released their third studio album, The Queen Is Dead. Andy played cello on several Smiths tracks, including "Shakespeare's Sister", "Rubber Ring", "Oscillate Wildly", and the Troy Tate version of "Pretty Girls Make Graves". The Smiths released their fourth and final studio album Strangeways, Here We Come, in 1987 to critical acclaim, and broke up soon after.

Dave Rowberry   The Animals

Dave Rowberry died aged sixty-two on the 6th of June 2003 in Hackney, East London, U.K. He was survived by his wife, Cheryl and his sons, Philip, Alan and Steven.

Dave had entered the Newcastle-upon-Tyne blues and jazz music scene in the early 1960's, while he was attending Newcastle University and joined The Mike Cotton Jazzmen in 1962, who then made a living backing American blues and pop acts touring England. Dave played on the group's singles from 1962 until 1965, including their hit, "Swing That Hammer", as well as their eponymous album.

The Animals were already a major British group in May 1965 when founding keyboardist Alan Price suddenly left due to fear of flying and other issues. According to lead singer Eric Burdon, Dave, while considered a good musician, was chosen partly because of his passing physical resemblance to Alan Price. Dave played many of the group's big hits, including "We Gotta Get Out of This Place", "It's My Life", "Don't Bring Me Down", "Inside-Looking Out", and "See See Rider". For a number of songs, Dave was also credited as the arranger.

In the early to mid-1990s, Dave was a member of Shut Up Frank, a band formed by Mick Avory, of The Kinks. In 1999, Dave joined "Animals II", formed in 1993 by original Animals guitarist Hilton Valentine. During this period Dave also worked as a freelance musician on the London jazz scene.

Jimmy Ruffin   Solo Artiste

Jimmy Ruffin died aged seventy-eight on the 17th of November 2014, in Las Vegas, U.S.A. He was interred in the Garden of Eternal Life Section at Palm Memorial Park Northwest Cemetery, Las Vegas, Clark County, Nevada, U.S.A.

In 1961, Jimmy became a singer as part of the Motown stable, mostly on sessions but also recording singles for its subsidiary Miracle label, but was then drafted for national service. After leaving the Army in 1964, he returned to Motown. In 1966, Jimmy heard a song about unrequited love written for The Spinners, and persuaded the writers that he should record it himself. His recording of "What Becomes of the Brokenhearted" became a major success. The song reached number seven on the American Billboard Hot 100 and number six on the Rythm&Blues Chart. It also initially reached number eight in the UK singles chart, rising to number four when it was reissued in the UK in 1974.

In the 1980s, Jimmy moved to live in Great Britain, where he continued to perform successfully. In December 1984 he collaborated with Paul Weller of The Style Council for his benefit single "Soul Deep", produced to raise money for the families of striking miners affected by the UK miners' strike. This went under the name of The Council Collective and he appeared with Paul on Radio 1 to say he is involved because his father worked down the mines and "he understands the suffering."

Leon Russell died aged seventy-four in his sleep at his home in Tennessee, U.S.A. on the 13th of November 2016. He was survived by his wife, Janet and his son, Teddy Jack and his daughters, Blue, Tina, Sugaree, Honey and Coco.

Leon began playing the piano at the age of four and attended Will Rogers High School in Tulsa, Oklahoma in the same 1959 class as power-pop musician David Gates with whom he played and recorded with as the Fencemen.

After moving to Los Angeles in 1958, Leon became a session musician, working as a pianist on the recordings of many notable 1960s musical artists. By the late 1960s, he had diversified, becoming successful as an arranger and songwriter. By 1970, he had become a solo recording artist. Leon Russell released his first solo single, "Everybody's Talking 'Bout the Young", for Dot Records in 1965. The 1968 release of Look Inside the Asylum Choir by Smash Records was a recording of a studio group consisting of Leon Russell and Marc Benno.

Leon l performed as a member of Delaney & Bonnie and Friends in 1969 and 1970, playing guitar and keyboards on their albums and as part of the touring band.

Leon's first commercial success as a songwriter came when Joe Cocker recorded the song "Delta Lady" for his 1969 album, Joe Cocker! The album, co-produced and arranged by Leon, reached number eleven on the Billboard 100. Leon went on to organize and perform in the 1970 Mad Dogs and Englishmen tour, using many of the musicians from Delaney and Bonnie's band.

Paul Ryan died aged forty-four of lung cancer on the 29th of November 1992 in London, U.K. He was survived by nobody traceable.

Paul was born Paul Sapherson in 1948 and was the son

of 1950's pop singer Marion Ryan. Paul began performing with his twin brother Barry at the age of sixteen. In 1965 they signed a recording contract with Decca under the name of Paul & Barry Ryan. Within two years they had amassed eight Top 50 singles in the UK. Their best sellers were "Don't Bring Me Your Heartaches", a number thirteen hit in 1965, "I Love Her", a number seventeen hit in 1966 and "Have Pity on the Boy", a number eighteen hit the same year.

This success took its toll on Paul, who was unable to cope any longer with the stress of show business. It was decided that Barry would now continue as a solo artist, enabling him to stay out of the limelight and write songs for his twin to perform.

Their greatest achievement as a composer-singer duo, was "Eloise", a number two hit in 1968. It sold over one million copies and was awarded a gold disc. "Love is Love", their next chart entry, also became a million-seller.

In the 1970s, Paul relocated to the United States. In 1976, he released an album, Scorpio Rising. After returning to the U.K. in 1985, he earned his living from operating a chain of hairdressing salons.

Barry Ryan   **Paul & Barry Ryan**

Barry Ryan died of cancer aged seventy-two on the 28th of September 2021. He was survived by his wife, Christine, his son, Jack and his daughter, Sophia.

Barry achieved his initial pop success in the mid 1960s in a duo with his twin brother Paul. After Paul ceased performing to concentrate solely on songwriting, Barry became a solo artist. Barry's most successful hit, "Eloise", reached number 2 on the UK Singles Chart in 1968.

In the mid-1970s, Barry began a forty year career as a fashion and portrait photographer. He worked for magazines such as Italian Vogue and David Bailey's Ritz; he sold six photographs to the National Portrait Gallery; and he made portraits of celebrities such as Ronald Reagan, Margaret Thatcher, Stephen Hawking, Sting, Paul McCartney, and Björk.

Paul Ryder   Happy Mondays

Paul Ryder died of heart disease and diabetes aged fifty-eight on the 15th of July 2022. He was survived by his wife, Linda and his son, Chico.

Paul was a bass player and was a founding member of the Manchester band Happy Mondays along with his brother Shaun.

Paul was an active member of the band through most of its history from its inception in 1983 through to his death. It was during his tenure with the band that it had its biggest successes with albums such as Pills 'n' Thrills and Bellyaches.

Paul left Happy Mondays to write music for several television shows, and formed a new band, Big Arm, who released an album in 2008 entitled Radiator.

Peter Sarstedt   Solo Artiste

Peter Sarstedt died on the 8th of January 2017 at the age of seventy-five. He was survived by his wife, Joanna, his son, Daniel and his daughter, Anna. He had progressive supranuclear palsy, diagnosed in 2015, but originally misdiagnosed as dementia in 2013.

Peter was a younger brother of the 1960's pop star Eden Kane, for whom he briefly played bass. He was best known for his 1969 UK number-one single, released on the United Artists label, "Where Do You Go To My Lovely?". The song topped the charts in fourteen countries and was also awarded the 1970 Ivor Novello Award for Best Song Musically and Lyrically. Peter cited his first wife Anita as the inspiration for the song.

In the 1980s and 1990s, Peter frequently toured the

southern UK as part of the "Solid Silver '60s" package tours, having returned to England after several years residing in Denmark. In the 1990s and 2000s, he continued to release new albums and tour. In 1997 he released the album England's Lane, and in 2007 an album of new material called On Song.

Peter's final album, released in 2013, was entitled Restless Heart and he last performed live in 2010.

Ray Sawyer   Dr. Hook & the Medicine Show

Ray Sawyer died aged eighty-one of undisclosed causes on the 31st of December 2018 at Daytona Beach, Florida, U.S.A. He was survived by his wife, Linda, and his son, Cayse.

Ray lost his right eye in an automobile accident in 1967. As Dr. Hook, Ray had many hit singles such as "Sylvia's Mother", "A Little Bit More", "Only Sixteen", "Walk Right In", "Sharing the Night Together", "When You're in Love with a Beautiful Woman", "Better Love Next Time", "Sexy Eyes", "Girls Can Get It", and "Baby Makes Her Bluejeans Talk".

Bon Scott   AC/DC

Bon Scott died aged thirty-three of acute alcohol poisoning on the 19th of February 1980. He was survived by his wife, Irene.

Bon grew up in Kirriemuir, Scotland and was his parents' second child. The Scott family emigrated from Scotland to Australia in 1952.

Bon's vocals were inspired by his idol, Little Richard. After working as a postman, bartender and truck packer, Scott started his first band, the Spektors, in 1964 as drummer and occasional lead singer. In 1966 they merged with another local band, the Winstons, and formed the Valentines, in which Scott was co-lead singer with Vince Lovegrove. The Valentines recorded several songs written by

George Young of the Easybeats. "Every Day I Have to Cry" made the local record chart. In 1970, after gaining a place on the National Top 30 with their single "Juliette", the Valentines disbanded due to artistic differences after a much-publicised drug scandal.

Bon moved to Adelaide in 1970 and joined the progressive rock group Fraternity. Fraternity released the LPs Livestock and Flaming Galah before touring the UK in 1973, where they changed their name to Fang. During this time they played support slots for Status Quo and Geordie.

Bon replaced Dave Evans as the lead singer of AC/DC in October 1974, when it became obvious the band and Evans were heading in different directions. Scott's appointment coincided with him working as a chauffeur for the band at the time until an audition promoted him to lead singer.

With the Young brothers as lead and rhythm guitarists, session drummer Tony Currenti and George Young as a temporary bassist, AC/DC released High Voltage, their first LP in Australia, in February 1975. The album was not released in the USA until March 1981.

In the following years, AC/DC gained further success with their albums Let There Be Rock and Powerage. In February 1980, AC/DC appeared on Aplauso TV in Spain where they played "Beating Around the Bush", "Girls Got Rhythm", and "Highway to Hell", This was be Bon Scott's last public appearance with AC/DC before his death.

Jim Seals   **Seals & Crofts**

Jim Seals died aged seventy-nine on the 6th of June 2022 after a long illness. He was survived by his wife, Ruby and his sons Joshua and Sutherland.

Jim Seals and Dash Crofts were both born in Texas and they first met when Dash was a drummer for a local band. Later, Jim joined an outfit called Dean Beard and the Crew Cats, in which he played sax and later on Dash joined Jim in the band.

After the failure of a band called the Dawnbreakers, the Jim and Dash decided to play as a duo, with Jim on guitar, saxophone and violin and Dash on guitar and mandolin. They signed a contract with the record division of Talent Associates (TA) in 1969 and released two LPs, of which only the second reached the Billboard 200 chart, peaking at number 122 in October 1970.

The pair also recorded songs that appeared in the feature films One on One in 1977 and Foolin' Around in1980, as well as the song "First Years".

In 1991, Seals and Crofts officially reunited and made concert appearances once again until disbanding a year later.

In 2004, the duo reunited again and recorded their first new album since 1980, released as Traces.

In the early 2000s up to 2008, Jim Seals embarked on various tours with his brother Dan, billing themselves as Seals & Seals and performing their successful hits from Seals & Crofts. A few shows featured Jim's sons Joshua on bass guitar and backing vocals and Sutherland on electric guitar.

Pete Seeger   Solo Artiste

Pete Seeger died aged ninety-four on the 27th of January 2014 at the Presbyterian Hospital, New York, U.S.A. He was survived by his wife, Toshi and his sons, Peter and Daniel and his daughters, Mika and Tinya.

To earn money during the blacklist period of the late 1950s and early 1960s, Pete worked gigs as a music teacher in schools and summer camps, and travelled the college campus circuit. He also recorded as many as five albums a year for Moe Asch's Folkways Records label. As the nuclear disarmament movement picked up steam in the late 1950s and early 1960s, Pete's anti-war songs, such as, Where Have All the Flowers Gone? & Turn! Turn! Turn! gained wide currency. Pete Seeger also was closely associated with the Civil Rights Movement and in 1963 helped organize a landmark Carnegie Hall concert, featuring the youthful Freedom Singers, as a benefit for the Highlander Folk School in Tennessee. This event and Martin Luther King's March on Washington in August of that year brought the Civil Rights anthem We Shall Overcome to wide audiences where he sang it on the 50-mile walk from Selma to Montgomery, Alabama, along with 1,000 other marchers. By this time, Pete Seeger was a senior figure in the 1960s folk revival centred in Greenwich Village, as a longtime columnist in Sing Out!, the successor to the People's Songs Bulletin, and as a founder of the topical Broadside magazine.

Pete toured Australia in 1963 and his single Little Boxes, written by Malvina Reynolds, was number one in the nation's Top 40. That tour sparked a folk boom throughout the country. In November 1976, Pete wrote and recorded the anti-death penalty song Delbert Tibbs about the eponymous death-row inmate, who was later exonerated.

Ravi Shankar   Solo Artiste

Ravi Shankar died aged ninety-two on the 11th of December 2012 after receiving heart valve replacement surgery at Scripps Memorial Hospital in La Jolla, San Diego, California, U.S.A. He was survived by his wife Sukanya and his son, Shubhendra and his daughters Norah and Anoushka.

At the age of ten, after spending his first decade in Benares, Ravi Shankar went to Paris with the dance group of his brother, choreographer Uday Shankar. By the age of thirteen he had become a member of the group, accompanied its members on tour and learned to dance and play various Indian instruments. Uday's dance group toured Europe and the United States in the early to mid-1930s and Ravi Shankar learned French, discovered Western classical music, jazz, cinema and became acquainted with

Western customs. Ravi was sporadically trained on tour, and Allauddin offered Ravi training to become a serious musician.

Ravi gave up his dancing career in 1938 to go to Maihar and study Indian classical music as Allauddin Khan's pupil, living with his family in the traditional gurukul system. Allauddin Khan was a rigorous teacher and Ravi Shankar had training on sitar and surbahar, learned ragas and the musical styles dhrupad, dhamar, and khyal, and was taught the techniques of the instruments rudra veena, rubab, and sursingar. He often studied with Khan's children Ali Akbar Khan and Annapurna Devi. Ravi began to perform publicly on sitar in December 1939 and his debut performance was a jugalbandi.

In 1967, Ravi performed a well-received set at the Monterey Pop Festival in America. Ravi's live album from Monterey peaked at number 43 on the American Billboard's pop LPs chart in the US, which remains the highest placing he achieved on that chart. Ravi performed his final concert, with daughter Anoushka, on the 4th of November 2012 at the Terrace Theatre in Long Beach, California.

Del Shannon   Solo Artiste

Del Shannon died on the 8th of February 1990 aged fifty-five by suicide, killing himself with a rifle at his home in Santa Clarita, California, U.S.A. He was survived by his wife, Bonnie and his sons, Craig and Jody and his daughter, Kyra.

Del was born in 1934 and was an American rock and roll and country musician and singer-songwriter, best known for his 1961 number one Billboard hit "Runaway".

Del learned to play the ukulele and guitar and listened to country-and-western music, by artists such as Hank Williams, Hank Snow, and Lefty Frizzell. He was drafted into the Army in 1954, and while in Germany played guitar in a band called The Cool Flames. When his service ended, he returned to Battle Creek, Michigan, U.S.A. and worked as a carpet salesman and as a truck driver for a furniture factory. He found part-time work as a rhythm guitarist in the singer Doug DeMott's group, The Moonlight Ramblers.

In July 1960, Del signed to become a recording artist and composer for Bigtop Records. He flew to New York City. In January 1961, he recorded Runaway, which was released as a single in February 1961, reaching number One on the American Billboard chart that April.

In 1963, Del became the first American to record a cover version of a song by the Beatles. His version of From Me to You charted in the U.S.A., before the Beatles' version.

Del Shannon's UK chart hits include: "Runaway" in 1961, "Hey Little Girl" in 1962, "Little Town Flirt" in 1963, "Two Kinds of Teardrops" in 1963 and "Keep Searchin' (We'll Follow the Sun)" in 1965.

Kim Shattuck   The Muffs

Kim Shattuck died aged fifty-six at her home in Los Angeles, California, U.S.A. on the 2nd of October, 2019, from complications of amyotrophic lateral sclerosis. She was survived by her husband, Kevin and her mother and by her brother, Kirk and her sister, Kristen. Kim was a singer, musician, and songwriter and was the lead vocalist, guitarist, and primary songwriter of the American punk rock band the Muffs.

Growing up in Orange County, California, Kim discovered the principles of singing harmony by singing along to her parent's McGuire Sisters albums but later gravitated towards the rock music of bands including the Who, Blondie and the Sex Pistols. She did not learn to play guitar until she attended Orange Coast College. where she majored in photography and then began writing her own songs.

During the 1980's Kim played bass guitar for the Pandoras, an all-female garage band. When she had written sufficient songs to launch her own band, she quit the Pandoras, along with their keyboard player and together they started the Muffs.

The Muffs released their self-titled debut album in 1993 and recorded their second album, Blonder and Blonder which was released on Warner's subsidiary Reprise Records in 1995. The album included the college radio hit single, Sad Tomorrow. The Muffs made their third album, Happy Birthday to Me, in 1997, and it proved to be their final release through Warner Bros. Moving to independent label Honest Don's Records, they released Alert Today, Alive Tomorrow in 1999.

Burke Shelley   Budgie

Burke Shelley died aged seventy-one, in his sleep, on the 10th of January, 2022. He was survived by his sons, Osian, Dimitri and Nathaniel and his daughter, Ela.

In the final years of his life, Burke suffered from Stickler syndrome, and on two occasions had an aortic aneurysm. He died at the University Hospital of Wales in Cardiff.

In 1967, Cardiff-born Burke co-founded the band Hills Contemporary Grass with Tony Bourge on guitar and vocals and Ray Phillips on drums. The following year they changed their name to Budgie.

In addition to singing and playing bass for the group, Burke also performed keyboards on its early albums.

Budgie attained one minor UK chart hit in 1981 called "Keeping A Rendezvous".

Pete Shelley   The Buzzcocks

Pete Shelley died aged sixty-three on the 6th of December 2018 of a heart attack whilst in Tallinn, Estonia. He was survived by his second wife, Greta, his son and younger brother, Gary.

Pete was born in Leigh, Lancashire, England, U.K. and formed the Buzzcocks with Howard Devoto after they met at the Bolton Institute of Technology in 1975.

In 1977 the Buzzcocks released an EP called Spiral Scratch, on their independent label, New Hormones. When Howard Devoto left them that year, Pete Shelley took over as the lead vocalist and chief songwriter. They created the punk/new wave singles Orgasm Addict, What Do I Get? and Ever Fallen in Love (With Someone You Shouldn't've), along with three LPs: Another Music in a Different Kitchen in 1978, Love Bites in 1978 and A Different Kind of Tension in 1979.

In 1981 Pete released his first solo single, the song Homosapien, on which he returned to his original interests in electronic music and shifted emphasis from guitar to synthesiser.

The Buzzcock's UK chart hits include: "Ever Fallen in Love" in 1978 and "Promises" in 1978.

Ray Shulman   Gentle Giant

Ray Shulman died aged seventy-three in London on the 30th of March 2023. He was survived by his wife, Barbara Tanner, and his two elder brothers, Derek and Phil.

Ray was a British musician, songwriter, and record producer and with his brothers Derek and Phil, he co-founded the progressive rock band Gentle Giant. He also worked as record producer in the late 1980s and early 1990s for alternative rock artists including The Sundays and The Sugarcubes.

Ray' father was a trumpet player in a jazz band, and that was the first instrument he learned to play. He went on to learn violin and guitar and was primed for the National Youth Orchestra of Great Britain, but his brother Derek convinced him to join his band Simon Dupree and the Big Sound, which later evolved into Gentle Giant. Ray was in Gentle Giant from the beginning in 1970 until the last tour in 1980.

Nina Simone died in her sleep aged seventy at her home in Carry-le-Rouet, Bouches-du-Rhône, France on the 21st of April 2003. Nina's ashes were scattered in several African countries. She is survived by her daughter, Lisa Celeste Stroud, an actress and singer, who took the stage name Simone.

Nina was diagnosed with bipolar disorder in the late 1980s and she had suffered from breast cancer for several years.

Nina began playing piano at the age of three and demonstrating a talent with the instrument, she performed at her local church. Her concert debut, a classical recital, was given when she was aged twelve. Nina later said that during this performance, her parents, who had taken seats in the front row, were forced to move to the back of the hall to make a way for white people. She said that she refused to play until her parents were moved back to the front, and that the incident contributed to her later involvement in the civil rights movement.

To fund private lessons, Nina Simone performed at the Midtown Bar & Grill on Pacific Avenue in Atlantic City, whose owner insisted that she sing as well as play the piano, which increased her income to ninety dollars a week.

In 1958, Nina's debut album 'Little Girl Blue' came out on Bethlehem Records and after the success of Little Girl Blue, she signed a contract with Colpix Records and recorded a number of studio and live albums.

Nina recorded her last album for RCA, It Is Finished, in 1974, and did not make another record until 1978. During the 1980s, Nina performed regularly at Ronnie Scott's Jazz Club in London,U.K. where she recorded the album Live at Ronnie Scott's in 1984. Although her early on-stage style could be somewhat haughty and aloof, in later years, Nina particularly seemed to enjoy engaging her audiences sometimes by recounting humorous anecdotes related to her career and music and by soliciting requests.

Frank Sinatra   Solo Artiste

Frank Sinatra died of a heart attack aged eighty-two on the 14th of May 1998 at Cedars-Sinai Medical Centre in Los Angeles, USA. He was survived by his wife, Barbara, his son, Frank Jnr and his daughters, Nancy and Tina.

The night after Frank's death, the lights on the Empire State Building in New York City were turned blue, the lights at the Las Vegas Strip were dimmed in his honor, as well as the casinos stopped spinning for a minute. Frank was buried in a blue business suit with mementos from family members—cherry-flavoured Life Savers, Tootsie Rolls, a bottle of Jack Daniel's, a pack of Camel cigarettes, a Zippo lighter, stuffed toys, a dog biscuit, as well as a roll of dimes that he always carried, next to his parents in section B-8 of Desert Memorial Park in Cathedral City, California.

Frank developed an interest in music, particularly big bas well as jazz, at a young age. His maternal uncle, Domenico, gave him a ukulele for his fifteenth birthday, then he soon began performing at family gatherings.

Frank began singing professionally as a teenager, but he learned music by ear and never learned to read music. He got his first break in 1935 when his mother persuaded a local singing group, the Three Flashes, to let him join.

In 1938, Frank found employment as a singing waiter at a roadhouse called The Rustic Cabin in Englewood Cliffs, New Jersey, for which he was paid fifteen dollars per week.

Band leader Harry James, who had heard Frank sing on Dance Parade, signed a two-year contract of seventy-five dollars per week one evening after a show at the Paramount Theatre in New York. It was with the James band that Frank Sinatra released his first commercial record "From the Bottom of My Heart".

In November 1939 he left James to replace Jack

Leonard as the lead singer of the Tommy Dorsey band. Frank Sinatra signed a contract with Dorsey for one-hundred-and-twenty-five dollars per week at Palmer House in Chicago, plus James agreed amicably to release Frank Sinatra from his contract. On January 26th 1940, Frank made his first public appearance with the band at the Coronado Theatre in Rockford, Illinois. Tommy Dorsey was a major influence on Frank as well as becoming a father figure.

In his first year with Dorsey, Frank recorded over forty songs. Frank's first vocal hit was the song Polka Dots as well as Moonbeams in late April 1940. It Started All Over Again, In the Blue of Evening as well as It's Always You in 1943. As his success as well as popularity grew, Frank pushed Dorsey to allow him to record some solo songs. Dorsey eventually relented.

After his 1942 recordings, Frank believed he needed to go solo, with an insatiable desire to compete with Bing Crosby, but he was hampered by his contract which gave Dorsey 43% of his lifetime earnings in the entertainment industry. A legal battle ensued, eventually settled in August 1943.

By May 1941, Frank had topped the male singer polls in Billboard as well as Down Beat magazines. His appeal to bobby soxers, as teenage girls of that time were called, uncovered an undiscovered fresh audience for popular music, which up until that time had been recorded mainly for an adult market.

The release of the movie 'From Here to Eternity' in August Nineteen-fifty-three marked the beginning of a remarkable career revival. Frank began to bury himself in his work, with an unparalleled frenetic schedule of recordings, movies as well as concerts.

In 1955 Frank Sinatra released 'In the Wee Small Hours', his first twelve-inch LP, featuring songs including "In the Wee Small Hours of the Morning" and "Mood Indigo".

In 1957, Frank released 'Close to You, A Swingin' Affair!' as well as 'Where Are You?' – his first Long Playing Record in stereo. In 1959, Frank released Come Dance with Me!, a highly successful, critically acclaimed LP which stayed on Billboard's Pop Long Playing Record chart for 140 weeks, peaking at Number two.

In 1975, Frank performed in concerts in New York with Count Basie as well as Ella Fitzgerald, as well as at the London Palladium with Sarah Vaughan, as well as in Tehran at Aryamehr Stadium, giving one-hundred and forty performances in one hundred-and-five days.

Frank was noted for his impeccable sense of style. He always dressed immaculately, both in his professional as well as private life. He believed that as he was the best, he had to give his best to the audience, as well as would wear expensive custom-tailored tuxedos on stage as a sign of respect as well as to look important. He spent lavishly on stylish pin-striped suits as well as other clothing, more-over, later admitted that clothing made him feel wealthy as well as important.

Peter Skellern   Solo Artiste

Peter Skellern died of a brain tumour aged sixty-nine on the 17th of February 2017 at Lanteglos-by-Fow in Cornwall, UK. He was survived by his wife Diana, his son: Timothy, his daughter: Katherine and four grandchildren.

Peter's first charting hit song was You're a Lady in 1972. The record featured the Congregation, who had previously recorded the top ten hit Softly Whispering I Love You. You're a Lady reached number three on the UK Singles Chart and number fifty in the United States Billboard Hot 100. More success for Peter followed three years later with Hold On to Love which reached number fourteen on the UK chart. He also sang the theme song to the London Weekend Television series Billy Liar . For three years in the 1970s he worked on BBC Radio 4's Stop the Week.

In 1984, Peter performed the theme song for the London Weekend Television programme Me and My Girl. In the same year, he formed a group with cellist Julian Lloyd Webber and singer Mary Hopkin. The group released an album called Oasis in 1984 on the Warner Bros. Records label which earned a silver record.

In 1987, Peter wrote and performed the theme music and song for the Yorkshire Television series Flying Lady. He also collaborated with Richard Stilgoe in cabaret and in musical comedy with comic songs such as Joyce the Librarian and they released three live albums.

Percy Sledge   Solo Artiste

Percy Sledge died aged seventy-four of liver cancer at his home in Baton Rouge, Louisiana, U.S.A. on the 14th of April 2015. His interment was in Baton Rouge's Heavenly Gates Cemetery.

Percy married twice and was survived by his second wife, Rosa, whom he married in 1980. They had twelve children, three of whom became singers.

When a Man Loves a Woman was Percy Sledge's first song recorded under a record contract, and was released in March 1966, it reached number one in the U.S.A. and went on to become an international hit. When a Man Loves a Woman was a hit twice in the UK, reaching number 4 in 1966 and, on reissue, peaked at number 2 in 1987. The soul anthem became the cornerstone of Percy Sledge's career, and was followed by "Warm and Tender Love", "It Tears Me Up", "Take Time to Know Her", "Love Me Tender", and "Cover Me". In 2011 Percy toured with Sir Cliff Richard during his Soul-icious tour.

Mike Smith   The Dave Clark Five

Mike Smith died aged sixty-four of pneumonia on the 28th of February 2008 at Stoke Mandeville Hospital in Aylesbury, Buckinghamshire, United Kingdom, just eleven days before he was due to be inducted into the Rock and Roll Hall of Fame as a member of the Dave Clark Five.

When young, Mike started lessons in classical piano, and at age thirteen, passed the entrance exams at Trinity Music College in London.

Mike first met Dave Clark when they were both members on the same football team for the St. George Boys Club. By his mid-teens, Mike had developed a strong vocal delivery, while idolising Little Richard, among other American rock & roll stars. At age seventeen, while working for a finance company, Mike was invited by Dave Clark to join his band, which was busy rebuilding itself around the core of Clark and rhythm guitarist, later bassist, Rick Huxley, after having recently lost its lead singer.

With Mike on vocals, piano or organ the new Dave Clark Five was completed with the additions of saxophonist Denis Payton and lead guitarist Lenny Davidson, who was auditioned on Mike Smith's recommendation.

Mike made his recording debut, at age eighteen, with the single "I Knew It All the Time" b/w "That's What I Said" produced by Pye Records in June 1962.

Mike continued working with Dave Clark until 1973, mainly to help the drummer/bandleader fulfill contractual commitments, as "Dave Clark & Friends." Mike Smith & Clark released cover versions of popular hits such as "Rub It In," "Sweet City Woman," and "Na Na Hey Hey (Kiss Him Goodbye)." .

In 1976, Mike recorded an album with former Manfred Mann singer Michael d'Abo.

Most of Mike Smith's work in the 1970s and 1980s, however, was as a producer and songwriter, and he was successful working on commercials, authoring jingles for many products.

Beginning in March 2003, Mike Mike Smith's Rock Engine occasional tours generated very enthusiastic responses from audiences, despite being prevented from mentioning the Dave Clark Five in his advertising, Mike Smith appeared to be emerging as a popular star in his own right.

The Dave Clark Five's UK chart hits include: "Glad All Over" in 1963, "Bits and Pieces" in 1964, "Catch Us If You Can" in 1965, "Everybody Knows" in 1967, "Red Balloon" in 1968 and "Everybody Get Together" in 1970.

O.C. Smith   Solo Artiste

O.C. Smith, born Ocie Lee Smith, died aged sixty-nine of heart attack on the 23rd of November 2001. He was survived by his wife Robbie and his son, Robert and daughters, Sherryn, Ocie and Kelly.

In 1961, O.C. Smith was recruited into the Count Basie Orchestra, to be the vocalist, a position he held until 1965. He also continued to record with different labels, but a hit remained elusive. By 1968, O.C. Smith's then label, Columbia Records, was ready to release him from his recording contract, when he entered the charts for the first time with "The Son of Hickory Holler's Tramp", which got into the Top 40 in the United States.

O.C. Smiths UK chart entries include: "Son of Hickory Holler's Tramp" in 1968 and "Together" in 1977.

Jerome Smith   K.C.& the Sunshine Band

Jerome Smith died aged forty-seven on the 28th of July, 2000, in an accident on a construction site in Miami, Florida, United States of America, where he was working as a bulldozer operator.

Jerome was born on the 18th of June, 1953 and was a guitarist at TK Records in Miami, Florida, and who was a member of KC and the Sunshine Band. Jerome's rhythm guitar playing was a key part of the studio's propulsive disco sound, first gaining international attention on George McRae's hit recording of "Rock Your Baby" in 1974.

Jerome's high-pitched, restless guitar solo on "Get Down Tonight" by KC and the Sunshine Band; their first American number 1 single, resembled the sound of a synthesizer. It was achieved by speeding up the solo guitar track against a normal-speed rhythm guitar track in the studio. He was also sought after as a session guitarist and contributed to the soundtrack of the television series 'Melrose Place'.

KC & The Sunshine Band's UK chart entries include: "Queen of Clubs" in 1974, "That's The Way I Like It" in 1975, "Shake Your Booty" in 1976, "Please Don't Go" in 1979 and "Give It Up" in 1983.

Joe South   Solo Artiste

Joe South died of heart failure aged seventy-two at his home in Buford, Georgia, U.S.A. on the 5th of September 2012, of heart failure. He was survived by his second wife, Jan and his son, Craig.

Joe started his pop career in July 1958 with the NRC Records novelty hit "The Purple People Eater Meets the Witch Doctor". After this hit, Joe's music grew increasingly serious.

In 1959, Joe wrote two songs which were recorded by Gene Vincent: "I Might Have Known", which was on the album Sounds Like Gene Vincent , and "Gone Gone Gone" which was included on the album The Crazy Beat of Gene Vincent.

Joe began his recording career in Atlanta with the National Recording Corporation, where he served as staff guitarist along with other NRC artists Ray Stevens and Jerry Reed. Joe's earliest recordings have been re-released by NRC on CD.

Responding to late 1960s issues, Joe's style changed radically, most evident in his biggest single, 1969's "Games People Play" , a hit on both sides of the Atlantic. Accompanied by a lush string sound, an organ, and brass, the production won the Grammy Award for Best Contemporary Song and the Grammy Award for Song of the Year.

Joe's most commercially successful composition was Lynn Anderson's 1971 country/pop monster hit "Rose Garden", which was a hit in sixteen countries worldwide.

Joe South's UK chart entries include: "Games People Play" in 1969.

Ronnie Spector   The Ronnettes

Ronnie Spector died aged seventy-eight from cancer on the 12th of January, 2022 in Danbury, Connecticut, USA. She was survived by her second husband, Jonathan and her sons, Louise, Donte, Gary, Jason and Austin.

Ronnie was born Veronica Yvette Bennett in East Harlem, New York City, and grew up in the Washington Heights section of Manhattan. Ronnie and her sister Estelle were encouraged to sing by their large family, as was their cousin Nedra. The trio formed the Darling Sisters, known later as the Ronettes. They performed locally and sang at school events, and had a residency at the Peppermint Lounge, a nightspot in Manhattan, the birthplace of the Twist and go-go dancing.

The Ronettes became a popular live attraction around the greater New York area in the early 1960s. Looking for a recording contract, they initially were signed to Colpix Records and produced by Stu Phillips. After releasing a few singles on Colpix without success, they tracked down record producer Phil Spector, who signed them to his own label in 1963. Their relationship with Spector brought chart success with their biggest hit "Be My Baby" in 1963, which peaked at number two on the American Billboard Hot 100. A string of top 40 pop hits followed with "Baby, I Love You" in 1963, "(The Best Part of) Breakin' Up" in 1964, "Do I Love You?" in 1964, and "Walking in the Rain" in 1964.

In 1965, the Ronettes were voted the third-top singing

group in England behind the Beatles and the Rolling Stones. They opened for the Beatles on their 1966 US tour without Ronnie. Phil had forbidden Ronnie to tour with the Beatles, so her cousin Elaine stood in as a third member. The group's last charting single, "I Can Hear Music", was produced by Jeff Barry and reached number 100 on the Billboard Hot 100 in 1966.

The Ronettes broke up in early 1967, following a European concert tour. It was only after Ronnie married Phil in 1968 that she began to use the name Ronnie Spector, but she withdrew from the spotlight because Phil prohibited her from performing and limited her recordings.

In February 1971, Ronnie recorded the song "Try Some, Buy Some/Tandoori Chicken" at Abbey Road Studios during Phil's work with George Harrison. Written by Harrison, and produced by both Harrison and Phil Spector, her debut solo single was released on Apple Records in April 1971.

After separating from Phil Spector in 1972, Ronnie reformed the Ronettes. They released a few singles on Buddah Records. By 1975, Ronnie was recording as a solo act. She released the single "You'd Be Good For Me" on Tom Cat Records in 1975.

Dusty Springfield   Solo Artiste

Dusty Springfield died of cancer aged fifty-nine on the 2nd of March 1999 in Henley-on-Thames, Oxfordshire, United Kingdom. She was survived by her brother, Tom.

Dusty's funeral service was attended by hundreds of fans and people from the music business. It was a Catholic funeral, which took place at the ancient parish church of St. Mary the Virgin in Henley-on-Thames, where Dusty had been living during her final years. A marker dedicated to her memory was placed in the church graveyard. Dusty was cremated and some of her ashes were buried at Henley, while the rest were scattered by her brother, Tom, at the Cliffs of Moher in Ireland.

Dusty Springfield was raised in a music-loving family. She listened to a wide range of music, including George Gershwin, Rodgers and Hart, Rodgers and Hammerstein, Cole Porter, Count Basie, Duke Ellington, and Glenn Miller.

At the age of twelve, she made a recording of herself performing the Irving Berlin song "When the Midnight Choo Choo Leaves for Alabam" at a local record shop in Ealing.

After finishing school, Dusty sang with her brother Tom in local folk clubs. In 1957 the pair worked together at holiday camps. The following year Dusty responded to an advertisement in The Stage to join The Lana Sisters, an "established sister act". She had changed her name to Shan, and "cut her hair, lost her glasses, experimented with makeup to become one of the 'sisters'. As a member of the pop vocal trio, Dusty developed skills in harmonising and microphone technique and recorded, performed on TV, and played at live shows in the United Kingdom and at United States Air Force bases in continental Europe.

In 1960, Dusty left The Lana Sisters and formed a pop-folk trio, The Springfields, with her brother, Tom and Reshad Feild, who was replaced by Mike Hurst in 1962.

Dusty left the Springfields after their final concert in October 1963. In November 1963 Dusty released her first solo single, "I Only Want to Be with You." In April 1964 Dusty issued her debut album 'A Girl Called Dusty' which included mostly remakes of her favourite songs. The album reached Number 6 in the UK in May 1964. The chart hits "Stay Awhile," "All Cried Out," and "Losing You" followed the same year.

By the start of the 1970's Dusty Springfield was a major star, though her record sales were declining. Her intimate companion, Norma Tanega, had returned to the US after their relationship had become stressful, and Dusty Springfield was spending more time in the USA herself. In January 1970 her second and final album on Atlantic Records,

'A Brand New Me' was released; it featured tracks written and produced by Gamble and Huff. The album and related singles only sold moderately and Dusty was unhappy with both her management and record company. She sang back up vocals with her friend Madeline Bell on two tracks on Elton John's 1971 hit album 'Tumbleweed Connection'. She recorded some songs with producer Jeff Barry in early 1971, which were intended for an album to be released by Atlantic Records.

In early 1979, Dusty Springfield played club dates in New York City. In London, she recorded two singles with David Mackay for her UK label, Mercury Records . The first was the disco-influenced "Baby Blue", co-written by Trevor Horn and Geoff Downes which reached Number 61 in the UK. The second, "Your Love Still Brings Me to My Knees", released in January 1980, was Dusty Springfield's final single for Mercury Records; she had been with them for nearly 20 years.

In 1987, Dusty accepted an invitation from Pet Shop Boys to duet with their lead singer, Neil Tennant, on the single "What Have I Done to Deserve This?".

The very last song Dusty recorded was George and Ira Gershwin's song "Someone to Watch Over Me" while in London in 1995. .

Chris Squire   Yes

Chris Squire died aged sixty-seven on the 27th of June 2015, while receiving treatment for acute erythroid leukemia in his adopted hometown of Phoenix, Arizona, U.S.A. He was survived by his third wife, Scotty and his daughters; Carmen, Chandrika, Camille, Cameron and Xilan.

Chris was the longest-serving original member of YES, having remained in the band until his death and appearing on every studio album released from 1969 to 2014.

Chris was born in Kingsbury, northwest London and

took an early interest in church music and sang in the local church and school choirs. After he took up the bass guitar at age sixteen, his earliest gigs were in 1964 for the Selfs, which later evolved into the Syn. In 1968, however, Chris formed Yes with singer Jon Anderson.

As the band developed, they brought in drummer Bill Bruford, keyboardist Tony Kaye and Peter Banks for rehearsals. The five agreed to drop their former name, Mabel Greer's Toyshop, and settled on the name Yes. The band played their first show as Yes at a youth camp in East Mersea, Essex during August 1968.

A year later, Yes released their self-titled debut album. Chris took writing credits on four of the album's eight tracks, these being, "Beyond & Before", "Looking Around", "Harold Land", and "Sweetness".

Chris was the only member to play on each of Yes's 21 studio albums released from 1969 to 2014. Heaven & Earth was his final studio album.

Yes's single chart entries in the UK include: "Wonderous Stories" in 1977, "Going For The One" in 1977, "Don't Kill The Whale" in 1978, "Owner of a Lonely heart" in 1983, "Leave It" in 1984 and "Love Will Find A Way" in 1987.

Dorothy Squires   Solo Artiste

Dorothy Squires died of lung cancer aged eighty-three on the 14th of April 1998 at Llwynypia Hospital, Rhondda, Wales, U.K. Her remains are interred in a family plot in Streatham Park Cemetery, London, U.K.

Dorothy was given birth to in her parents' carnival caravan in Pontyberem, Carmarthenshire, Wales,U.K. Her mother bought young Dorothy a ukulele. While working in a tin plate factory, Dorothy began to perform professionally as a singer at the age of sixteen in the working men's club of Pontyberem.

In London, Dorothy did most of her work with the orchestra of Billy Reid, who was her partner for many years. After she joined his orchestra in 1936, he began to write songs for her to perform.

In the immediate post-war, she worked on the BBC radio show Variety Bandbox, which subsequently made her the highest paid female singer in the UK. Dorothy and Reid bought a 16-bedroom house in Bexhill on Sea, and working with him she recorded the original version of Reid's composition, "A Tree in the Meadow", best known in the United States for the recording by Margaret Whiting, which reached No.1 on the US pop chart.

Dorothy met Roger Moore who was twelve years her junior at one of her lavish parties at her mansion in Old Bexley, Kent. He later became her second husband when they married in New Jersey in July 1953 and their marriage lasted until 1961.

Returning to living in the UK, Dorothy Squires had a career revival in the late 1960s at the age of fifty-five with a set of three singles making the UK Singles Chart. New albums and concerts followed included a sell out set of concerts at the London Palladium. Dorothy herself had hired the Palladium for a series of shows, and they exceeded expectations and sold out of tickets within hours. A double album of the event was issued.

Dorothy's UK chart entries include: "I'm Walking Behind You" in 1953, "Say It With Flowers" in 1961, "For Once In My Life" in 1969, "Till" in 1970 and "My Way" in 1970.

Crispian St Peters   Solo Artiste

Crispian St. Peters died on the 8th of June 2010 aged seventy-one after a protracted illness. He was survived by his wife, Collette, a daughter, Samantha, and a son, Lee.

Crispian learned guitar and left school in 1954 to become an assistant cinema projectionist. As a young man, he performed in several lesser known bands in England, U.K. Through the late 1950s and early 1960s, he was a member of 'The Country Gentlemen', 'Beat Formula Three', and 'Peter & The Wolves'.

While a member of Beat Formula Three in 1963, he was heard by David Nicholson, an EMI publicist who became his manager. Nicholson suggested he use the stage name : Crispian St. Peters. In 1964, as a member of Peter & The Wolves, Crispian made his first commercial recording. He was persuaded to turn solo by Nicholson, and was signed to Decca Records in 1965. His first two singles on this record label, "No No No" and "At This Moment", proved unsuccessful on the charts.

In 1965 a Crispian St. Peters' single eventually hit number 2 in the UK and was then released in the USA on the Philadelphia-based Jamie Records label. "The Pied Piper," became known as Crispian's signature song and became a Top 10 hit in the United States and the UK.

In 1967, Crispian released his first album, Follow Me.., which included several of his own songs, as well as the single "Free Spirit". One of them, "I'll Give You Love," was recorded by Marty Kristian in a version produced by Crispian, and became a big hit in Australia. Crispian's album was followed by his first EP, Almost Persuaded, yet by 1970, he was dropped by Decca. "You Were on My Mind" was featured in the 1996 German film Jenseits Der Stille.

Later in 1970, Crispian was signed to Square Records. Under this new record deal, he released a second LP, 'Simply', that year, predominantly of country and western songs. Later still, they released his first cassette, The Gospel Tape, in 1986, and a second cassette, New Tracks on Old Lines in 1990. His third cassette, Night Sessions, Vol. 1 was released in 1993.

Mark St John   Kiss

Mark St.John died aged fifty-one suddenly on the 5th of April 2007 under suspicious circumstances just several months after being badly beaten during a short stay in

Orange County jail, California, USA. Mark died, due to what the coroner described as a brain hemorrhage brought on by an accidental overdose of methamphetamines. His girlfriend was with him the night before he died and she has been adamant that he wasn't taking drugs, refuting the coroner's official ruling. She is convinced the bleeding was caused by his assault at the jail several months earlier.

Before joining Kiss, Mark was a well-known and respected teacher and guitarist for the Southern California cover band Front Page. Mark was with Kiss only a short time; but he was featured on the album 'Animalize', the second album of the non-makeup period. This turned out to be one of Kiss' most successful studio albums, aside from those made by the original lineup. Mark's only video appearance with Kiss is in the video for the hit single "Heaven's on Fire". During the sessions for the album, which was recorded in mid-1984, Mark clashed with the other members of the band.

In January 1985 Mark teamed up with vocalist David Donato and drummer Barry Brandt of Angel to work on developing some demo ideas and he and Donato soon formed White Tiger. They had written most of the material for the album by mid-1985 and set out to complete a lineup with which to record. The band also included Mark's younger brother, Michael, on bass, and was completed with the addition of Brian James Fox on drums. In his later years, Mark did not make many public appearances.

Layne Staley   **Alice N' Chains**

Layne Staley died aged thirty-four on the 5th of April 2002 at his home in Seattle, Washington, U.S.A. The autopsy and toxicology report on Layne's body was released on 6th May 2002 which stated that he died from a mixture of heroin and cocaine, known as "speedball".

Layne began playing drums at age twelve and played in

several glam bands in his early teens, but at that point, he had aspirations of becoming a singer.

In 1985, Layne and his band Sleze made a cameo in Father Rock, a low-budget movie from Seattle's Public Access Channel.

In 1986, Sleze morphed into Alice N' Chains, a band which Layne said dressed in drag and played speed metal. The new band performed around the Seattle area playing Slayer and Armored Saint covers.

In October 1996, Layne's former fiancée, Demri Lara Parrott, died of a drug overdose. Layne was reported to have been placed on a twenty-four hour suicide watch and had fallen into a deep depression and that he never recovered from Demri's death.

Alice In Chains had UK chart entries including: "Would" in 1993, "Them Bones" in 1993, "Angry Chair" in !993, "Down A Hole" in 1993, "Grind" in 1995 and "Heaven Beside You" in 1996, .

Viv Stanshall   The Bonzo Dog Dooda Band

Vivian Stanshall died aged fifty-one on the 5th of March 1995 in a house fire in his top floor flat in Muswell Hill, North London, U.K. His private funeral service was held at the Golders Green Crematorium, North London. He was survived by his wife, Pamela and his daughter, Silky.

Viv attended Southend High School for Boys until 1959. As a young man, he earned money doing various odd jobs at the Kursaal fun fair in nearby Southend-on-Sea. They included working as a bingo caller and spending the winter painting the fairground attractions. To set aside enough money to get through art school he spent a year in the merchant navy.

Viv enrolled at the Central School of Art and Design in London. He joined fellow students in forming a band including Neil Innes, who was studying art at Goldsmiths College.

The Bonzo Dog Doo-Dah Band was named after a word game that Viv played, in which they cut up sentences and juxtaposed fragments to form new ones.

In 1968 the Bonzos scored a surprise top-ten hit with a "I'm the Urban Spaceman" . The band toured incessantly and recorded several albums, which led to a tour of the United States that was so successful they were booked for another soon after. In March 1970, the band played their last show at Loughborough University.

In early 1971 Viv returned to touring with a new band called Freaks. This group soon recorded a BBC radio session for John Peel that featured solo numbers by Viv and Neil Innes alongside tracks from the Bonzos' yet to be recorded reunion album of 1972.

In early 1974, Viv wrote, arranged, and quickly recorded his first solo album, 'Men Opening Umbrellas Ahead'. A rather more serious work than many would have expected, its darkly-comic lyrics detailed Viv's alcoholism and troubled emotional state, laced with surreal poetic imagery and literary reference.

Viv collaborated on numerous musical projects, including Robert Calvert's 1974 concept album Captain Lockheed and the Starfighters, and Mike Oldfield's 1973 Tubular Bells, where he played the Master of Ceremonies; he also recorded this role for Tubular Bells II in 1992 although the main album release featured Alan Rickman instead. Viv performed with Grimms , as well as occasionally working with The Alberts and The Temperance Seven.

In 1975 Viv provided the narration for a rock music version of 'Peter and the Wolf', produced by Robin Lumley and Jack Lancaster and featuring, among others, Gary Moore, Manfred Mann, Phil Collins, Bill Bruford, Stéphane Grappelli, Alvin Lee, Cozy Powell, Brian Eno and Jon Hiseman.

Yvonne Staples died aged eighty from Colon Cancer on the 10th of April 2018 at her home in Chicago, Illinois, U.S.A. She was survived by her sister, Mavis and her brother, Pervis.

Yvonne performed with her sisters Mavis and Cleotha and their father, Roebuck "Pops" Staples, on hits such as "Respect Yourself" and "I'll Take You There," their first number one hit.

The family's music career had its roots with Pops Staples, a manual laborer who strummed a ten dollar guitar while teaching his children gospel songs to keep them entertained in the evenings. They sang in church one Sunday morning in 1948, and three encores and a heavy church offering basket convinced Pops that music was in the family's future — and the Staple Singers group was born. Two decades later, the group became an unlikely hit maker for the Stax label. The Staple Singers had a string of Top 40 hits with Stax in the late 1960s, earning them the nickname "God's greatest hit makers." .

The family also became active in the civil rights movement after hearing the Rev. Martin Luther King Jr. deliver a sermon while they were on tour in Montgomery, Alabama, U.S.A. in 1962 and went on to perform at events at King's request.

Alvin Stardust   Solo Artiste

Alvin Stardust died of prostate cancer aged seventy-two on the 23rd of October 2014. He was survived by his wife, Julie, his sons Shaun and Adam and his daughter, Sophie.

Alvin made his stage debut in pantomime at the age of four years and in the early 1960s took the performing name, Shane Fenton. The Fentones were a teenage band who recorded a demo tape and mailed it in to a BBC programme with the hope of being picked to appear on television and received a letter from the BBC inviting them to come to London to audition in person for the programme. Alvin, who was a roadie with them at the time, was asked to join the band and to use Shane Fenton as a pseudonym. The combo had a number of hits in the UK Singles Chart.

Alvin disappeared from the spotlight for a decade after the break-up of the Fentones, working in music management and performing at small venues with his wife Iris, the sister of Rory Storm. During the early 1970s, however, he acquired his new persona, 'Alvin Stardust', cashing in on the glam rock bandwagon.

Alvin participated in A Song for Europe, the UK qualifying heat of the Eurovision Song Contest, in 1985, with the song "The Clock on the Wall" and finished in third place.

Edwin Starr   Solo Artiste

Edwin Starr died aged sixty-one on the 2nd of April 2003 from a heart attack while taking a bath at his home in Nottinghamshire, U.K. He was survived by his wife, Annette and his son André. He was buried in Wilford Hill Cemetery in Nottingham where his headstone reads "Agent 00 Soul".

The song which launched Edwin's career was "Agent Double-O-Soul" in 1965. Other early hits included "Headline News", "Back Street" and "S.O.S. (Stop Her on Sight)". At Motown he recorded a string of singles before enjoying an international success with "25 Miles", which he co-wrote with producers Johnny Bristol and Harvey Fuqua. The biggest hit of Edwin's career, which cemented his reputation, was the Vietnam War protest song "War".

Moving to England in 1973, Edwin continued to record, most notably the song "Hell Up in Harlem" for the 1974 movie Hell Up in Harlem.

Edwin remained a hero on England's Northern Soul circuit and continued living in England for the remainder of his life.

Joe Strummer died aged fifty on the 22nd of December 2002 from a congenital heart defect. He was survived by his wife Lucinda.

After finishing his time at City of London Freemen's School, in 1970, Joe moved on to the Central School of Art and Design in London, where he briefly flirted with the idea of becoming a professional cartoonist and completed a one-year foundation course.

In 1973 Joe moved to Newport, Wales and met up with college musicians in the Students' Union in Stow Hill and became vocalist for Flaming Youth, renaming the band the Vultures. For the next year he was the band's part-time singer and rhythm guitarist. During this time Joe also worked as a gravedigger in St Woolos Cemetery. In 1974, the band fell apart and he moved back to London where he became the lead singer of the 101ers and began to write original songs for the group. One song he wrote was inspired by his girlfriend at the time, The Slits' drummer Palmolive. The group liked the song "Keys to Your Heart", and picked it as their first single.

In April 1976, the then-unknown Sex Pistols opened for The 101ers at a venue called the Nashville Rooms in London, and Joe was impressed by them. Sometime after the show, Joe was approached by Bernie Rhodes and Mick Jones. Jones was from the band London SS and wanted Joe to join as lead singer. Joe agreed to leave the 101ers and join Jones, bassist Paul Simonon, drummer Terry Chimes and guitarist Keith Levene. The band was then named the Clash.

During his time with the Clash, Joe, along with his bandmates, became notorious for getting into trouble with the law.

In September 1983, Joe issued the infamous "Clash Communique", and fired Mick Jones. Topper Headon had earlier been kicked out of the band because of his heroin addiction, and Terry Chimes was brought back temporarily to fill his place until the permanent replacementcould be found. This left the band with only two of its original members. Rhodes persuaded Joe Strummer to carry on.

In the mid-to-late 1990s, Joe gathered top-flight musicians into a backing band he called the Mescaleros and the band signed with Mercury Records, and released their first album in 1999, which was co-written with Antony Genn, called Rock Art and the X-Ray Style. A tour of England, Europe, and North America soon followed.

Joe Strummer's final gig was at Liverpool Academy on the 22nd of November 2002, yet his final performance, just two weeks before his death, was in a small club venue 'The Palace' in Bridgwater, Somerset, near his home. .

Levi Stubbs   The Four Tops

Levi Stubbs died aged seventy-two in from failing health on the 17th of October 2008, at his home in Detroit, Michigan, U.S.A. A memorial service for Levi was held at the Greater Grace Temple in Detroit and he was interred at Detroit's historic Woodlawn Cemetery. He was survived by his wife, Clineice, his sons, Raymond and Levi.Jnr and his daughters, Beverly, Kelly and Deborah.

Levi began his professional singing career with friends Fakir, Renaldo "Obie" Benson and Lawrence Payton, forming a singing group called the Four Aims in 1954. Two years later, after signing with Chess Records, the group changed their name to the Four Tops. The Four Tops began as a supper-club act before signing to Motown Records in 1963. By the end of the decade, they had over a dozen hits. The most popular of their hits, all of which featured Levi on lead vocals, include "Baby I Need Your Loving", "I Can't Help Myself (Sugar Pie, Honey Bunch)", "It's the Same Old Song", "Reach Out I'll Be There", "Standing in the Shadows of Love", "Bernadette", "If I Were A Carpenter", "Walk Away Renee", as well as the late hit "Loco In Acapulco".

Donna Summer   Solo Artiste

Donna Summer died from lung cancer, aged sixty-three at her home in Naples, Florida,U.S.A. on the 17th of May 2012. Her funeral service was held in Christ Presbyterian Church in Nashville, Tennessee. She was survived by her husband, Helmuth and her daughter, Mimi.

Donna's performance debut occurred at church when she was eight years old, replacing a vocalist who failed to show up. Donna later attended Boston's Jeremiah E. Burke High School where she performed in school musicals. In 1967, just weeks before graduation, Donna left for New York where she auditioned for a role in the counter-culture musical, 'Hair'. She landed the part of Sheila, and agreed to take the role in the Munich production of the show, moving there after getting her parents' reluctant approval.

Donna eventually became fluent in German, singing various songs in that language, and participated in the musicals Ich bin ich, Godspell, and Show Boat. Within three years, Donna moved to Vienna, Austria, and joined the Vienna Volksoper. She briefly toured with an ensemble vocal group called FamilyTree, the creation of producer Günter "Yogi" Lauke. In 1968, Donna Summer released, as Donna Gaines, on Polydor, her first single, a German version of the title "Aquarius" from the musical Hair, followed in 1971 by a second single, a remake of the Jaynetts' 1963 hit, "Sally Go 'Round the Roses", from a one-off European deal with Decca Records. In 1969, she issued the single "If You Walkin' Alone" on Philips Records.

Donna's first album was 'Lady of the Night'. It became a hit in the Netherlands, Sweden, Germany and Belgium on the strength of two songs, "The Hostage" and the title track "Lady of the Night". "The Hostage" reached the top of the charts in France.

In early 1976, Donna, single "Love to Love You Baby" had reached Number two on the U.S. Billboard Hot 100 chart and had become a Gold single, while the album had sold over a million copies. The song generated controversy due to Donna Summer's moans and groans, and some American stations, like those in Europe with the initial release, refused to play it. Despite this, "Love to Love You Baby" found chart success in several European countries, and made the Top five in the United Kingdom despite the BBC ban.

Donna Summer achieved four number-one hits on the American Hot 100 chart within a twelve month period. Donna recorded and delivered the album 'She Works Hard for the Money' and Polygram released it on its Mercury imprint in 1983. The title song became a major hit, reaching Number three on the US Hot 100, as well as number one on Billboard's R&B chart for three weeks.

In 2008, Donna released her first studio album of fully original material in 17 years, entitled 'Crayons'. Released on the Sony BMG label Burgundy Records, it peaked at Number seventeen on the U.S. Top 200 Album Chart, her highest placing on the chart since 1983.

Iain Sutherland   The Sutherland Brothers

Iain Sutherland died from failing health aged seventy-one on the 25th of November, 2019, in Wollerton, Shropshire, U.K. He was survived by his brother, Gavin, his wife Patricia, their son James, daughter Virginia, and three grandchildren.

When they were children, Iain and Gavin would learn chords and harmonies by listening to Everly Brothers records over and over again and then trying to copy them.

Iain eventually got a place at Manchester University and might have gone on to become an architect, but he decided instead to try to make a living with his band.

In the early 1960s Iain and Gavin Sutherland moved to London, which was essentially the location of the British music industry at that time, sharing a room in a flat in West Kensington. They were always close. And although he was the quieter of the two, Iain was always protective and supportive of his younger sibling.

Iain and Gavin saw themselves primarily as songwriters, rather than singers, but got themselves a contract with Island Records and in 1971 they released their first album entitled "Sutherland Brothers Band".

Iain and Gavid Sutherland drew on their childhood in the North-East of Scotland to write two of the best-known songs of the 1970s, although it took a cover version by Rod Stewart to propel their composition, "Sailing" to number one position in the UK pop charts and into the public consciousness.

The Sutherland Brothers released eight albums during the 1970s, six of them with Quiver, and had a few other minor hits before going on to solo careers in the 1980s. Iain had returned to the Stoke area, where he had his own music studio and stated that he just wrote and recorded for his own purposes and if anyone was interested, then that was all well and good!   .

Dave Swarbrick   Fairport Convention

Dave Swarbrick died aged seventy-five from pneumonia on the 3rd of June 2016, in hospital in Aberystwyth, Wales, U.K. Dave was survived by his wife Jill, daughters; Emily and Isobel, son; Alexander, eight grandchildren, and two great-grandchildren.

Dave was born in London but his family moved to North Yorkshire, where he learned to play the violin and in the late 1940s they moved to Birmingham. After winning a talent contest with his skiffle band playing guitar, he was introduced to Beryl and Roger Marriott, influential local folk musicians. The Marriotts took him under their wing and Beryl discovering that he had played the violin classically up until the skiffle craze, actively encouraged him to switch back to the fiddle whence he joined the Beryl Marriott Ceilidh Band.

Dave joined the Ian Campbell Folk Group in 1960 and embarked on his recording career, playing on one single, three EPs and seven albums with the group over the next few years.

From 1965 Dave began to work with Martin Carthy, supporting him on his eponymous first album. The association was such a success that the next recording, Second Album in 1966, gave them equal billing. They produced another four highly regarded recordings between 1967 and 1968, including Byker Hill in 1967.

Originally, it was as a session musician that Swarbrick was called in by the manager of rising folk rock group Fairport Convention, in 1969, to undertake some overdubs. Fairport had decided to play a traditional song "A Sailor's Life", which Dave had previously recorded with Carthy in 1969, and he was asked to contribute violin to the session. The result was an eleven-minute mini-epic that appeared on the 1969 album Unhalfbricking and which marked out a new direction for the band. Subsequently, Dave was asked to join the group and was the first fiddler on the folk scene to electrify the violin.

Felice Taylor   Solo Artiste

Felice Taylor died aged seventy-three on 12th of June 2017 and was interred at the Riverside National Cemetery in Riverside, California, U.S.A. She was survived by her second husband, Walter.

Felice was born Florine Corella Flanagan in Richmond, California, U.S.A. and began singing with her sisters Norma and Darlene in a trio called 'The Sweets', who recorded two singles, "The Richest Girl", for the Valiant label in 1965 and "Satisfy Me Baby" on the Soul Town label.

Felice recorded her solo hit "Think About Me", as Florain Felice Taylor, on the Groovy label. Her greatest success came after signing for Bob Keane's Mustang label, a subsidiary of Bronco Records. There she was teamed with the songwriters and record producers, Barry White and Paul Politi, who co-wrote "It May Be Winter Outside (But in My Heart It's Spring)", a minor hit reaching number forty-two on the Billboard Hot 100 and number forty-four on the Rythm & Blues chart in early 1967. The follow-up single was "I'm Under the Influence of Love" but third single, "I Feel Love Comin' On", also written and produced by White and Politi was not released in the U.S.A, but reached number eleven in the UK Singles Chart, when leased to President Records later in 1967.

After leaving Bronco, Felice recorded for Kent Records, and later in the U.K. with members of The Equals. In 1973, White's protegées Love Unlimited recorded new versions of "It May Be Winter Outside" and "Under the Influence of Love" and Barry White recorded "I Feel Love Comin' On" on The Love Unlimited Orchestra's top ten album Rhapsody in White.

Larry Taylor died from cancer aged seventy-seven on the 19th of August 2019 at Lake Balboa, California, U.S.A. He was survived by his wife, Andrea and his son Danny and his two daughters, Rebecca and Molly.

As a young man Larry Taylor played bass guitar in The Gamblers, one of the earliest pioneering rock groups to play instrumental surf music. The Gamblers had a local hit in the Los Angeles area with "Moon Dawg".

Larry, before joining Canned Heat, had been a session bassist for both The Monkees and Jerry Lee Lewis. Larry played with Canned Heat from 1967 to 1970, and appeared with them at various festivals including the Monterey International Pop Festival, held from 16th to 18th June 1967 near Monterey, California, and the Woodstock music festival held from 15th to 18th of August, 1969 at Max Yasgur's six hundred acre dairy farm in Bethnal, New York State, U.S.A.

Larry's Canned Heat nickname was "The Mole." In addition to playing bass, Larry also played lead guitar on occasion. An example can be heard on the track "Down In the Gutter, But Free," on the album Hallelujah. In 1970, when John Mayall moved to Los Angeles, Larry and Harvey Mandel quit Canned Heat to join John in the Bluesbreakers.

In 1974, Larry became part of The Hollywood Fats Band led by Mike "Hollywood Fats" Mann. The pair joined Canned Heat for a King Biscuit Flower Hour concert in 1979. Larry recorded Reheated in 1988, again with Canned Heat. He toured and recorded with his former band a few more times until 1999.

Larry became a leading exponent and practitioner of the acoustic upright bass in the contemporary blues scene. He was quite prominently seen with his upright bass in the live blues film, 'Lightning in a Bottle'. He was also featured in a concert DVD released in winter 2013, from the album Time Brings About A Change by Floyd Dixon.

Larry played on numerous Tom Waits albums and was the bass player in Tom's touring band.

Tami Terrell   Solo Artiste

Tammi Terrell died aged twenty-four on the 16th of March 1970 due to complications from brain cancer. Since early 1970, Tami had been confined to a wheelchair and had suffered from blindness, hair loss and weight loss.

In 1960, Tammi signed under the Wand subsidiary of Scepter Records after being discovered by Luther Dixon, recording the ballad, "If You See Bill", under the name Tammy Montgomery and doing demos for The Shirelles. After another single, Tammi left the label and, after being introduced to James Brown, signed a contract with him and began singing backup for his Revue concert tours. In 1963, she recorded the song "I Cried". Released on Brown's Try Me Records, it became her first charting single, reaching number 99 on the American Billboard Hot 100.

After this tenure ended, Tammi Terrell signed with Checker Records and released the Bert Berns produced duet, "If I Would Marry You" with Jimmy Radcliffe, which Tammi co-composed. Following this relative failure, Tammi announced a semi-retirement from the music business and enrolled in the University of Pennsylvania where she majored in pre-med, staying at the school for two years. In April 1965, during a performance at the Twenty Grand Club in Detroit, she was spotted by Motown CEO Berry Gordy, who promised to sign her to Motown. Tammi agreed and signed with the label on April 29th, her 20th birthday. Before releasing her first single with Motown's Tamla subsidiary, "I Can't Believe You Love Me", Gordy suggested a name change. Figuring "Tammy Montgomery" was too long of a name to put on a single, Gordy changed it to "Tammi Terrell". He felt this name screamed "sex appeal".

In early 1967, Motown hired Tammi to sing duets with Marvin Gaye, who had achieved duet success with Mary Wells and Kim Weston as well as having recorded duets with Oma Heard. During recording sessions, Marvin Gaye would recall later that he did not realise how gifted Tammi Terrell was until they began singing together. At first the duets were recorded separately. For sessions of their first recording, the Ashford & Simpson composition, "Ain't No Mountain High Enough", both Marvin Gaye and Tammi Terrell recorded separate versions. The song became a crossover pop hit in the spring of nineteen-sixty-seven, reaching number 19 on the Billboard Hot 100 and number three on the Rythm&Blues charts and making Tammi Terrell a star.

Gary Thain   Uriah Heep

Gary Thain died aged twenty-seven on the eighth of December 1975, from respiratory failure due to a heroin overdose, at his flat in Norwood Green, London, United Kingdom. He was survived by his second wife, Mika.

Gary Thain joined the Keef Hartley Band and, in 1971, they toured with Uriah Heep. Uriah Heap asked him to join them in February 1972, and he stayed in the band until February 1975. He played on four studio albums: Demons & Wizards, The Magician's Birthday, Sweet Freedom and Wonderworld as well as their live album, titled Uriah Heep Live.

During his last tour in the United States with Uriah Heep, Gary Thain suffered an electric shock at the Moody Coliseum in Dallas, Texas in September 1974, and was seriously injured. Due to his drug addiction he was not able to perform properly, and was fired by the band in early 1975.

Ray Thomas   The Moody Blues

Ray Thomas died aged seventy-six on the 4th of January 2018 from prostate cancer at his home in Surrey, U.K. He was survived by his second wife, Lee, by his son, Adam and by daughters Nancy and Zoe.

In the early nineteen sixties, Ray joined the Birmingham Youth Choir then began singing with various Birmingham blues and soul groups including The Saints and Sinners and The Ramblers. He was then inspired to learn the flute from a grandfather who played the instrument. Taking up the harmonica he started a band, El Riot and the Rebels, with bassist John Lodge. After a couple of years their friend Mike Pinder joined as keyboardist. On Easter Monday 1963 the band opened for The Beatles at the Bridge Hotel, Tenbury Wells. Ray and Mike were later in a band called Krew Cats, formed in 1963, who played in Hamburg and at other music venues in northern Germany.

They then recruited guitarist Denny Laine, drummer Graeme Edge, and bassist Clint Warwick to form a new, blues-based band, The Moody Blues. Signed to Decca Records, their first album, The Magnificent Moodies, yielded a Number One UK hit called "Go Now".

Following the lead of Pinder, Hayward, and Lodge, Ray also started writing songs. The first he contributed to the group's repertoire were "Another Morning" and "Twilight Time" on the 1967 Days of Future Passed. The album is regarded a prog rock landmark, and Ray's flute solo on the single "Nights in White Satin" one of its defining moments. His flute would become an integral part of the band's music, even as Mike started to use the Mellotron keyboard.

Johnny Thunders   New York Dolls

Johnny Thunders died aged thirty eight from drug related causes on the 23rd of April, 1991 in New Orleans, Louisiana, U.S.A. He was survived by his ex-wife Julie, sons John, Vito and Dino, and daughter Jamie.

Johnny's first musical performance was in the winter of 1967 with The Reign. Shortly thereafter, he played with

Johnny and the Jaywalkers, under the name Johnny Volume, at Quintano's School for Young Professionals, around the corner from Carnegie Hall, on 56th Street near 7th Avenue, New York.

Towards the end of 1970, Johnny started hanging out at Nobodys, a club also on Bleecker Street in the West Village. It was near there that he met future Dolls Arthur Kane and Rick Rivets. He joined their band Actress, which later, after firing Rivets and adding David Johansen, Sylvain Sylvain and Billy Murcia, became the New York Dolls. It was then that he adopted the stage name "Johnny Thunders", inspired by a comic book hero. Johnny recorded two albums with the New York Dolls.

Johnny Thunders formed The Heartbreakers with former New York Dolls drummer Jerry Nolan and former Television bassist Richard Hell.

With Johnny Thunders leading the band, the Heartbreakers toured America before going to Britain to join the Sex Pistols, The Clash and The Damned on the now-legendary Anarchy Tour. While in Britain they were signed to Track Records and released their only official studio album, L.A.M.F., an abbreviation for "Like A Mother Fucker". L.A.M.F. was received positively by critics and fans alike, but was criticised for its poor production. Shortly thereafter, the Heartbreakers officially disbanded.

Johnny Thunders stayed in London and recorded the first of a number of solo albums, beginning with So Alone in 1978.

During the early 1980s, Johnny Thunders re-formed The Heartbreakers for various tours; the group recorded their final album, Live at the Lyceum, in 1984. The concert was also filmed and released as a video and later a DVD titled Dead Or Alive.

Johnny's final recording was a version of "Born To Lose", with German punk rock band Die Toten Hosen, recorded just thirty-six hours before his death in New Orleans.

Peter Tork died aged seventy-seven on the 21st of February 2019 from a cancer of the throat at his home in Mansfield, Connecticut, U.S.A. He was survived by his wife, Pamela, his son, Ivan and daughters Hallie and Erica.

Peter began studying piano at the age of nine, showing an aptitude for music by learning to play several different instruments, including the banjo, acoustic bass, and guitar. He attended college before he moved to New York City, where he became part of the folk music scene in Greenwich Village during the first half of the 1960s. While there, he befriended other up-and-coming musicians including Stephen Stills who had auditioned for the new television series about four pop-rock musicians but was turned down. When asked if he knew of someone with a similar "open, Nordic look", Stills suggested that Peter Tork should audition. Peter got the job and became one of the four members of the Monkees, a pop band of the mid-nineteen-sixties, created for a television sitcom. Peter Tork was the oldest member in the group.

Six albums were produced with the original Monkees lineup, four of which went to number one on the Billboard chart. This success was supplemented by two years of the TV show, a series of successful concert tours both across America and abroad, and a trippy-psychedelic movie called Head.

A chance meeting with Sire Records executive Pat Horgan at the Bottom Line in New York City in 1980 led to Peter recording a six-song demo, his first recording in many years.

Since 1986, Peter had intermittently toured with his former bandmates and also played with his own bands The Peter Peter Tork Project and Shoe Suede Blues. In 1991, Peter formed a band called the Dashboard Saints and played at a pizza restaurant in Guerneville, California. In 1994, he released his first album length solo project, Stranger Things Have Happened, which featured brief appearances by Micky Dolenz and Michael Nesmith.

In 2002, Peter Tork resumed working with his band Shoe Suede Blues. The band performed original blues music, Monkees' covers (blues versions of some), and covers of classic blues hits by greats such as Muddy Waters and has shared the stage with bands such as Captain Zig. The band toured extensively in 2006-2007 following the release of the album "Cambria Hotel". In 2011, Peter joined Mickie and Davy for their 45th Anniversary Tour.

Berne Torme   Gillan, Atomic Rooster

Bernie Tormé died aged sixty-six from pneumonia on the 17th of March 2019. He was survived by his wife Lisa, his sons Jimi and Eric and his daughter, Tuli.

Bernie formed his first band at at around sixteen years of age and played in Dublin band The Urge in the early 1970s before relocating to London in 1974, where he initially played with heavy rockers Scrapyard then formed the Bernie Tormé Band in 1976.

Frustrated by a lack of commercial success, Bernie accepted the invitation of former Deep Purple vocalist Ian Gillan in 1979 to join his band, Gillan.

In 1981 Bernie left Gillan then played as a live session man for Atomic Rooster and was hired in March 1982 by Jet Records to replace the recently deceased Randy Rhoads in Ozzy Osbourne's band.

Beginning in 1982 Bernie led his own band under various names and lineups and spent several years with the band Desperado. Bernie successfully released four albums between 2014 and 2018, and his last album 'Shadowland', was released in November 2018.

Allen Toussaint   Various

Allen Toussaint died of a heart attack aged seventy-seven on the 10th of November 2015 whilst in Madrid, Spain, on tour. He was survived by his son, Clarence and daughter, Alison, and several grandchildren.

Allen learned piano as a child and took informal music lessons from an elderly neighbour. In his teens he played in a band, the Flamingos, before dropping out of school. A significant early influence on Allen Toussaint was the syncopated "second-line" piano style of Professor Longhair.

After a lucky break at age seventeen, in which he stood in for Huey "Piano" Smith at a performance with Earl King's band in Prichard, Alabama, Allen was introduced to a group of local musicians who performed regularly at the Dew Drop Inn, a nightclub in Uptown New Orleans. His first recording was in 1957 as a stand-in for Fats Domino on Domino's record "I Want You to Know", on which Allen played piano and Domino overdubbed his vocals.

After being spotted as a sideman by the A&R man Danny Kessler, he initially recorded for RCA Records as Al Tousa and in early 1958 he recorded an album of instrumentals.

Allen played piano, wrote, arranged and produced a string of hits in the early and mid-1960s for New Orleans Rhythm & Blues artists and Lee Dorsey, whose first hit "Ya Ya" he produced in 1961.

Allen was drafted into the US Army in 1963 but continued to record when on leave. After his discharge in 1965, he joined forces with Marshall Sehorn to form Sansu Enterprises, which included a record label, Sansu and recorded Lee Dorsey, Chris Kenner, Betty Harris, and others. Lee Dorsey had hits with several of Allen's songs, including "Ride Your Pony" in 1965, "Working in the Coal Mine" in 1966, and "Holy Cow" in 1966.

In 2008, Allen Toussaint's song "Sweet Touch of Love" was used in a deodorant commercial for the Axe brand. The commercial won a Gold Lion at the 2008 Cannes Lions International Advertising Festival.

Mary Travers died aged seventy-two on the 16th of September 2009, in hospital in Connecticut, U.S.A. from complications related to a bone marrow transplant and other treatments. She was survived by her husband, Ethan and her daughters Erika and Alicia and was buried in a cemetery in Redding, Connecticut, U.S.A.

Mary Travers was born in Louisville, Kentucky and in 1938, the family moved to Greenwich Village in New York City. Mary attended the progressive Little Red School House, where she met musical icons including Pete Seeger and Paul Robeson and left school in the 11th grade to become a member of the Song Swappers folk group.

The group Peter, Paul and Mary was formed in 1961, and was an immediate success. They shared a manager, Albert Grossman, with Bob Dylan. Their success with Bob Dylan's song "Don't Think Twice, It's All Right" helped propel Dylan's Freewheelin' album into the U.S. Top 30 four months after its release.

Peter, Paul and Mary broke up in 1970 shortly after having their biggest U.K. hit, "Leaving on a Jet 'Plane" which made number 1 on both the U.S. Billboard and Cash Box charts in December 1969 and was the group's only number one hit.

Mary Travers subsequently pursued a solo career and recorded five albums: Mary in 1971, Morning Glory in 1972, "All My Choices" in 1973, "Circles" in 1974 and "It's in Everyone of Us" in 1978.

Peter, Paul and Mary's UK chart entries include: "Blowing In The Wind" in 1963, "Tell It to The Mountain" in 1964 and "Leavin' On A Jet Plane" in 1970.

Mick Tucker   **The Sweet**

Mick Tucker died of leukemia aged fifty-four on the 14th of February 2002 in Welwyn Garden City, Hertfordshire,

U.K. He was survived by his wife, Janet and his daughter, Alison.

As a boy, Mick's first interest was art but by fourteen he had changed his interest to the drums and by the age of nineteen, he had embarked on a career in pop music, playing around pubs and clubs in a band called Wainwright's Gentlemen and was later joined by vocalist Brian Connolly playing a mixture of R&B, Motown, and early psychedelic sounds but this band split in 1968.

Mick was a founding member of the band Sweetshop in January 1968 then "Sweetshop" was shortened to "The Sweet" in 1968.

The Sweet's UK chart entries include: "Co-Co" in 1971, "Little Willy" in 1972, "Wig-Bam-Bam" in 1972, "Blockbuster" in 1973, "Hell Raiser" in 1973, "Ballroom Blitz" in 1973, "Teenage Rampage" in 1974, "Fox on the Run" in 1975 and "Love is Like Oxygen" in 1978.

Mark Tulin   **The Electric Prunes**

Mark Tulin died aged sixty-two on 26th of February 2011 in Avalon, California, U.S.A. He was survived by his ex-wife, Lani and his daughter, Samantha.

In 1965, Mark was playing in a band called the Sanctions, which became The Electric Prunes and they had hit singles internationally with "I Had Too Much To Dream (Last Night)" and "Get Me To The World on Time". Mark Tulin continued playing with the Electric Prunes until 1968.

In 1999, renewed interest in The Electric Prunes led to a reunion including Mark Tulin and then after he remained a member until he died.

The Electric Prunes' UK chart entries include: "I Had Too Much To Dream Last Night" in 1967 and "Get Me To The World On Time" in 1967.

Charlie Tumahai   Be-Bop Deluxe

Charlie Tumahai died aged forty-six of a heart attack on the 21st of December 1995 while working in New Zealand where he had joined the popular New Zealand reggae band Herbs. He was survived by his wife, Susan and their two progeny.

Besides music, Charlie became involved in Maori affairs, working as a voluntary member of a scheme set up to assist young Maori offenders in Auckland. He was also developing plans for an arts programme for Maori prisoners and for exploring new ways he could help young Maori people connect with their culture.

Charlie was born in Orakei, Auckland, New Zealand, where he began his music career before moving to Australia in the late 1960's.

He was a member of several notable Australian bands including Chain, Healing Force, Friends and Mississippi. Charlie then travelled to the UK with Mississippi in 1974 and remained there when Mississippi broke up. Later that year he joined Be-Bop Deluxe, with whom he played and recorded until 1978.

Be-Bop Deluxe's UK chart entries include: "Ships In The Night" in 1976.

Ike Turner   The Ike & Tina Turner Revue

Ike Turner died aged seventy-six from emphysema on the 12th of December 2007 at his home in San Marcos, California, U.S.A. He was survived by several ex-wives, including Tina, and by his sons Ike Jnr, Ronnie and Michael and his daughters, Mia, Linda and Twanna.

At around his eighth year, Ike began frequenting the local Clarksdale radio station, WROX, located in the Alcazar Hotel in downtown Clarksdale. WROX was notable as one of the first radio stations to employ a black DJ.

Ike was inspired to learn the piano on a visit to his friend's house, where he heard someone playing the friend's father's piano. Ike then persuaded his mother to pay for piano lessons and he taught himself to play guitar by playing along to old blues records. At some point in the 1940s, Ike moved into Clarksdale's Riverside Hotel. The Riverside played host to touring musicians, including Sonny Boy Williamson II and Duke Ellington. Ike associated with many of these guests and played music with them.

In high school, Ike Turner joined a local rhythm ensemble called the Tophatters who played dances around Clarksdale, Mississippi. Ike, who was trained by ear and could not sight read, would learn the pieces by listening to a version on record at home, pretending to be reading the music during rehearsals.

Ike became a session musician and production assistant for Philips and the Bihari Brothers, commuting to Memphis from Clarksdale. He began by contributing piano to a B.B. King track, "You Know I Love You", which brought him to the attention of Modern Records' Joe Bihari, who requested Ike's services on another King track, 3 O'Clock Blues. It became King's first hit.

In 1957, 16-year-old Anna Mae Bullock accompanied her sister Aillene to watch Ike Turner and the Kings of Rhythm at the Club Manhattan. Aillene was a barmaid at the club and was dating Ike Turner's drummer. After seeing the band, Anna Mae asked to sing with the Kings of Rhythm, finally being given the chance to do so during an intermission. Impressed by her voice, Ike Turner invited her to join the band, giving her the stage name "Little Ann".

In March 1960, Ike used Anna Mae's voice on a recording of his self-penned song "A Fool in Love" to lay down a guide track for a male singer who did not attend the recording. He sent the recording to Sun Records in New York, where label owner Juggy Murray insisted on putting out the track with Bullock's vocal. Murray offered twenty-five thousand dollars for the song, convinced it was a hit. Around the time of the recording, Anna Mae had been pursued by Raymond Hill to join his band and leave Ike Turner's. When Ike Turner asked her to use his last name as an attempt to discourage Hill, Anna Mae took the offer. Ike added a backing girl group he renamed the Ikettes, and this also led to the first name change of the Kings of Rhythm as they began performing as the Ike & Tina Turner Revue. There was never any doubt that Tina Turner was the star.. the electrifying performer audiences came to see. Ike kept his own stage presence deliberately low-key, avoiding flamboyant moves and directing the band with underplayed, economical gestures. His songwriting, production and musical direction were geared toward showcasing Tina.

Phil Spector sought out the duo to work with on 1965's "River Deep – Mountain High". The song was not a success in the States, causing Spector's retreat from the music industry, but was a big hit in Europe, reaching number 3 in the UK singles chart. This brought the duo to the attention of Mick Jagger, who in 1966 and in 1969, invited them to tour with and open for the Rolling Stones, bringing them to a wider audience outside of soul.

The success of the Ike and Tina Ike Turner Revue gave Ike Turner the finances to create his own recording studio, the Los Angeles-based Bolic Sounds next door to his mansion in Inglewood.

Ike's partnership ended abruptly in 1976 with Tina leaving after the last in a series of violent altercations with Ike him. On 1st July 1976, Ike and Tina were en route from Los Angeles to Dallas where the Revue had a gig at the Dallas Statler Hilton. They got into a fight during their ride to the hotel. Shortly after arriving at the hotel, Tina fled and later hid at a friend's house. That July, Tina sued for divorce on the grounds of irreconcilable differences.

Tina Turner died, aged eighty-three on the 24th of May 2023, at her home in Küsnacht, Switzerland from natural causes after years of illnesses. In the UK, King Charles III paid tribute by allowing "The Best" to be performed during the changing of the guard.

After moving to St. Louis, Missouri, USA Tina and her sister Alline became acquainted with Ike Turner's Kings of Rhythm. Alline was dating the band's drummer and Tina began dating the saxophonist Raymond Hill. After Tina became pregnant during her senior year of high school, she moved in with Hill, who lived with Ike Turner. Their relationship ended after Hill broke his ankle and he returned to his hometown of Clarksdale before their son Craig was born in August 1958, leaving Tina to become a single parent. t.

Tina likened her early relationship with Ike Turner to that of a "brother and sister from another lifetime." They were platonic friends from the time they met in 1957 until 1960. Their affair began while Ike was with his live-in girlfriend Lorraine Taylor. They had sex when she went to sleep with him after another musician threatened to go into her room.

After recording "A Fool in Love" in 1960, a pregnant Tina told Ike that she did not want to continue their relationship and he responded by striking her in the head with a wooden shoe stretcher. After the birth of their son Ronnie in October 1960, they moved to Los Angeles in 1962 and married in Tijuana. In 1963, Ike purchased a house in the View Park area. They brought their son Ronnie, Tina's son Craig, and Ike's two sons from St. Louis to live with them.

Tina abruptly left Ike after they got into a fight on their way to the Dallas Statler Hilton in 1976. She fled with only 36 cents and a Mobil credit card in her pocket to the Ramada Inn across the freeway. Later, she filed for divorce on the grounds of irreconcilable differences. The divorce was finalized in March, 1978.

In 1986, Tina met German music executive Erwin Bach, who was sent by her European record label (EMI) to greet her at Düsseldorf Airport. Bach was over sixteen years her junior. Initially friends, they began dating later that year. In July 2013, after a 27-year romantic relationship, they married in a civil ceremony on the banks of Lake Zurich in Küsnacht, Switzerland.

Tina began living at Château Algonquin in Küsnacht on the shore of Lake Zurich in 1994. She previously owned property in Cologne, London, and Los Angeles, and a villa on the French Riviera named Anna Fleur.

In 2013, Turner applied for Swiss citizenship, stating she would relinquish her US citizenship and she became a citizen of Switzerland and was issued a Swiss passport.

In 1977, she re-emerged with a sexier image and costumes created by Bob Mackie. She headlined a series of cabaret shows at Caesars Palace in Las Vegas and took her act to smaller venues in the United States. Later that year, she embarked on her first solo concert tour in Australia.

In 1978, Tina released her third solo album, Rough, on United Artists with distribution in North America and Europe on EMI. That album, along with its 1979 follow-up, Love Explosion, which included a brief diversion to disco music, failed to chart, so United Artists Records and Turner parted ways. Without the premise of a hit record, she continued performing and headlined her second tour.

In 1979, Australian manager Roger Davies agreed to manage Tina after seeing her perform at the Fairmont Hotel in San Francisco. In early 1979, Tina worked in Italy as a regular performer on the Rete 1 TV series Luna Park, hosted by Pippo Baudo and Heather Parisi. Later that year, she embarked on a controversial five-week tour of South Africa during the apartheid regime.

Until 1983, Turner was considered a nostalgia act, performing mostly at hotel ballrooms and clubs in the United

States. During her second stint at the Ritz, she signed with Capitol Records in 1983. In November 1983, she released her cover of Al Green's "Let's Stay Together", which was produced by B.E.F. It reached several European charts, including number six in the UK. In the US, the song peaked at number twenty-six on the Billboard Hot 100.

Following the single's success, Capitol Records approved a studio album and Tina had two weeks to record her Private Dancer album, which was released in May 1984. It reached Number three on the Billboard 200 and number two in the United Kingdom. Private Dancer was certified 5× Platinum in the United States, and sold 10 million copies worldwide, becoming her most successful album. Also in May 1984, Capitol issued the album's second single, "What's Love Got to Do with It". The song had previously been recorded by the pop group Bucks Fizz. Following the album's release, Tina joined Lionel Richie as the opening act on his tour.

At the beginning of September, 1984, Tinar achieved her first and only number one on the Billboard Hot 100 with "What's Love Got to Do with It". The follow-up singles "Better Be Good to Me" and "Private Dancer" were both US top 10 hits. The same year, she duetted with David Bowie on a cover of Iggy Pop's "Tonight".

Tina culminated her comeback when she won three Grammys at the 27th Annual Grammy Awards, including the Grammy Award for Record of the Year for "What's Love Got to Do with It". In February 1985, she embarked on her second world tour to support the Private Dancer album. Two nights were filmed at Birmingham, England's NEC Arena and later released as a concert on home video.

Tina's success continued when she travelled to Australia to star opposite Mel Gibson in the 1985 post-apocalyptic film Mad Max Beyond Thunderdome. The movie provided her with her first acting role in ten years; she portrayed the glamorous Aunty Entity, the ruler of Bartertown. Upon release, critical response to her performance was generally positive. The film was a global success, grossing more than $36 million in the United States. Tina later received the NAACP Image Award for Outstanding Actress for her role in the film. She recorded two songs for the film, "We Don't Need Another Hero (Thunderdome)" and "One of the Living"; both became hits, with the latter winning her a Grammy Award for Best Female Rock Vocal Performance. In July 1985, Tina performed at Live Aid alongside Mick Jagger. Their performance surprised observers when Mick ripped her skirt off.

In 1986, Tina released her sixth solo album, Break Every Rule, which reached number one in four countries and sold over five million copies worldwide within its first year of release. The album featured the singles "Typical Male", "Two People", "What You Get Is What You See ", and the Grammy-winning "Back Where You Started". Prior to the album's release, Tina published her autobiography I, Tina, which became a bestseller. That year, she received a star on the Hollywood Walk of Fame. Her Break Every Rule World Tour, which began in March 1987 in Munich, Germany, was the third highest-grossing tour by a female artist in North America that year. In January 1988, Tina performed in front of approximately 180,000 at Maracanã Stadium in Rio de Janeiro, Brazil, setting a Guinness World Record at the time for the largest paying concert attendance for a solo artist. In April 1988, Tina released the Tina Live in Europe album, which won a Grammy Award for Best Female Rock Vocal Performance. After taking time off following the end of the tour, she emerged with the Foreign Affair album in 1989. It reached Number one in eight countries, including in the UK, her first number-one album there. The album sold over six million copies worldwide and included the international hit single "The Best".

In 1990, Tina embarked on her Foreign Affair European Tour, which drew in nearly four million spectators—breaking the record for a European tour that was previously set by the Rolling Stones. In October 1991 Tina released her first greatest hits compilation Simply the Best, which sold seven million copies worldwide. The album is her biggest seller in the UK, with more than two million copies sold. In 1995 Tina returned to the studio, releasing "GoldenEye", which was written by Bono and the Edge of U2 for the James Bond film GoldenEye. In 1996 Tina released the Wildest Dreams album, accompanied by her "Wildest Dreams Tour". In September 1999, before celebrating her 60th birthday, Tina released the dance-infused song "When the Heartache Is Over" as the leading single from her tenth and final solo album, Twenty Four Seven. The success of the single and the following tour helped the album become certified Gold by the RIAA. The Twenty Four Seven Tour was the highest-grossing tour of 2000, grossing over $120 million. Her two concerts at Wembley Stadium were recorded by the director David Mallet and released in the DVD One Last Time Live in Concert. At a July 2000 concert in Zürich, Switzerland, Tina announced that she would retire at the end of the tour.

In November 2004, Tina released All the Best, which debuted at No. 2 on the Billboard 200 in 2005, her highest charting album in the United States. The album went platinum in the US three months after its release and reached platinum status in seven other countries, including the UK.

In October 2008, Tina embarked on her first tour in nearly ten years with the Tina!: 50th Anniversary Tour. In support of the tour, Turner released a greatest hits compilation. The tour was a huge success and became one of the bestselling tours of all time. In 2009, Tina officially retired from performing.

Richie Valens   Solo Artiste

Richie Valens died aged seventeen on the 3rd of February 1959 in a plane crash. Following a performance in Clear Lake, Iowa, USA which ended around midnight, Richie, along with Buddy Holly and The Big Bobber flew out of the Mason City airport in a small chartered plane. The three-passenger Beechcraft Bonanza departed for Fargo, North Dakota, and crashed a few minutes after take-off killing all three passengers and the pilot. Richie's remains were buried at San Fernando Mission Cemetery, Mission Hills, California, U.S.A.

Richie was born Richard Steven Valenzuela in Pacoima, a neighborhood in the San Fernando Valley region of Los Angeles and was brought up hearing traditional Mexican mariachi music, as well as flamenco guitar, R&B, and jump blues. Richie expressed an interest in making music of his own by the age of five, and he was encouraged by his father to take up guitar and trumpet, and later taught himself the drums. Though Richie was left-handed, he was so eager to learn the guitar that he mastered the traditionally right-handed version of the instrument. By the time Richie was attending junior high school, he brought the guitar to school and would sing and play songs to his friends. When he was sixteen years old, he was invited to join a local band, the Silhouettes as a guitarist, and when the main vocalist left the group, he assumed the position. During October, 1957, he made his performing debut with the Silhouettes.

Richie demonstrated several songs in a studio that he later recorded at Gold Star Studios in Hollywood. The first songs recorded at Gold Star Studios, at a single studio session one afternoon in July nineteen fifty-eight, were "Come On, Let's Go", an original credited to Richie Valens/Kuhn, and "Framed", a Leiber and Stoller tune. Pressed and released within days of the recording session, the record was a success. Richie Valens's next record, a double A-side, the final record to be released in his lifetime, had the song "Donna" coupled with "La Bamba". It sold over one million copies, and was awarded a gold disc by the Record Industry Association of America. By the autumn of nineteen fifty-eight, the demands of Richie Valens' career forced him to drop out of high school.

In early 1959, Richie was travelling the Midwest on a multiple-act rock-and-roll tour dubbed "The Winter Dance Party" which led to his death in the plane crash.

Dickie Valentine   Solo Artiste

Dickie Valentine died aged forty-one on the 6th of May 1971 in a car crash in Wales, U.K. He was survived by his wife, Wendy, his son, Richard and his daughter, Kim.

Dickie developed a flexible vocal style and skills as an impersonator of famous singers. Later, he sang in clubs and learned stagecraft to help gain confidence and experience. While he was in his late teens, he was singing at the Panama Club one night when music publisher Sid Green saw him and brought him to the attention of bandleader Ted Heath.

In 1949, Dickie, then an unknown, was signed by Ted Heath to join his band. He was voted the Top UK Male Vocalist in 1952 while singing with the Ted Heath Orchestra, the most successful of all British big bands.

In November 1954, Dickie was invited to sing at the Royal Command Performance, and in February 1955 he was top billed at the London Palladium. He also recorded two number one hits, "Christmas Alphabet" and "Finger of Suspicion".

In 1961, Dickie had a television series called 'Calling Dickie Valentine'. Although his fame began to slew off during the 1960s, he remained a popular live performer until his death.

Hilton Valentine   The Animals

Hilton Valentine died on the 29th of January 2021 at the age of seventy-seven. No cause or place of death was revealed. He was survived by his wife, Germaine and their daughter Samantha.

Hilton was born in North Shields, Northumberland,

England, and was soon influenced by the 1950s skiffle music. His mother bought him his first guitar in 1956 when he was thirteen he taught himself some chords from a book. He continued to develop his musical talent at Tynemouth High School and formed his own skiffle group called the Heppers. They played local gigs and a newspaper described them at the time as, "A young but promising skiffle group". The Heppers eventually evolved into a rock and roll band, the Wildcats in 1959. During this period Hilton played a Futurama III solid guitar. The Wildcats were a popular band in the Tyneside area, getting a lot of bookings for dance halls, working men's clubs, church halls etc., and it was during this period that they decided to record a 10" acetate LP titled Sounds of the Wild Cats.

In 1963, the Animals had began to form and Chas Chandler heard about Hilton Valentine's wild guitar playing and asked him to join what was then the Alan Price Combo. Eric Burdon was already a member and John Steel joined immediately following Hilton's arrival. Within a few months, this group changed their name to the Animals.

While the Animals are often remembered most for Eric Burdon's vocals and Price's organ, Hilton is credited with the electric guitar arpeggio introduction to the Animals' 1964 signature song "The House of the Rising Sun", which inspired countless beginning guitarists. It was played on his Gretsch Tennessean guitar which he bought in Newcastle in early 1962 while he was still with the Wildcats.

Hilton continued to play and record with the Animals, until the first incarnation of the band dissolved in September 1966. In 1977, Hilton rejoined the group and recorded a reunion album called Before We Were So Rudely Interrupted.

After he left The Animals, Hilton moved to California and in 1969 recorded a solo album entitled All In Your Head, which was not successful. He then returned to the UK, and over the years joined several Animals reunions.

Along with Eric Burdon, Chas Chandler, Alan Price and John Steel, Hilton Valentine was inducted into the Rock and Roll Hall of Fame in 1994. Along with the other Animals, Hilton was inducted into Hollywood's Rock Walk of Fame in May 2001. He released a new album, It's Folk 'n' Skiffle, Mate! in 2004.

Hilton's last recording was "River Tyne", a 2019 video that celebrated the river close to his boyhood home.

Eddie Van Halen

Eddie Van Halen died aged sixty-five of a stroke on the 6th of October, 2020 whilst in Santa Monica, California, United States of America. He was survived by his ex-wife Valerie, their son Wolfgang and his second wife, Janie.

In 1962, the Van Halen family moved from the Netherlands to the United States, settling in Pasadena, California where Eddie and his older brother, Alex, became naturalized U.S. citizens. The brothers learned to play the piano as children starting at the age of six and they commuted from Pasadena to San Pedro to study with an elderly piano teacher.

Eddie was never taught to read music but would watch recitals of Bach or Mozart and improvise. From 1964 through 1967, he won first place in the annual piano competition held at Long Beach City College. His parents wanted the boys to be classical pianists, but Eddie Van Halen gravitated towards rock music. Consequently, when Alex began playing the guitar, Eddie bought a drum kit for himself but he then gave Alex the drums and began learning how to play the electric guitar. Eddie and his brother Alex formed their first band with three other boys, calling themselves 'The Broken Combs'.

Whilst Eddie and Alex Van Halen formed a band in 1972, they changed its name to "Van Halen" and, simultaneously , became a staple of the Los Angeles music scene and then in 1977, Warner Records offered them a recording contract.

Soon after its release in nineteen seventy-eight, , their eponymous album ' Van Halen', reached number nineteen on the American Billboard pop music charts, becoming one of rock's most commercially successful debut LP's.

By the early 1980s, Van Halen was one of the most successful rock acts of the time and the album, "1984", went five-times Platinum a year after its release. The lead single "Jump" became the band's first and only number-one pop hit and garnered them a Grammy nomination.

In February 2017, Eddie donated seventy-five guitars from his personal collection to a program that provides musical instruments to students in low income schools.

Van Halen's UK chart entries include; "Jump" in 1984 and "Why Can't This Be Love" in 1986.

Ronnie Van Zant   Lynard Skynard

Ronnie Van Zant died aged twenty-nine on the 20th of October 1977 after an aircraft carrying Lynyrd Skynyrd between shows crashed near Gillsburg, Mississippi, U.S.A. Ronnie was survived by his wife Judy, daughters Tammy and Melody. He was buried in Orange Park, Florida.

Ronnie was born and raised in Jacksonville, Florida,U.S.A. and aspired to be many things before finding his love for music. Idolising boxer Muhammad Ali, he considered a career in the ring, and while playing American Legion baseball dreamed of Minor League success.

Ronnie formed a band called My Backyard late in 1964 with friends and schoolmates Allen Collins, Gary Rossington, Larry Junstrom, and Bob Burns . The foursome went through several names before deciding on Lynyrd Skynyrd, a mock tribute to a gym teacher that all but Collins had had at Robert E. Lee High School, Leonard Skinner, who disapproved of male students with long hair.

The band's national exposure began in 1973 with the release of their debut album, which had a string of hits that included "I Ain't the One", "Tuesday's Gone", "Gimme

Three Steps", "Simple Man," and what became their signature song, "Free Bird".

Luther Vandross   **Solo Artiste**

Luther Vandross died aged fifty-four of a heart attack on the 1st of July 2005 at the JFK Medical Center in Edison, New Jersey, U.S.A. He was survived by his mother, Mary.

Luther had suffered from diabetes and hypertension and had, in 2003, suffered a severe stroke and was in a coma for almost two months. The stroke impaired his ability to speak and sing and forced him to use a wheelchair.

Before his solo breakthrough, Luther was part of a singing quintet in the late 1970s named Luther. Although the singles "It's Good for the Soul", "Funky Music", and "The Second Time Around" were relatively successful, their two albums, the self-titled Luther in 1976 and This Close to You in 1977 did not sell enough to make the charts.

Luther also wrote and sang commercial jingles from 1977 until the early 1980s, for companies including NBC, Mountain Dew, Kentucky Fried Chicken, Burger King, and Juicy Fruit. He continued his successful career as a popular session singer during the late 1970s.

Luther made his career breakthrough as a featured singer with the vaunted pop-dance act Change, a studio concept created by French-Italian businessman Jacques Fred Petrus. Their 1980 hits, "The Glow of Love" and "Searching", featured Luther as the lead singer.

Luther released a series of successful r&b albums during the 1980s and continued his session work. More albums followed in the 1990s, beginning with 1991's Power of Love which spawned two top ten pop hits. Luther hit the top ten again in 1994, teaming with Mariah Carey on a cover version of Lionel Richie and Diana Ross's duet "Endless Love". It was included on the album Songs, a collection of songs which had inspired Luther over the years.

Luther Vandross' UK chart hits included: "I Really Didn't Mean It" in 1987, "Never Too Much" in 1989, "The Best Things In Life Are Free" in 1992, "Endless Love" in 1994, "Ain't No Stopping Us Now" in 1995 and "Your Secret Love" in 1996.

Vangelis   Solo Artiste

Evangelos Papathanassiou died aged seventy-nine of heart failure on the 17th of May 2022, at a hospital in Paris from COVID-19 complications. He was survived by his wife, Veronique.

Vangelis developed an interest in music at age four, composing on the family piano. When he was six his parents enrolled him for music lessons, but Vangelis later said that his attempts to study "failed" as he preferred to develop technique on his own. He considered himself fortunate to have not attended music school, as he believed that it would have impeded his creativity. He never learned to read or write music, instead played from memory.

Vangelis acquired his first Hammond organ at age eighteen and in 1963, he and three school friends started a five-piece rock band called, The Forminx. Following the split of The Forminx, Vangelis spent the next two years mostly studio-bound, writing and producing for other Greek artists and he scored music for three Greek movies.

In 1968, Vangelis wished to further his career and, amidst the political turmoil surrounding the 1967 coup, left Greece for London. However, he was denied entry into the UK and settled in Paris for the next six years. Later in 1968 he formed the progressive rock band Aphrodite's Child with Demis Roussos, Loukas Sideras, and Anargyros "Silver" Koulouris. Their debut single, "Rain and Tears", was a commercial success in Europe which was followed by the albums End of the World in 1968 and It's Five O'Clock in 1969.

The group split in 1971 but Vangelis produced future albums and singles for their singer Demis Roussos. From 1970 to 1974, Vangelis took part in various solo projects in film, television, and theatre. He also provided music for the Henry Chapier movie, Amore, in 1973.

Also in 1973, he released his second solo album Earth, a percussive-orientated album with various additional musicians, including Robert Fitoussi and Aphrodite's Child bandmate Silver Koulouris.

In August 1975, after Vangelis had settled in a flat in Marble Arch, London, where he set up his new 16-track studio, Nemo Studios, which he named his "laboratory", he secured a recording deal with RCA Records. He released a series of electronic albums for RCA until 1979. The first of these, Heaven and Hell, features the English Chamber Choir and Yes singer Jon Anderson.

In 1980, Vangelis agreed to record the score for the movie Chariots of Fire. The choice of music was unorthodox as most period films featured orchestral scores, whereas Vangelis's music was modern and synthesiser-oriented. It gained mainstream commercial success which increased Vangelis's public rofile.

The soundtrack album was number one on the American Billboard 200 for four weeks and sold one million copies in the United States.

Vangelis wrote the score for the film Bitter Moon, directed by Roman Polanski in 1992, and The Plague directed by Luis Puenzo. He performed his only concert in the U.S.A in November 1986.

Randy Vanwarmer   Solo Artiste

Randy Vanwarmer died from leukemia aged forty-eight on the 12th of January 2004 in Seattle, U.S.A. He was survived by his wife, Suzi.

Before his death, Randy had continued to write music for others and for his own recordings, which continued to be artistically successful but commercially less-so. He also helped other younger artists with their own songwriting efforts.

Randy Vanwarmer's only UK chart hit was: "Just When I Needed You Most" in 1979.

Stevie Ray Vaughan   Double Trouble

Stevie Ray Vaughan died aged thirty-five on the 27th of August 1990 in East Troy, Wisconsin, U.S.A. when his helicopter crashed. He was survived by his wife, Lenora and his brother, Jimmie.

In 1961, for his seventh birthday, Stevie received his first guitar and learning by ear, he diligently committed himself, following along to songs by the Nightcaps, particularly "Wine, Wine, Wine" and "Thunderbird". He listened to blues artists such as Albert King, Otis Rush, and Muddy Waters, and rock guitarists such as Jimi Hendrix and Lonnie Mack, as well as jazz guitarists including Kenny Burrell. In 1963, he acquired his first electric guitar, a Gibson ES-125T, as a hand-me-down from his brother.

Soon after he acquired the electric guitar, Stevie Ray joined his first band, the Chantones, in 1965. Their first gig was at a talent contest held in Dallas' Hill Theatre, but after realizing that they could not perform a Jimmy Reed song in its entirety, Stevie left the band and joined the Brooklyn Underground, playing professionally at local bars and clubs.

In September 1970, Stevie made his first studio recordings with the band Cast of Thousands. They recorded two songs, "Red, White and Blue" and "I Heard a Voice Last Night", for a compilation album, A New Hi, that featured various teenage bands from Dallas. In late January 1971, feeling confined by playing pop hits, Stevie formed his own band, Blackbird. After growing tired of the Dallas music scene, he dropped out of school and moved with the band to Austin, Texas, for the more liberal and tolerant audiences there.

Blackbird played at several clubs in Austin and opened shows for bands such as Sugarloaf, Wishbone Ash, and Zephyr, but could not maintain a consistent lineup. In early December 1972, Stevie left Blackbird and joined a rock band named Krackerjack. However, he performed with them for less than three months.

In 1975, Stevie joined a six-piece band called Paul Ray and the Cobras which included guitarist Val Swierczewski and saxophonist Joe Sublett. For the next two-and-a-half years, he earned a living performing weekly at a popular venue in town.

In 1978, Stevie renamed the band Double Trouble, taken from the title of an Otis Rush song. Later, Stevie and Double Trouble earned a frequent residency performing at one of Austin's most popular nightspots, the Rome Inn.

Although popular in Texas at the time, Double Trouble failed to gain national attention. The group's luck progressed when record producer Jerry Wexler recommended them to Claude Nobs, organizer of the Montreux Jazz Festival. He insisted the festival's blues night would be good for Stevie, whom he called "a jewel", and Nobs agreed to book Double Trouble.

Frankie Vaughan   Solo Artiste

Frankie Vaughan died from heart failure aged seventy-one on the 17th of September 1999 in High Wycombe, Buckinghamshire, United Kingdom. He was survived by his wife, Stella, his sons David and Andrew and daughter, Susan.

Frankie, in his early life, was a member of the Lancaster Lads' Club, a member group of the National Association of Boys' Clubs in the UK, and in his career he was a major contributor to the clubs, dedicating his monetary compensation from one song each year to them. Frankie was an evacuee during World War II and started out at the club intending to be a boxer. Frankie attended the Lancaster College of Art on a scholarship and was a vocalist in their dance band. After a stint in the Royal Army Medical Corps in World War II he returned to art school, this time at the Leeds College of Art. When he won a prize in a design contest, he left for London, where he won second prize on a radio talent show.

Frankie Vaughan's career began in the late 1940s performing song and dance routines. He was known as a fancy dresser, wearing top hat, bow tie, tails, and cane. In the 1950s he worked for a few years with the band of Nat Temple, and after that period he then began making records under his own name. In 1955, he recorded what was to become his trademark song, "Give Me the Moonlight".

In 1994, Frankie was one of a few to be honoured by a second appearance on BBC show 'This Is Your Life', when he was surprised by the host.

Despite frequent bouts of ill-health, Frankie continued performing until shortly before his death. Frankie's UK chart hits include: "Green Door" in 1956, "Garden of Eden" in 1957, "Man of Fire" in 1957, "Kisses Sweater Than Wine" in 1957, "Kewpie Doll" in 1958, "Come Softly To Me" in 1959, "The Heart of a Man" in 1959, "Tower of Strength" in 1961, "Loop-de-Loop" in 1963 and "There Must Be A Way" in 1967.

Bobby Vee   Solo Artiste

Bobby Vee died aged seventy-three from the complications of Alzheimer's disease on the 24th of October 2016. He was survived by his wife Karen, their sons Jeffrey, Thomas, and Robert, and daughter Jennifer.

Bobby's first single, "Suzie Baby," was written by himself and recorded for the Soma label, based in Minneapolis in 1959. It was a hit in Minnesota and drew enough national attention to be purchased by Liberty Records, which signed him later that year. His follow-up single, a cover of Adam Faith's UK number-one "What Do You Want?", charted in the lower reaches of the American Billboard pop chart in early 1960. His fourth release, a revival of the Clovers' doo-wop ballad "Devil or Angel", brought him into the big time with U.S. buyers. His next single, "Rubber Ball" in 1961, a U.S. number six and Australian number one, made him an international star.

Bobby Vee's UK chart hits include: "Rubber Ball" in 1961, "More Than I Can Say" in 1961, "How Many Tears" in 1961, "Take Good Care of My Baby" in 1961, "Run To Him" in 1961, "Sharing You" in 1962 and "The Night Has a Thousand Eyes" in 1963.

Henry Vestine   Canned Heat

Henry Vestine died aged fifty-two on the 20th of October, 1997 whilst in Paris, France. He had finished a European tour with Canned Heat when he died from heart and respiratory failure in a Paris hotel just as the band were awaiting their return to America. He was survived by his wife, Lisa and his son, Jesse.

Henry's love of music and the blues in particular was fostered at an early age when he accompanied his father on canvasses of black neighbourhoods for old recordings. Like his father, Henry became an avid collector, eventually owning tens of thousands of recordings of blues, hillbilly, country, and Cajun music. At Henry's urging, his father also used to take him to blues shows at which he and Henry were often the only white people present. Later Henry was instrumental in the "rediscovery" of Skip James and other Delta blues musicians.

Soon after the family moved to California, Henry joined his first junior high band. On his first LSD trip with a close musician friend, he went to an East LA tattoo parlor and got the first of what was to be numerous tattoos: the words "Living The Blues".

Throughout the early to mid-1960s Henry played in various musical line-ups and eventually was hired by Frank

Zappa for the original Mothers of Invention in October 1965.

Bob Hite and Alan Wilson started Canned Heat with Kenny Edwards as a second guitarist, but then Henry was asked to join. The first notable appearance of the band was the following year when they played at the Monterey Pop Festival, held from sixteenth to eighteenth of June, 1967. Shortly after, Canned Heat's first album, "Canned Heat", was released and Henry burst into musical prominence as a guitarist who stretched the idiom of the blues with long solos that moved beyond the conventional genres with his own style and a trademark piercing treble guitar sound.

Sid Vicious   The Sex Pistols

Sid Vicious died aged twenty-one on the 1st of February 1979 of heroin overdosing whilst in Manhattan, New York, U.S.A. He was survived by his mother Anne.

Sid first met John Lydon in 1973, when they were both students at Hackney Technical College. John Lydon described Sid at this time as a David Bowie fan and a "clothes hound".

Sid began his musical career in 1976 as a member of the Flowers of Romance along with former co-founding member of the Clash, Keith Levene. He appeared with Siouxsie and the Banshees, playing drums at their notorious first gig at the 100 Club Punk Festival in London's Oxford Street. According to members of the Damned, Sid was considered, along with Dave Vanian, for the position of lead singer for the Damned, but Sid failed to show up for the audition.

After Sid had joined the Sex Pistols, they embarked on a US tour which would only last one to two weeks because of multiple show cancellations and deterioration within the group.

After the show at Winterland in San Francisco, the group fell apart, freeing Sid to embark on a path to destruction, while recording lead vocals on three cover songs at the same time for the soundtrack album for the film The Great Rock 'n' Roll Swindle. "My Way" was released in 1978, "C'mon Everybody" was released in 1979, and "Something Else" was released in 1979 after Sid's death.

Gene Vincent   Solo Artiste

Gene Vincent died aged thirty-six on the 12th of October 1971, from a ruptured stomach ulcer, whilst in California, U.S.A. He was survived by his wife, Jackie, his son Gene Jnr and his daughters, Melody and Sherri Anne.

Gene showed his first real interest in music while his family lived in Virginia Beach, Virginia, where they ran a country store and he received his first guitar at the age of twelve as a gift from a friend.

Gene planned a career in the Navy and, in 1955, used his re-enlistment bonus to buy a new Triumph motorcycle. In July 1955, while he was in Norfolk, Virginia, his left leg was shattered in a motorcycle crash. He refused to allow the leg to be amputated, and the leg was saved, but the injury left him with a limp and pain and he wore a steel sheath around the leg for the remainder of his life.

Gene became involved in the local music scene in Norfolk and he formed a rockabilly band, Gene Vincent and His Blue Caps.

In 1956 Gene wrote "Be-Bop-A-Lula", a huge pop hit and he also made an appearance in the film The Girl Can't Help It, with Jayne Mansfield, performing "Be-Bop-A-Lula" with the Blue Caps in a rehearsal room. "Dance to the Bop" was released by Capitol Records in October 1957. In November, 1957, Gene and His Blue Caps performed the song on the nationally broadcast television program The Ed Sullivan Show. The song spent nine weeks on the Billboard chart and it was Gene's last American hit single.

Gene Vincent's UK chart hits include: "Be Bop A Lula"

in 1956, "Blue Jean Bop" in 1956, "My Heart" in 1960 and "Pistol Packin' Mama" in 1960.

Don Glen Vliet   Captain Beefheart Magic Band

Captain Beefheart died aged sixty-nine on 17th of December 2010 from complications of multiple sclerosis at a hospital in Arcata, California, U.S.A He was survived by his wife, Janet.

Captain Beefheart was born Don Glen Vliet in 1941 in Glendale, California, U.S.A. He began painting and sculpting at age three and his subjects reflected his "obsession" with animals, particularly dinosaurs, fish, African mammals and lemurs. At the age of nine he won a children's sculpting competition organised for the Los Angeles Zoo in Griffith Park by a local tutor.

During his early teenage years, Don would sometimes socialize with members of local bands. Later on, conducting a rotating ensemble known as the Magic Band, he recorded thirteen studio albums between 1967 and 1982. His music blended elements of blues, free jazz, rock, and avant-garde composition with idiosyncratic rhythms, absurdist wordplay, a loud, gravelly voice. Known for his enigmatic persona, Don frequently constructed myths about his life and was known to exercise an almost dictatorial control over his supporting musicians. Although he achieved little commercial success, he sustained a cult following as an influence on an array of experimental rock and punk-era artists.

A prodigy sculptor in his childhood, Don developed an eclectic musical taste during his teen years in Lancaster, California, and formed friendship with musician Frank Zappa, with whom he sporadically competed and collaborated. He began performing with his Captain Beefheart persona in 1964 and joined the original Magic Band line-up, the same year. The group released their debut album Safe as Milk in 1967 on Buddah Records. After being dropped by two consecutive record labels they signed to Frank Zappa's Straight Records, where they released 1969's Trout Mask Replica; the album would later rank 58th in Rolling Stone magazine's 2003 list of the 500 greatest albums of all time. In 1974 Don pursued a more conventional rock sound, but the ensuing albums were critically panned which led his entire band quitting.

Don eventually formed a new Magic Band with a group of younger musicians and regained critical approval through three final albums, these being, Shiny Beast in 1978, Doc at the Radar Station in 1980 and Ice Cream for Crow in 1982. Don made few public appearances after his retirement from music in 1982. He also pursued a career in art, an interest that originated in his childhood talent for sculpture, and a venture which proved to be his most financially secure. His abstract expressionist paintings and drawings command high prices, and have been exhibited in art galleries and museums across the world.

Bunny Wailer   The Wailers

Bunny Wailer, born, Neville O'Riley Livingston, died aged seventy-three of complications from a stroke in Andrews Memorial Hospital in Saint Andrew Parish, Kingston, Jamaica on the 2nd of March 2021. He was survived by his missing wife, Sis Jean and his son, Abijah.

In his earliest years Neville first met Bob Marley, and the two young boys befriended each other quickly. Neville had originally gone to audition for Leslie Kong at Beverley's Records in 1962, around the same time Bob Marley was cutting "Judge Not". He had intended to sing his first composition, "Pass It On", which at the time was more ska-oriented, however, he was late getting out of school and missed his audition. A few months later, in 1963, he formed "The Wailers" with Bob Marley and friend Peter Tosh, and other short-term members Junior Braithwaite and Beverley Kelso. Neville tended to sing lead vocals less often than Bob Marley and Tosh in the early years.

As The Wailers regularly changed producers in the late 1960s, Neville continued to contribute songs to the group's repertoire and he sang lead on such songs as "Dreamland", a cover of El Tempos' "My Dream Island", which soon became his signature song.

Neville toured with The Wailers in England and the United States, but soon became reluctant to leave Jamaica. Moreover, attention was increasingly getting focused on Bob Marley and Neville subsequently left The Wailers in 1973 when he adopted the name "Bunny" in pursuit of his solo career.

Junior Walker   Solo Artiste

Junior Walker died from cancer aged sixty-four whilst in

Battle Creek, Michigan, U.S.A. on the 23rd of November 1995. He was survived by his wife, Gwen.

Junior's career started when he formed his own band in the mid-1950s called the "Jumping Jacks." His long-time friend Billy Nicks, a drummer, would sit in on Jumping Jack's shows, and Junior would sit in on the Rhythm Rockers shows and obtained a permanent gig at a local TV station in South Bend, Indiana. Billy then asked Junior to join him permanently. The original name, "The Rhythm Rockers," was changed to "The All Stars". Junior Walker's style was inspired by jump blues and early Rhythm & Blues.

The group was recommended to Harvey Fuqua who had his own record labels and once they started recording on the Harvey label, their name was changed to Jr. Walker All Stars. The name was modified again when Fuqua's labels were taken over by Motown's Berry Gordy, and they became Jr. Walker & the All Stars becoming members of the Motown family, recording for their Soul imprint in 1964.

Their first and signature hit was "Shotgun," written and composed by Junior Walker and produced by Berry Gordy. "Shotgun" reached number four on the American Billboard Hot 100 and number one on the Rhythm & Blues chart in 1965, and was followed by many other hits, such as " Road Runner," "Shake and Fingerpop" and remakes of two Motown songs "Come See About Me" and "How Sweet It Is (To Be Loved by You)".

Junior Walker's UK chart hits include: "How Sweet It Is" in 1966, "Road Runner" in 1969, "What Does It Take" in 1969, "Walk In The Night" in1972 and "Take Me Girl, I'm Ready" in 1973.

John Walker   The Walker Brothers

John Walker died aged sixty-seven from liver cancer at his Los Angeles home on the 7th of May 2011. He was survived by his fifth wife Cynthia and their two children and three grandchildren.

John began learning saxophone, clarinet and guitar as a child, and by the age of eleven also began acting and appearing in TV talent shows. He had a role in a regular sitcom, Hello Mom, and small uncredited parts in the movies: The Eddy Duchin Story in 1956 and The Missouri Traveller in 1958.

From 1957 onwards, John worked as singer and guitarist with his sister, as the duo John and Judy. They recorded several singles for the Aladdin, Dore, Arvee and Eldo labels between 1958 and 1962. In 1961, they formed a backing band and performed as John, Judy and the Newports, until the band split up after an engagement in Hawaii. They then met Scott Engel, who had been playing bass in The Routers, and, with drummer "Spider" Webb, formed a new band, Judy and the Gents. John obtained an ID card in the name of John Walker, in order to perform in clubs around Los Angeles while under the legal age. In 1963, John and Scott, with two other musicians, toured the Midwest as "The Surfaris".

John released his first solo record, "What a Thrill", on the Almo label, with The Blossoms as backing singers. He formed The Walker Brothers in 1964, with himself as lead vocalist and guitarist, Scott Engel on bass and harmony vocals, and Al Schneider on drums. John and Scott were signed as a duo by Mercury Records, and recorded their first single, "Pretty Girls Everywhere" in Los Angeles.

In the UK, "Love Her" was released on the Philips label, an affiliate of Mercury, and reached number twenty on the UK singles chart. John and Scott signed a new recording contract, and, with Gary Leeds, began performing live in England, to considerable press attention and with growing numbers of - predominantly female teenage - fans. Their next record, a version of the Bacharach and David song "Make It Easy On Yourself", produced like their other British recordings, reached number one in the UK chart in September 1965. Over the next two years the Walker Brothers became, with the Beatles and the Rolling Stones, one of the most popular groups in the United Kingdom. Their second British number one, "The Sun Ain't Gonna Shine Anymore" in 1966, was also their biggest hit in the US, where it made number thirteen on the Billboard Hot 100.

In 1986, John took part in a 1960s revival tour, before finally moving from England to San Diego. He took an electronics course, and became a technical consultant to manufacturing companies, while developing his own recording studio. He also began writing and composing material, mainly for other artists, and formed his own publishing company, Arena. In 2000, he set up his own record label and released a CD, You. He toured Britain again as part of a nostalgia package tour in 2004, and released an album, Silver Sixties Tour 2004, as well as resuming extensive touring in his own right. In 2007, he released two new CDs, Just For You, a collection of love songs, and Songs of Christmas and Inspiration. He toured the UK again in 2009, as part of an "oldies" package.

Scott Walker   The Walker Brothers

Scott Walker died of cancer aged seventy-six on the 22nd of March 2019. He was survived by his partner Beverly, his daughter Lee and grand-daughter Emmi-Lee.

Scott was born Scott Engel. He and his mother settled in California in 1959 and Scott was interested in both music and performance and spent time as a child actor and singer in the late 1950s and recorded some songs.

In between attending art school and furthering his interests in cinema and literature, Scott played bass guitar and, as a teenager, was proficient enough to get session work in Los Angeles.

In 1961, after playing with The Routers, he met guitarist and singer John Maus, who was already using the stage name John Walker as a fake ID to enable him to perform in clubs while under age. At first they formed a new band,

Judy and the Gents, backing John Walker's sister Judy Maus, before joining other musicians to tour as The Surfaris. In early 1964, Scott and John Walker began working together as The Walker Brothers, later in the year linking up with drummer Gary Leeds, whose father financed the trio's first trip to the UK.

As a trio, the Walker Brothers cultivated a glossy-haired and handsome familial image and each of the members took " Walker" as their stage surname. Scott continued to use the name Scott Walker thereafter, with the brief exception of returning to his birth name for the original release of his fifth solo album Scott 4, and in song-writing credits.

Scott's final solo album, Bish Bosch, was released on the 3rd of December 2012 and was received with wide critical acclaim.

Ian Wallace   King Crimson

Ian Russell Wallace died aged sixty from esophageal cancer on the 22nd of February, 2007 in Los Angeles, California, U.S.A. He was survived by his wife, Marjorie.

In the UK, Ian formed his first band, the Jaguars, whilst at school, before going on to join The Warriors with Jon Anderson, then in his pre-Yes days. From The Warriors, Ian went on to join Big Sound, who, in the 1960s, worked in Denmark, Norway and Sweden. When the Big Sound split at the end of 1967 during a tour of Norway, some members, including Ian, moved to London to back other artists including Sandie Shaw, David Garrick, Marv Johnson and Lou Christie.

Ian later joined several more bands before joining King Crimson. He subsequently worked with Steve Marriott's All-Stars and was invited to join Bob Dylan's band in 1978 and accompanied Bob Dylan during a tour of Japan. Ian's heavy drum style was the driving force behind Bob Dylan's album, Street-Legal. Ian toured again with Bob Dylan in the early 1990s and in 1977 he worked briefly with Foreigner.

Following a move to Nashville, Tennessee, U.S.A. in 1998, Ian worked as a producer and in 2003, he joined the 21st Century Schizoid Band, and released his only solo album, 'Happiness With Minimal Side Effects'.

In 2005 Ian formed the Crimson Jazz Trio with Tim Landers on bass and Jody Nardone on piano, which released two albums; in 2005 and in 2009.

Gordon Waller   Peter & Gordon

Gordon Waller died aged sixty-four of a heart attack on the 17th of July 2009 whilst in hospital in Norwich, Connecticut, U.S.A. He was survived by his wife, Josenia, his daughters, Phillippa and Natalie his granddaughter, Tyla, and his two sisters, Diana and Annie.

Gordon was born in Scotland, U.K. and his family later moved to England when he was a child. He gained entrance to Westminster School where he met fellow student Peter Asher and they began playing together as the duo, Peter and Gordon.

Peter is the brother of actress Jane Asher, who in the mid-1960s was girlfriend of The Beatles' Paul McCartney and through this connection he and Gordon Waller were often given unknown Lennon–McCartney songs to perform, most notably their first and biggest hit, "A World Without Love" in 1964.

Peter and Gordon parted company in 1968 and, after this break, Gordon attempted a solo career with partial success, releasing one record. In the mid-1970's Gordon worked as a photocopier salesman in Bedford, Bedfordshire, U.K. then in 1995, he moved to Los Angeles, California, U.S.A. and started a publishing company.

Micky Waller   The Bruvvers

Micky Waller died aged sixty-six of liver failure in London

on the 29th of April 2008. He was survived by his daughter, Louise.

Micky was a drummer, who played with many of the biggest names on the UK rock and blues scene, after he became a professional musician in 1960. Micky's first professional band, The Flee-Rekkers, had a number 23 hit in the UK Singles Chart in 1960, with their recording of "Green Jeans". Micky shortly afterwards left to join a well-known band of the day, Joe Brown and the Bruvvers. In July 1963, he joined the Cyril Davies R&B All Stars. Micky also went on to play with Marty Wilde as one of the Wildcats.

After a short stint with Georgie Fame and the Blue Flames, a band he was to rejoin several times, he joined Brian Auger to become part of The Trinity. In April 1965, the group was expanded by Rod Stewart and Julie Driscoll and evolved into a new band, The Steampacket.

In 1969, Micky sat in on 'An Old Raincoat Won't Ever Let You Down', Rod Stewart's first solo album. Micky's relationship with Rod Stewart and Ronnie Wood served him well, as he would go on to join them on the next three Rod Stewart solo albums, 'Gasoline Alley', 'Every Picture Tells a Story' and 'Never A Dull Moment'.

Micky continued to play intermittently with a number of blues bands in the London area, including the eponymous Micky Waller Band. In his later years, he took a degree in law, and used his gained knowledge to win court claims for unpaid royalties.

Clifford T Ward   Solo Artiste

Clifford T. Ward died aged fifty-seven of Pneumonia on the 18th of December, 2001 in a hospital at Kidderminster, Worcestershire, U.K. He was survived by his wife, Pat.

In 1962, shortly after leaving school and supporting himself with a series of clerical jobs, Clifford formed a beat band called Cliff Ward and the Cruisers, which won the

1963 Midland Band of the Year contest in Birmingham. The band was popular in Birmingham and also in demand at American Army bases in France.

After signing a recording contract with Charisma Records, Clifford went on to have a hit with the single "Gaye". It sold over a million copies worldwide and reached number eight in the UK Singles Chart in July 1973.

Following the success of "Gaye", Clifford's second album "Home Thoughts" achieved healthy sales and reached number 40 in the UK Albums Chart. He made a rare public appearance in July 1973, performing "Gaye" on Top of the Pops. In January 1974 Clifford entered the singles chart again at number 37 with "Scullery", a track from his third album Mantle Pieces. Clifford recorded his eleventh and final album, "Julia and Other New Stories" whilst crawling on hands and feet into his home-based recording studio to finish it.

Charlie Watts   The Rolling Stones

Charlie Watts died aged eighty of cancer at a London hospital on the 24th of August 2021. He was survived by his wife, Shirley, his daughter, Seraphina and grand-daughter, Charlotte.

It was during the middle of 1962 that Charlie first met Brian Jones, Ian "Stu" Stewart, Mick Jagger and Keith Richards, who also frequented the London rhythm and blues clubs, but it was not until January 1963 that he agreed to join the Rolling Stones.

Initially, the band could not afford to pay Charlie, who had been earning a regular salary from his gigs. His first public appearance as a permanent member was at the Ealing Jazz Club in February 1963. Charlie was often introduced as "The Wembley Whammer" by Mick Jagger during live concerts.

Besides his work as a musician, Charlie contributed

graphic art and comic strips to early Rolling Stones records such as the Between the Buttons record sleeve and was responsible for the 1975 tour announcement press conference in New York City. The band surprised the throng of waiting reporters by driving and playing "Brown Sugar" on the back of a flatbed truck in the middle of Manhattan traffic, Charlie remembering that this was a common way for New Orleans jazz bands to promote upcoming dates. Moreover, with Mick Jagger, he designed the elaborate stages for tours, first contributing to the lotus-shaped design of the Tour of the Americas, as well as the Steel Wheels/Urban Jungle Tour, the Bridges to Babylon Tour, the Licks Tour, and the A Bigger Bang Tour.

Charlie was involved in many activities outside his life as a member of the Rolling Stones. In December 1964, he published a cartoon tribute to Charlie Parker titled Ode to a High Flying Bird. Although he made his name in rock, his personal tastes lay principally in jazz.

Charlie's last live concert with the Rolling Stones was on the 30th of August 2019 at Hard Rock Stadium in Miami, Florida. He had never missed a single concert throughout his career with the band. Besides Mick Jagger and Keith Richards, he was, at his time of death, the only member to have appeared on every album in the Rolling Stones discography.

Peter Overend Watts   Mott the Hoople

Peter Overend Watts died aged sixty-nine from throat cancer on the 22nd of January 2017. He was survived by his sister, Jane.

Peter began playing the guitar at the age of thirteen and by 1965, he had switched to bass guitar, and became a professional musician alongside Mick Ralphs in a group, the Buddies, that played in German clubs. The group later became the Doc Thomas Group, and then Shakedown Sound, before finally changing their name to Silence and settling in London in 1969. The group then added singer Ian Hunter, became Mott the Hoople.

Before his death Peter completed his solo album that he had been promising to deliver to his legion of fans for the past decade plus. In keeping with his legendary witty humour, he decreed that as the album would be released after his passing it would not be called "She's Real Gone" as planned but changed to "He's Real Gone."

Carl Wayne   The Move

Carl Wayne died from oesophageal cancer aged sixty-one on the 31st of August 2001. He was survived by his wife, Susan, and their son, Jack.

Carl was born in Birmingham, U.K. and he was later inspired by the American rock'n'roll of Elvis Presley, Eddie Cochran and Gene Vincent and joined local band the Vikings, where his powerful baritone and pink stage suit helped make them one of the leading rock groups in the Midlands of their time. In 1963 they followed in the footsteps of the Beatles by performing in the clubs of Frankfurt, Stuttgart, Nuremberg, etc. On returning to Birmingham, in the wake of the Beatles' success, record companies were keen to sign similar guitar bands. The Vikings went with Pye Records, but all three of their singles failed to chart.

In December 1965 Carl joined the Move, a Birmingham beat-group drawn from the top local bands. They included three members of the Vikings, bass guitarist Chris Kefford, drummer Bev Bevan and Carl Wayne himself, alongside Trevor Burton and Roy Wood. They enjoyed three years of hits with singles including "Night of Fear", "I Can Hear The Grass Grow", "Flowers in the Rain", "Fire Brigade", and their only number one chart success "Blackberry Way".

In their early years the Move had a stage act which occasionally saw Carl taking an axe to television sets, or chainsawing a Cadillac to pieces at the Roundhouse, London, during "Fire Brigade". However , Carl left the Move shortly after their number twelve hit "Curly" in 1969.

Carl went solo and made several singles and record albums, some including songs written and produced by Roy Wood. In 1977, Carl took part in the Song for Europe contest, hoping to represent the UK in the Eurovision Song Contest. His song, "A Little Give, A Little Take" finished in eleventh place out of twelve songs.

Carl also made a few recordings with the Electric Light Orchestra as guest vocalist, though these remained unreleased, until they appeared as bonus tracks on a remastered re-issue of the group's second album, ELO 2 in 2003. He never made the charts after leaving the Move, but still enjoyed a steady career in cabaret and on TV, recording versions of songs from the shows of Andrew Lloyd Webber and Tim Rice, as well as voiceovers and jingles. He also sang backing vocals on Mike Oldfield's Earth Moving, released in 1989.

In 2000, on the retirement of their the lead vocalist , Carl joined the Hollies, touring Europe and Australasia with them, as well as playing venues all over the United Kingdom. Carl played what turned out to be his last concert with the Hollies on the 10th of July 2004 at Iggesund, Norway.

Bob Welch   Fleetwood Mac

Bob Welch died aged sixty-six on the 7th of June 2012 via suicide at his Nashville home. He was survived by his wife Wendy.

Bob was born in Los Angeles, California, U.S.A. and a boy, he learned clarinet, switching to guitar in his early teens. He had received his first guitar at the age of eight. The young Bob developed an interest in jazz, rhythm and blues, and rock music. After graduating from high school, he declined attending Georgetown University, where he had been accepted, to move to Paris and spoke in an 1979 interview that, in Paris, he mostly smoked hash with bearded guys five years older. He spent time sitting in the Deux Magots café rather than attending to his intended studies and eventually returned to Southern California, where he studied French at the University of California, Los Angeles.

Dropping out of UCLA before graduation, Bob joined the Los Angeles-based vocal group The Seven Souls as a guitarist in 1964. Then he moved back to Paris and started a trio, Head West, which was not a success. He struggled with a variety of marginal bands until 1971, when he was invited to join Fleetwood Mac, a British blues band that had lost two of its three front-line members. Along with fellow newcomer Christine McVie, Bob helped to steer Fleetwood Mac in a more melodic and less bluesy direction.

In September 1971, Fleetwood Mac released the album Future Games, with the title song written by Bob and this was different from anything Fleetwood Mac had done before, up to that point. In 1972, six months after the release of Future Games, Fleetwood Mac released Bare Trees, which featured Bob's song "Sentimental Lady".

In 1974, for the first time, Fleetwood Mac had only one guitarist, Bob, who took over lead guitarist duties. The quartet of Bob Welch, Mick Fleetwood, and the McVies represented the ninth line-up in Fleetwood Mac's seven-year history. Warner Bros. made a new record deal with Fleetwood Mac, which recorded and released the album Heroes Are Hard to Find on Reprise in September 1974. The album became Fleetwood Mac's first to crack the Top forty in the United States, reaching number 34 on the Billboard album chart. Bob, however, resigned from Fleetwood Mac in December 1974 and was replaced by Lindsey Buckingham and Stevie Nicks.

In September 1977, Bob released his first solo album, French Kiss, , a mainstream pop collection featuring contributions from Fleetwood, Buckingham and Christine McVie. This album, ultimately certified platinum by RIAA, marked Bob's commercial highest point, peaking at number twelve on the Billboard album chart in 1978.

Bob released solo albums into the early 1980s. During this period, he partied with nouveau hard rock band Guns N' Roses who rehearsed in his garage and developed a cocaine and heroin addiction for less than a year before being hospitalized in the spring of 1985. The day he got out of detox, he was introduced to Wendy whom he married in December 1985, and they remained together as husband and wife and business partners until his death.

Mary Wells   **Solo Artiste**

Mary Wells died aged forty-nine of pneumonia and cancer on the 26th of July 1992 in Los Angeles, California, U.S.A. She was survived by sons Cecil, Jr. and Harry, and daughters Stacy and Sugar. After her funeral, which included a eulogy given by her old friend and former collaborator, Smokey Robinson, Mary Wells was cremated, and her ashes were laid to rest in Glendale's Forest Lawn Memorial Park.

During her early years, Mary lived in a poor residential Detroit district. By age twelve, she was helping her mother with house cleaning work. Mary used singing as her comfort from her pain and by age ten had graduated from church choirs to performing at local nightclubs in the Detroit area. Mary graduated from Detroit's Northwestern High School at the age of seventeen and set her sights on becoming a scientist, but after hearing about the success of Detroit musicians such as Jackie Wilson and the Miracles, she decided to try her hand at music as a singer-songwriter.

In 1960, seventeen-year-old Mary approached Tamla Records founder Berry Gordy at Detroit's Twenty Grand club with a song she had intended for Jackie Wilson to record, since Mary knew of Gordy's collaboration with Wilson. However, a tired Gordy insisted Mary sing the song in front of him. Impressed, Gordy had Mary enter

Detroit's United Sound Systems to record the single, titled "Bye Bye Baby". After a reported twenty-two takes, Gordy signed Mary to the Motown subsidiary of his expanding record label and released the song as a single in September 1960; it peaked at number eight on the Rhythm & Blues chart in 1961, and later crossed over to the pop singles chart, where it peaked at number forty-five. In the fall of that year, Motown issued Mary's first album and released a third single, the bluesy ballad "Strange Love". When that record slumped, Gordy set Mary up with the Miracles' lead singer Smokey Robinson.

Mary's teaming with Robinson led to a succession of hit singles over the following two years. Their first collaboration, 1962's "The One Who Really Loves You", was Mary's first smash hit, peaking at number two on the Rhythm & Blues chart and number eight on the Hot Hundred. The song featured a calypso-styled soul production that defined Mary Wells' early hits. Motown released the similar-sounding "You Beat Me to the Punch" a few months later. The song became her first Rhythm & Blues number one single and peaked at number nine on the pop chart. The success of "You Beat Me to the Punch" helped to make Mary Wells the first Motown star to be nominated for a Grammy Award when the song received a push in the Best Rhythm & Blues Recording category.

Mary Wells' success continued in 1963 when she hit the Top twenty with the doo-wop ballad "Laughing Boy". In 1964, Mary recorded "My Guy". The Smokey Robinson song became her trademark single, reaching number one on the Cashbox Rhythm & Blues chart for seven weeks and becoming the number one Rhythm & Blues single of the year. The song successfully crossed over to the Billboard Hot Hundred, where it eventually replaced Louis Armstrong's "Hello, Dolly!" at number one , remaining there for two weeks. The song became Mary Wells' second million-selling single. "My Guy" was one of the first Motown songs to break on the other side of the Atlantic, eventually

379

peaking at number five on the UK chart and making Mary an international star.

John Wetton   King Crimson, Asia

John Wetton died aged sixty-seven on the 31st of January 2017 from complications of colorectal cancer whilst in hospital in Christchurch, Dorset, U.K. He was survived by his wife Lisa, son Dylan, brother Robert and his mother Margaret .

John was born in Derbyshire, U.K. and grew up in Bournemouth, Dorset, U.K. He was in a number of early bands including Mogul Thrash and after live work with Renaissance, he joined Family and also did various sessions.

John's first big break came when he joined Robert Fripp in a then new line-up of King Crimson in 1972, allowing him to come to the fore as a lead singer and composer. John remained with the band until Robert Fripp disbanded it in 1974. John continued to work on various projects, including a tour with Roxy Music and two albums with Uriah Heep.

John released his first solo album, Caught in the Crossfire, in 1980. Later that year he had a brief stint in Wishbone Ash, contributing bass and vocals to their album Number the Brave in 1981. Also in 1981, John started working and writing with Steve Howe, who had most recently been in Yes. They went on to form Asia with whom John worked until 1983.

Roger Whittaker   Solo Artiste

Roger Whittaker died, aged eighty-seven from a stroke at a hospital near Toulouse, in France. He was survived by his wife, Natalie and his sons, Guy and Alexander and his daughters, Emily, Lauren and Jessica.

Roger was born in Nairobi to English parents. Upon

completing his primary education, Roger was admitted to Prince of Wales School (now Nairobi School), and whilst there sang in the choir at Nairobi Cathedral. Upon completing his high-school education, he was called up for national service and spent two years in the Kenya Regiment fighting the Mau Mau in the Aberdare Forest. He said that he was "stupid, selfish, and angry" in his youth, and that the army "made a man" out of him. After demobilization in 1956, he enrolled at the University of Cape Town in South Africa to pursue a career in Medicine, performing at the Equator Club in Nairobi during breaks. However, he left after eighteen months and joined the civil service education department as a teacher, following in his mother's footsteps.

Roger moved to Britain in September 1959. to continue his teaching career For the next three years, he studied zoology, biochemistry and marine biology at University College of North Wales and earned a Bachelor of Science degree while singing in local clubs, and released songs on flexi discs included with the campus newspaper, the Bangor University Rag. Reflecting upon this time in his life, he said later that "I guess I was an entertainer who was a biochemist for a while, rather than the other way around".

Roger was shortly signed to Fontana Records, which released his first professional single, "The Charge of the Light Brigade", in 1962. That summer, he performed in Portrush, Northern Ireland and achieved a breakthrough when he was signed to appear on an Ulster Television show called This and That. His second single was a cover version of "Steel Men", released in June 1962.

In 1966, Roger switched from Fontana to EMI's Columbia label, and was billed as Roger Roger from this point forward. His fourth single for the imprint was his self-composed Durham Town (The Leavin'), which in 1969 became Roger's first UK Top twenty hit in the UK Singles Chart. Roger's US label, RCA Victor, released the uptempo "New World in the Morning" in 1970, where it became a Top 20 hit in Billboard magazine's Easy Listening chart. That same year, his downbeat theme song "No Blade of Grass", written for the film adaptation of the same name that was sung during both the opening and ending titles, became his first film credit.

In 1975, EMI released "The Last Farewell", a track from Roger's 1971 New World in the Morning album. It became his biggest hit and a signature song, selling more than eleven million copies worldwide. In 1979, he wrote the song "Call My Name" which, performed by Eleanor Keenan, reached the final of the UK Eurovision selection, A Song For Europe, and came third. Roger recorded the song himself and the single charted in several European countries. Released in December 1983, his version of Leon Payne's "I Love You Because" spent four weeks in the US Hot Country charts, peaking at number ninety-one.

Throughout the 1970s and 1980s, Roger had success in Germany, with German-language songs produced by Nick Munro. Unable to speak German, Roger sang the songs phonetically. His biggest hits in Germany included "Du Warst Mein Schönster Traum" (a rerecording of "The Last Farewell") and "Abschied ist ein Scharfes Schwert" ("parting is a sharp sword"). He appeared regularly on the TV series ZDF-Hitparade, received numerous awards, and was West Germany's bestselling artist of 1977, when he completed a 41-concert tour of the country. Roger's German-language songs were not initially well received by some critics, who derided the songs as "meaningless folk music". Notwithstanding this, Roger released twenty-five albums in Germany and gained a considerable fan base in that country; he felt his most loyal fans were there, saying at one point: "The past few decades have been wonderful ... My relationship with the German fans is great." In March 2006, Roger announced on his website that a 2007 Germany tour would be his last, and that he would limit future performances to "occasional concerts". Now more fluent in German, he was seen singing and was interviewed in German on Danish television in November 2008. In a 2014 interview, Roger reiterated that he had retired from touring in 2013, but said that he had written eighteen new songs for an album and said that he could still whistle very well.

Alan White   Yes

Alan White died aged seventy-two on the 26th of May 2022, in Newcastle, UK, following a brief illness. He was survived by his wife, Gigi, his son, Jesse and by his daughter, Cassie.

At age six, Alan began to take piano lessons, playing the instrument "very percussively", which his uncle noticed and informed his parents who bought him an Ajax drum kit for Christmas when he was twelve. Alan named his uncle as a big influence and felt he was pushed to learn and play like his drum instructor and wished "to be more individual" on the instrument, so he began to develop his own style. His parents went on to buy him a metallic silver Ludwig kit.

Several months into formal drumming lessons, Alan joined his first band, a local group named the Downbeats, when thirteen. They performed songs by the Beatles, the Searchers, and Gerry and the Pacemakers. The group became well known in the Newcastle area, playing working men's clubs and dance halls as much as seven nights a week until late hours. In 1964, the Downbeats changed their name to the Blue Chips and travelled to London to enter an amateur band contest held at the London Palladium. They won the contest and were awarded money, new equipment, and a recording contract and recorded several singles, which did not chart. They returned home, and disbanded soon after.

At seventeen, Alan pursued music and toured the cabaret circuit as part of Billy Fury's band the Gamblers, which included several gigs in Germany. He went on to play in Happy Magazine, later known as Griffin, with Alan

Marshall and Kenny Craddock, then continued to tour and play in the Alan Price Set, and took up several jobs as a session musician.

In July 1972, after Yes had finished recording Close to the Edge, Bill Bruford left to join King Crimson and with their supporting tour less than a week away, the band were desperate for a replacement. Alan then got a call informing him that Yes wanted him to join. He spent the following days learning the Yes's repertoire before the Close to the Edge Tour began in Dallas, Texas in July 1972. Alan played over 3,070 live shows during his tenure with Yes. In 2018 he toured with Yes celebrating their 50th anniversary.

Barry White   Solo Artiste

Barry White died aged fifty-eight from kidney failure and stroke on the 4th of July 2003 at Cedars-Sinai Medical Center in Los Angeles, California, U.S.A. He was survived by his ex-wife, Glodean, his sons Barry Jnr. and Daryl and his daughter, Dennise.

Barry's voice deepened suddenly when he was fourteen he recalled. As a child he had a normal squeaky kid voice. Then as a teenager, that completely changed.

Barry began a musical career at the beginning of the 1960s in singing groups. He first released "Too Far to Turn Around" in 1960 as part of The Upfronts before working for various small independent labels in Los Angeles. He also recorded several singles under his own name in the early 1960's.

In 1972, Barry got his big break producing a girl group he had discovered called Love Unlimited. Their 1972 album, From A Girl's Point of View We Give to You.. Love Unlimited, became a million album seller and the first of Barry's string of long-titled albums and singles.

Barry then wrote several other songs and recorded them for what eventually became an entire album of music. He was going to use the name "White Heat," but decided on using his given name instead. He was still hesitating up to the time the label copy was made. It eventually became his first solo album, 'I've Got So Much to Give' in 1973. It included the title track and his first solo chart hit, "I'm Gonna Love You Just a Little More Baby", which also rose to number one on the Billboard R&B charts as well as number three on the Billboard Pop charts in 1973 and stayed in the top forty for many weeks.

In 1973, Barry formed The Love Unlimited Orchestra, a 40-piece orchestral group. In 1973 he released a single with "Love's Theme",written by him and played by the Orchestra, That same track reached number one on the Billboard Pop charts. Later, in 1974, he made the first album of the Love Unlimited Orchestra, 'Rhapsody in White', containing "Love's Theme". Barry's final album, 1999's Staying Power, resulted in his last hit song "Staying Power," which placed number forty-five on the Billboard R&B charts.

Barry White's UK chart hits include: "Can't Get Enough Of Your Love Babe" in 1974, "You're The First The Last My Everything" in 1974, "What Am I Gonna Do With You" in 1975, "You See The Trouble With Me" in 1976, "Baby We Better Try To Get It Together" in 1976, "Just The Way You Are" in 1978 and "Sho' You Right" in 1987.

Maurice White   Earth Wind & Fire

Maurice White died aged seventy-four from Parkinson's disease at his home in Los Angeles, California, U.S.A. on the 4th of February 2016. He was survived by his wife, Marilyn, his sons, Kahbran and Eden, his daughter, Hamia, his brothers, Verdine, Fred, Monte and Ron and his sister, Jeri.

Maurice was born in Memphis, Tennessee and during his teenage years, he moved to Chicago where he studied at the Chicago Conservatory of Music, and played drums in local nightclubs. By the mid-1960s he found work as a session drummer for Chess Records. While at Chess, he played on the records of artists including Etta James, Chuck Berry, Sonny Stitt, Muddy Waters, the Impressions, the Dells, Betty Everett, Sugar Pie DeSanto and Buddy Guy. Maurice also played the drums on Fontella Bass's "Rescue Me", Billy Stewart's "Summertime" and Jackie Wilson's Higher and Higher.

In 1969, Maurice joined his two friends, Wade Flemons and Don Whitehead, to form a songwriting team who wrote songs for commercials in the Chicago area. The three friends got a recording contract with Capitol Records and called themselves the Salty Peppers. They had a moderate hit in the Midwest area with their single "La La Time", but their second single, "Uh Huh Yeah", was not as successful. Maurice then moved from Chicago to Los Angeles, and altered the name to Earth, Wind and Fire.

Earth Wind and Fire's UK chart hits include: "September" in 1978, "Boogie Wonderland" in 1979, "After The Love Has Gone" in 1979 and "Let's Groove" in 1981.

Tony Joe White   Solo Artiste

Tony Joe White died aged seventy-five of a heart attack on the 24th of October, 2018 at his home in Leiper's Fork, Nashville, Tennessee, U.S.A. He is survived by his wife Leann, his sons Jody and JimBob and his daughter, Michelle.

Tony first began performing music at school dances, and after graduating from high school he performed in night clubs in Texas and Louisiana.

In 1967, Tony signed with Monument Records, which operated from a recording studio in the Nashville suburb of Hendersonville, Tennessee. Over the next three years, Tony Joe released four singles with no commercial success in the U.S.A., although "Soul Francisco" was a hit in France. "Polk Salad Annie" had been released for nine months and written off as a failure by his record label, when it finally entered the American charts in July 1969. It climbed to the Top Ten by early August, and eventually reached No. 8, becoming Tony Joe's biggest hit there.

Tony's first album, 1969's Black and White, was recorded with Muscle Shoals/Nashville musicians David Briggs, Norbert Putnam, and Jerry Carrigan, and featured "Willie and Laura Mae Jones" and "Polk Salad Annie", along with a cover of Jimmy Webb's "Wichita Lineman".

In the 1990s, Tony toured Germany and France with Joe Cocker and Eric Clapton, and in 1992 he played the Montreux Festival.

In May 2016, Tony Joe released 'Rain Crow' on Yep Roc Records. The album 'Bad Mouthin' was released in September 2018 again on Yep Roc Records. The album contains six self-penned songs and five blues standards. On the album Tony also performs a cover of the Elvis Presley song "Heartbreak Hotel". He plays acoustic and electric guitar on the album which was produced by his son Jody White. Tony's only UK chart hit was "Groupie Girl" in 1970.

Slim Whitman   Solo Artiste

Slim Whitman died aged ninety of heart failure on the nineteenth of June 2013. He was survived by his daughter; Sharron Beagle, his son; Byron Keith, and two great-grandchildren.

Growing up, Slim liked the country music of Jimmie Rodgers and the songs of Gene Autry, but he did not embark on a musical career of his own until the end of World War II, after he had served in the South Pacific with the United States Navy.

While aboard ship he would sing and entertain members aboard. This resulted in the captain blocking his transfer to another ship, which saved his life, as the other ship later sank with no surviving hands. Slim's early ambitions were to become either a boxer or a professional baseball player.

Slim Whitman's UK chart hits include: "Rose Marie" in 1955, "Indian Love Call" in 1955, "Serenade" in 1956 and "I'll Take You Home Again, Kathleen" in 1957.

Andy Williams   Solo Artiste

Andy Williams died aged eighty-four from bladder cancer on the 25th of September 2012 at his home in Branson, Missouri, U.S.A. He was survived by his wife, Debbie, his sons, Christian and Robert and his daughter, Noelle.

Andy's first performance was in a children's choir at a Presbyterian church. He and his brothers formed the Williams Brothers quartet in late 1938, and they performed on radio in the Midwest of America.

Moving to Los Angeles in 1943, the Williams Brothers sang with Bing Crosby on his 1944 hit record "Swinging on a Star". They appeared in four musical films: Janie in 1944, Kansas City Kitty in1944, Something in the Wind in 1947 and Ladies' Man in 1947.

The Williams Brothers were signed by Metro-Goldwyn-Mayer to appear in Anchors Aweigh and Ziegfeld Follies in 1945 but, before they went before the cameras, the oldest brother, Bob, was drafted into military service and the group's contract was cancelled. Kay Thompson, a former radio star who was then head of the vocal department at MGM, had a nose for talent and hired the remaining three Williams brothers to sing in her large choir on many soundtracks for MGM films, including The Harvey Girls in 1946. When Bob completed his military service, Kay hired all four brothers to sing on the soundtrack to Good News in 1947.

Andy's solo career began in 1953 when he recorded six sides for RCA Victor. In 1961, Andy moved to Los Angeles, California, and signed with Columbia Records. His first album with Columbia, Danny Boy and Other Songs I Love to Sing, was a chart success, peaking at number 19. He was then asked to sing "Moon River", the theme from Breakfast at Tiffany's, at the 1962 Academy Awards, where it won Best Original Song.

From 1962 to 1972, Andy was one of the most popular vocalists in the U.S.A. and was signed to what was at that time the biggest recording contract in history. He was primarily an album artist, and at one time he had recorded more gold albums than any solo performer except Frank Sinatra, Johnny Mathis, and Elvis Presley.

Andy Williams' UK chart hits include: "Butterfly" in 1957, "Can't Get Used To Losing You" in 1963, "Almost There" in 1965, "Can't Take My Eyes Off You" in 1968, "Can't Help Falling In Love" in 1970 and "Solitaire" in 1973.

Don Williams   Solo Artiste

Don Williams died from emphysema aged seventy-eight in Mobile, Alabama, U.S.A. on the 8th of September 2017. He was survived by his wife, Joy and his sons, Gary and Tim.

Prior to forming the folk-pop group Pozo-Seco Singers, Don served with The United States Army Security Agency for two years then, after his honorable discharge, worked various odd jobs in order to support himself and his family.

In 1972, Don got a contract with JMI Records as a solo country artist. At the height of the country and western boom in the UK in 1976, he had pop chart hits with "You're My Best Friend" and "I Recall a Gypsy Woman".

Larry Williams   Solo Artiste

Larry Williams died of suicide aged forty-four on the seventh of January 1980 in his home in Los Angeles, California, U.S.A. He was survived by his wife, Ina and his daughter, Michelle.

Larry learned how to play piano at a young age. The family moved to Oakland, California when he was a teenager, and there he joined the Lemon Drops, a Rythm

& Blues group. Larry returned to New Orleans in 1954 and began working for his cousin, singer Lloyd Price, as a valet and played in the bands there. In 1955, Larry met and developed a friendship with Little Richard, who was recording at the time in New Orleans. Larry was introduced to Specialty's house producer, and was signed to record.

Larry's three biggest successes were "Short Fat Fannie", which was his best seller, reaching number 5 in Billboard's pop chart, "Bony Moronie", which peaked at number 14, and its flip "You Bug Me Baby" which made it to number 45. "Dizzy, Miss Lizzy" charted at number 69 on Billboard the following year. Both "Short Fat Fannie" and "Bony Moronie" sold over one million copies, gaining gold discs.

Larry recorded a number of songs in 1958 and 1959, including "Heebie Jeebies" but was convicted of dealing narcotics in 1960 and served a three-year jail term, setting back his career considerably. Larry also began acting in the 1960s, appearing on film in Just for the Hell of It in 1968, The Klansman in 1974, and Drum in 1976.

Larry Williams' UK chart hits include: "Short Fat Fannie" in 1957 and "Bony Moronie" in 1958.

Milan Williams   The Commodores

Milan Williams died aged fifty-eight from cancer on the 9th of July, 2006 at a hospital in Houston, Texas, United States of America. He was survived by his ex-wife, Gwedolyn his sons, Jason ans Ricci.

Milan began playing the piano after being inspired by his older brother Earl, who was a multi-instrumentalist. Milan's first band was called The Jays and after they disbanded he met the other founding members of the Commodores in 1967. In 1969 he travelled with the band to New York City, where they recorded a single called "Keep on Dancing" on Atlantic Records.

Milan wrote the Commodores' first hit record, the instrumental track, "Machine Gun". Other Commodores songs penned by him are; "The Bump", "Rapid Fire", "I'm Ready", "Better Never Than Forever", "Mary Mary", "Quick Draw", "Patch It Up", "X-Rated Movie", "Wonderland", "Old-Fashion Love", "Only You", "You Don't Know That I Know", "Let's Get Started" and "Brick House". He left the Commodores in 1989, allegedly after refusing to perform with them in South Africa.

The Commodores' UK chart hits include: "Easy" in 1977, "Three Times A Lady" in 1978, "Sail On" in 1979, "Still" in 1979 and "Nightshift" in 1985. .

Tony Williams   The Tony Williams Lifetime

Tony Williams died aged fifty-one of a heart attack on the 23rd of February 1997 in Daly City, California, U.S.A. He was survived by his wife, Shirley.

Tony was born in Chicago and grew up in Boston, Massachusetts, U.S.A. He studied with drummer Alan Dawson at an early age, and began playing professionally at the age of thirteen with saxophonist Sam Rivers.

At age seventeen Tony gained attention by joining Miles Davis in what was later dubbed Mile's Second Great Quintet. Tony was a vital element of the group, called by Miles in his autobiography "the centre that the group's sound revolved around." His playing helped redefine the role of the jazz rhythm section through the use of poly-rhythms and metric modulation. Meanwhile, he recorded his first two albums as leader for Blue Note label, 'Life Time' in 1964 and 'Spring' in 1965.

In 1969, he formed a trio, the Tony Williams Lifetime, with John McLaughlin on guitar and Larry Young on organ. Lifetime was a pioneering band of the fusion movement, a combination of rock, Rhythm & Blues, and jazz.

Tony Williams also played drums for the band Public

Image Limited, fronted by John Lydon, on an album. One of his final recordings was 'The Last Wave' by the jazz-rock trio called Arcana.

Dennis Wilson   The Beach Boys

Dennis Wilson accidentally drowned aged thirty-nine on the 28th of December,1983 whilst swimming at the Marina Del Rey in Los Angeles, California, U.S.A. He was survived by his wife, Shawn and his son, Gage Dennis and his daughters, Jennifer and Carole.

Dennis' mother forced brother Brian to include him in the original lineup of the Beach Boys. Urged by older cousin Mike Love, Dennis had approached Brian to form a group and compose a song about surfing. The Beach Boys formed in August 1961 and were immediately successful.

Although the Beach Boys developed their image based on the California surfing culture, Dennis was the only actual surfer in the band. In the early years of the Beach Boys, Brian gave Dennis the role of the drummer. Dennis quickly learned the basics of drumming at school lessons and, like the other members, he picked up more on the job.

Though given few important lead vocals on the early Beach Boys recordings, Dennis did sing lead on "Do You Wanna Dance?," the group's 1965 hit.

Carl Wilson   The Beach Boys

Carl Wilson died aged fifty-one of lung cancer in Los Angeles on the 6th of February 1998. He was survived by his wife, Gina, and by his sons, Justyn and Jonah.

As a boy, Carl practiced harmony vocals under the guidance of his brother Brian, who often sang in the family music room. At the age of twelve Carl asked his parents to buy him a guitar and he then took some lessons. While brother Brian perfected the band's vocal style and keyboard base, Carl's styled guitar playing became an early

Beach Boys trademark. While in high school, Carl also studied saxophone.

Carl was just fifteen as the Beachboy's first hit, "Surfin'", broke locally in Los Angeles, and his father and manager, Murry, bought him a Fender Jaguar guitar. Carl developed as a musician and singer through the band's early recordings, and the early "surf lick" sound quickly evolved into the rock sophistication of "Fun, Fun, Fun", recorded in 1964 when Carl was seventeen. By the end of nineteen-sixty-four, he was diversifying, favoring the twelve-string Rickenbacker.

By the early 1980's the Beach Boys were in disarray and Carl took a leave of absence in 1981. He quickly recorded and released a solo album, 'Carl Wilson', composed largely of rock n' roll songs. Carl also undertook a solo tour to promote the album, becoming the first member of the Beach Boys to break ranks. Carl recorded a second solo album, 'Youngblood', in a similar vein, but by the time of its release in 1983 he had re-joined the Beach Boys.

Carl continued recording through the 1990's while continuing to tour with the Beach Boys until the last months of his life.

Al Wilson   Canned Heat

Al 'Blind Owl' Wilson died from suicide aged twenty-seven on the third of September 1970 in California, U.S.A.

Some of Al's first efforts at performing music publicly came during his teen years with a jazz ensemble he formed with other musically oriented friends from school. It was around this same time that he developed a fascination with blues music after a friend played a Muddy Waters record for him. After graduating from Arlington High School, he majored in music at Boston University and played the Cambridge, Massachusetts coffee-house folk-blues circuit.

During this time he met American guitarist John Fahey

from whom he acquired the nickname "Blind Owl" owing to his extreme nearsightedness, roundish facial features and scholarly nature.

With Canned Heat, Al performed at two prominent concerts of the 1960s era, the Monterey Pop Festival in 1967 and Woodstock in 1969. Al also wrote and sang the hit record "On the Road Again."

Canned Heat's UK chart hits include: "On The Road Again" in 1968, "Going Up The Country" in 1969, "Let's Work Together" in 1970 and "Sugar Bee" in 1970.

B.J.Wilson   Procol Harum

B.J.Wilson died aged forty-three on the 8th of October 1990 from pneumonia whilst in Eugene, Oregon, USA. He was survived by his wife, Susan and his daughters, Sarah and Nicola.

B.J. was born Bary Wilson, in London, U.K. He joined a group, The Paramounts, from Southend on Sea, Essex who scored a hit with the song "Poison Ivy" in 1964. After follow up singles failed to chart, the Paramounts disbanded in 1966 and Barrie worked doing session drumming, playing with stars including Cat Stevens and Lulu.

While Barrie was busy with session drumming, his former bandmate Gary Brooker had assembled Procol Harum which he joined in the summer of 1967, along with fellow ex-Paramount member, Robin Trower. After Procol Harum disbanded in 1977, Barrie played on Frankie Miller's Double Trouble album in 1978 and was a member of Joe Cocker's touring band between 1979 and 1984 and is featured on several live Joe Cocker DVD's. He was the drummer on Joe Cocker's number one hit single, "With a Little Help from My Friends", recorded in 1968.

Barrie's last recorded work was on the 1985 Gary Brooker solo album, Echoes in the Night on tracks "Ghost Train", "The Long Goodbye" "Hear What You're Saying" and "Mr. Blue Day".

Procol Harum's UK chart hits include: "A Whiter Shade Of Pale" in 1967, "Homburg" in 1967, "Conquistador" in 1972 and "Pandora's Box" in 1975.

Jackie Wilson   **Solo Artiste**

Jackie Wilson died aged forty-nine on the 21st of January 1984 from pneumonia. He was survived by his wife, Harlean, by his son, Bobby and by his daughter, Sandra.

In his early teens Jackie joined a quartet, the Ever Ready Gospel Singers, who gained popularity in local churches. Jackie was not very religious, but he enjoyed singing in public.

Jackie was discovered by talent agent Johnny Otis, who recruited him for a group called the Thrillers. Jackie signed on with manager Al Green who owned two music publishing companies, Pearl Music and Merrimac Music.

Jackie eventually was hired in 1953 to join a group formed in 1950 called the Dominoes and he was the group's lead singer for three years. They made appearances riding on the strength of the group's earlier hits, until 1956 when the Dominoes recorded Jackie Wilson with an unlikely interpretation of the pop hit "St. Therese of the Roses", giving the Dominoes a brief moment in the spotlight. In 1957 Jackie began a solo career, left the Dominoes, collaborated with his cousin Levi, and secured performances at Detroit's Flame Show Bar. Later his manager secured a deal with Decca Records, and was signed to its subsidiary label Brunswick.

Jackie's first single was released, "Reet Petite", which became a modest Rhythm & Blues success and many years later, an international smash hit. Jackie's late-1958 signature song, "Lonely Teardrops", which peaked at number seven on the pop charts, ranked number one on the Rhythm & Blues charts in the U.S.A., and established Jackie as a Rhythm & Blues superstar known for his extraordinary, operatic multi-octave vocal range. Jackie's

"Lonely Teardrops" sold over one million copies, and was awarded a gold disc by the RIAA.

Jackie scored hits as he entered the 1960s with the number fifteen "Doggin' Around", the number one pop ballad "Night", another million-seller, and "Baby Workout", another Top ten hit, which he composed with The Midnighters member Alonzo Tucker. His songwriting alliance with Tucker also turned out other songs, including "No Pity" and "I'm So Lonely." Top ten hits continued with "Alone At Last" and "My Empty Arms".

In 1966, Jackie Wilson scored the first of two big comeback singles with "Whispers" and "Higher and Higher", number six pop hit in 1967, became one of his final hits ; followed by "I Get the Sweetest Feeling".

Jackie Wilson's UK chart hits include: "Reet Petite" in 1957 and "I Get The Sweetest Feeling" in 1972.

Mary Wilson   The Supremes

Mary Wilson died aged seventy-six on the 8th of February, 2021 in Henderson, Nevada, United States of America; from hypertensive atherosclerotic cardiovascular disease. She was survived by her daughter, Turkessa.

In 1959, Florence Ballard asked Mary to audition for the Primettes with Diana Ross and Betty McGlown. The Primettes signed to Motown Records in 1961, changing the group's name to The Supremes and they scored their first hit in 1963 with the song, "When the Lovelight Starts Shining Through His Eyes", and reached Number one on the pop charts for the first time with the hit, "Where Did Our Love Go", becoming their first of twelve number one singles.

By 1964, the Supremes had become international superstars. However, in 1967, the Motown president changed the name of them to Diana Ross & The Supremes.

In late 1977, Mary left The Supremes, following a farewell performance at London's Drury Lane Theatre.

Mary then signed with Motown for solo work, releasing a disco-heavy self-titled album in 1979. A single from the album, "Red Hot", had a modest showing on the pop charts. Throughout the mid-1980s, Mary focused on performances in musical theatre productions, including Beehive, Dancing in the Streets, and Supreme Soul.

Nancy Wilson   Solo Artiste

Nancy Wilson died aged eighty-one on the 13th of December 2018 from renal cancer whilst at her home in California, U.S.A. She was survived by her first husband, drummer Kenny Dennis, their son Kenneth ("Kacy") Dennis Jr. , her second husband; Presbyterian minister, Reverend Wiley Burton, and their daughter, Samantha , and their adopted daughter, Sheryl .

Nancy was born in Ohio, U.S.A. and from an early age she became aware of her talent while singing in church choirs, imitating singers as a young child, and performing in her grandmother's house during summer visits. By the age of four, Nancy believed she would eventually become a professional singer.

At the age of fifteen whilst attending High School, Nancy won a talent contest sponsored by the local ABC television station. The prize was an appearance on a twice-a-week television show, Skyline Melodies, which she later hosted. She also worked clubs on the east side and north side of Columbus, Ohio, from the age of fifteen until she graduated from West High School at age seventeen. She spent one year at Ohio's Central State College before dropping out and following her original ambitions. She auditioned and won a spot with Rusty Bryant's Carolyn Club Big Band in nineteen-fifty-six. She toured with them throughout Canada and the Midwest in 1956 to 1958. While in this group, Nancy Wilson made her first recording under Dot Records.

In 1959, Nancy relocated to New York with a goal of

obtaining Capitol Records as her label. Within four weeks of her arrival in New York she got her first big break, a call to fill in for Irene Reid at "The Blue Morocco". The club booked Nancy on a permanent basis; she was singing four nights a week and working as a secretary for the New York Institute of Technology during the day. John Levy sent demos of "Guess Who I Saw Today", "Sometimes I'm Happy", and two other songs to Capitol. Capitol Records signed her in 1960.

Between March 1964 and June 1965, four of Nancy's albums hit the Top 10 on Billboard's Top LPs chart and after making numerous television guest appearances, Nancy eventually got her own series on NBC, The Nancy Wilson Show and, over the years she appeared on many popular television shows .

In 1964, Nancy Wilson won her first Grammy Award for the best rhythm and blues recording for the album How Glad I Am. She was featured as a "grand diva" of jazz in a 1992 edition of Essence. In the same year, she also received the Whitney Young Jr. Award from the Urban League. In 1998, she was a recipient of the Playboy Reader Poll Award for best jazz vocalist.

Rickie Wilson   Black Narsissus, The B.52's

Ricky Wilson died aged thirty-two from AIDs on the 12th of October, 1985 at the Memorial Sloan–Kettering Cancer Center, in New York City, U.S.A.

Ricky was born in Athens, Georgia U.S.A. and at an early age he developed an interest in music, and learned how to play folk guitar from television programmes. Upon entering high-school, Ricky upgraded to a Silvertone guitar and, to tape his music, bought a two-track tape recorder with money earned from a summer job at the local landfill.

From 1969 to 1971, Ricky and Keith Strickland collaborated with high school friends Pete Love and Owen Scott, in performing together as the four-member band Black

Narcissus. Upon graduation from the University of Georgia in 1976, Ricky kept in touch with Keith and they toured Europe.

In late 1976, Keith and Ricky returned to Athens in search of further employment. The two joined the B-52's when they and Ricky's sister Cindy, Kate Pierson and Fred Schneider of local protest band The Sun-Donuts, formed the group in an impromptu musical practice session after sharing a tropical flaming volcano drink at a Chinese restaurant. They played their first concert in 1977 at a Valentine's Day party for friends. The band's quirky take on the new wave sound of their era was a combination of dance and surf music set apart by the unusual guitar tunings used by Ricky.

Amy Winehouse   Solo Artiste

Amy Winehouse died aged twenty-seven of accidental alcohol poisoning on the 23rd of July 2011 at her home in Camden, London, U.K. She was survived by her brother, Alex, her father, Mitchell and her mother, Janis.

Some of Amy's maternal uncles were professional jazz musicians. Amy's paternal grandmother, Cynthia, was a singer, who, with Amy's parents, influenced Amy's interest in jazz. Her father, Mitch, often sang Frank Sinatra songs to her and whenever she got chastised at school, she would sing "Fly Me to the Moon" before going up to the headmistress to be told off. Amy's parents separated when she was nine, and she lived with her mother and stayed with her father and his girlfriend in Hatfield Heath, Essex, on weekends.

In 1992, her grandmother Cynthia suggested that Amy attend the Susi Earnshaw Theatre School, where she went on Saturdays to further her vocal education and to learn to tap dance. Amy attended the school for four years and founded a short-lived rap group called Sweet 'n' Sour, with her childhood friend, before seeking full-time training at Sylvia Young Theatre School. Amy also appeared in an episode of The Fast Show, 1997, with other children from the Sylvia Young School and later attended the Mount School, Mill Hill; the BRIT School in Selhurst, Croydon; Osidge JMI School and then Ashmole School.

After toying around with her brother Alex's guitar, Amy bought her own when she was fourteen and began writing songs a year later. Soon after, she began working for a living, including, at one time, as an entertainment journalist for the World Entertainment News Network, in addition to singing with local group the Bolsha Band. In July 2000, she became the featured female vocalist with the National Youth Jazz Orchestra; her influences were to include Sarah Vaughan and Dinah Washington, the latter whom she was already listening to at home. One of Amy's best friends sent her demo tape to an A&R person and she was signed to Simon Fuller's 19 Management in 2002 and was paid £250 a week against future earnings. While being developed by the management company, she was kept as a recording industry secret although she was a regular jazz standards singer at a club. Her future A&R representative at Island, Darcus Beese, heard of her by accident when the manager of The Lewinson Brothers showed him some productions of his clients, which featured Amy as key vocalist but Amy had already recorded a number of songs and signed a publishing deal with EMI by this time.

Amy's debut album, 'Frank', was released in October 2003. The album entered the upper levels of the UK album chart in 2004 when it was nominated for Brit Awards in the categories of "British Female Solo Artist" and "British Urban Act." It went on to achieve platinum sales.

A later album spawned a number of hit singles, the first being the Ronson-produced "Rehab." The song reached the top ten in the UK and the US. Time magazine named "Rehab" the Best Song of 2007. Amy's last recording was a duet with American singer Tony Bennett .

Johnny Winter died aged seventy on the 16th of July 2014 from emphysema combined with pneumonia. He was survived by his wife, Susan and his brother, Edgar.

Johnny's recording career began at the age of fifteen, when his band Johnny and the Jammers released "School Day Blues" on a Houston record label. In 1968, he released his first album 'The Progressive Blues Experiment', on Austin's Sonobeat Records.

Johnny caught his biggest break in December 1968, when Mike Bloomfield, whom he met and jammed with in Chicago, invited him to sing and play a song during a Bloomfield and Al Kooper concert at the Fillmore East in New York City. Johnny played and sang B.B. King's "It's My Own Fault" to loud applause and, within a few days, was signed to what was reportedly the largest advance in the history of the recording industry at that time; six hundred thousand dollars.

Johnny's first Columbia album, 'Johnny Winter', was recorded and released in 1969. The album's success coincided with Imperial Records picking up 'The Progressive Blues Experiment' for wider release. The same year, the Winter trio toured and performed at several rock festivals, including Woodstock. With brother Edgar added as a full member of the group, Johnny also recorded his second album, 'Second Winter', in Nashville in 1969. The two-record album, which only had three recorded sides (the fourth was blank), introduced a couple more staples of Johnny Winter's concerts, including Chuck Berry's "Johnny B. Goode" and Bob Dylan's "Highway 61 Revisited".

In 1973, Johnny returned to the music scene with the release of 'Still Alive and Well', a basic blend between blues and hard rock, whose title track was written by Rick Derringer. His comeback concert at Long Island, New York's Nassau Coliseum featured the "And" line-up minus

Rick Derringer and Bobby Caldwell. In 1975, Johnny returned to Bogalusa, Louisiana, to produce an album for Thunderhead, a Southern rock band which included Pat Rush and Bobby "T" Torello. A second live Winter album, 'Captured Live!', was released in 1976.

Johnny continued to perform live, including at festivals throughout North America and Europe. He headlined such prestigious events as the New Orleans Jazz & Heritage Festival, Chicago Blues Festival, the 2009 Sweden Rock Festival, the Warren Haynes Christmas Jam, and Rockpalast. He also performed with the Allman Brothers at the Beacon Theater in New York City on the 40th anniversary of their debut. In 2007 and 2010, Johnny performed at Eric Clapton's Crossroads Guitar Festival.

Bill Withers   Solo Artiste

Bill Withers died aged eighty-one on the 30th of March 2020 from a heart condition in Los Angeles, California, U S A. He was survived by his wife, Marcia and their son Todd and daughter Kori.

Bill enlisted with the United States Navy at the age of eighteen and served for nine years, during which time he became interested in singing and writing songs. Bill left the Navy in 1965 and relocated to Los Angeles in 1967 to start a musical career.

His album 'I Am' was released in 1971 with the tracks, "Ain't No Sunshine" and "Grandma's Hands" as singles. The album was a success, and Bill began touring with a backing band.

Bill Wither's UK chart hits include: "Lean On Me" in 1972 and "Lovely Day" in 1978.

Jimmy Witherspoon   Solo Artiste

Jimmy Witherspoon died aged seventy-seven from throat cancer on the 18th of September 1997, in Los Angeles, California, U.S.A. He was survived by his wife, Diana and his sister, Jimmie-Lois and his brother, Leonard and his three children, Angela, Regina and James.

Jimmy first recorded under his own name in 1947, and two years later with the McShann band, he had his first hit, "Ain't Nobody's Business," a song that came to be regarded as his signature tune. In 1950 he had hits with two more songs closely identified with him—"No Rollin' Blues" and "Big Fine Girl"—and also with "Failing by Degrees" and "New Orleans Woman", recorded with the Gene Gilbeaux Orchestra for Modern Records.

In 1961 Jimmy toured Europe with Buck Clayton and returned to the UK on many occasions, featuring on a mid-'60s live UK recording, Spoon Sings and Swings, in 1966.

Bobby Womack   Solo Artiste

Bobby Womack died aged seventy from cancer and Alzheimer's on the 27th of June 2014 at his home in Tarzana, California, U.S.A. He was survived by his wife, Regina, his sons, Bobby, Corrie and Jordan and his daughter, Ginare.

By the mid-1950s, the ten year-old Bobby was touring with his brothers on the midwest gospel circuit as The Womack Brothers, along with Naomi on organ and Friendly Sr. on guitar. In 1954, under the moniker Curtis Womack and the Womack Brothers, the group issued the single, "Buffalo Bill" and more records followed.

Sam Cooke, the lead singer of The Soul Stirrers, first saw the Womacks performing in the mid-1950s. He became their mentor and helped them go on tour. They also went on national tours with The Staple Singers. Even though Curtis often sang lead, Bobby was allowed to sing alongside him showcasing his gruff baritone vocals in contrast to his older brother's smoother tenor.

Bobby became a member of Sam Cooke's band, touring

and recording with him from 1961. In 1968, Bobby signed with Minit Records and recorded his first solo album, 'Fly Me to the Moon', and he scored a major hit with his cover of "California Dreamin'".

Chris Wood   Traffic

Chris Wood died aged thirty-nine of pneumonia on the 12th of July 1983 in hospital in Birmingham, U.K. He was survived by his sister, Stephanie.

At the time, Chris was working on a solo album that was to be titled Vulcan, and had recorded material for the album over the previous few years, mostly in London at Island's Hammersmith Studio.

Chris was self-taught on flute and saxophone, which he commenced playing at the age of fifteen. Aged eighteen, Chris joined the Steve Hadley Quartet, a jazz/blues group in 1962. His younger sister Stephanie designed clothes for the Spencer Davis Group, based in Birmingham, and it was through her that Chris was first introduced to fellow Birmingham native Steve Winwood. A well-known Birmingham club – the Elbow Room – was an after-hours haunt of local bands and musicians and it was here that Chris used to meet up with Steve Winwood and Jim Capaldi, and with Dave Mason before the quartet eventually formed Traffic.

Traffic's UK chart hits include: "Paper Sun" in 1967, "Hole In My Shoe" in 1967, "Here We Go Round The Mulberry Bush" in 1967 and "No Face,No Name,No Number" in 1968.

Ric Wright   Pink Floyd

Rick Wright died aged sixty-five at home in London from cancer on 15th of September 2008. At the time of his death, Ric had been working on a new solo album. He was survived by his son, Ben and his daughter, Gala.

Ric grew up in Hatch End, Middlesex,U.K. and taught

himself to play guitar, trumpet and piano at age twelve after he was recuperating from a broken leg. His mother helped and encouraged him to play the piano. He took private lessons in musical theory and composition at the Eric Gilder School of Music and became influenced by the trad jazz revival, learning the trombone and saxophone in addition to the piano. Uncertain about his future, he enrolled in 1962 at the Regent Street Polytechnic which was later incorporated into the University of Westminster. There he met fellow musicians Roger Waters and Nick Mason and the three formed a band called Sigma Six.

Through a friend, Ric arranged the fledgling group's first recording session in a West Hampstead studio, in December 1964 and guitarist Syd Barrett joined the band, which became Pink Floyd.

Pink Floyd had stabilised with a line-up of Barrett, Waters, Mason and Ric Wright by mid-1965, and after frequent gigging that year became regulars on the underground live circuit in London.

Ric later made significant contributions to Pink Floyd's long, epic compositions such as "Atom Heart Mother", "Echoes" (on which he harmonised with Gilmour for the lead vocals) and "Shine On You Crazy Diamond". On 1973's The Dark Side of the Moon he composed the music for "The Great Gig in the Sky" and "Us and Them". He also contributed to other album tracks such as "Breathe" and "Time", singing the lead vocals on the latter's chorus.

In 2006, Ric became a regular member of Dave Gilmour's solo touring band along with former Floyd sidemen Jon Carin, Dick Parry and Guy Pratt. He contributed keyboards and background vocals to Gilmour's solo album, On an Island, and performed live in Europe and North America that year. On stage with Gilmour he played keyboards, including a revival of the Farfisa for performing "Echoes". He declined an offer to join Waters and Mason on The Dark Side of the Moon Live tour to spend more time working on a solo project.

Tammy Wynette Solo Artiste

Tammy Wynette died from cardiac arrhythmia aged fifty-five on the sixth of April 1998. She was survived by her husband George and daughters, Tamala, Gwen, Jackie and Tina.

Tammy was born near Tremont, Mississippi, U.S.A. She grew up in her maternal grandparents' home, which had no indoor toilets or running water. She was raised with an aunt, Carolyn Russell, who was only five years older, thus more of a sister than an aunt. As a girl, Tammy taught herself to play a variety of musical instruments that had been left by her deceased father.

In 1966, she moved from Birmingham to Nashville, Tennessee, where she attempted to get a recording contract. After being turned down repeatedly by all of the other record companies, she auditioned for the producer Billy Sherrill, who was originally reluctant to sign her, but decided to do so after finding himself in need of a singer for "Apartment Number 9". When Sherrill heard Tammy sing it, he was impressed and decided to sign her to Epic Records in 1966. Tammy Wynette's UK chart hits include: "Stand By Your Man" in 1975, "D.I.V.O.R.C.E" in 1975, "I Don't Wanna Play House" in 1976 and "Justified And Ancient" in 1991

Zal Yanovsky The Lovin' Spoonful

Zal Yanovsky died from a heart attack aged fifty-seven on the 13th of December 2002 in Kingston, Ontario, Canada. He was survived by his wife, Rose.

Zal started his musical career playing folk music coffee houses in Toronto. He lived on a kibbutz in Israel for a short time before returning to Canada. Zal then teamed with fellow Canadian Denny Doherty in the Halifax Three. The two joined Cass Elliot in the Mugwumps. It was at this time that Zal met John Sebastian and they formed the

Lovin' Spoonful with Steve Boone and Joe Butler to go on to have many hit records. Zal sang and played lead guitar in the group.

The Lovin' Spoonful's UK chart hits include: "Daydream" in 1966, "Summer In The City" in 1966 and "Nashville Cats" in 1967.

George Young   The Easybeats

George Young died of undisclosed causes aged seventy on the 22nd of October 2017. George began his music career in Sydney, Australia, where on rhythm guitar he formed a beat pop band, the Easybeats and aside from performing and recording, George co-wrote nearly all of their songs. The Easybeats relocated to the UK to record and perform, however, they disbanded in late 1969.

After the Easybeats dissolved George formed a production and song writing duo with Vanda, as Vanda & Young in 1970, initially living in London where they provided pop and rock songs for other recording artists. After retiring from the music industry in the late 1990s, George resided mainly in Portugal with his family.

The Easybeats' only UK chart hits were: "Friday On My Mind" in 1966 and "Hello How Are You" in 1968.

Malcolm Young   AC/DC

Malcolm Young died of cancer aged sixty-four on the 18th of November 2017 in Elizabeth Bay, New South Wales, Australia. He was survived by his wife, Linda, his son, Ross and his daughter, Cara.

Malcolm was twenty years old when he and younger brother Angus formed AC/DC in 1973. Angus was on lead guitar, Malcolm on rhythm guitar, Colin Burgess on drums, Larry Van Kriedt on bass guitar and Dave Evans on vocals. "Can I Sit Next To You Girl," their first single, was later re-recorded with Bon Scott as their vocalist. They decided upon the name AC/DC after seeing the letters "AC/DC" on the back of their sister Margaret's sewing machine.

In 1975 AC/DC moved to Melbourne. In 1988, Malcolm missed the majority of AC/DC's Blow Up Your Video World Tour to address alcohol abuse issues. He eventually became sober and returned to the band but during his absence he was replaced by his nephew, Stevie Young.

Paul Young   Sad Café

Paul Young died aged fifty-three from a heart attack on the 15th of July 2000 at his home in Altrincham, Manchester, U.K.

After releasing a number of unsuccessful solo singles between 1967 and 1975, Paul Young came to prominence as the frontman of 1970s rock band Sad Café, with whom he achieved multiple UK Top 40 and US Billboard Hot 100 hits. Paul formed Sad Café in 1976 and recorded with them until 1989. He enjoyed further chart success sharing lead vocal duties with Paul Carrack in Mike & The Mechanics, the pop-rock band formed in 1985 by Genesis guitarist Mike Rutherford. In that band, Paul Young played various instruments as required, and served as de facto frontman during live performances.

During his career, Paul provided lead vocals on several chart hits, including Sad Café's "Every Day Hurts" and "My Oh My", and Mike + The Mechanics' "All I Need Is a Miracle", "Word of Mouth", "Taken In" and "Nobody's Perfect". Paul Young's power and range lent themselves to the band's heavier songs.

Sad Café's UK chart hits include: "Every Day Hurts" in 1979 and "My Oh My" in 1980.

Frank Zappa   The Mothers of Invention

Frank Zappa died aged fifty-two from prostate cancer on the 4th of December 1993. He was survived by his wife,

Gail, his sons Dweezil and Ahmnet and his daughters, Moon and Diva.

Frank joined his first band at Mission Bay High School in San Diego as the drummer. About the same time his parents bought a phonograph, which allowed him to develop his interest in music, and to begin building his record collection. R&B singles were early purchases, starting a large collection he kept for the rest of his life. He was interested in sounds for their own sake, particularly the sounds of drums and other percussion instruments. By age twelve he had obtained a snare drum and began learning the basics of orchestral percussion.

Frank started playing drums in a local band, the Blackouts. The band was racially diverse and included Euclid James "Motorhead" Sherwood who later became a member of the Mothers of Invention. Frank Zappa's interest in the guitar grew, and in 1957 he was given his first guitar.

Frank Zappa's interest in composing and arranging flourished in his last high-school years. By his final year, he was writing, arranging and conducting avant-garde performance pieces for the school orchestra.

During the early 1960's, Frank wrote and produced songs for other local artists. With Captain Beefheart, Frank recorded some songs under the name of the Soots. Frank started performing in local bars as a guitarist with a power trio, the Muthers, to support himself.

In 1965, someone asked Frank to take over as guitarist in local R&B band the Soul Giants and Frank accepted, and soon assumed leadership and the role as co-lead singer, even though he never considered himself a singer. He convinced the other members that they should play his music to increase the chances of getting a record contract. The band was renamed the Mothers, coincidentally on Mother's Day. They increased their bookings and gradually gained attention on the burgeoning Los Angeles underground music scene. In early 1966, they were spotted by leading record producer Tom Wilson when playing

"Trouble Every Day", a song about the Watts riots. Wilson signed the Mothers to the Verve division of MGM, which had built up a strong reputation for its releases of modern jazz recordings in the 1940s and 1950s, but was attempting to diversify into pop and rock audiences. Verve insisted that the band officially rename themselves the 'Mothers of Invention'.

With Wilson credited as producer, the Mothers of Invention, augmented by a studio orchestra, recorded the groundbreaking 'Freak Out'! in 1966. which immediately established Frank Zappa as a radical new voice in rock music, providing an antidote to the "relentless consumer culture of America". The sound was raw, but the arrangements were sophisticated. Released by Capitol Records in 1967 but due to contractual problems, the album was pulled. Frank took the opportunity to radically restructure the contents, adding newly recorded, improvised dialogue. After the contractual problems were resolved, the album was reissued by Verve in 1968. In it, Frank uniquely contributed to the avant-garde, anti-establishment music scene of the 1960s, sampling radio tape recordings and incorporating his own philosophical ideals to music and freedom of expression in his pieces.

Reflecting Frank's eclectic approach to music, the next album, 'Cruising with Ruben & the Jets', was very different. It represented a collection of doo-wop songs; listeners and critics were not sure whether the album was a satire or a tribute.

After he disbanded the Mothers of Invention, Frank released the acclaimed solo album 'Hot Rats'. It features, for the first time on record, Frank playing extended guitar solos and contains one of his most enduring compositions, "Peaches en Regalia", which came up again several times on subsequent recordings. It became a popular album in the UK and had a major influence on the development of the jazz-rock fusion genre.